FLY ME TO THE MOON

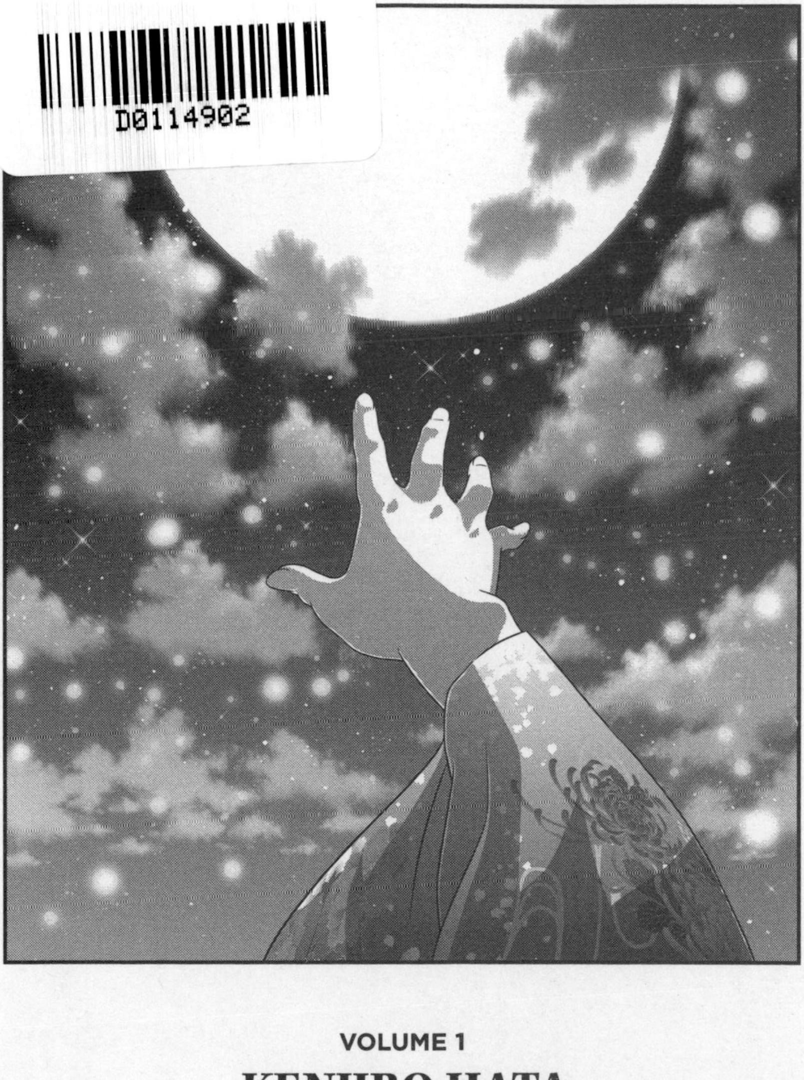

VOLUME 1

KENJIRO HATA

Contents

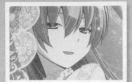
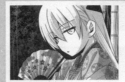
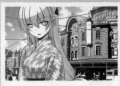
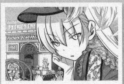
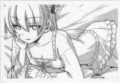
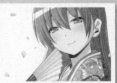
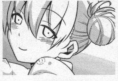
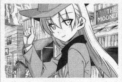
FLY ME TO THE MOON

Chapter 1: "The Moonlight Is a Message of Love"

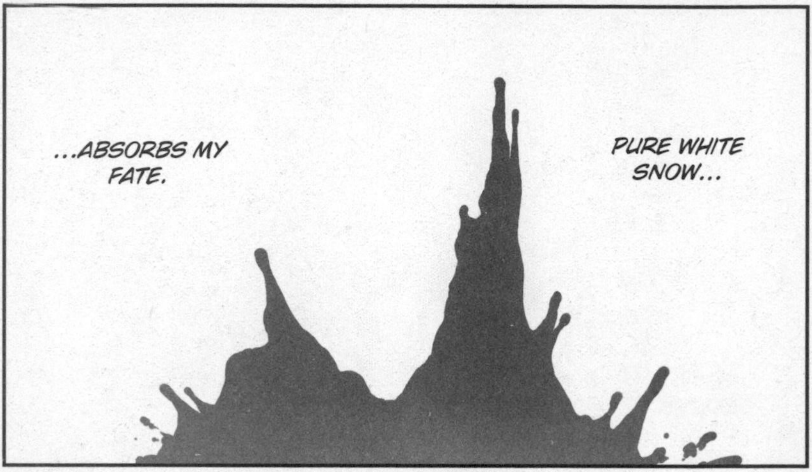
PURE WHITE SNOW...
...ABSORBS MY FATE.

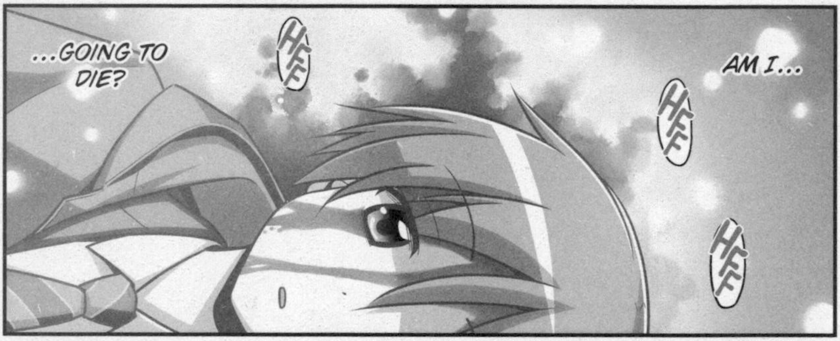
AM I...
HEFF
HEFF
HEFF
...GOING TO DIE?

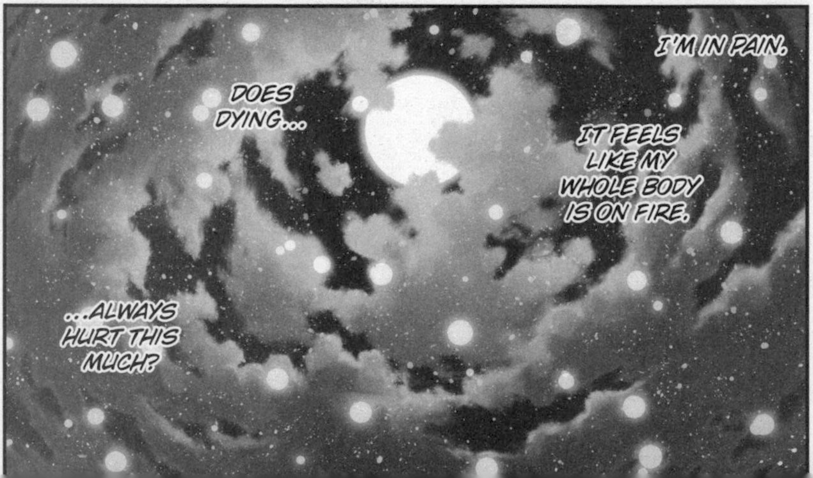
I'M IN PAIN.
IT FEELS LIKE MY WHOLE BODY IS ON FIRE.
DOES DYING...
...ALWAYS HURT THIS MUCH?

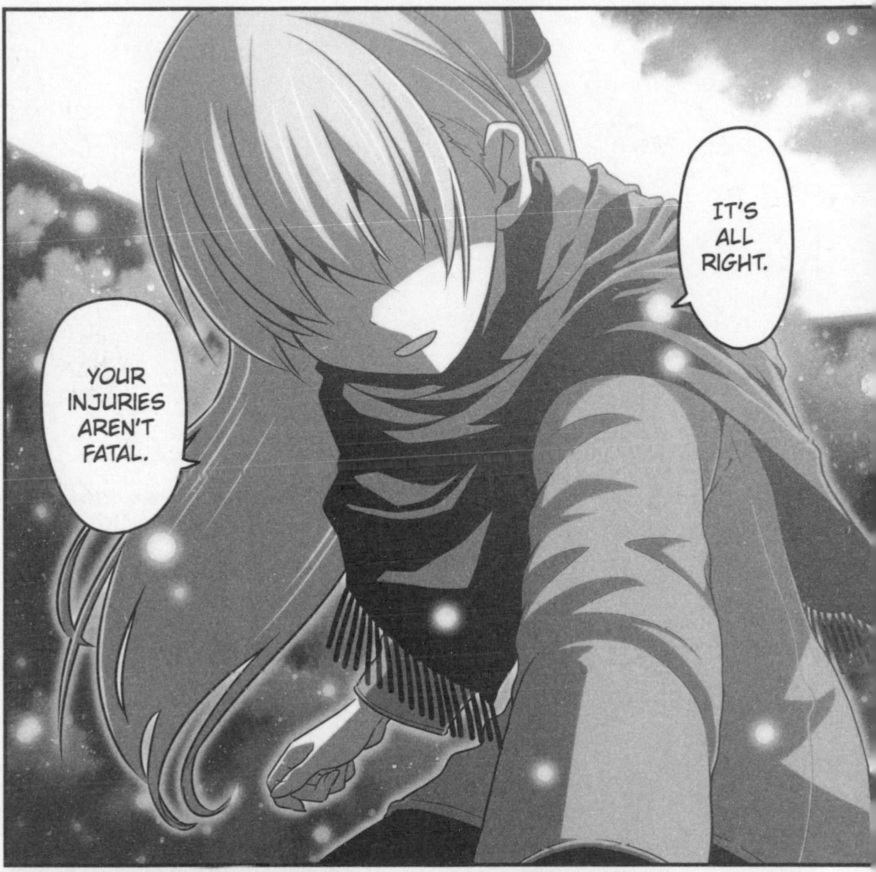
IT'S ALL RIGHT.
YOUR INJURIES AREN'T FATAL.

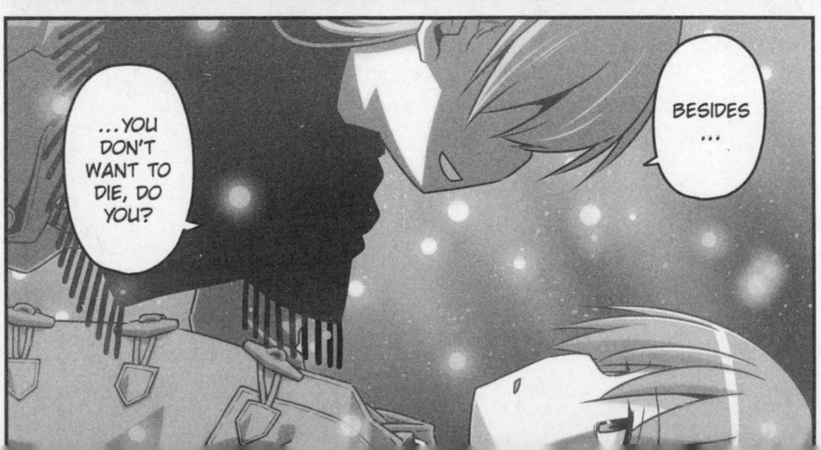
BESIDES ...
...YOU DON'T WANT TO DIE, DO YOU?

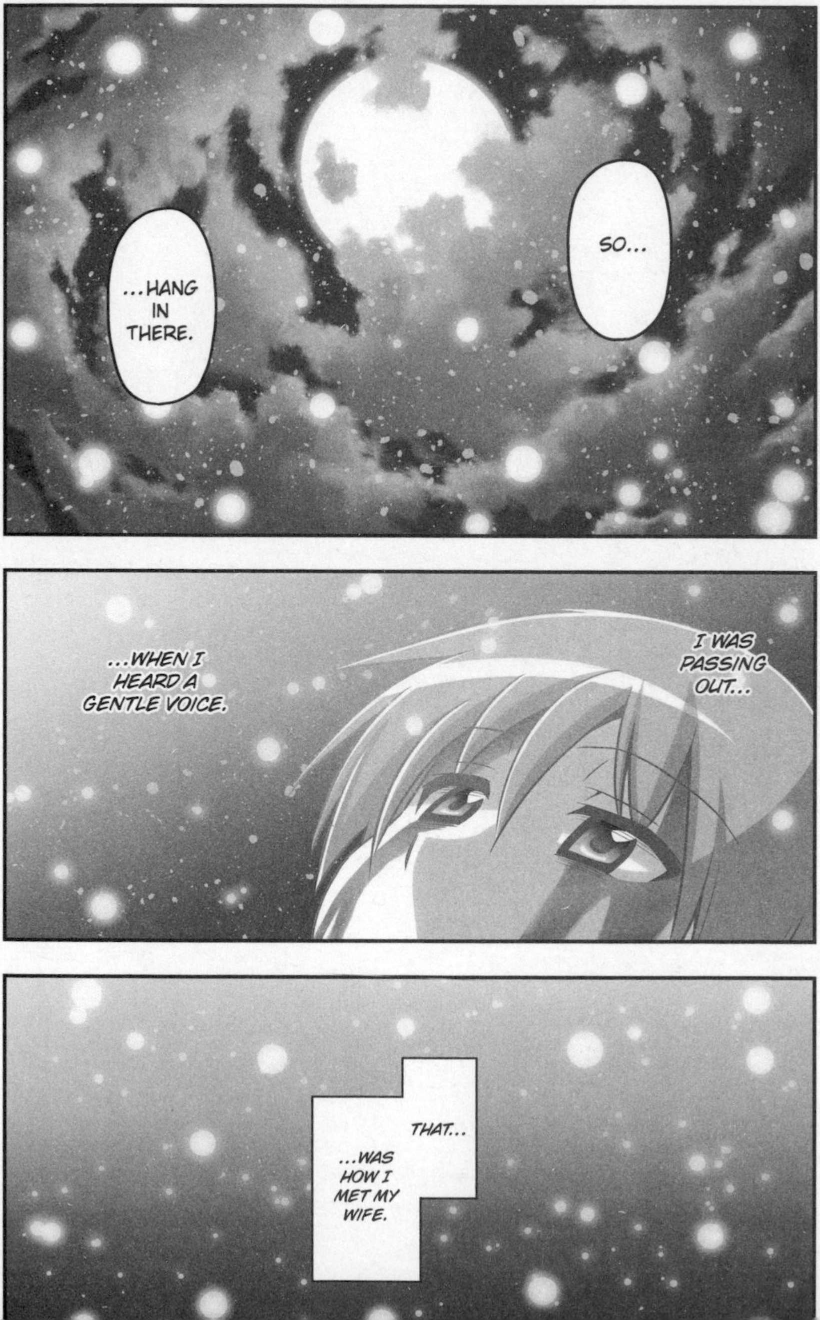
SO...
...HANG IN THERE.
I WAS PASSING OUT...
...WHEN I HEARD A GENTLE VOICE.
THAT...
...WAS HOW I MET MY WIFE.

Chapter 1: "The Moonlight Is a Message of Love"

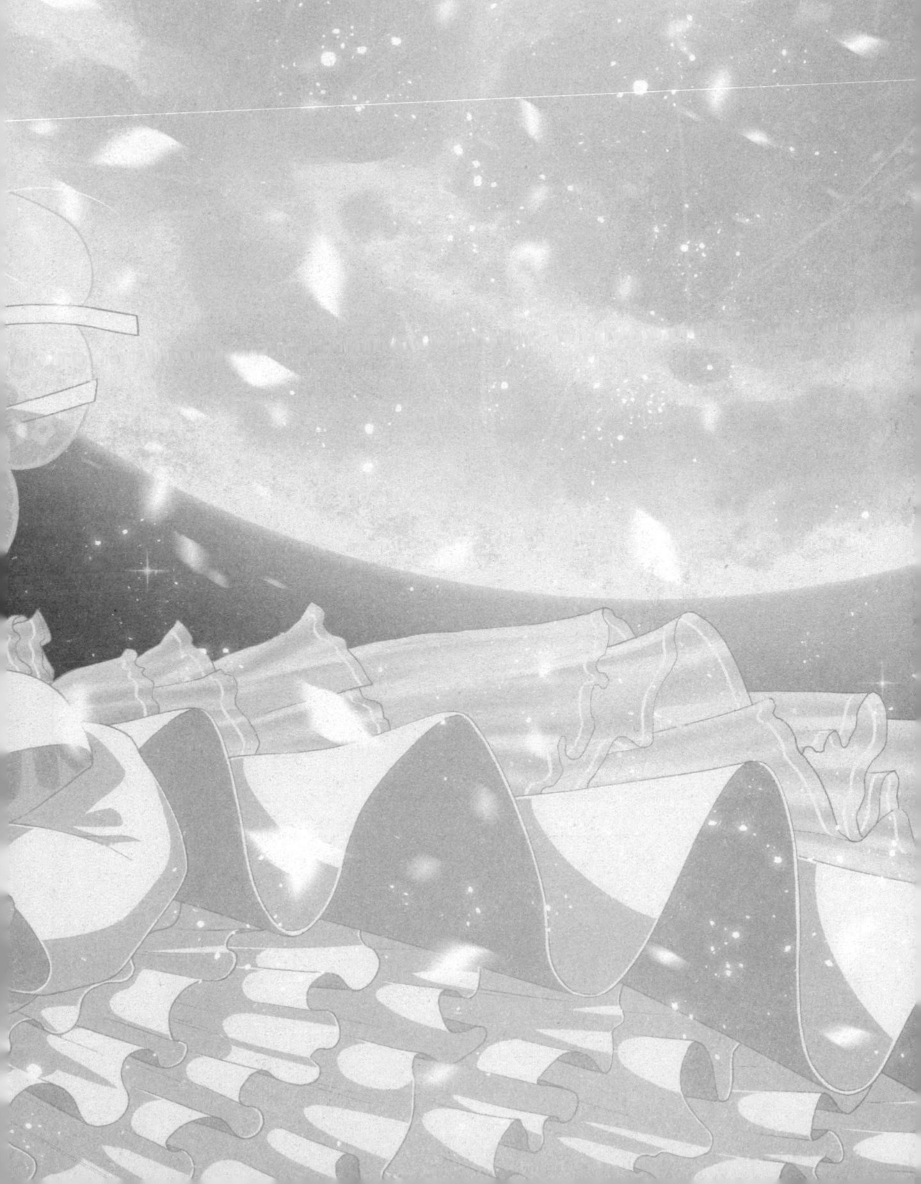

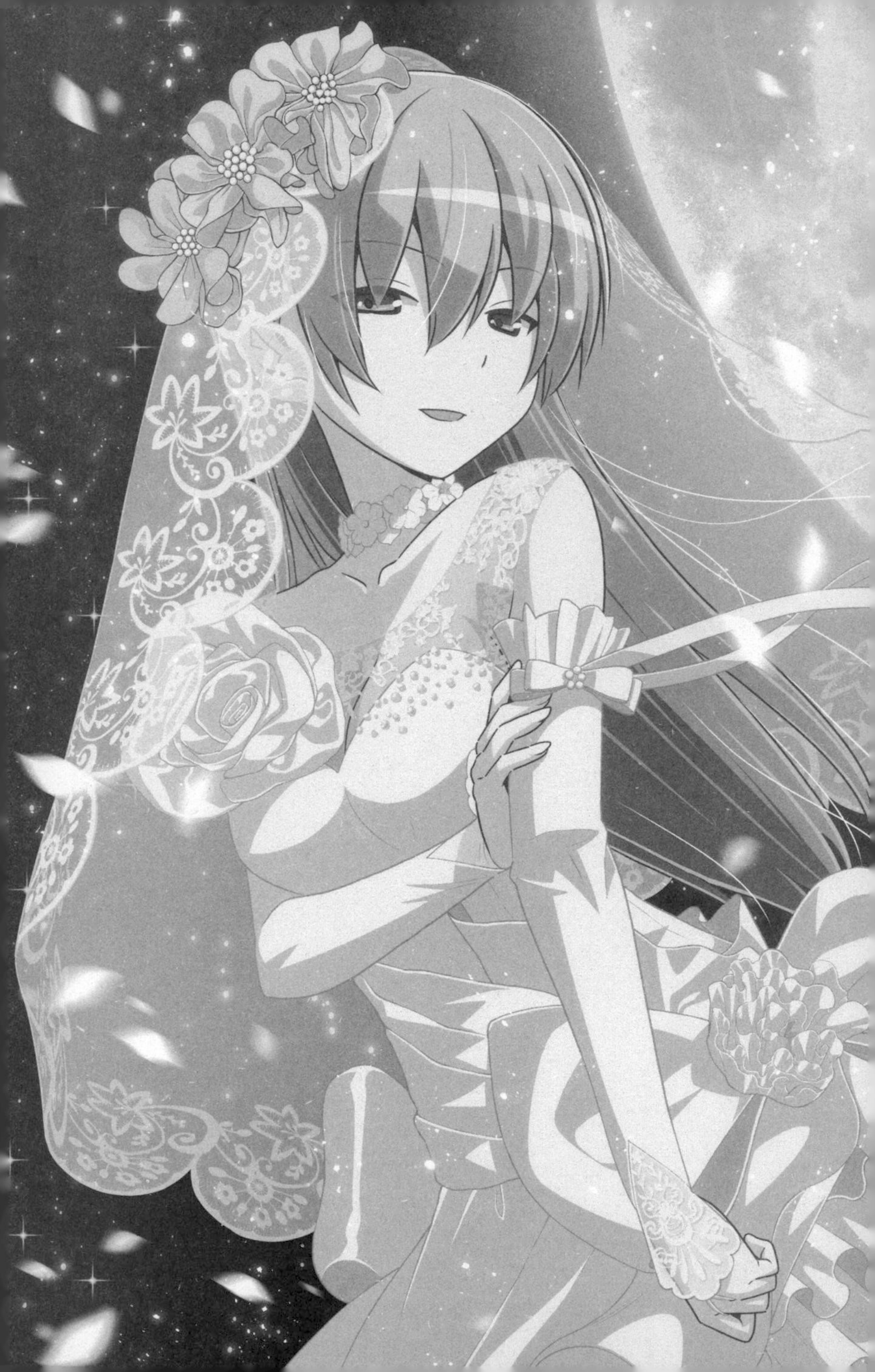

FLY ME _{TO} _{THE} MOON

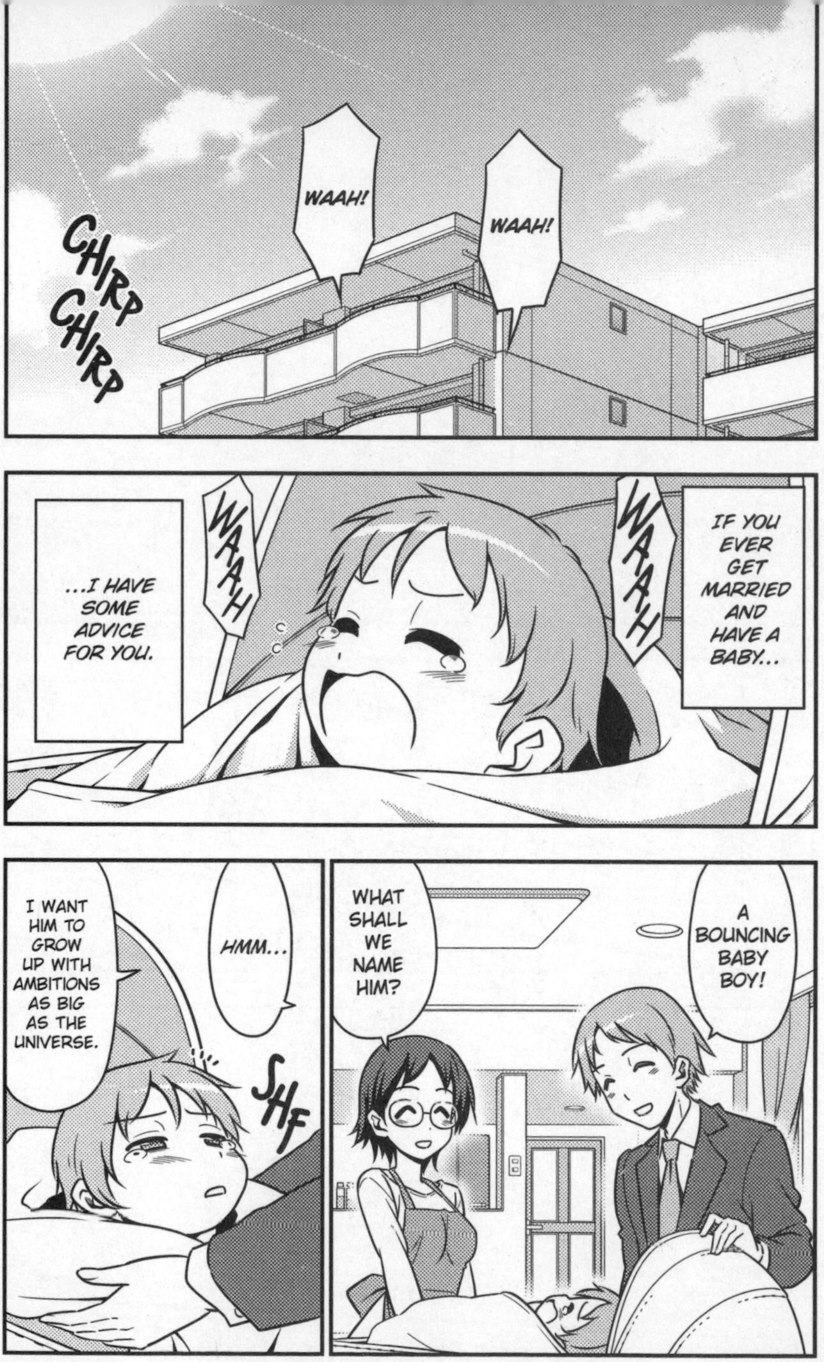
WAAH!
WAAH!
CHIRP CHIRP
IF YOU EVER GET MARRIED AND HAVE A BABY...
WAAAH
WAAH
...I HAVE SOME ADVICE FOR YOU.
A BOUNCING BABY BOY!
WHAT SHALL WE NAME HIM?
HMM...
I WANT HIM TO GROW UP WITH AMBITIONS AS BIG AS THE UNIVERSE.
SHF

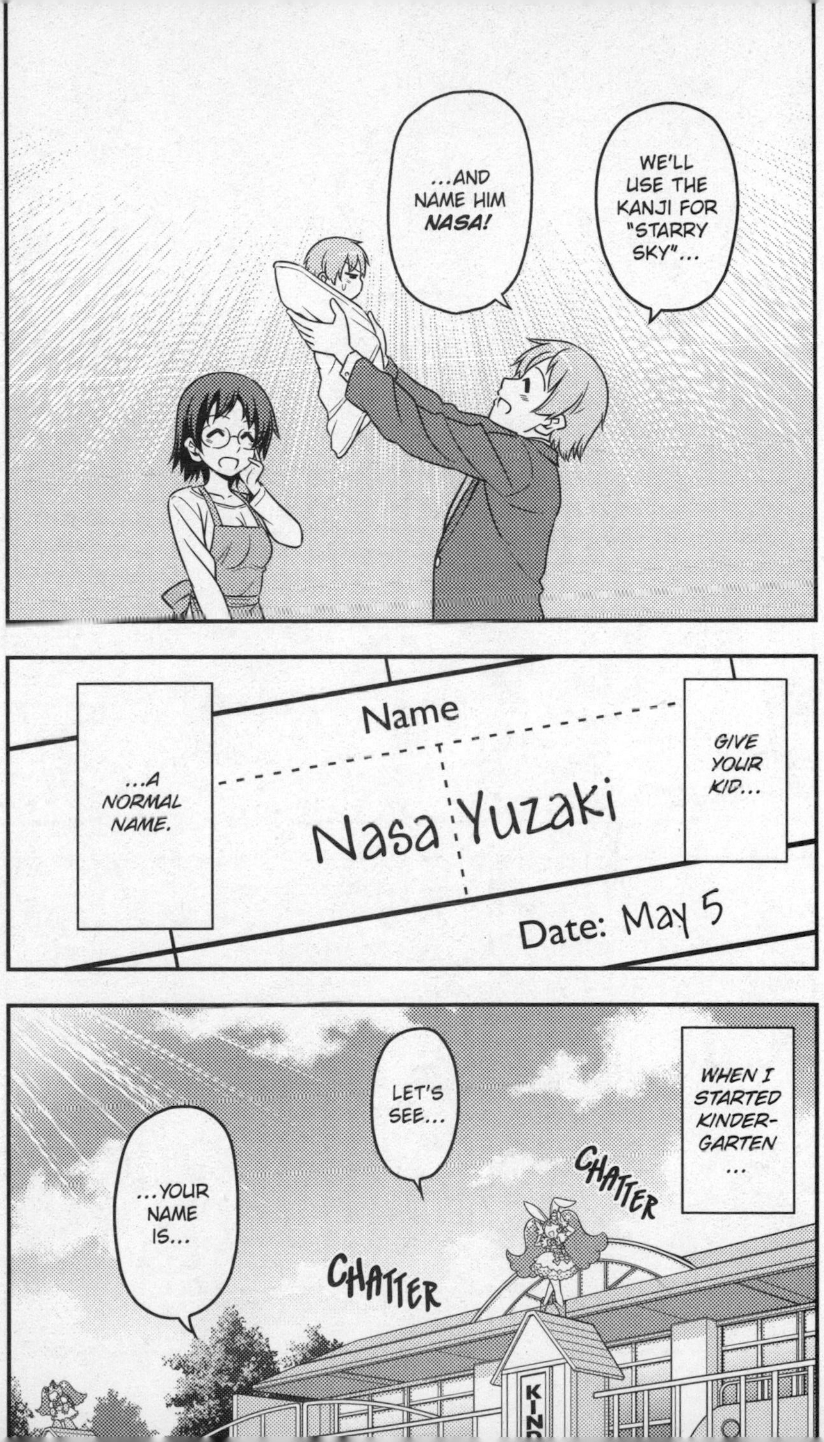
WE'LL USE THE KANJI FOR "STARRY SKY"...
...AND NAME HIM *NASA!*
GIVE YOUR KID...
Name
Nasa Yuzaki
Date: May 5
...A NORMAL NAME.
WHEN I STARTED KINDER-GARTEN ...
CHATTER
LET'S SEE...
CHATTER
...YOUR NAME IS...

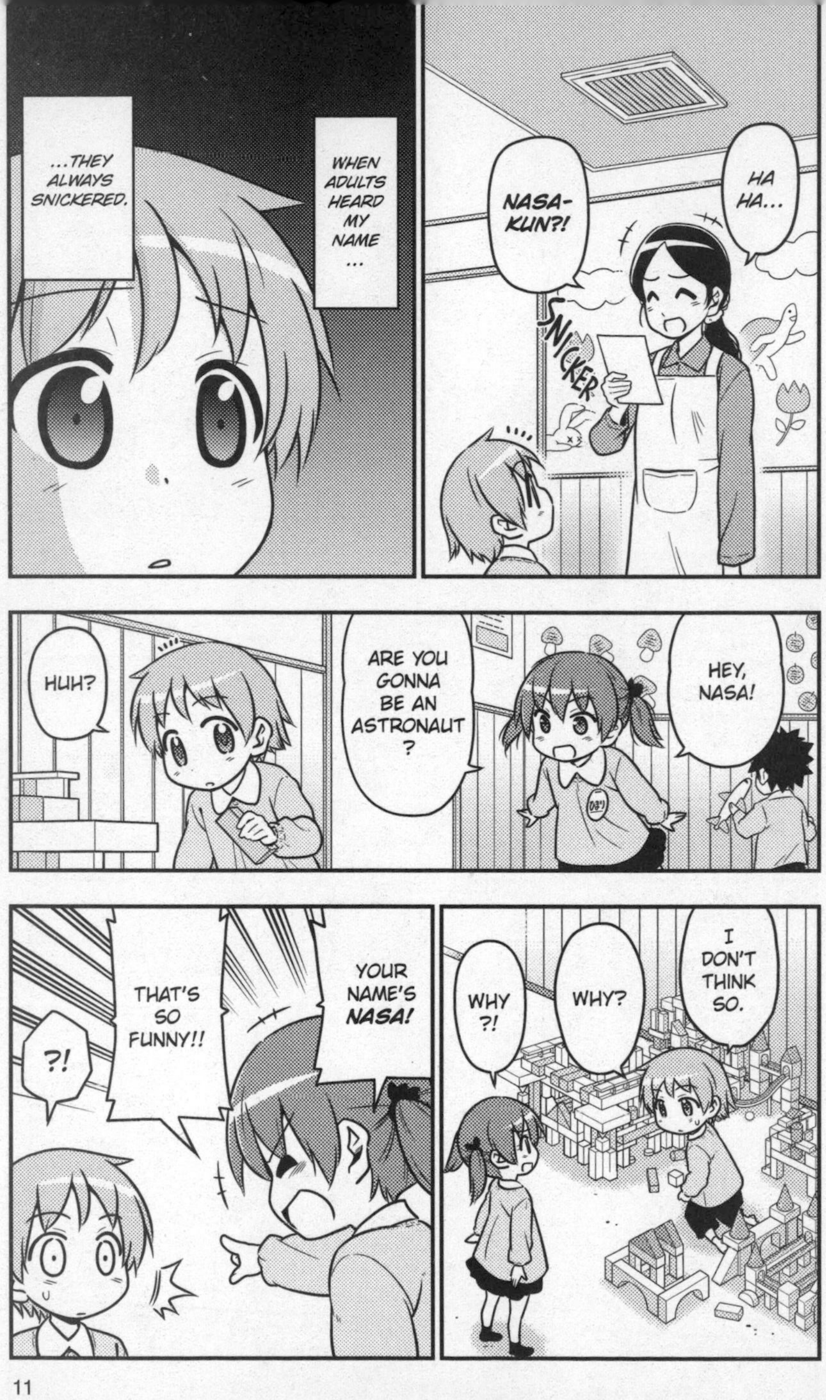
HA HA...
NASA-KUN?!
SNICKER
WHEN ADULTS HEARD MY NAME ...
...THEY ALWAYS SNICKERED.
HEY, NASA!
ARE YOU GONNA BE AN ASTRONAUT?
HUH?
I DON'T THINK SO.
WHY?
WHY?!
YOUR NAME'S NASA!
THAT'S SO FUNNY!!
?!

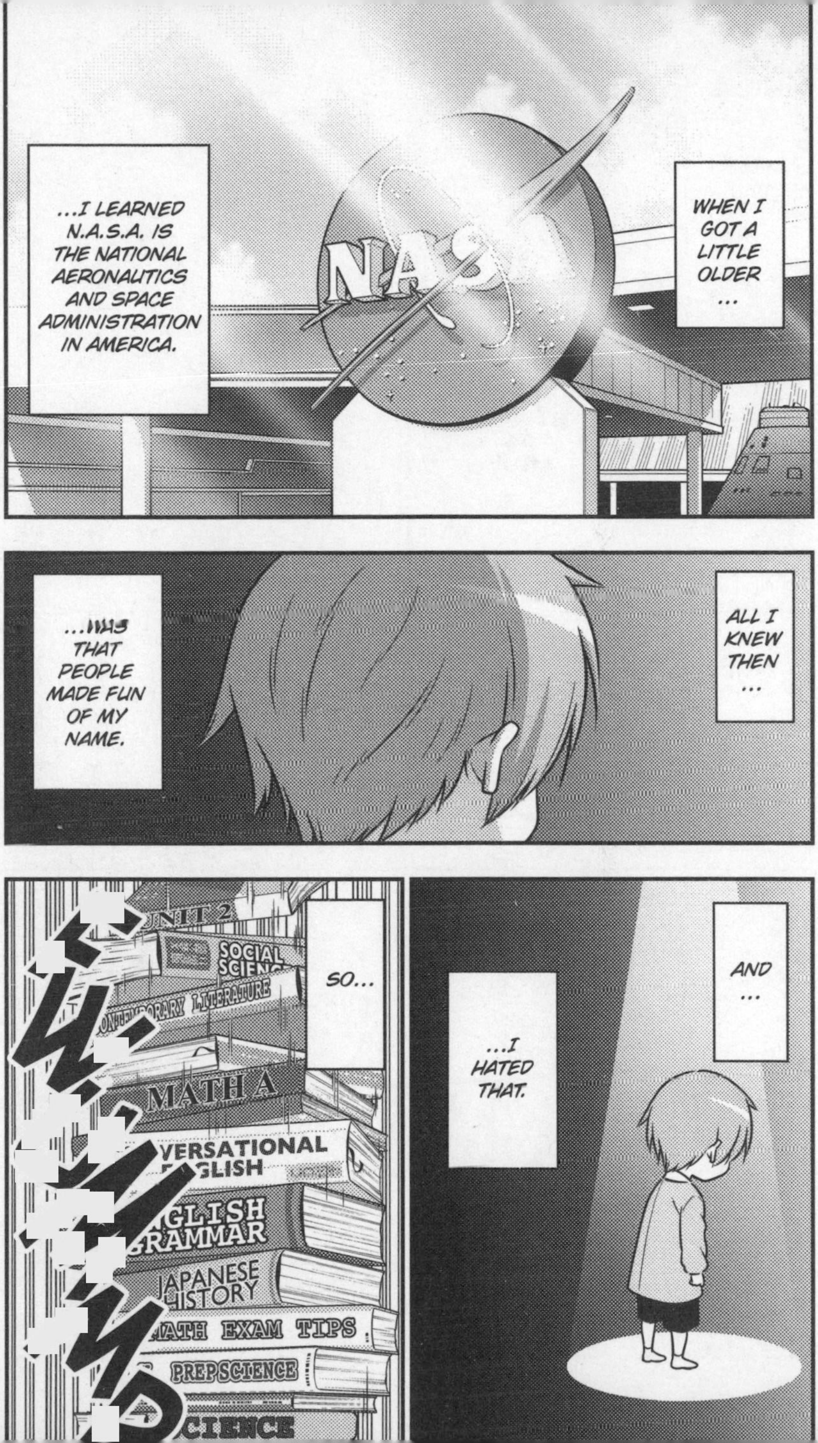
WHEN I GOT A LITTLE OLDER ...
...I LEARNED N.A.S.A. IS THE NATIONAL AERONAUTICS AND SPACE ADMINISTRATION IN AMERICA.
ALL I KNEW THEN ...
...WAS THAT PEOPLE MADE FUN OF MY NAME.
AND ...
...I HATED THAT.
SO...
UNIT 2
MATH A
PREP SCIENCE

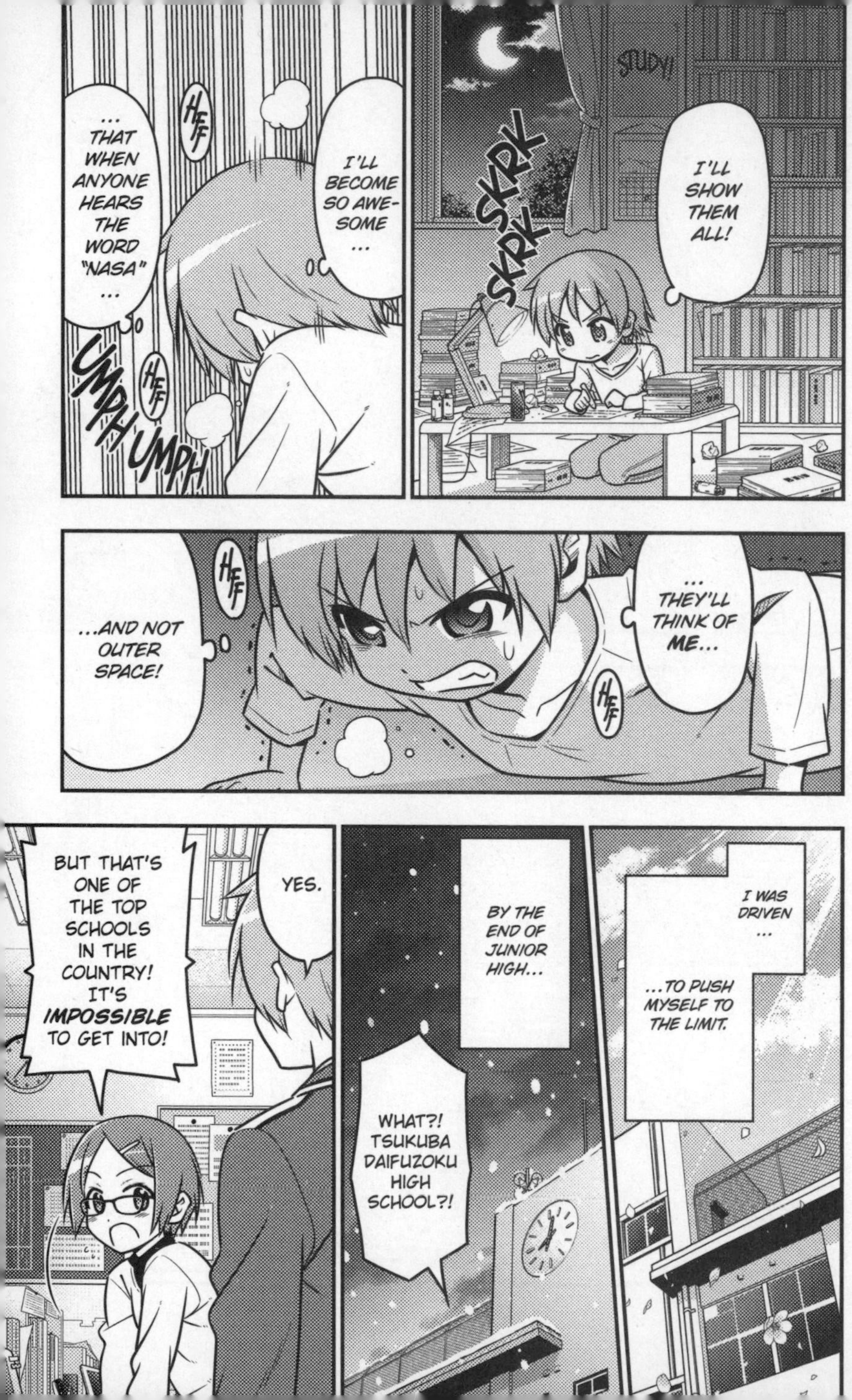
STUDY!!
I'LL SHOW THEM ALL!
SKRK SKRK
I'LL BECOME SO AWE-SOME...
HEFF
...THAT WHEN ANYONE HEARS THE WORD "NASA"...
HEFF
UMPH UMPH
...THEY'LL THINK OF ME...
HEFF
HEFF
...AND NOT OUTER SPACE!
I WAS DRIVEN...
...TO PUSH MYSELF TO THE LIMIT.
BY THE END OF JUNIOR HIGH...
WHAT?! TSUKUBA DAIFUZOKU HIGH SCHOOL?!
YES.
BUT THAT'S ONE OF THE TOP SCHOOLS IN THE COUNTRY! IT'S IMPOSSIBLE TO GET INTO!

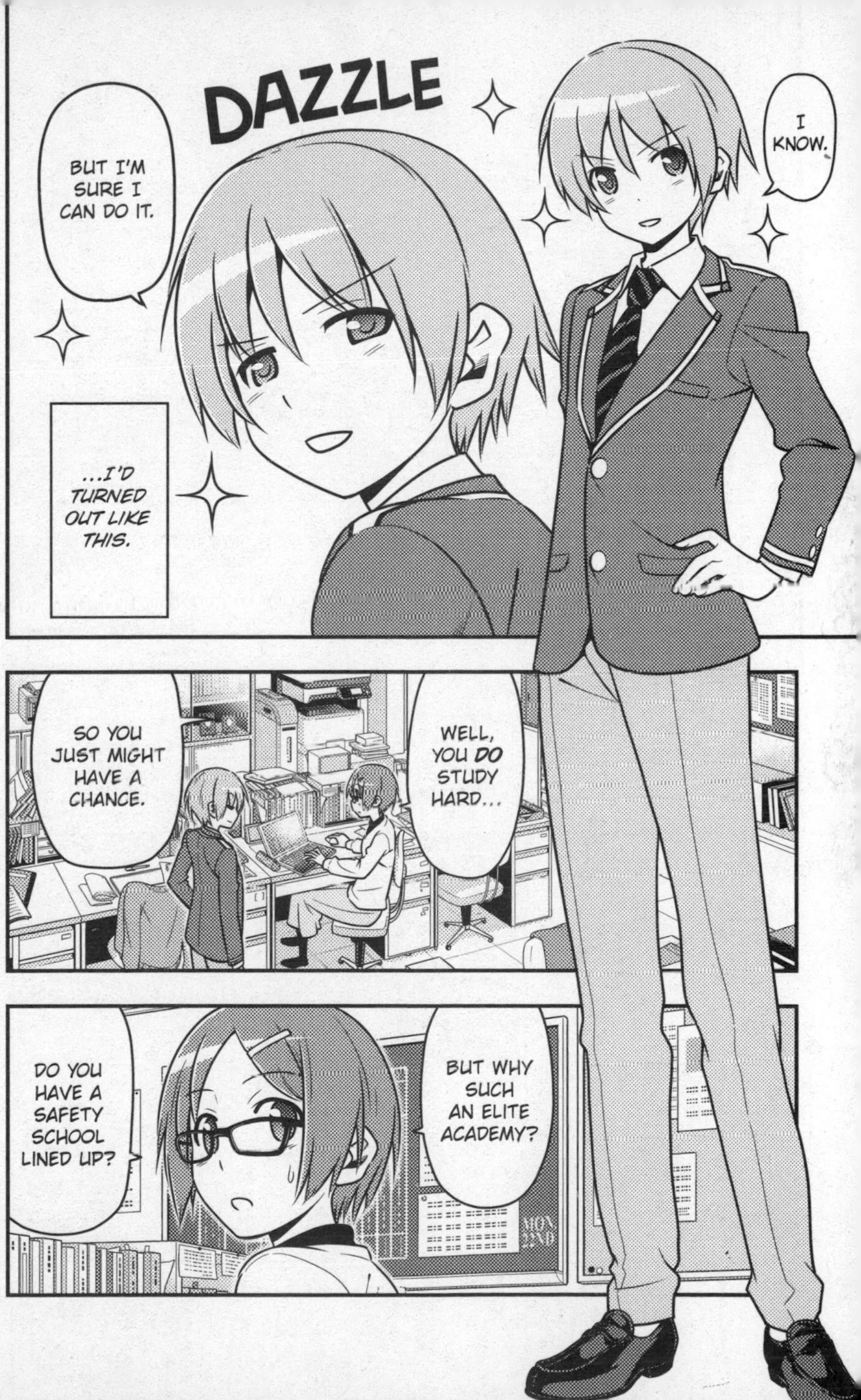
I KNOW.
DAZZLE
BUT I'M SURE I CAN DO IT.
...I'D TURNED OUT LIKE THIS.
WELL, YOU *DO* STUDY HARD...
SO YOU JUST MIGHT HAVE A CHANCE.
BUT WHY SUCH AN ELITE ACADEMY?
DO YOU HAVE A SAFETY SCHOOL LINED UP?

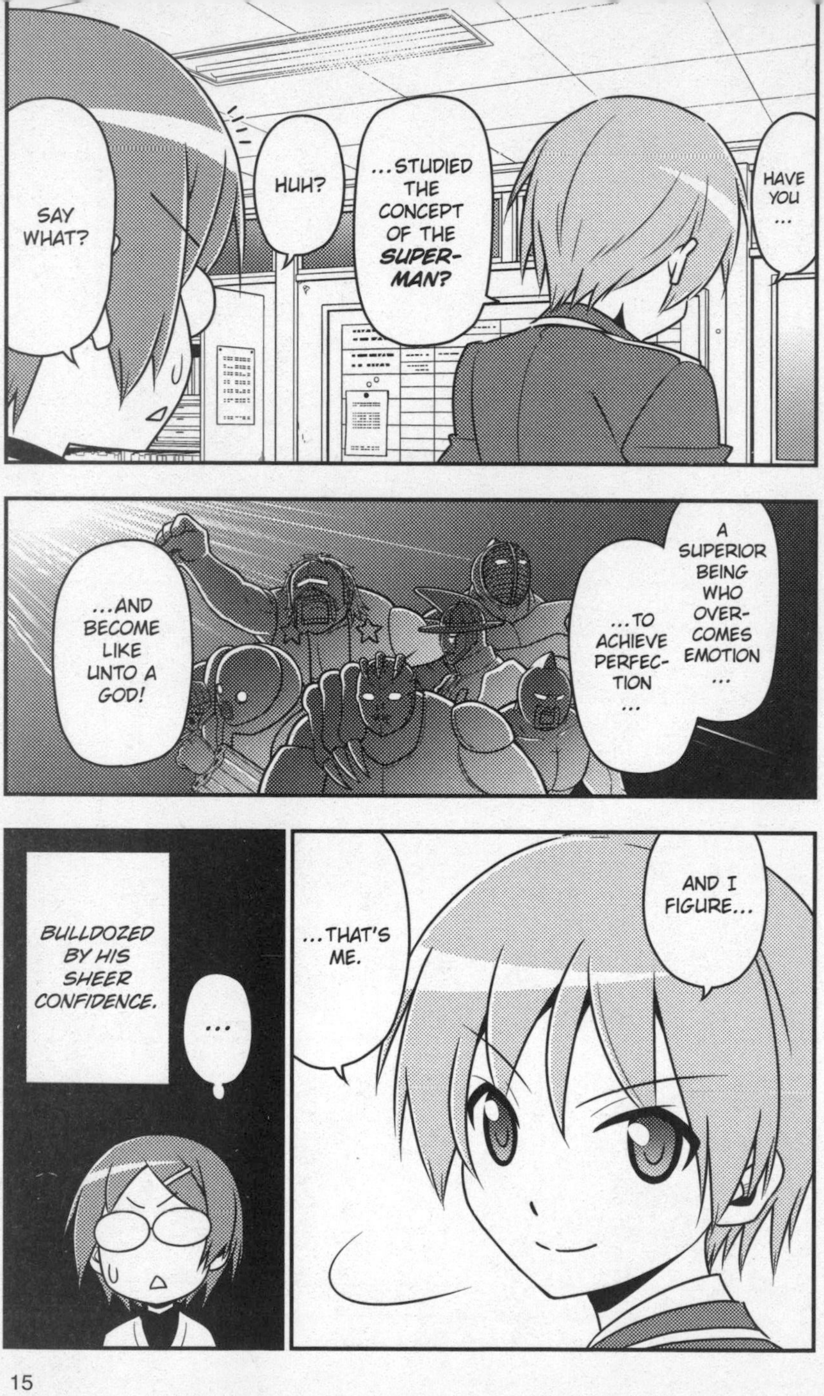
HAVE YOU ...
...STUDIED THE CONCEPT OF THE SUPER-MAN?
HUH?
SAY WHAT?
A SUPERIOR BEING WHO OVER-COMES EMOTION ...
...TO ACHIEVE PERFEC-TION ...
...AND BECOME LIKE UNTO A GOD!
AND I FIGURE...
...THAT'S ME.
BULLDOZED BY HIS SHEER CONFIDENCE.
...

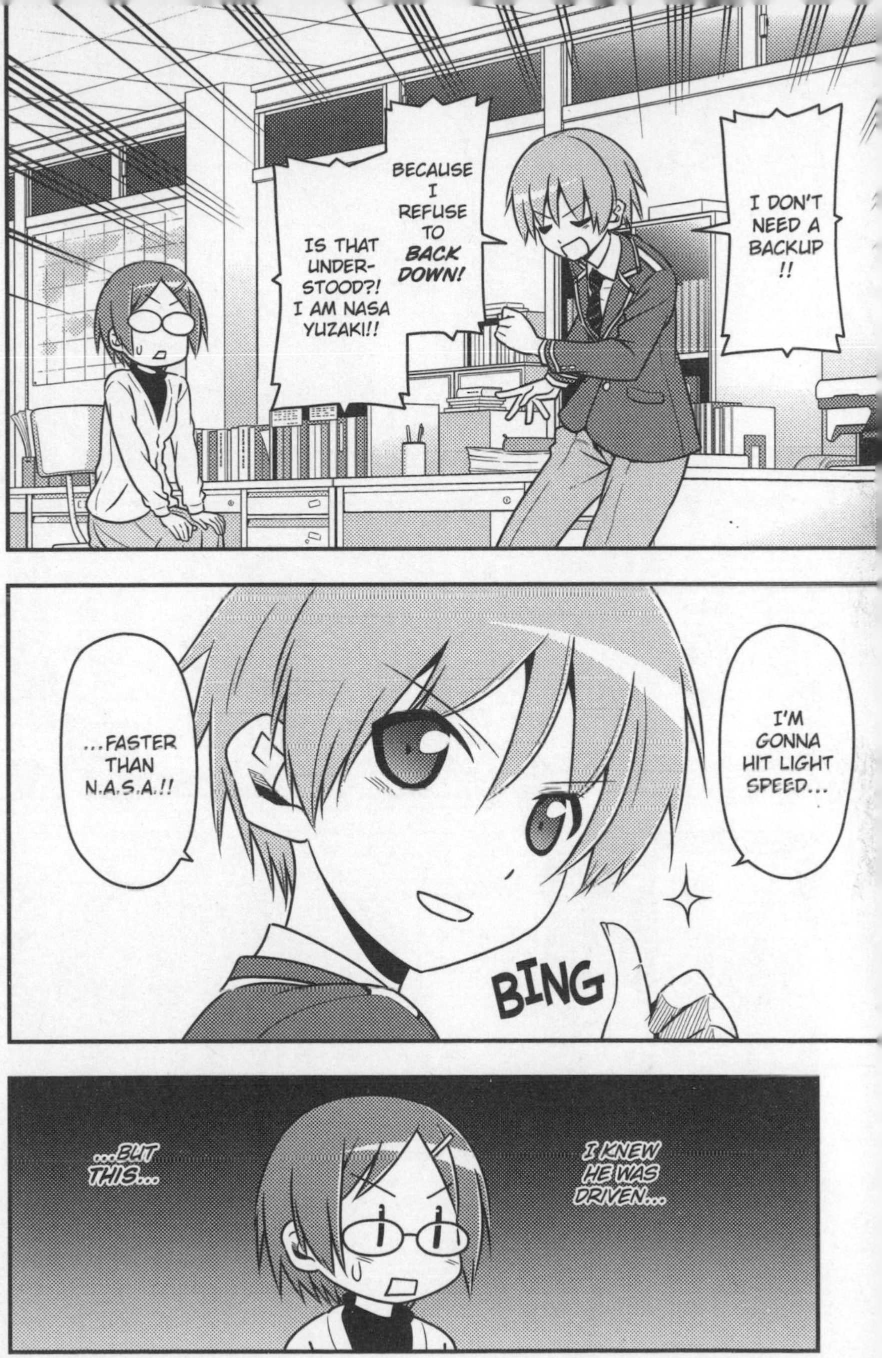
I DON'T NEED A BACKUP !!
BECAUSE I REFUSE TO ***BACK DOWN!***
IS THAT UNDER-STOOD?! I AM NASA YUZAKI!!
I'M GONNA HIT LIGHT SPEED...
BING
...FASTER THAN N.A.S.A.!!
I KNEW HE WAS DRIVEN...
...BUT THIS...

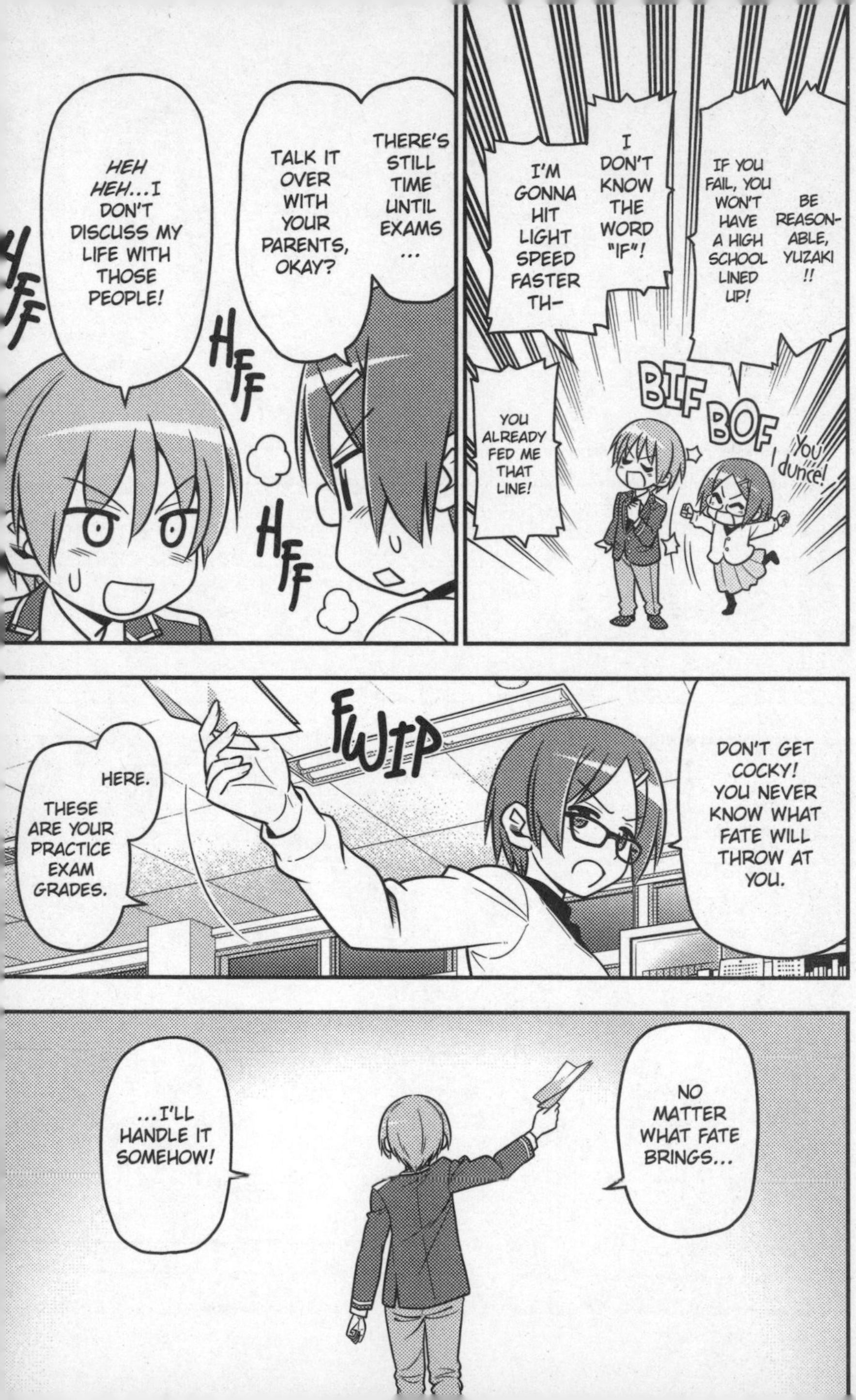
BE REASONABLE, YUZAKI!!
IF YOU FAIL, YOU WON'T HAVE A HIGH SCHOOL LINED UP!
I DON'T KNOW THE WORD "IF"!
I'M GONNA HIT LIGHT SPEED FASTER TH-
BIF BOF
You dunce!
YOU ALREADY FED ME THAT LINE!
THERE'S STILL TIME UNTIL EXAMS...
TALK IT OVER WITH YOUR PARENTS, OKAY?
HFF
HFF
HEH HEH...I DON'T DISCUSS MY LIFE WITH THOSE PEOPLE!
HFF
DON'T GET COCKY! YOU NEVER KNOW WHAT FATE WILL THROW AT YOU.
FWIP
HERE.
THESE ARE YOUR PRACTICE EXAM GRADES.
NO MATTER WHAT FATE BRINGS...
...I'LL HANDLE IT SOMEHOW!

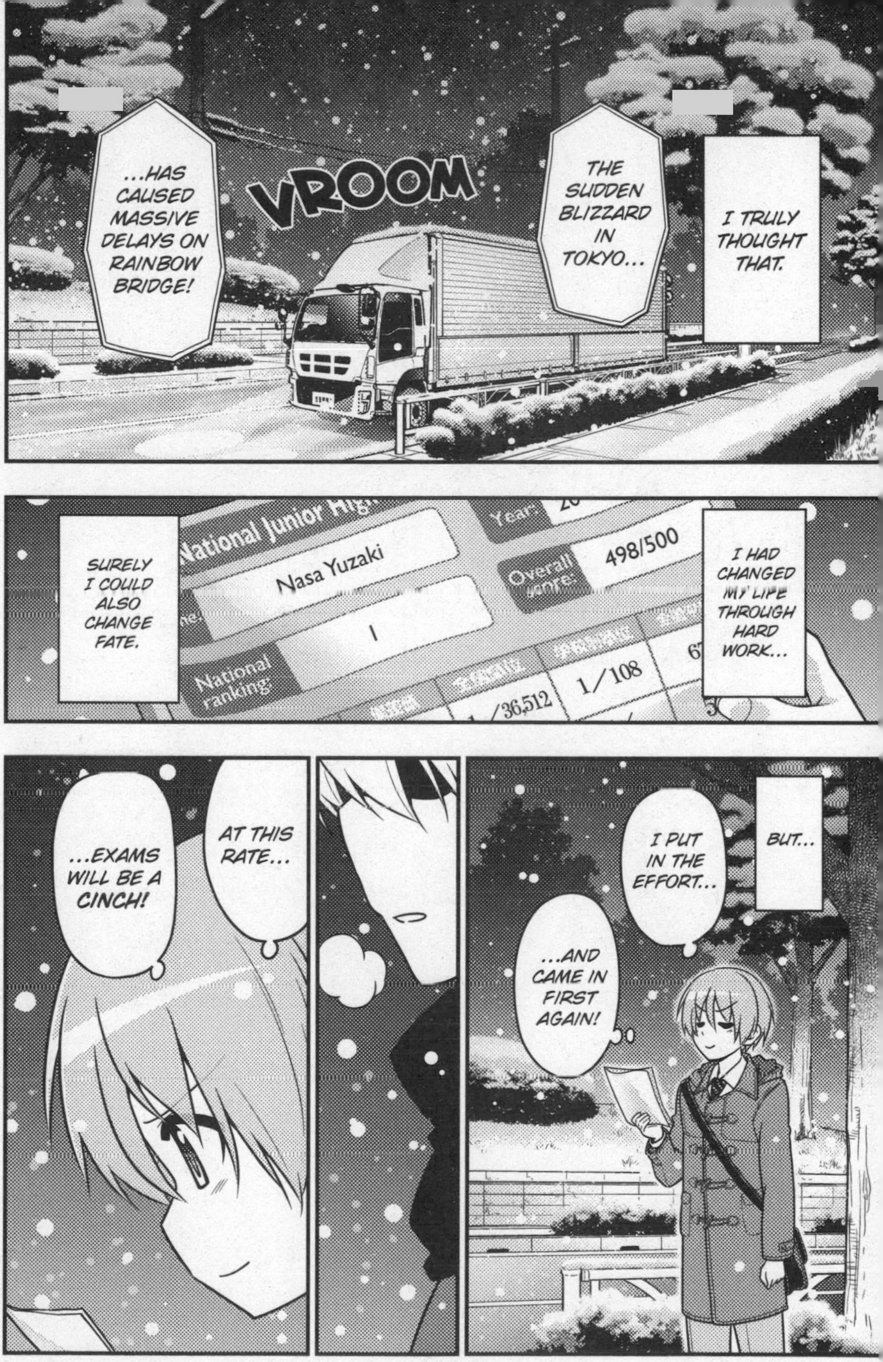
I TRULY THOUGHT THAT.
THE SUDDEN BLIZZARD IN TOKYO...
VROOM
...HAS CAUSED MASSIVE DELAYS ON RAINBOW BRIDGE!
I HAD CHANGED MY LIFE THROUGH HARD WORK...
National Junior High
Year:
Nasa Yuzaki
Overall score:
498/500
National ranking:
1
1/108
1/36,512
SURELY I COULD ALSO CHANGE FATE.
BUT...
I PUT IN THE EFFORT...
...AND CAME IN FIRST AGAIN!
AT THIS RATE...
...EXAMS WILL BE A CINCH!

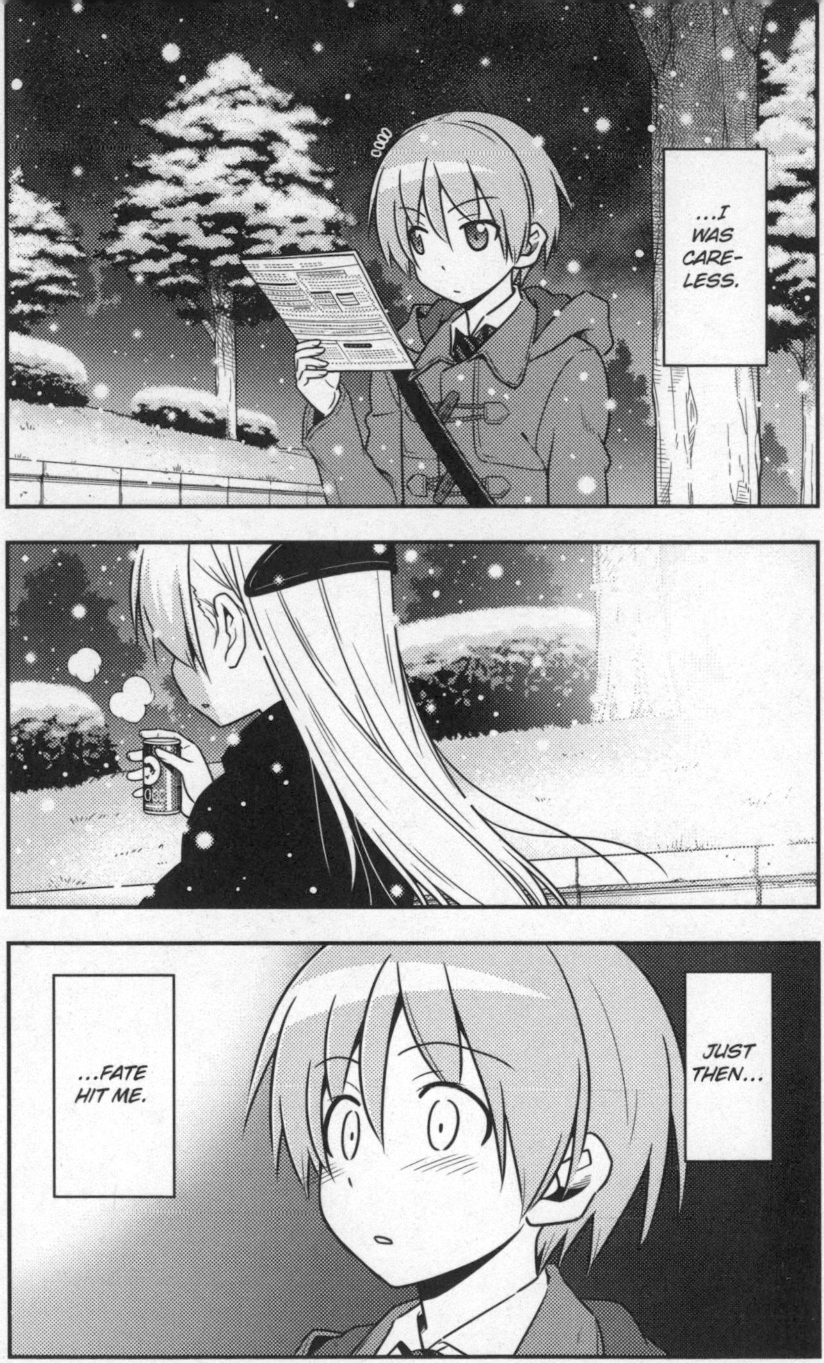
...I WAS CARE-LESS.
JUST THEN...
...FATE HIT ME.

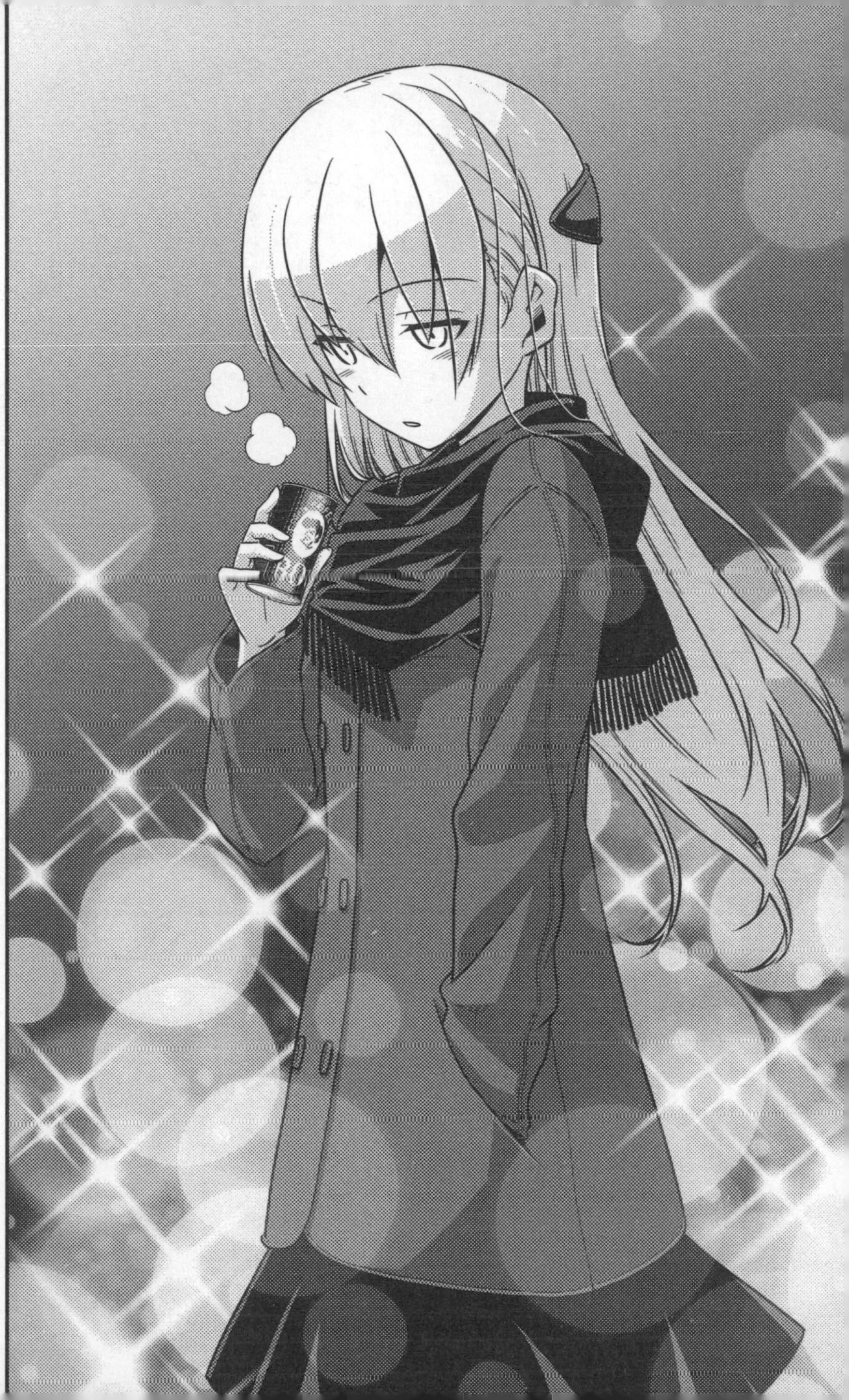

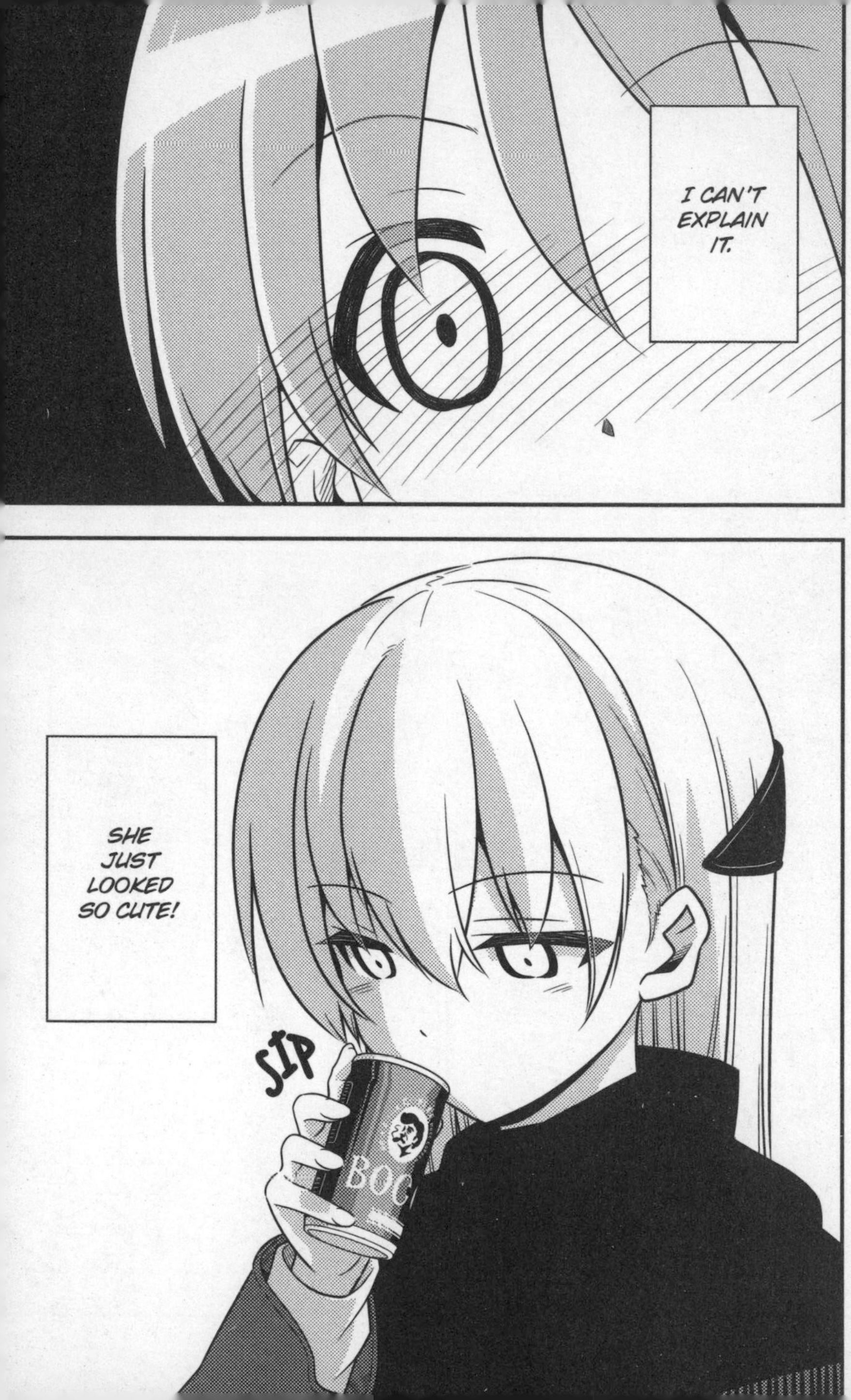
I CAN'T EXPLAIN IT.
SHE JUST LOOKED SO CUTE!
SIP

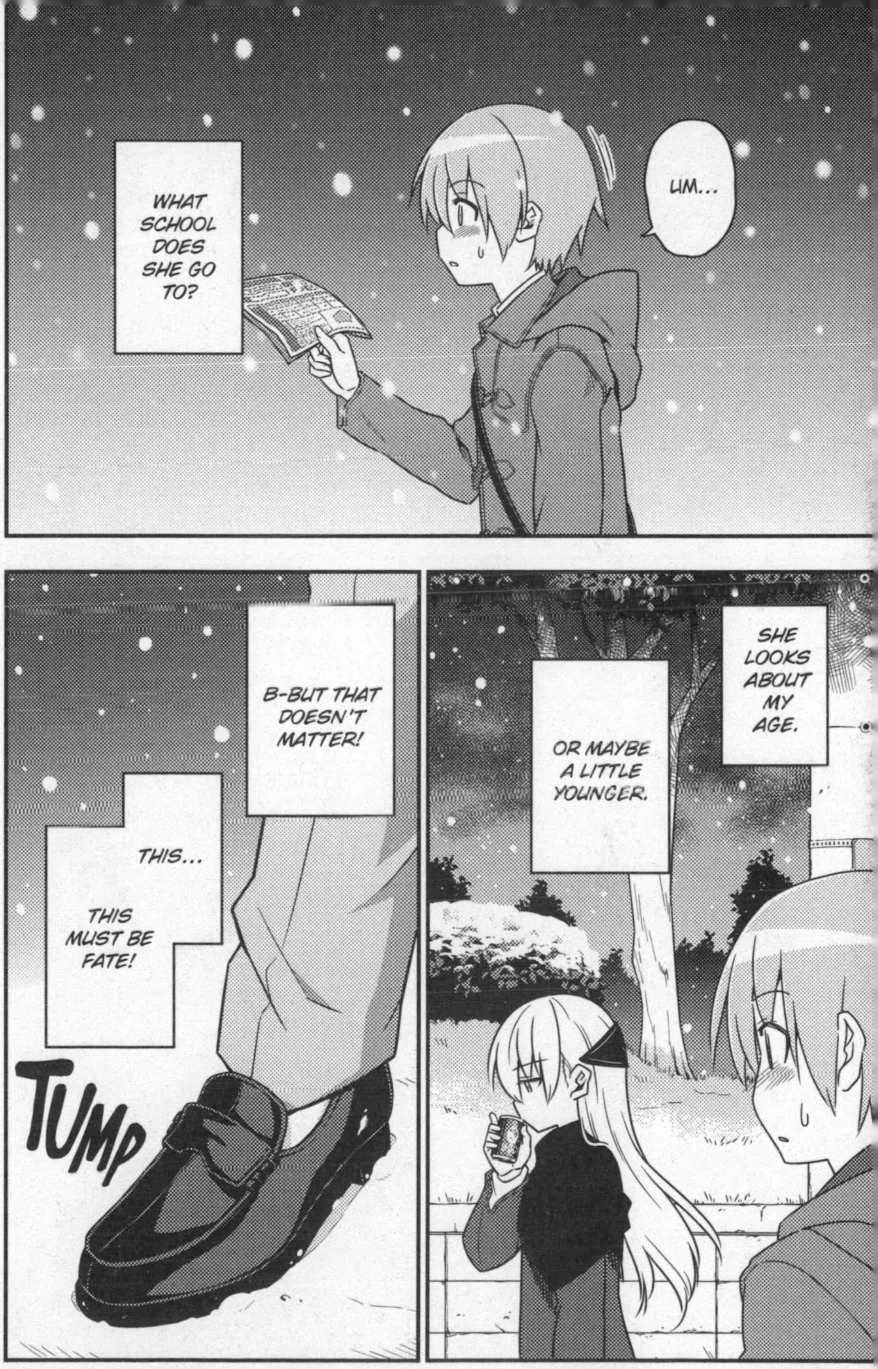
UM...
WHAT SCHOOL DOES SHE GO TO?
SHE LOOKS ABOUT MY AGE.
OR MAYBE A LITTLE YOUNGER.
B-BUT THAT DOESN'T MATTER!
THIS...
THIS MUST BE FATE!
TUMP

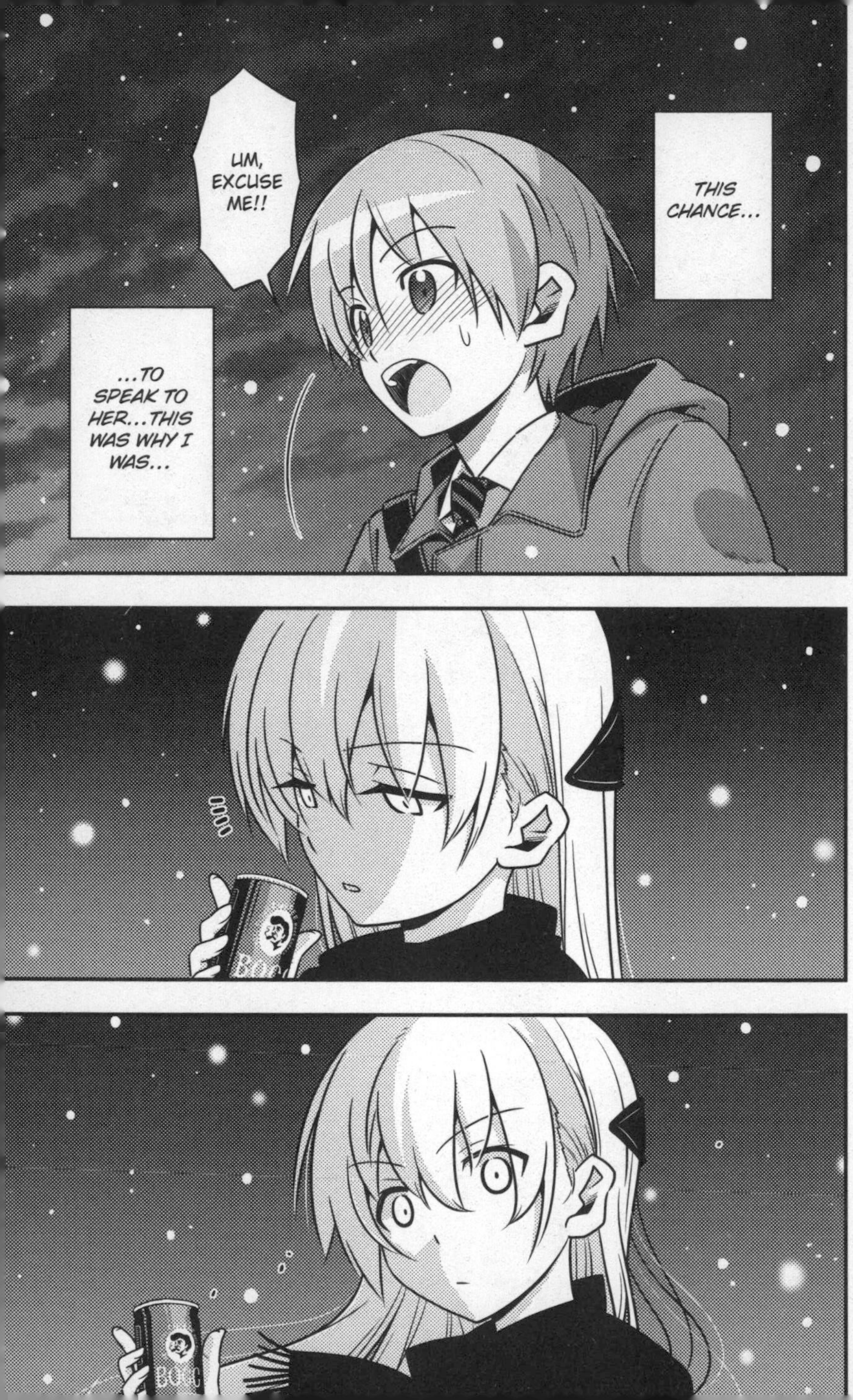
THIS CHANCE...
UM, EXCUSE ME!!
...TO SPEAK TO HER...THIS WAS WHY I WAS...

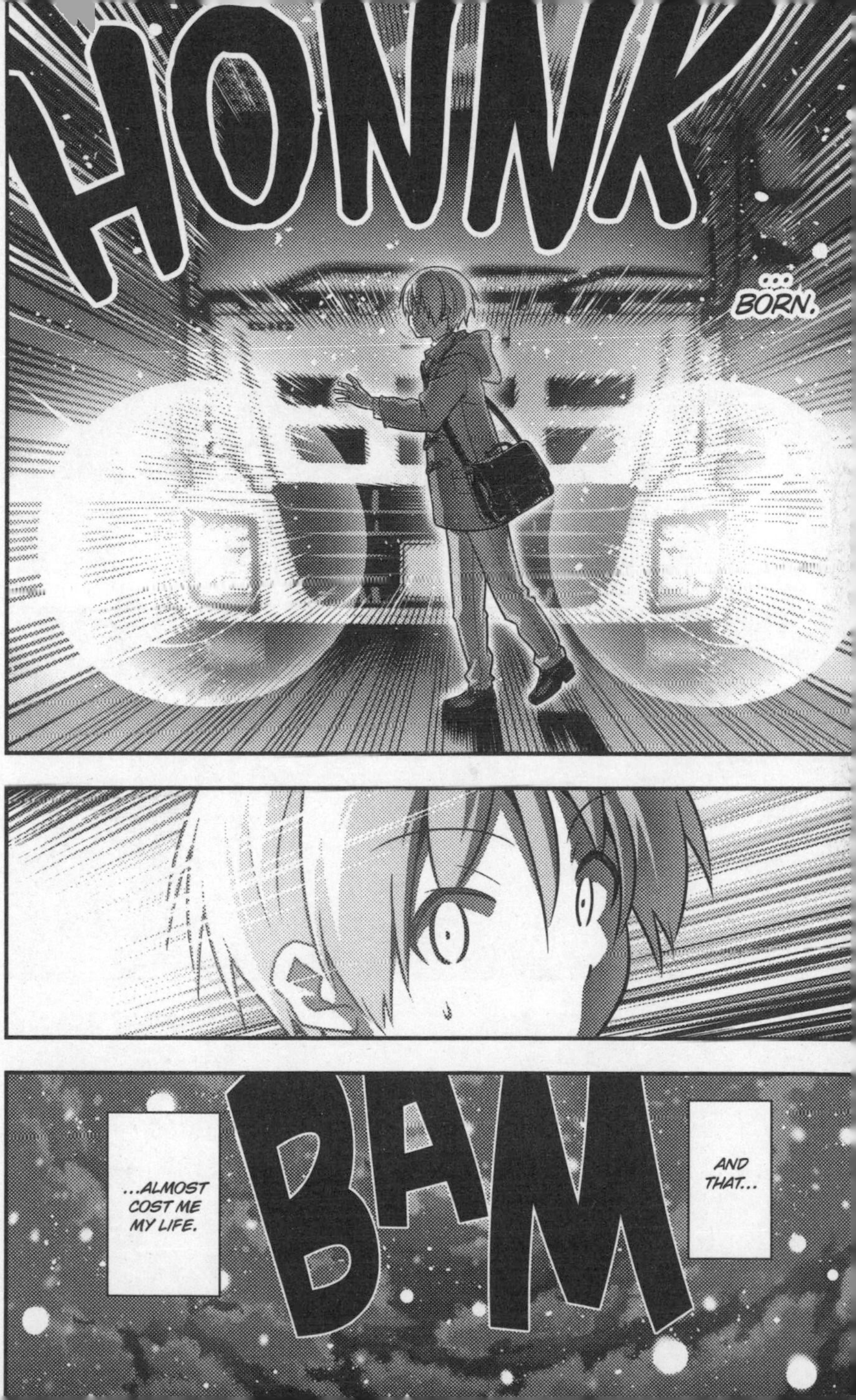
...BORN.
HONK
AND THAT...
BAM
...ALMOST COST ME MY LIFE.

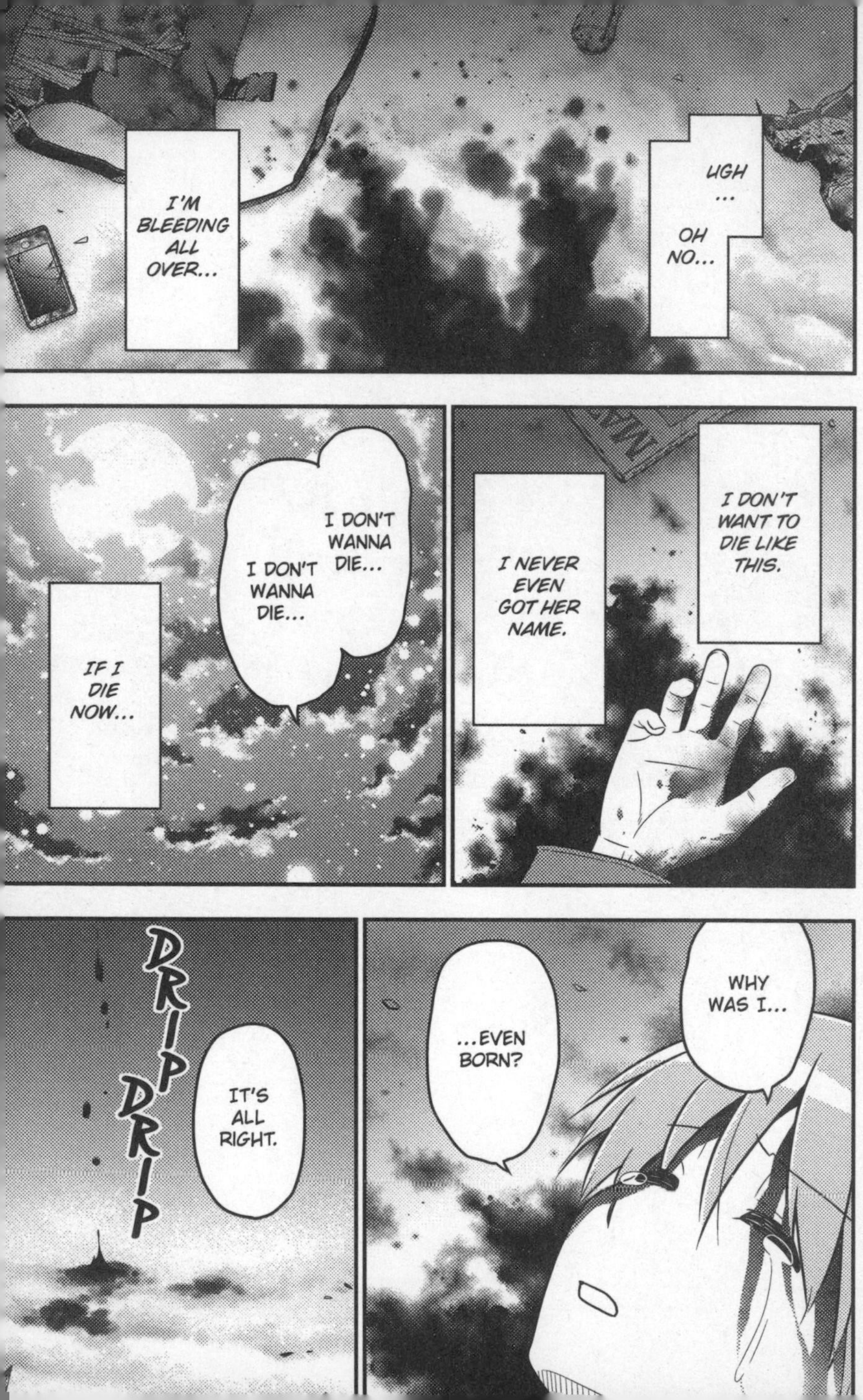
UGH... OH NO...
I'M BLEEDING ALL OVER...
I DON'T WANT TO DIE LIKE THIS.
I NEVER EVEN GOT HER NAME.
I DON'T WANNA DIE...
I DON'T WANNA DIE...
IF I DIE NOW...
WHY WAS I...
...EVEN BORN?
DRIP DRIP
IT'S ALL RIGHT.

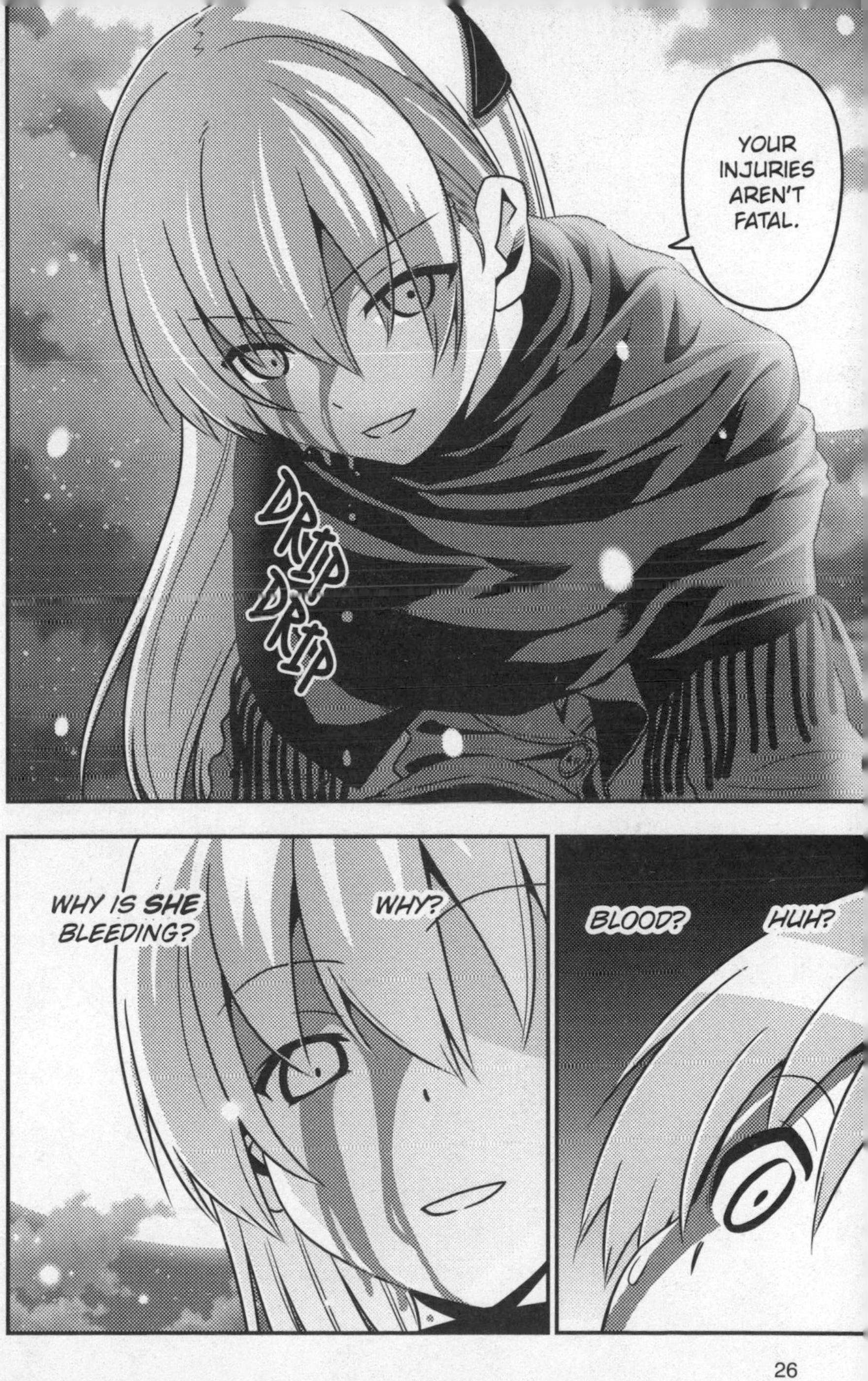
YOUR INJURIES AREN'T FATAL.
DRIP DRIP
HUH?
BLOOD?
WHY?
WHY IS SHE BLEEDING?

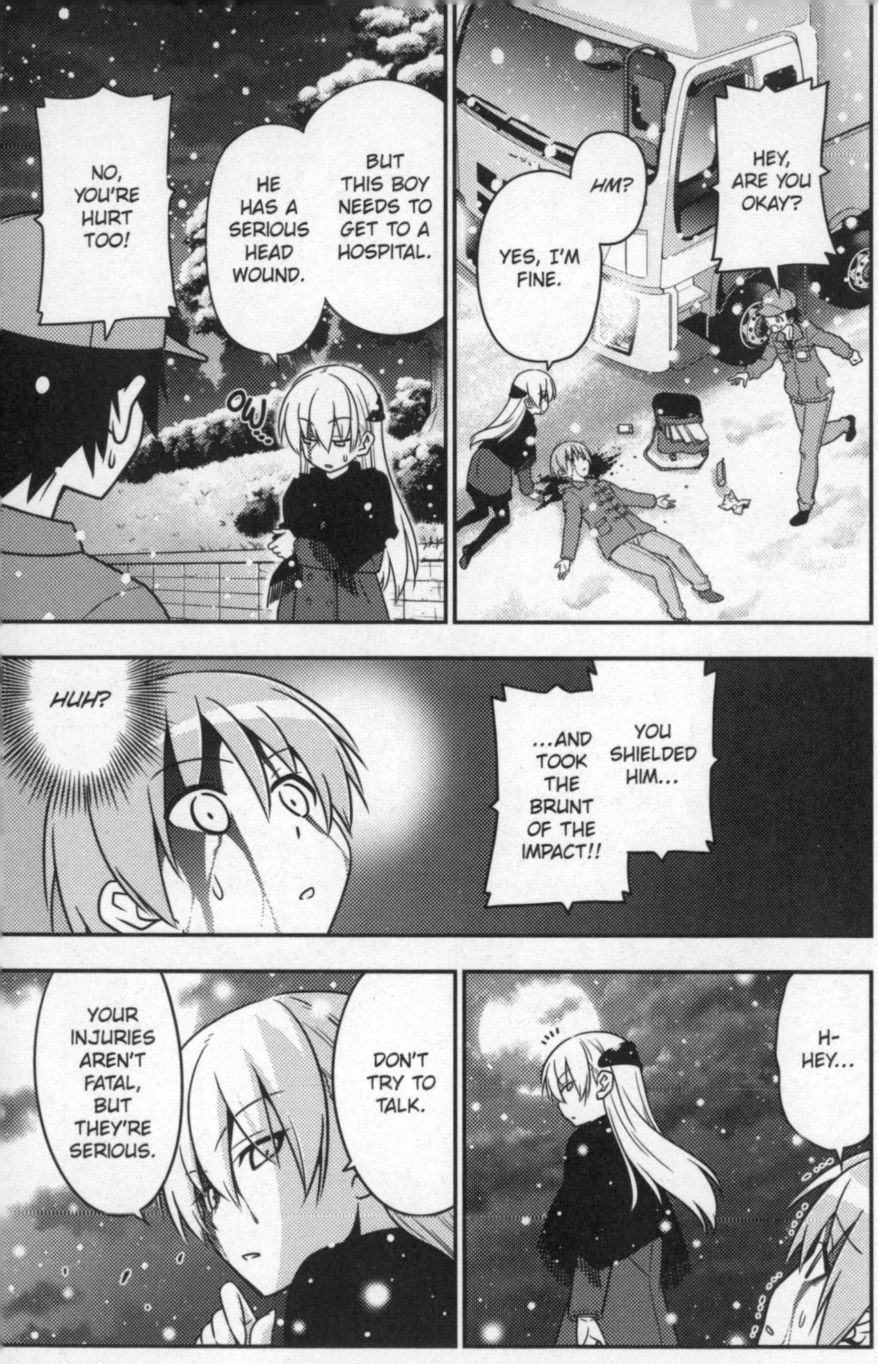
HEY, ARE YOU OKAY?
HM?
YES, I'M FINE.
BUT THIS BOY NEEDS TO GET TO A HOSPITAL.
HE HAS A SERIOUS HEAD WOUND.
OW...
NO, YOU'RE HURT TOO!
YOU SHIELDED HIM...
...AND TOOK THE BRUNT OF THE IMPACT!!
HUH?
H-HEY...
DON'T TRY TO TALK.
YOUR INJURIES AREN'T FATAL, BUT THEY'RE SERIOUS.

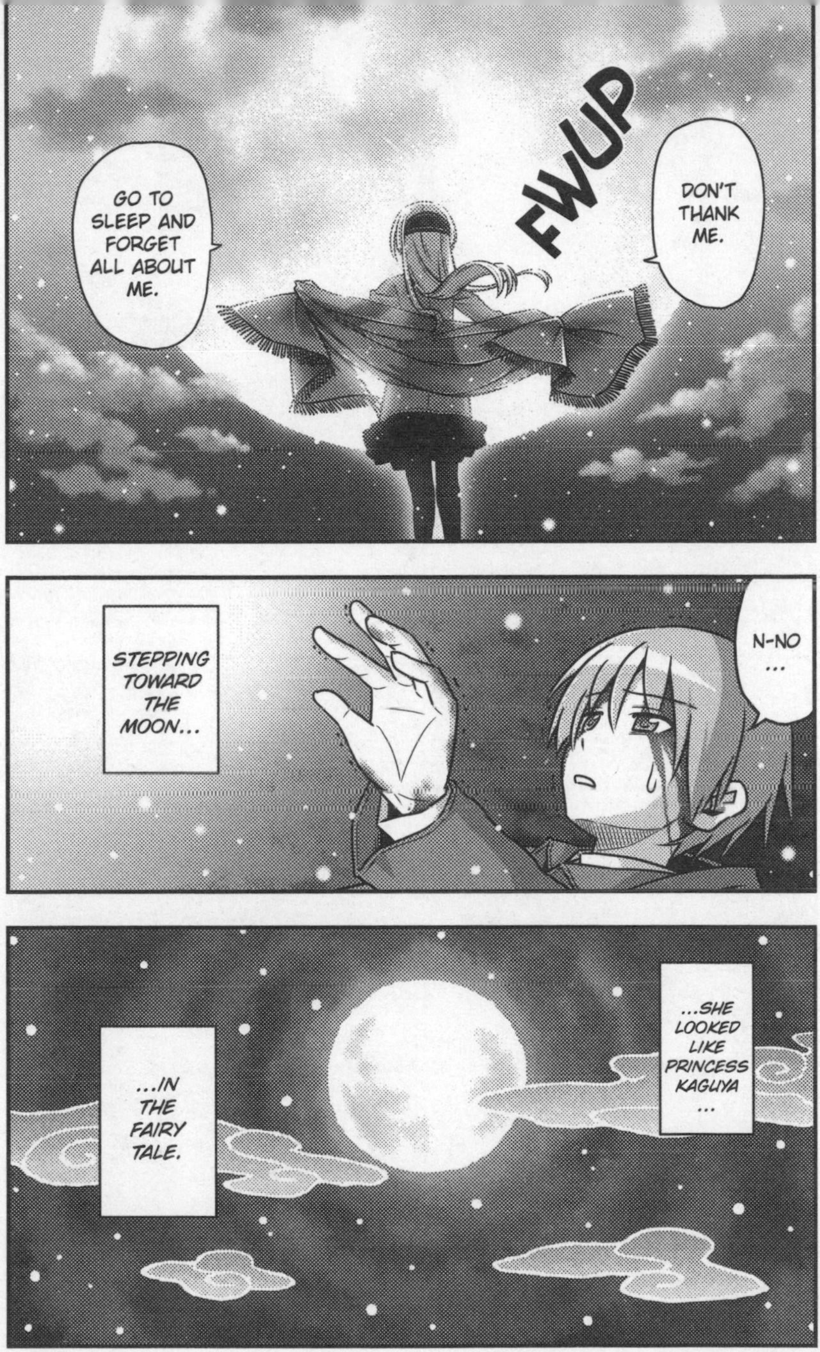
DON'T THANK ME.
FWUP
GO TO SLEEP AND FORGET ALL ABOUT ME.
N-NO ...
STEPPING TOWARD THE MOON...
...SHE LOOKED LIKE PRINCESS KAGUYA ...
...IN THE FAIRY TALE.

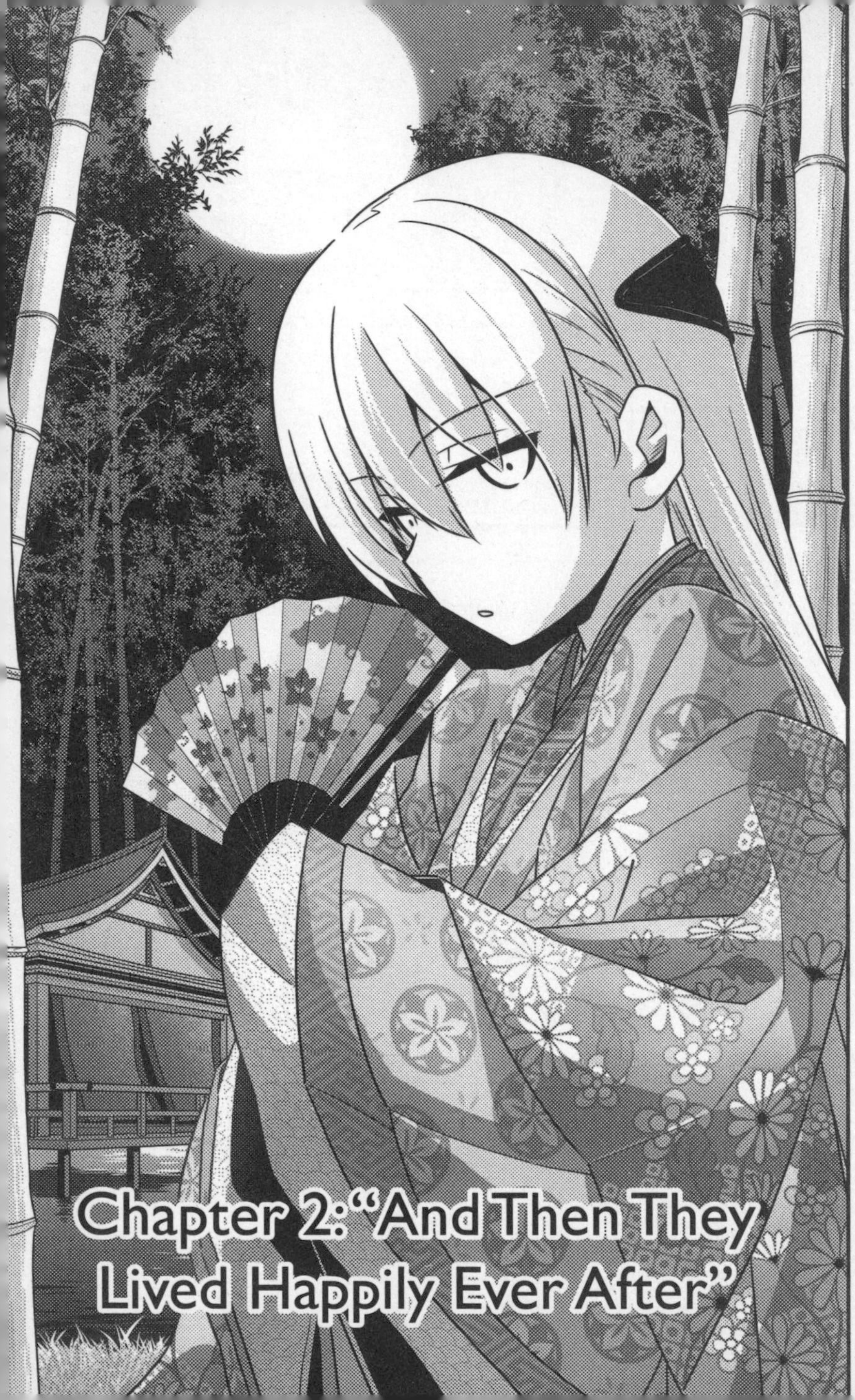
Chapter 2: "And Then They
Lived Happily Ever After"

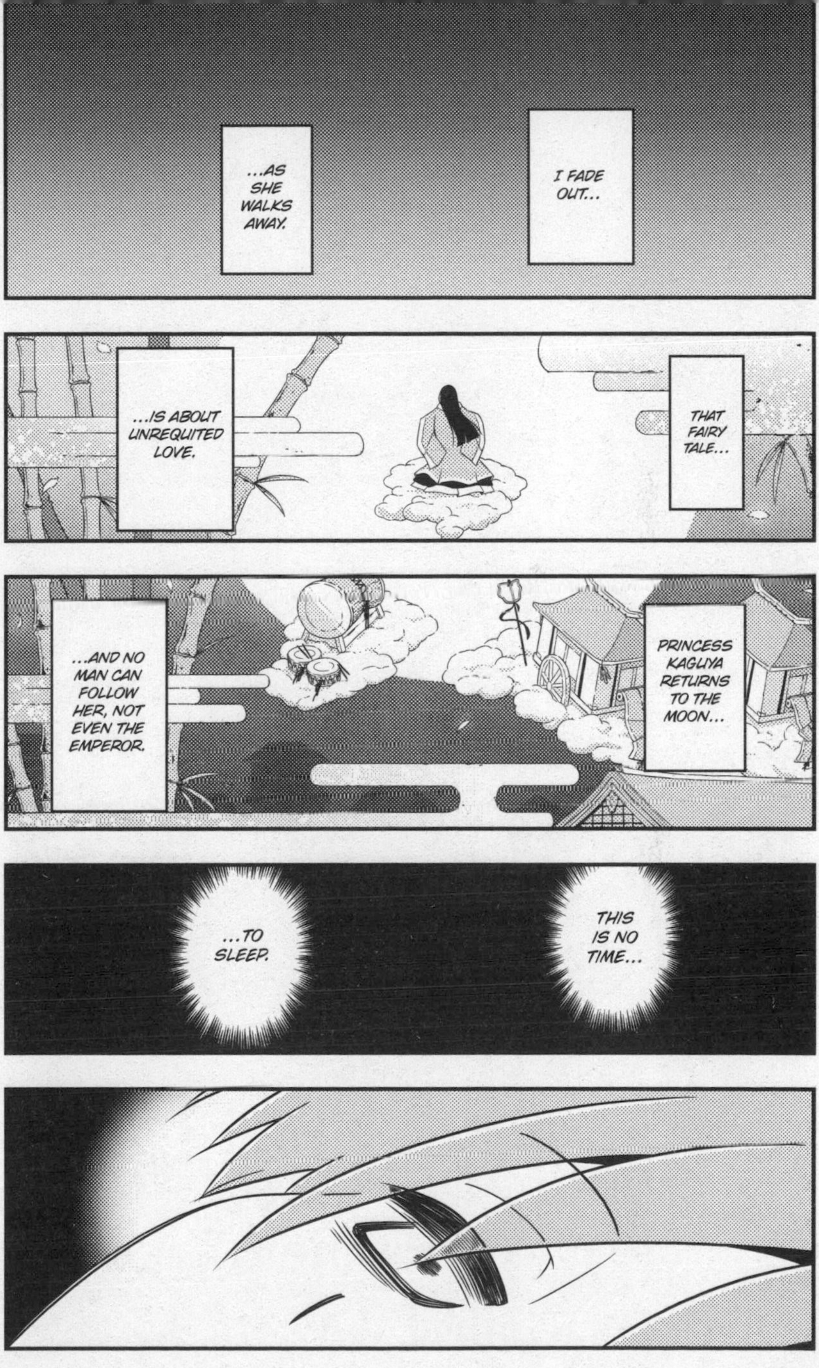
I FADE OUT...
...AS SHE WALKS AWAY.
THAT FAIRY TALE...
...IS ABOUT UNREQUITED LOVE.
PRINCESS KAGUYA RETURNS TO THE MOON...
...AND NO MAN CAN FOLLOW HER, NOT EVEN THE EMPEROR.
THIS IS NO TIME...
...TO SLEEP.

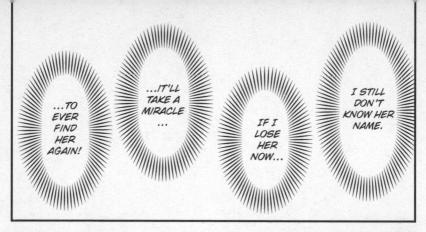

I STILL DON'T KNOW HER NAME.
IF I LOSE HER NOW...
...IT'LL TAKE A MIRACLE...
...TO EVER FIND HER AGAIN!
TWITCH
YES, PLEASE!!
SEND AN AMBULANCE RIGHT AWAY!
GRAB
?!

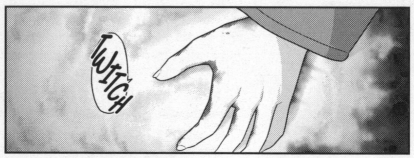

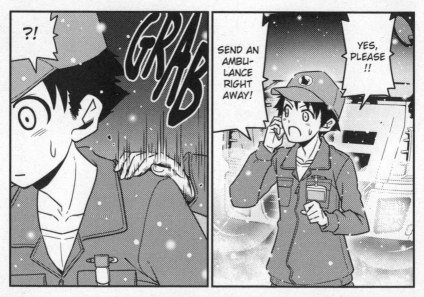

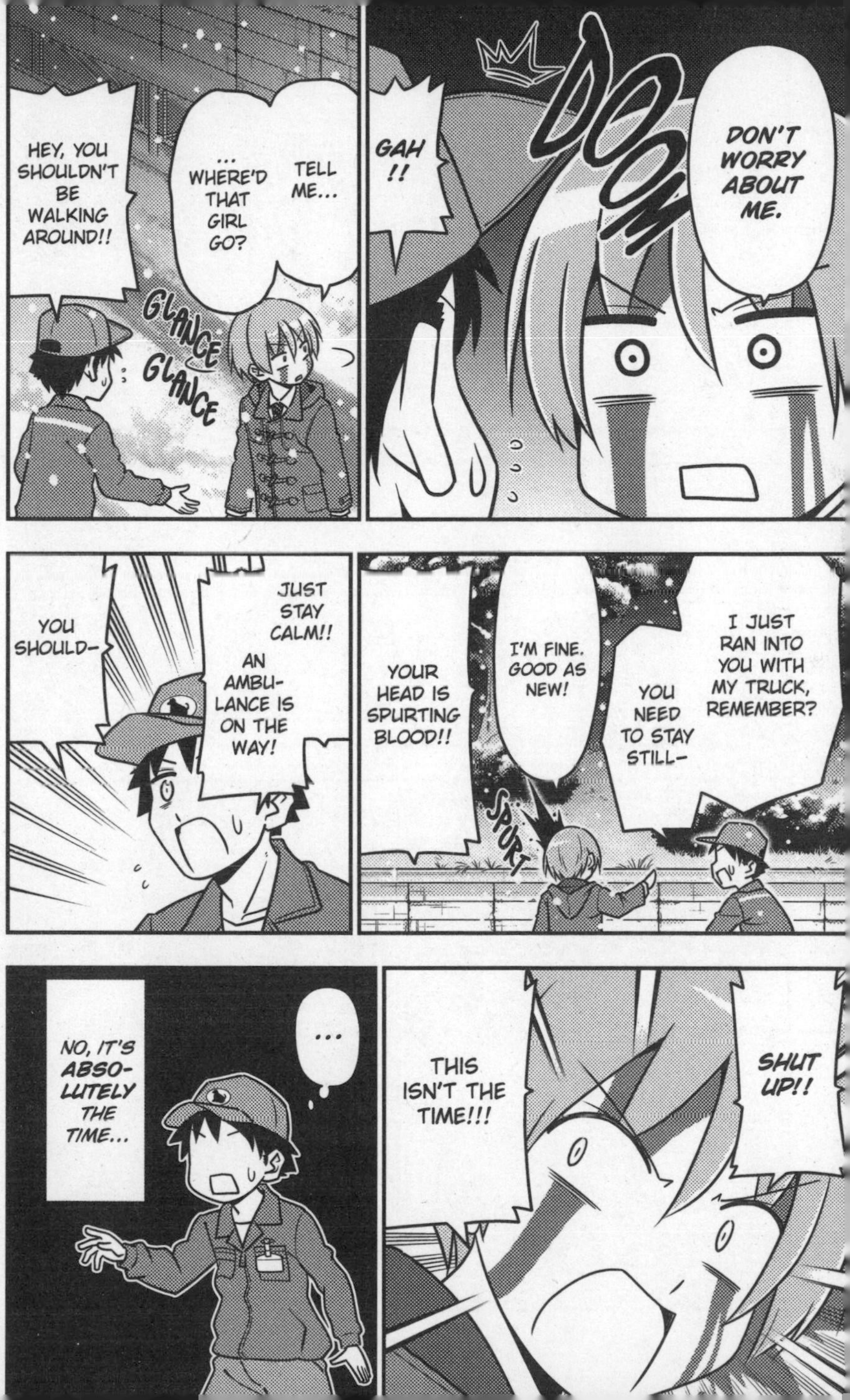
DON'T WORRY ABOUT ME.
DOOM
GAH!!
TELL ME... ...WHERE'D THAT GIRL GO?
HEY, YOU SHOULDN'T BE WALKING AROUND!!
GLANCE GLANCE
I JUST RAN INTO YOU WITH MY TRUCK, REMEMBER? YOU NEED TO STAY STILL-
I'M FINE. GOOD AS NEW!
SPURT
YOUR HEAD IS SPURTING BLOOD!!
JUST STAY CALM!! AN AMBULANCE IS ON THE WAY!
YOU SHOULD-
SHUT UP!!
THIS ISN'T THE TIME!!!
...
NO, IT'S ABSOLUTELY THE TIME...

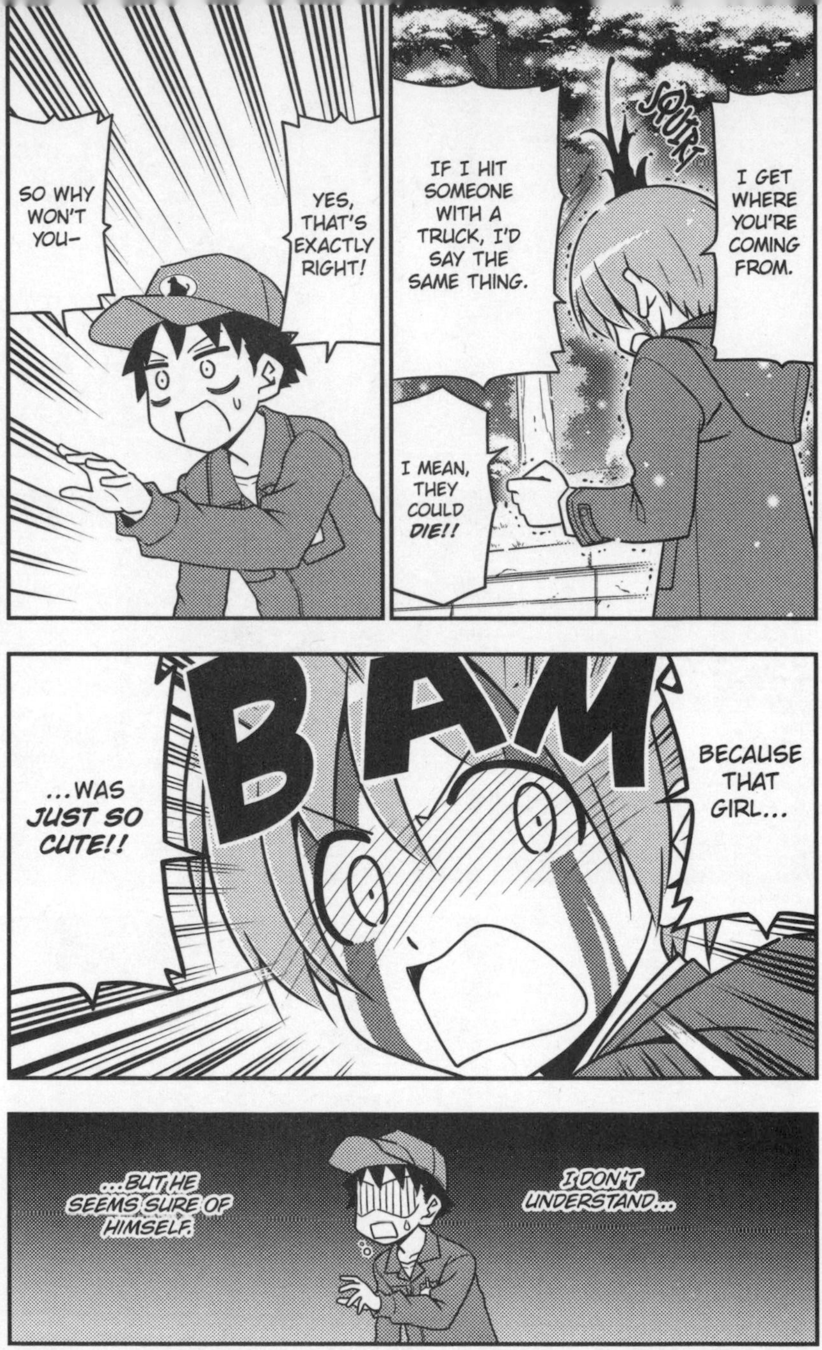
SQUIRT
I GET WHERE YOU'RE COMING FROM.
IF I HIT SOMEONE WITH A TRUCK, I'D SAY THE SAME THING.
I MEAN, THEY COULD DIE!!
YES, THAT'S EXACTLY RIGHT!
SO WHY WON'T YOU–
BAM
BECAUSE THAT GIRL...
...WAS JUST SO CUTE!!
I DON'T UNDERSTAND...
...BUT HE SEEMS SURE OF HIMSELF.

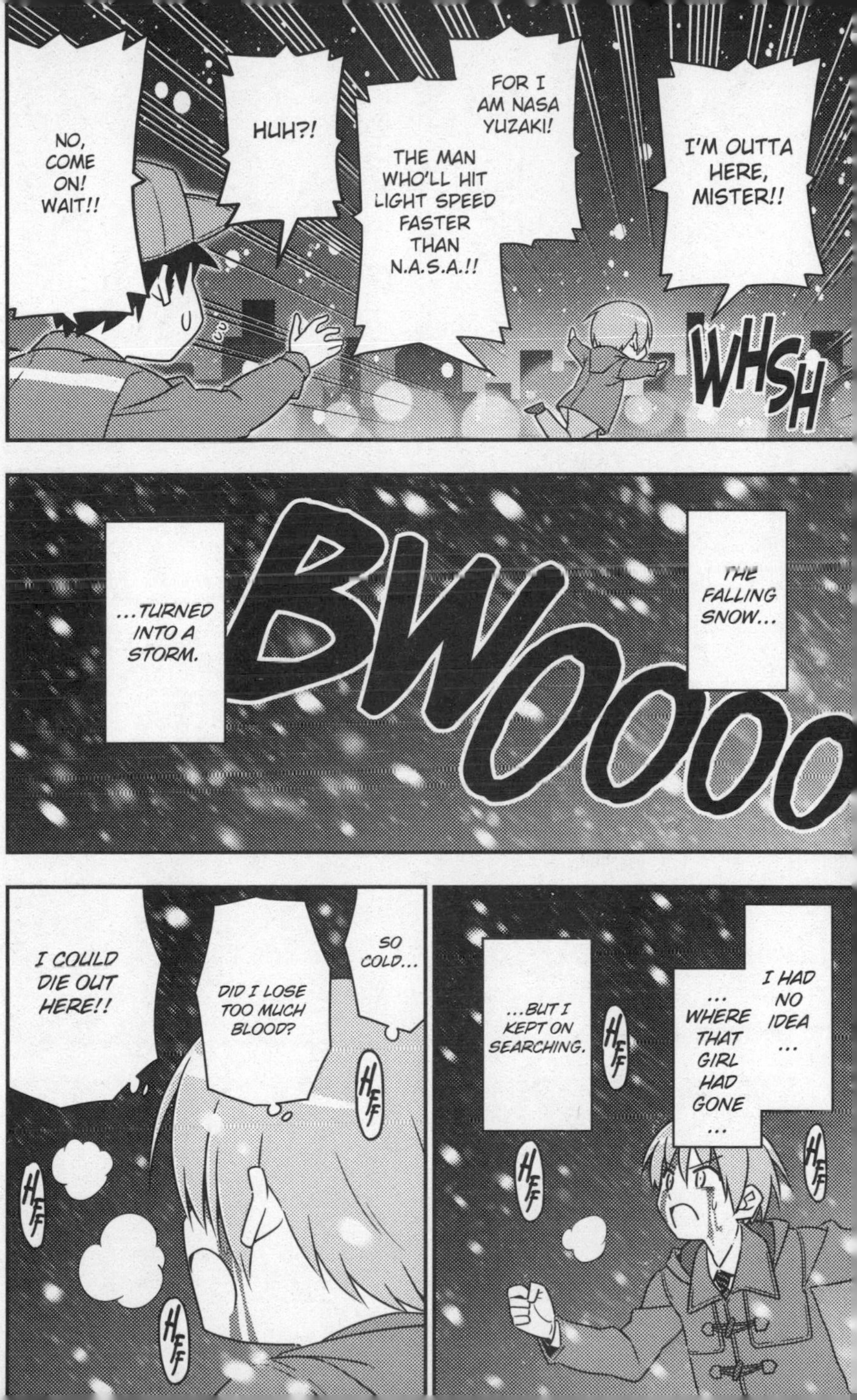
I'M OUTTA HERE, MISTER!!
WHSH
FOR I AM NASA YUZAKI!
THE MAN WHO'LL HIT LIGHT SPEED FASTER THAN N.A.S.A.!!
HUH?!
NO, COME ON! WAIT!!
THE FALLING SNOW...
BWOOOOO
...TURNED INTO A STORM.
I HAD NO IDEA...
...WHERE THAT GIRL HAD GONE...
HEFF
...BUT I KEPT ON SEARCHING.
HEFF
HEFF
SO COLD...
DID I LOSE TOO MUCH BLOOD?
HEFF
I COULD DIE OUT HERE!!
HEFF
HEFF

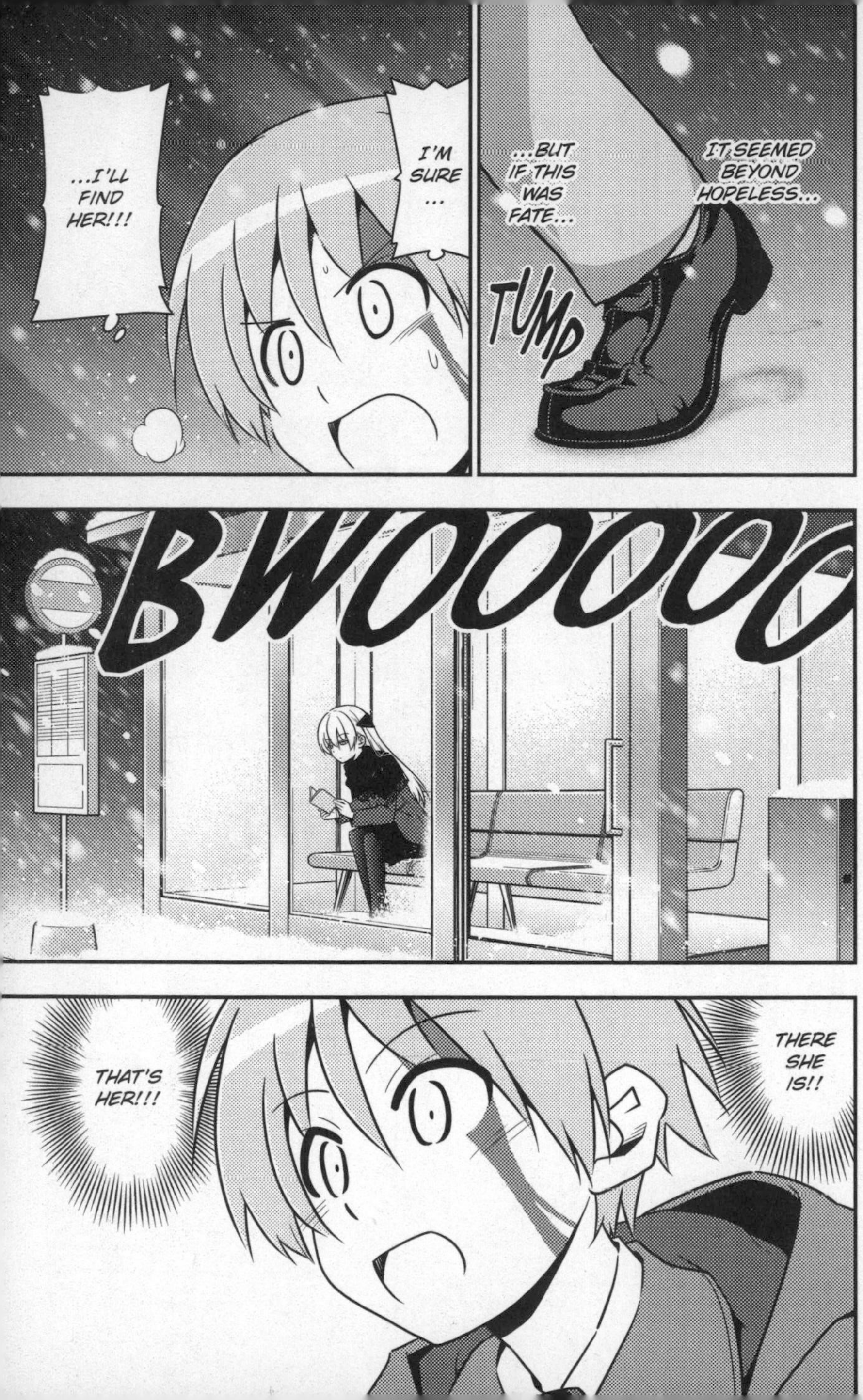
IT SEEMED BEYOND HOPELESS...
...BUT IF THIS WAS FATE...
TUMP
I'M SURE...
...I'LL FIND HER!!!
BWOOOOO
THERE SHE IS!!
THAT'S HER!!!

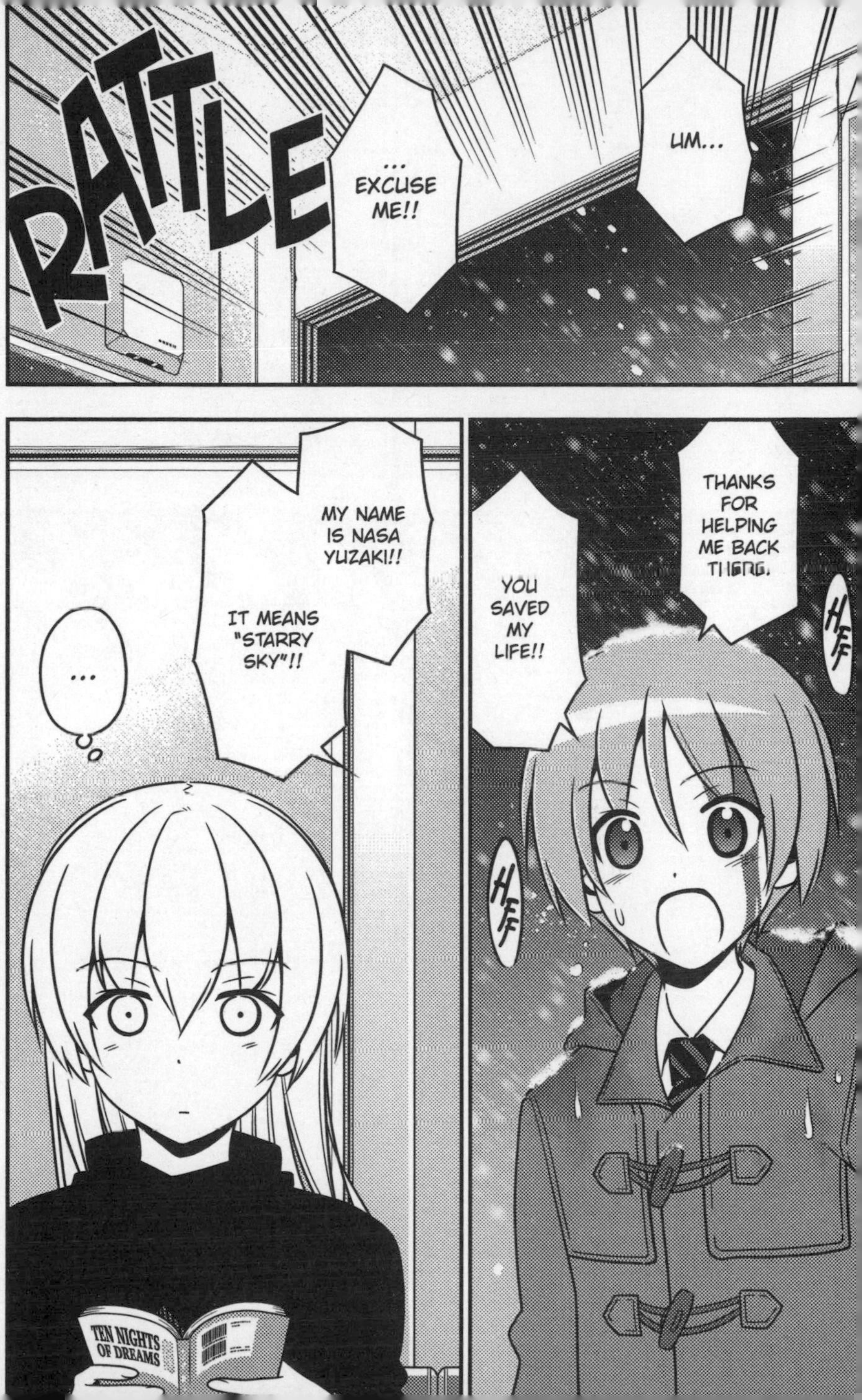
UM...
... EXCUSE ME!!
RATTLE
THANKS FOR HELPING ME BACK THERE.
HFF
YOU SAVED MY LIFE!!
HFF
MY NAME IS NASA YUZAKI!!
IT MEANS "STARRY SKY"!!
...
TEN NIGHTS OF DREAMS

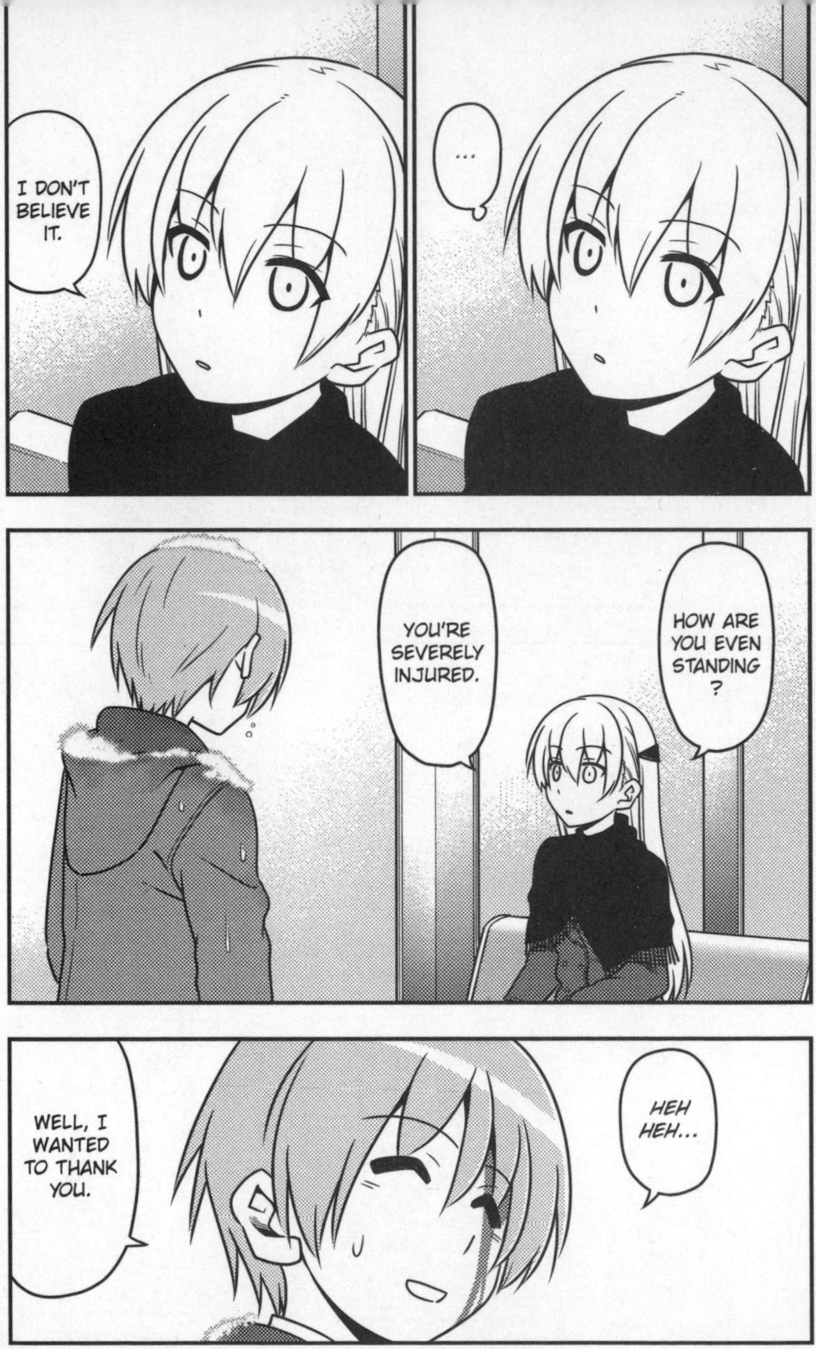
...
I DON'T BELIEVE IT.
HOW ARE YOU EVEN STANDING?
YOU'RE SEVERELY INJURED.
HEH HEH...
WELL, I WANTED TO THANK YOU.

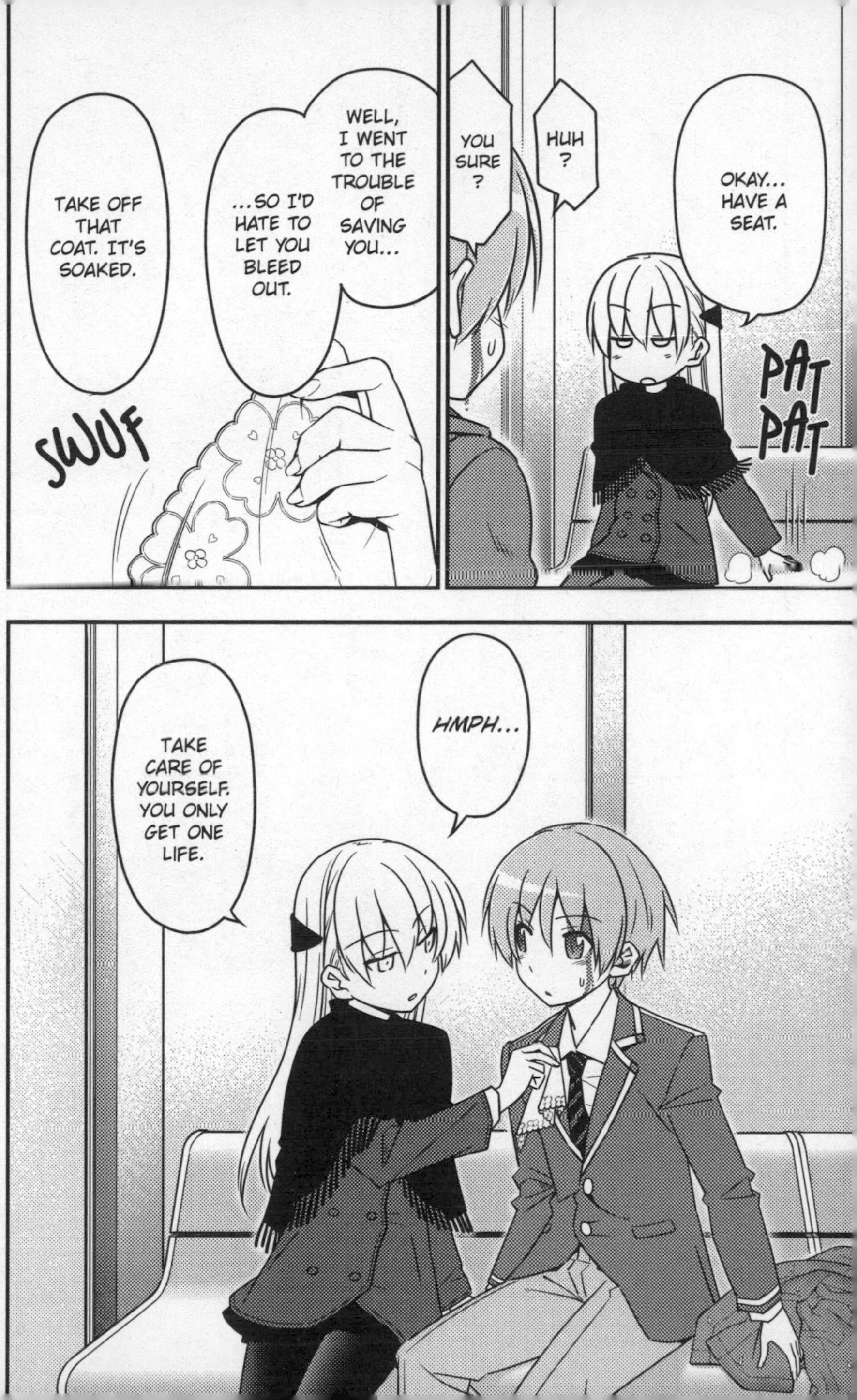
OKAY... HAVE A SEAT.
PAT PAT
HUH?
YOU SURE?
WELL, I WENT TO THE TROUBLE OF SAVING YOU...
...SO I'D HATE TO LET YOU BLEED OUT.
TAKE OFF THAT COAT. IT'S SOAKED.
SWUF
HMPH...
TAKE CARE OF YOURSELF. YOU ONLY GET ONE LIFE.

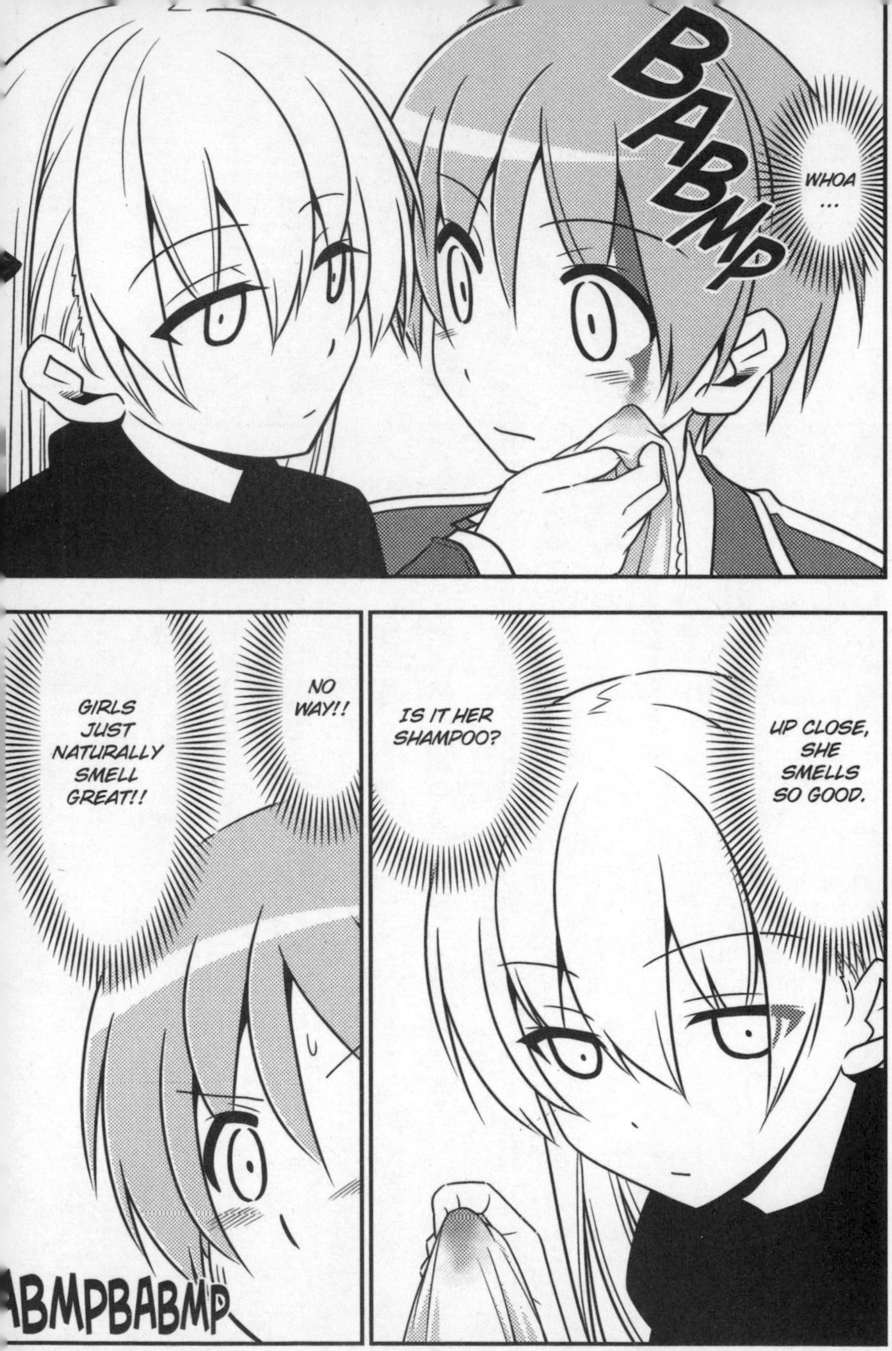
BABMP
WHOA ...
UP CLOSE, SHE SMELLS SO GOOD.
IS IT HER SHAMPOO?
NO WAY!!
GIRLS JUST NATURALLY SMELL GREAT!!
ABMPBABMP

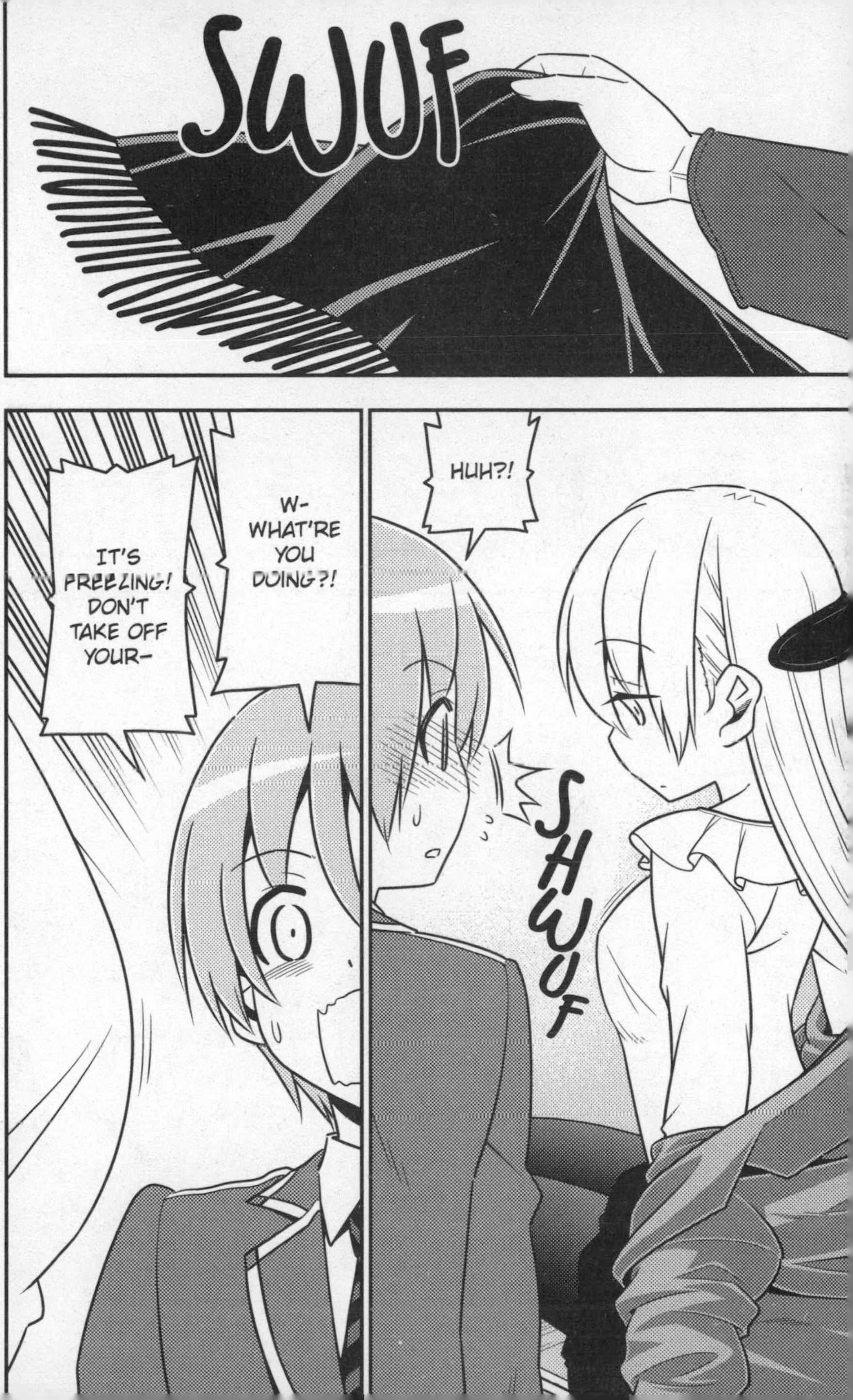
SWUF
HUH?!
SHWUF
W-WHAT'RE YOU DOING?!
IT'S FREEZING! DON'T TAKE OFF YOUR-

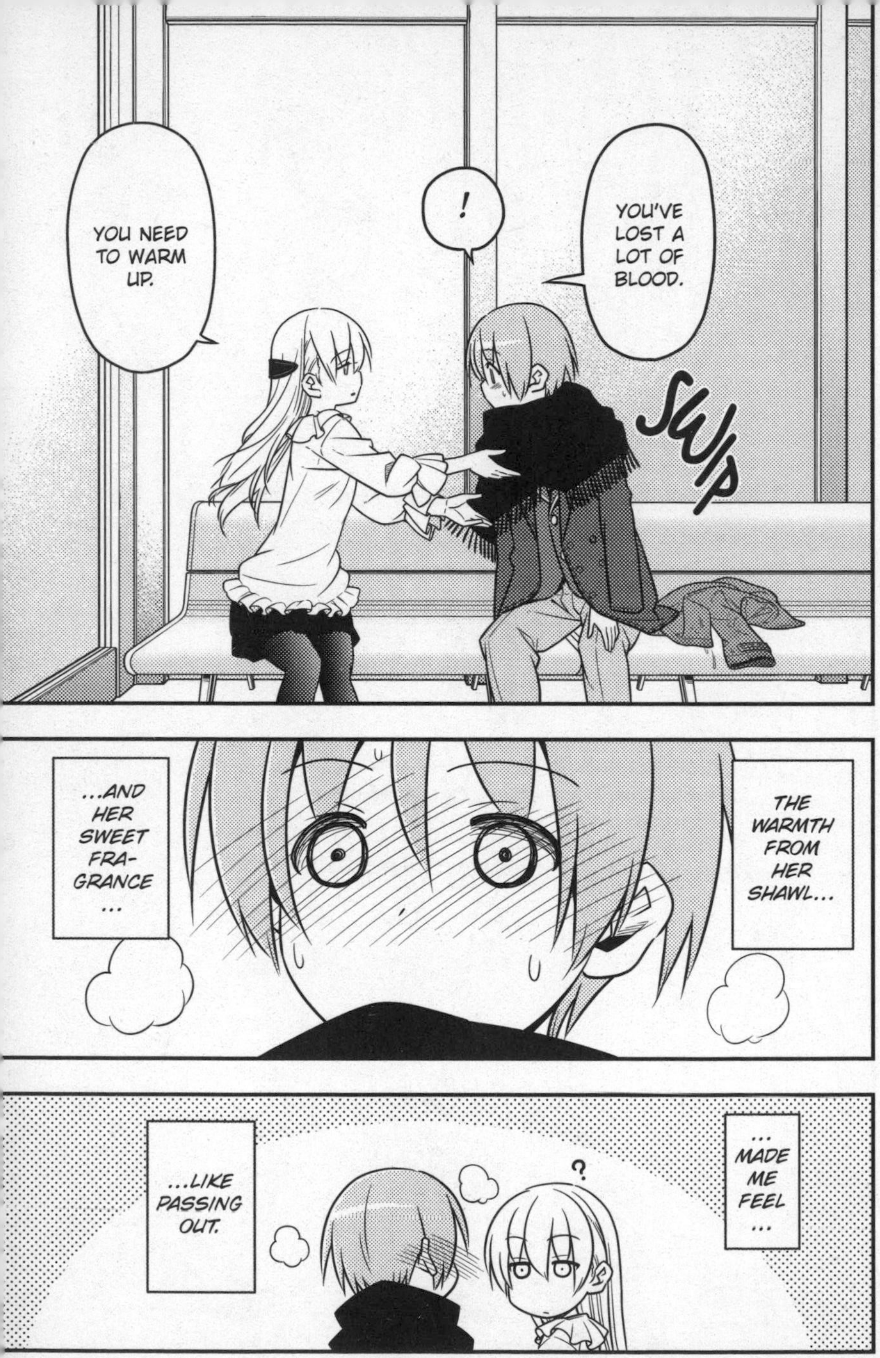
YOU'VE LOST A LOT OF BLOOD.
!
YOU NEED TO WARM UP.
SWIP
THE WARMTH FROM HER SHAWL...
...AND HER SWEET FRA-GRANCE...
...MADE ME FEEL...
?
...LIKE PASSING OUT.

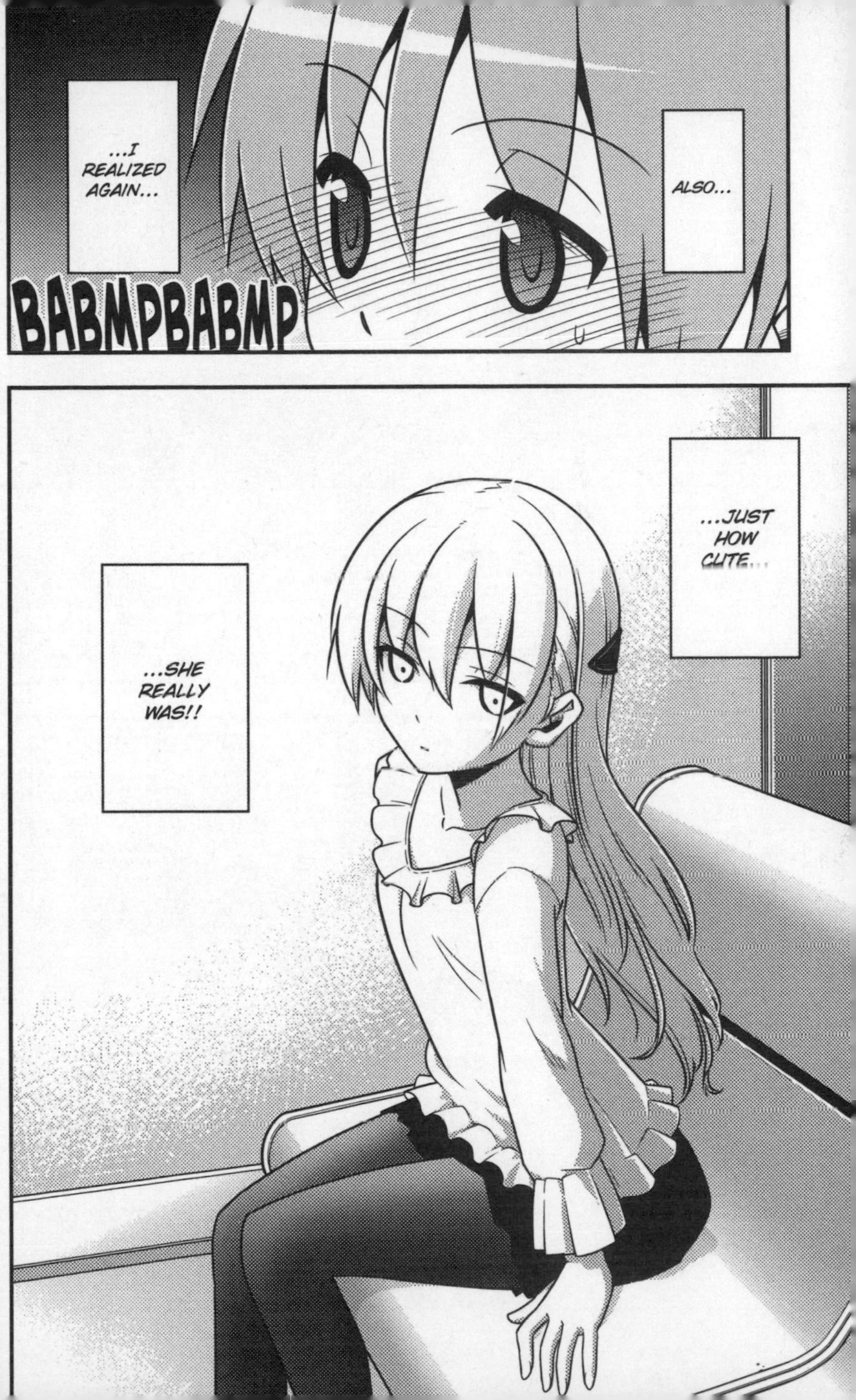
ALSO...
...I REALIZED AGAIN...
BABMPBABMP
...JUST HOW CUTE...
...SHE REALLY WAS!!

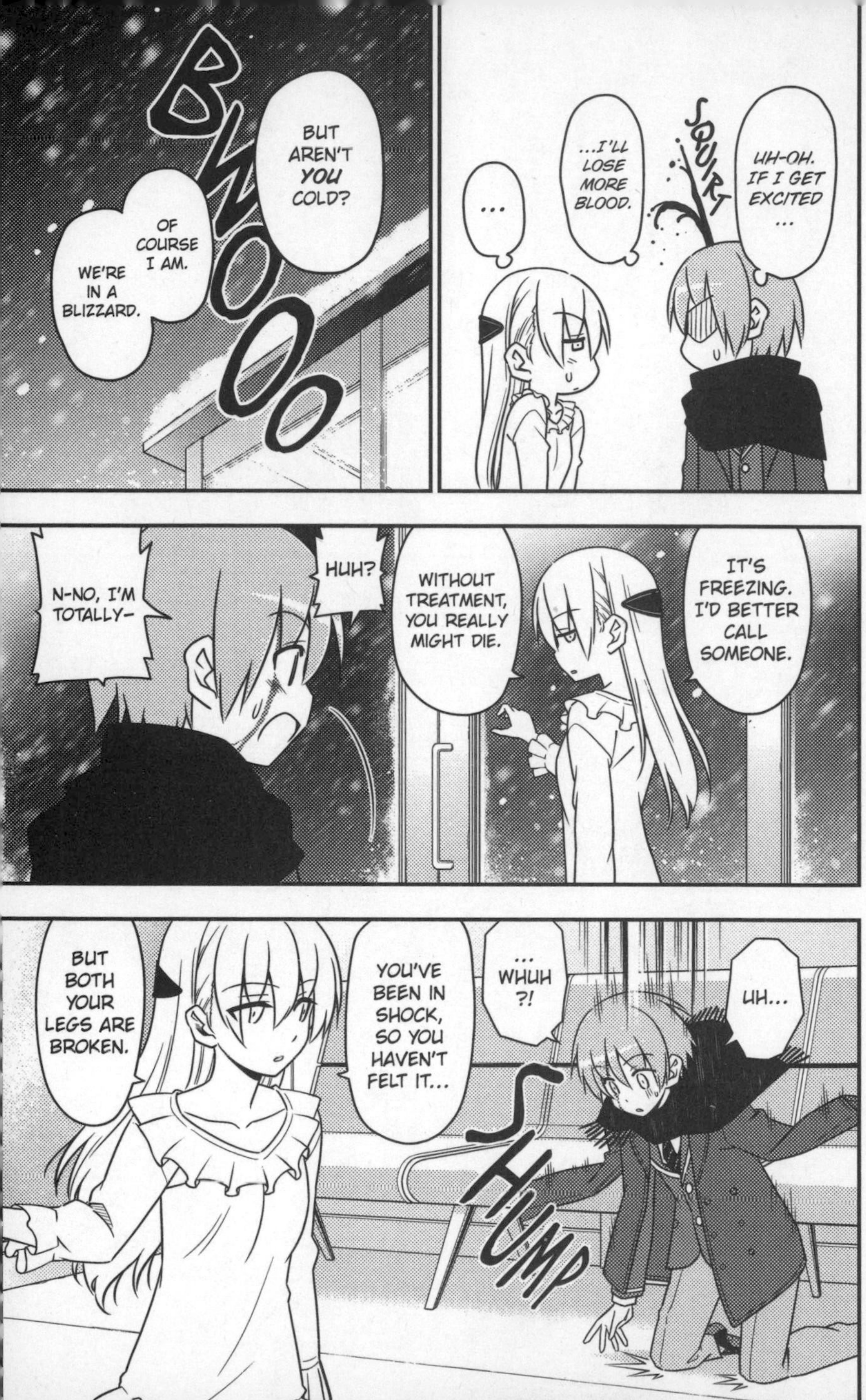
UH-OH. IF I GET EXCITED ...
SQUIRT
...I'LL LOSE MORE BLOOD.
...
BUT AREN'T YOU COLD?
OF COURSE I AM.
WE'RE IN A BLIZZARD.
BWOOOO
IT'S FREEZING. I'D BETTER CALL SOMEONE.
WITHOUT TREATMENT, YOU REALLY MIGHT DIE.
HUH?
N-NO, I'M TOTALLY-
UH...
...WHUH?!
YOU'VE BEEN IN SHOCK, SO YOU HAVEN'T FELT IT...
BUT BOTH YOUR LEGS ARE BROKEN.
SHUMP

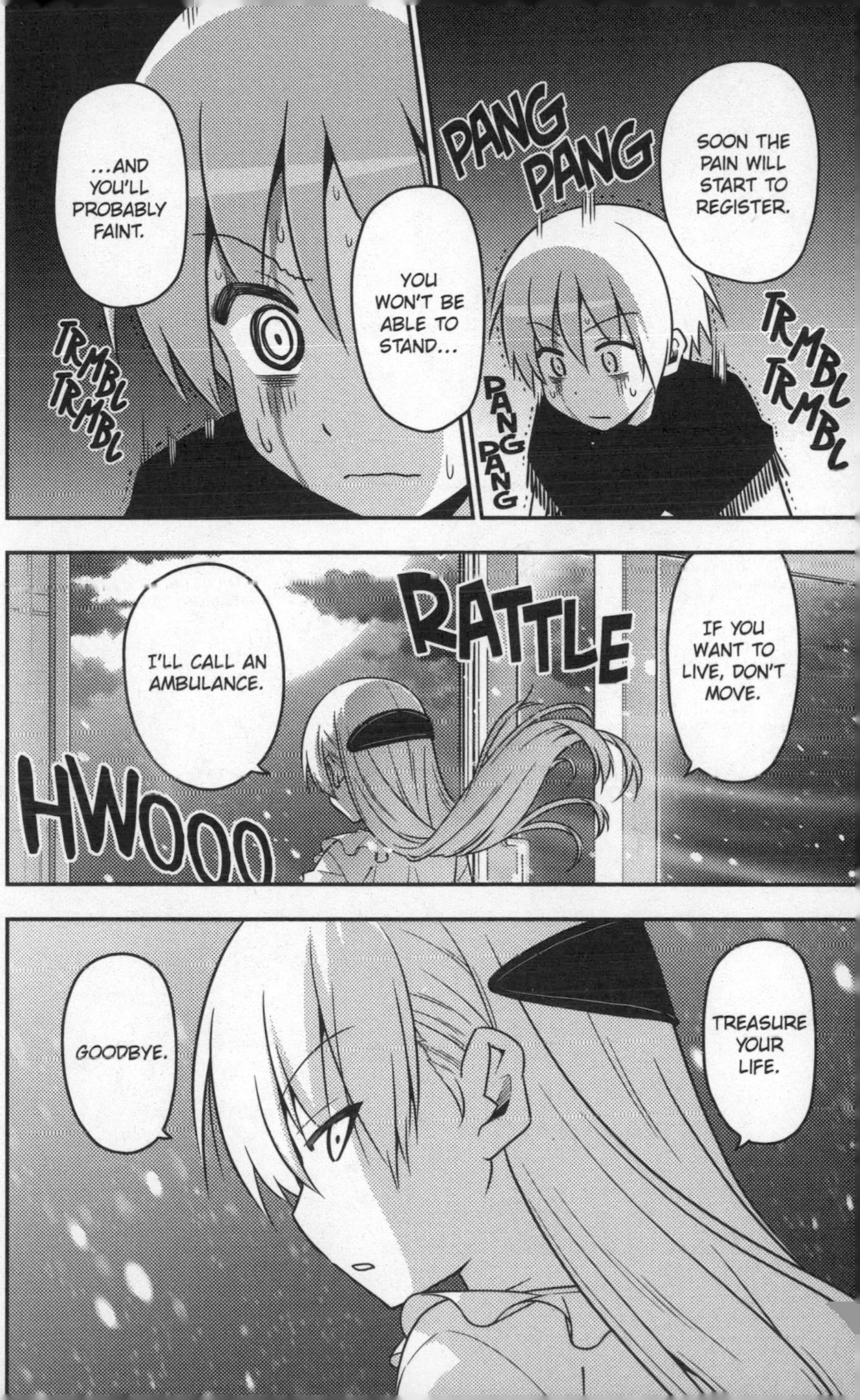
SOON THE PAIN WILL START TO REGISTER.
PANG PANG
TRMBL TRMBL
PANG PANG
YOU WON'T BE ABLE TO STAND...
...AND YOU'LL PROBABLY FAINT.
TRMBL TRMBL
IF YOU WANT TO LIVE, DON'T MOVE.
RATTLE
I'LL CALL AN AMBULANCE.
HWOOO
TREASURE YOUR LIFE.
GOODBYE.

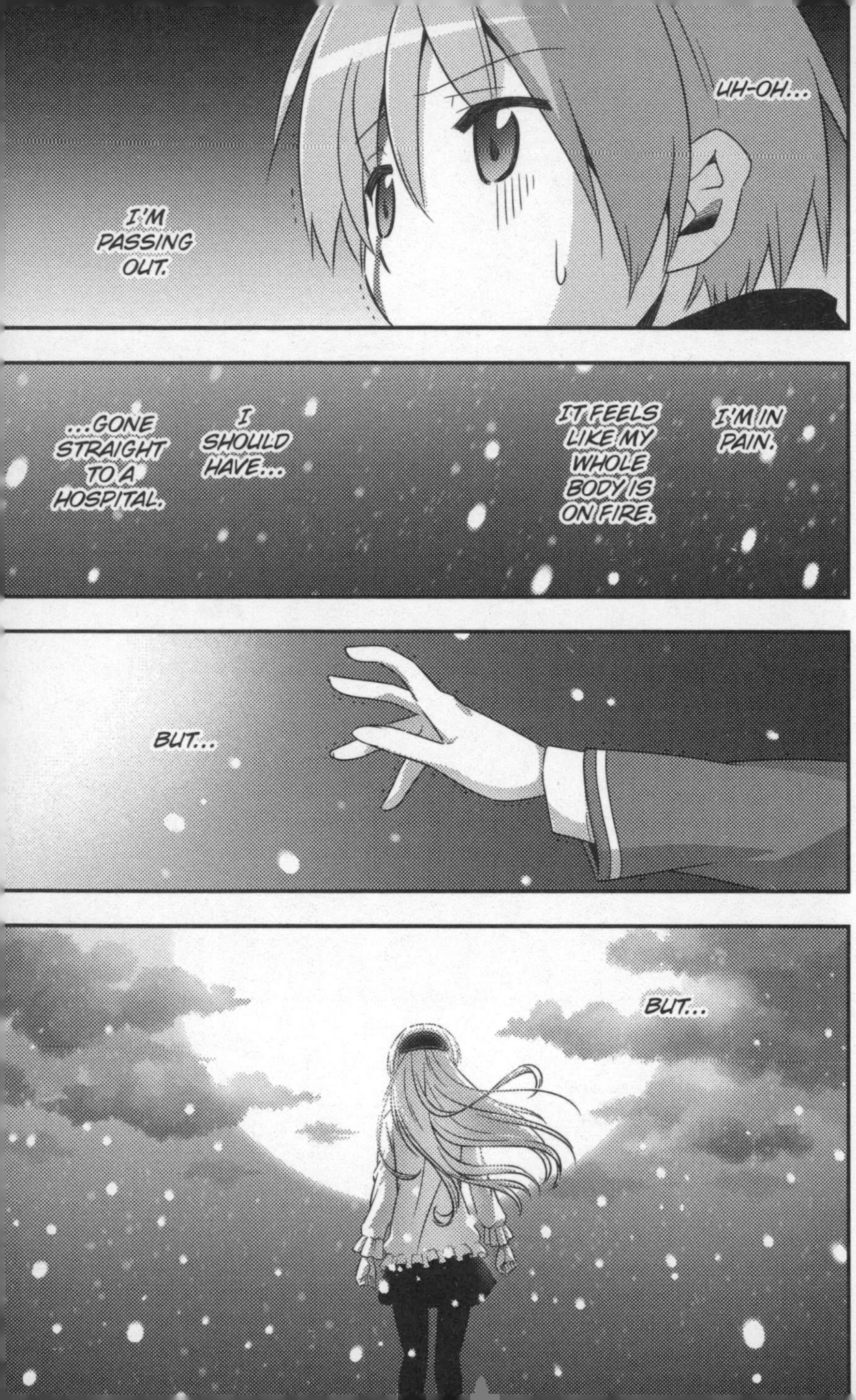
UH-OH...
I'M PASSING OUT.
I'M IN PAIN.
IT FEELS LIKE MY WHOLE BODY IS ON FIRE.
I SHOULD HAVE...
...GONE STRAIGHT TO A HOSPITAL.
BUT...
BUT...

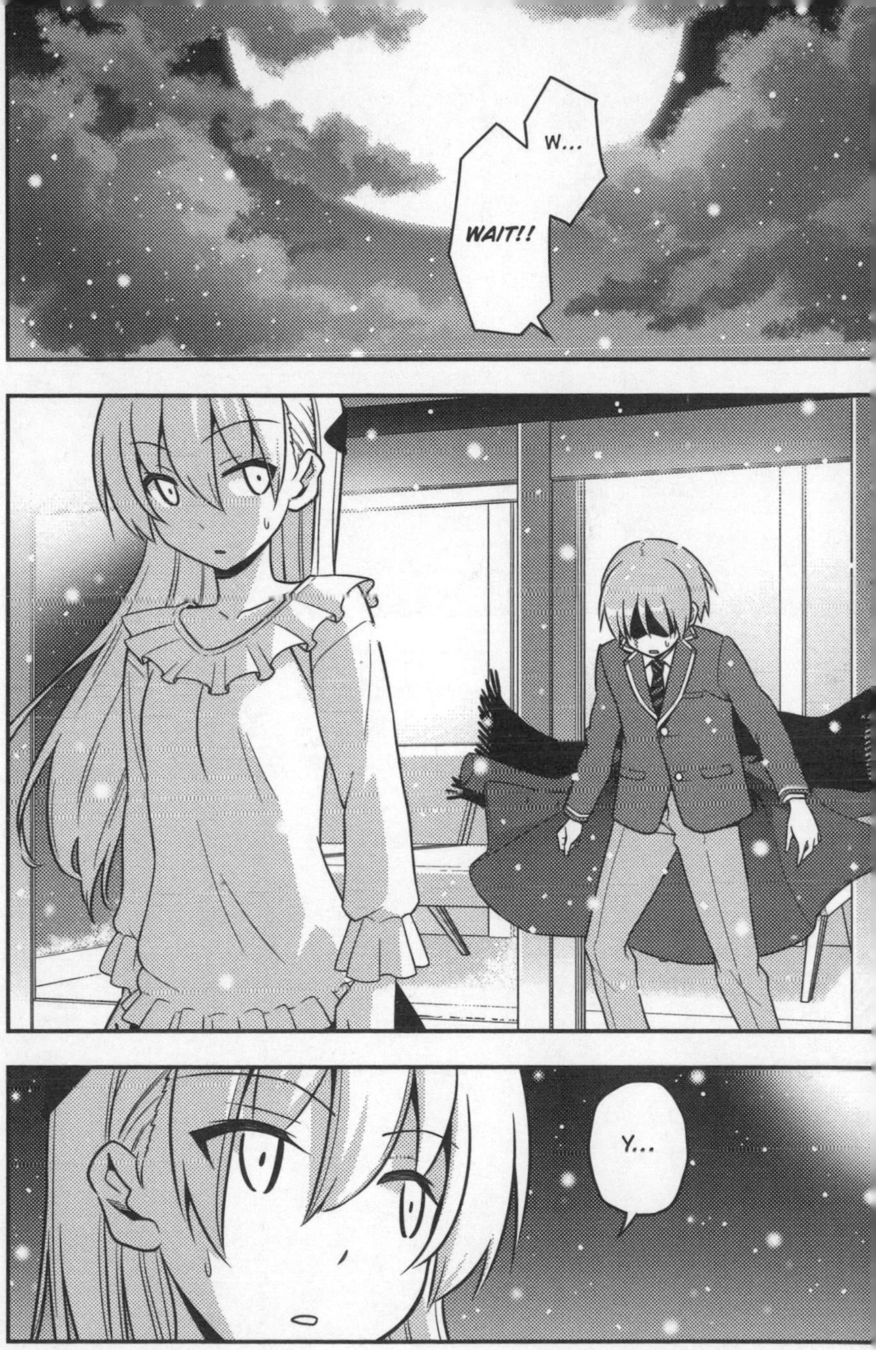
W...
WAIT!!
Y...

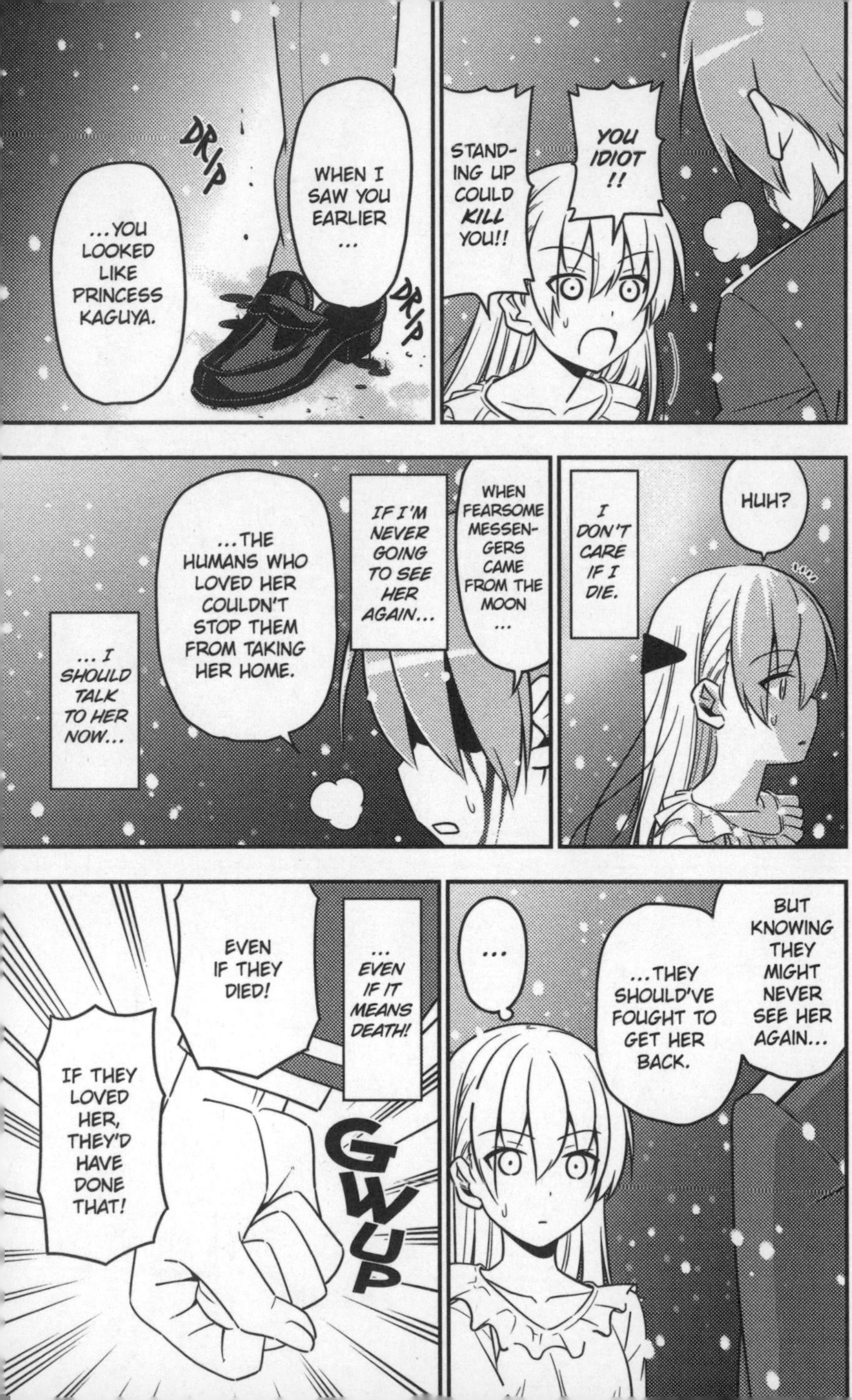
YOU IDIOT!!
STANDING-UP COULD KILL YOU!!
WHEN I SAW YOU EARLIER...
...YOU LOOKED LIKE PRINCESS KAGUYA.
DRIP
DRIP
HUH?
I DON'T CARE IF I DIE.
WHEN FEARSOME MESSEN-GERS CAME FROM THE MOON...
IF I'M NEVER GOING TO SEE HER AGAIN...
...THE HUMANS WHO LOVED HER COULDN'T STOP THEM FROM TAKING HER HOME.
...I SHOULD TALK TO HER NOW...
BUT KNOWING THEY MIGHT NEVER SEE HER AGAIN...
...THEY SHOULD'VE FOUGHT TO GET HER BACK.
...
...EVEN IF IT MEANS DEATH!
EVEN IF THEY DIED!
IF THEY LOVED HER, THEY'D HAVE DONE THAT!
GWUP

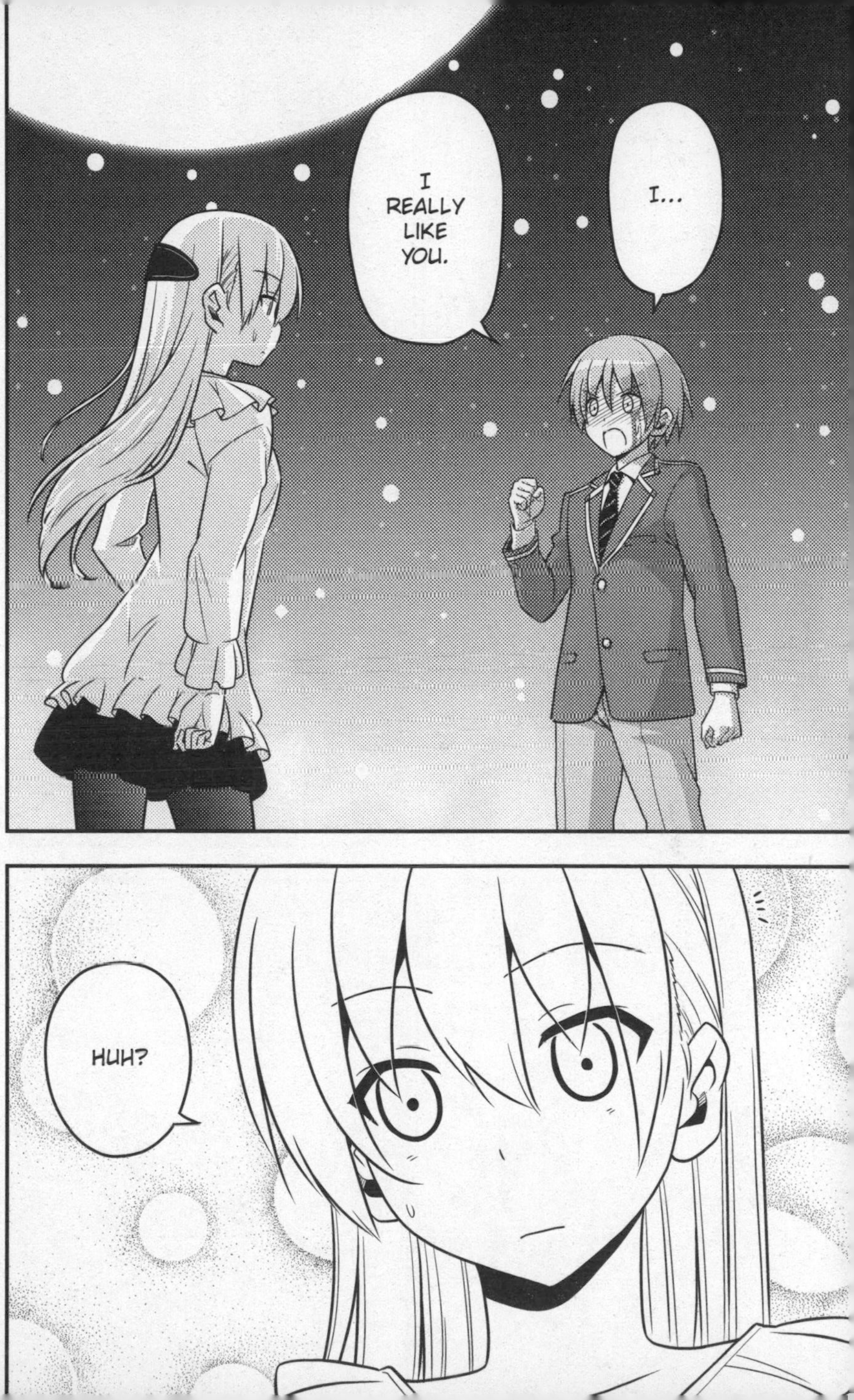
I...
I REALLY LIKE YOU.
HUH?

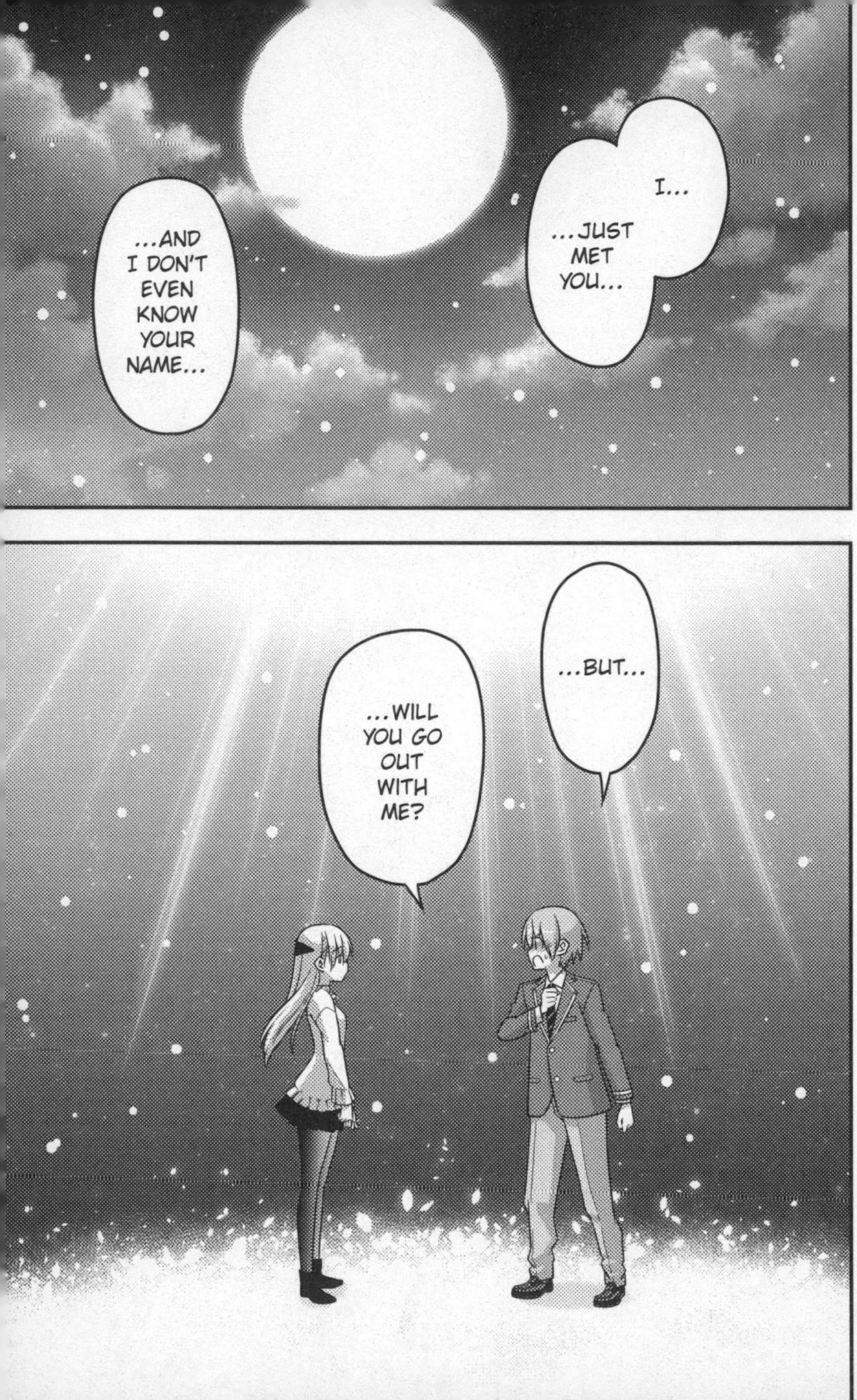
I... ...JUST MET YOU...
...AND I DON'T EVEN KNOW YOUR NAME...
...BUT...
...WILL YOU GO OUT WITH ME?

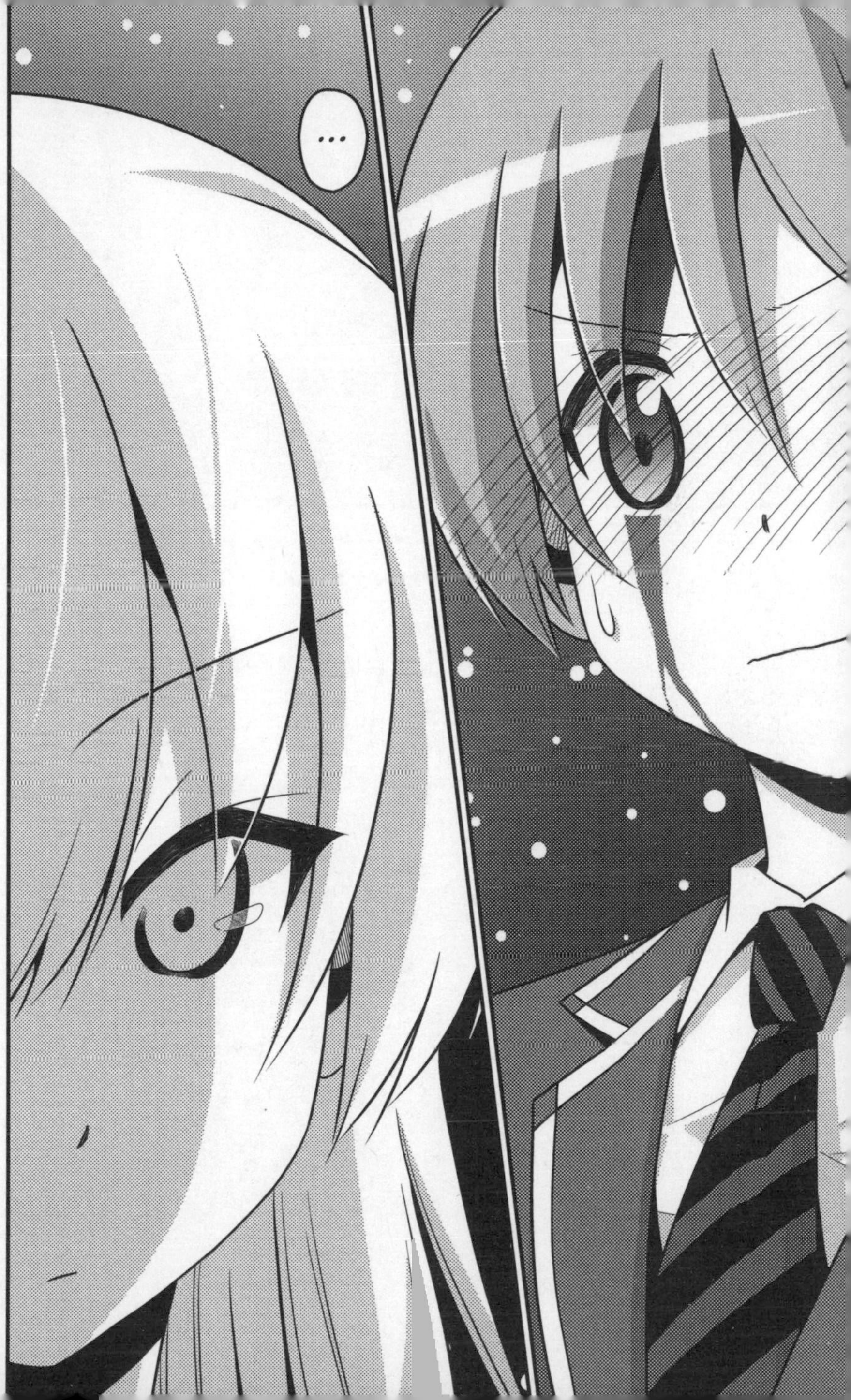
...

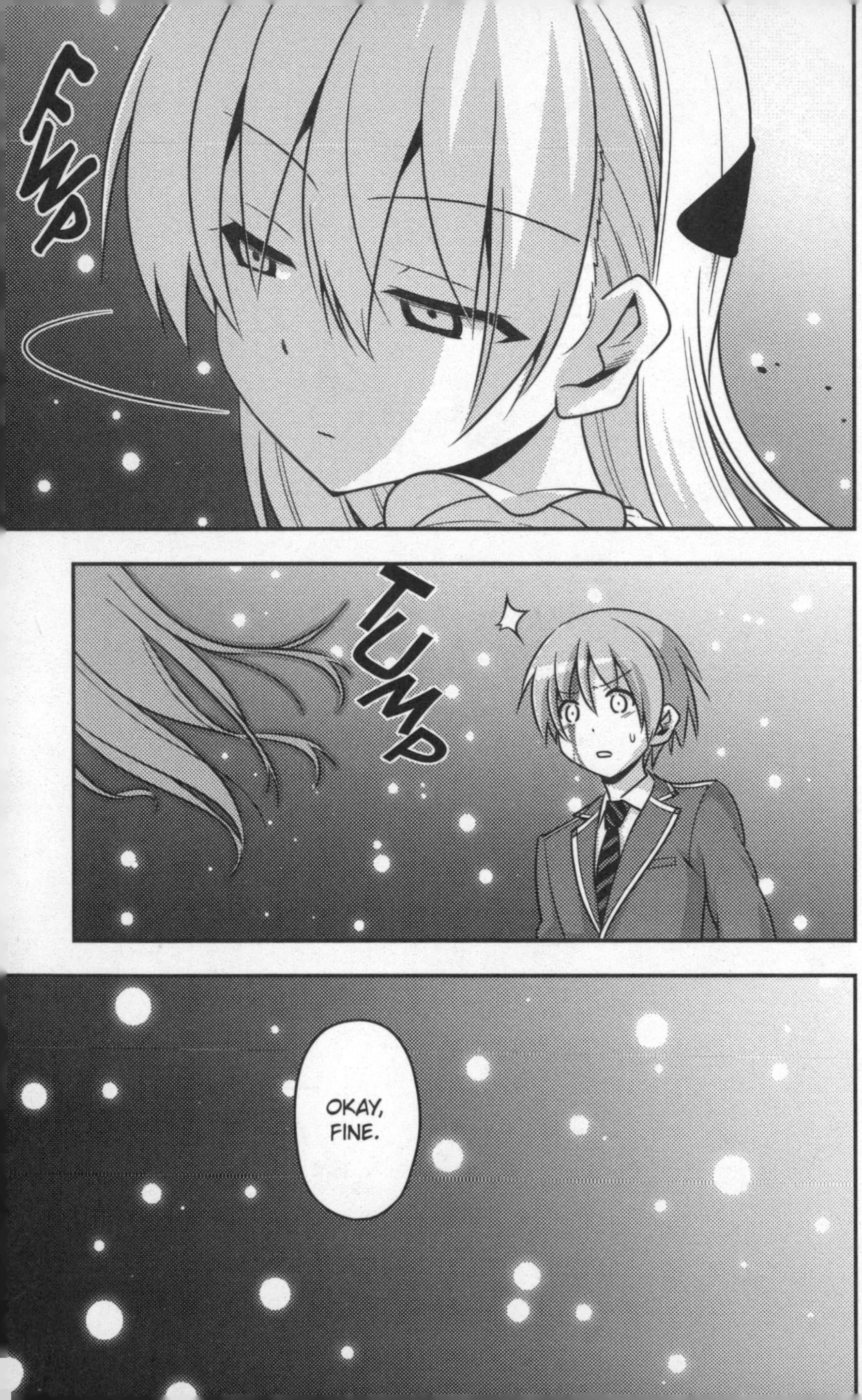
FWP
TUMP
OKAY, FINE.

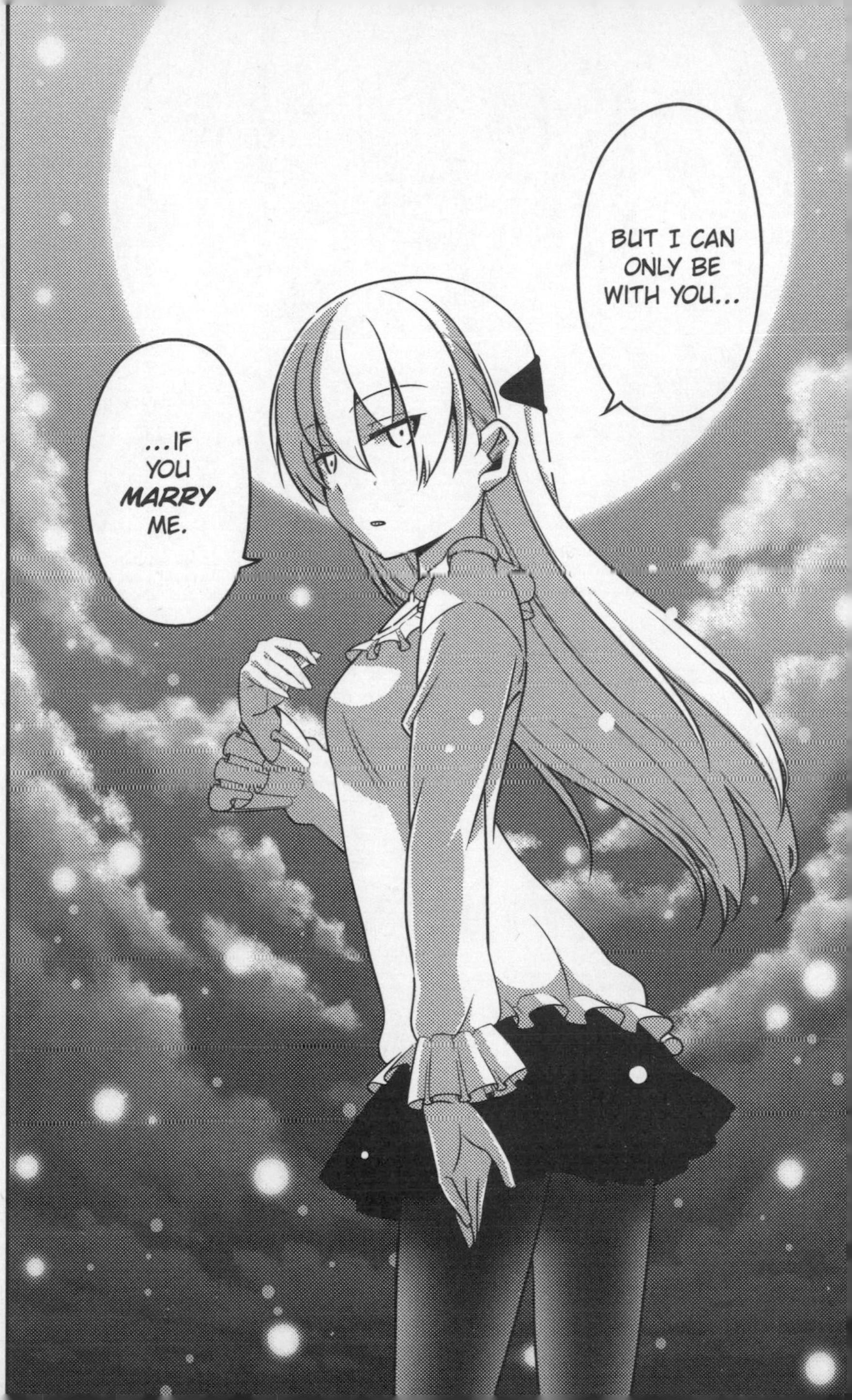
BUT I CAN ONLY BE WITH YOU...
...IF YOU *MARRY* ME.

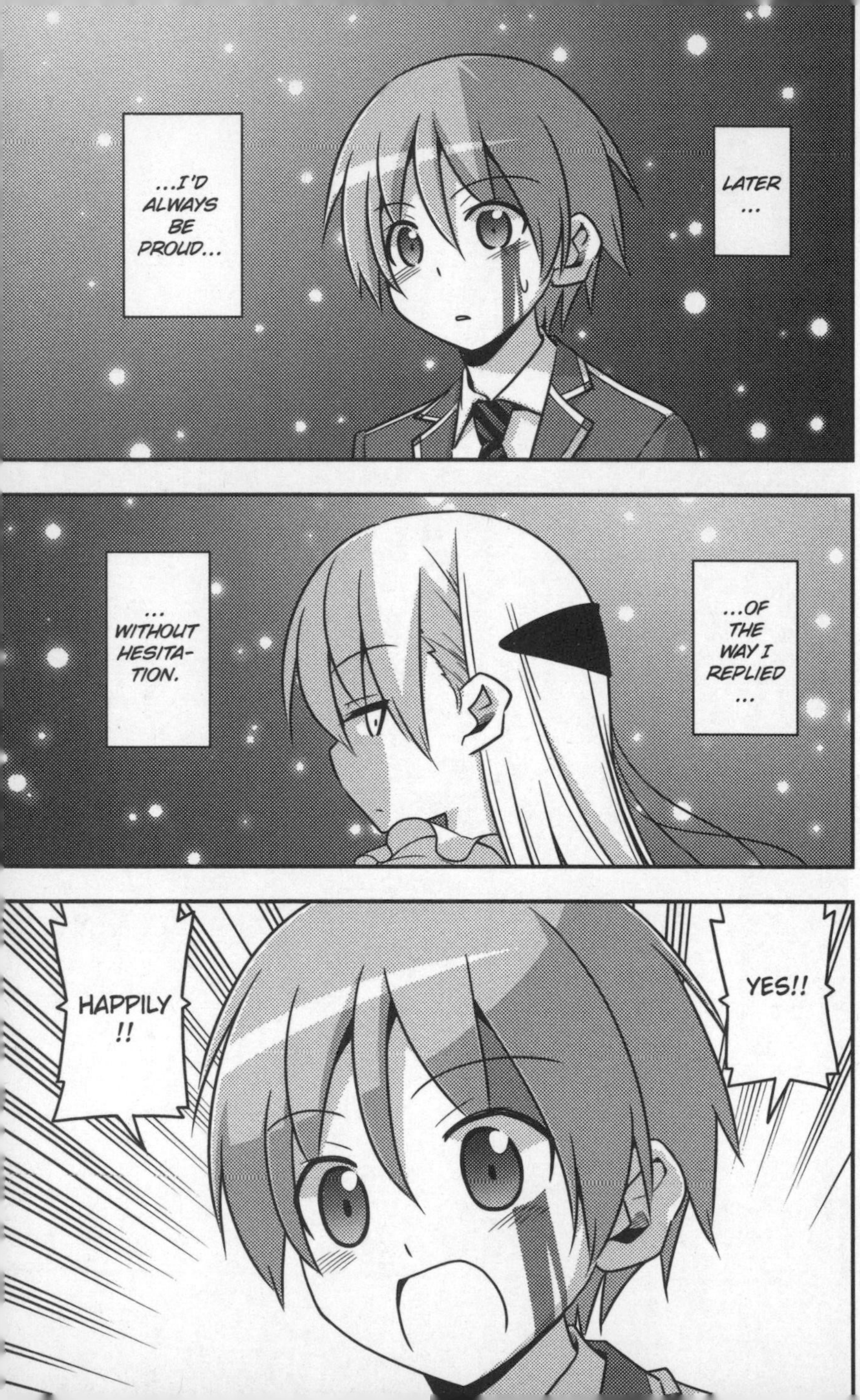
LATER...
...I'D ALWAYS BE PROUD...
...OF THE WAY I REPLIED...
...WITHOUT HESITA-TION.
YES!!
HAPPILY!!

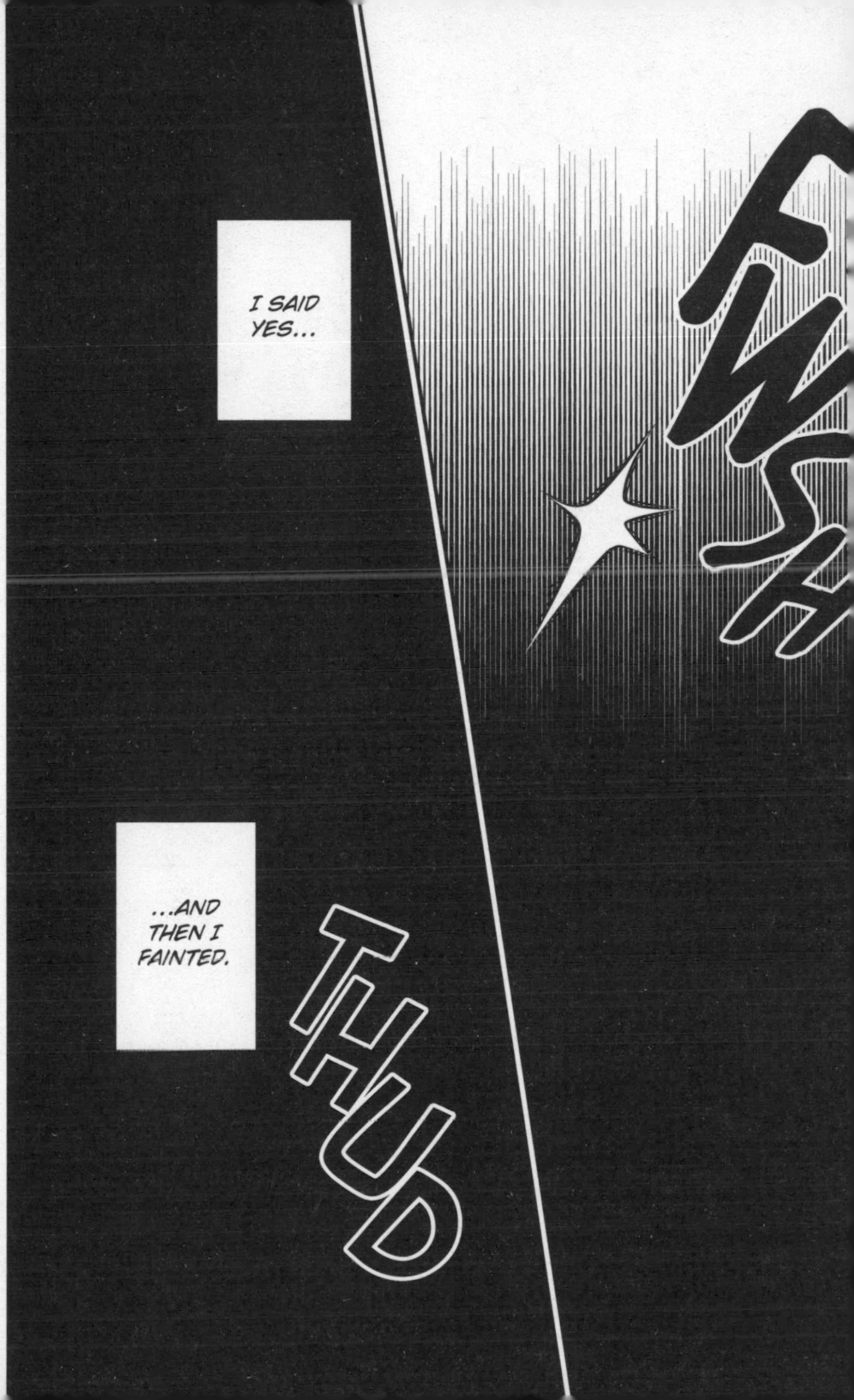
FWSH
I SAID YES...
...AND THEN I FAINTED.
THUD

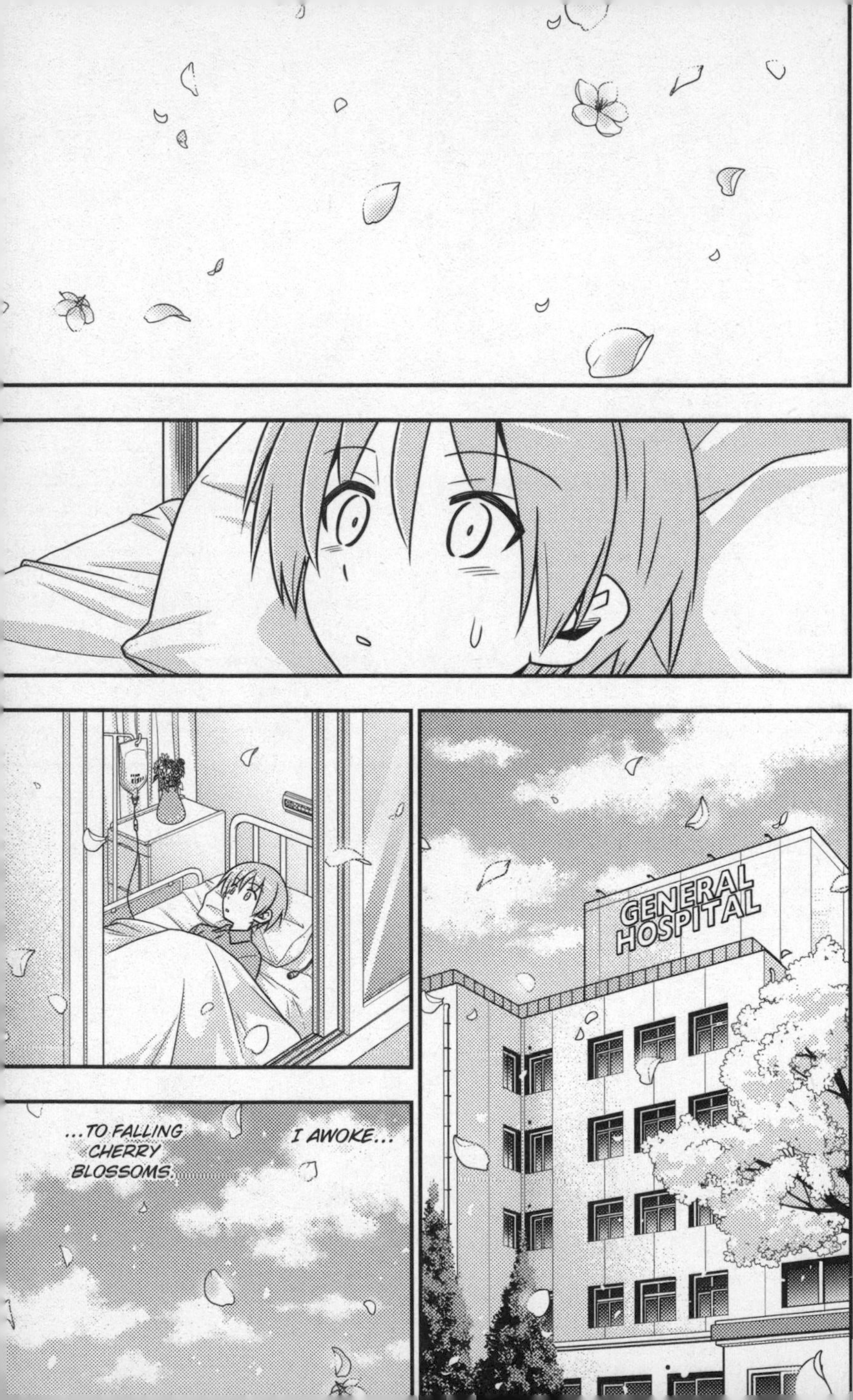
GENERAL HOSPITAL
I AWOKE...
...TO FALLING CHERRY BLOSSOMS.

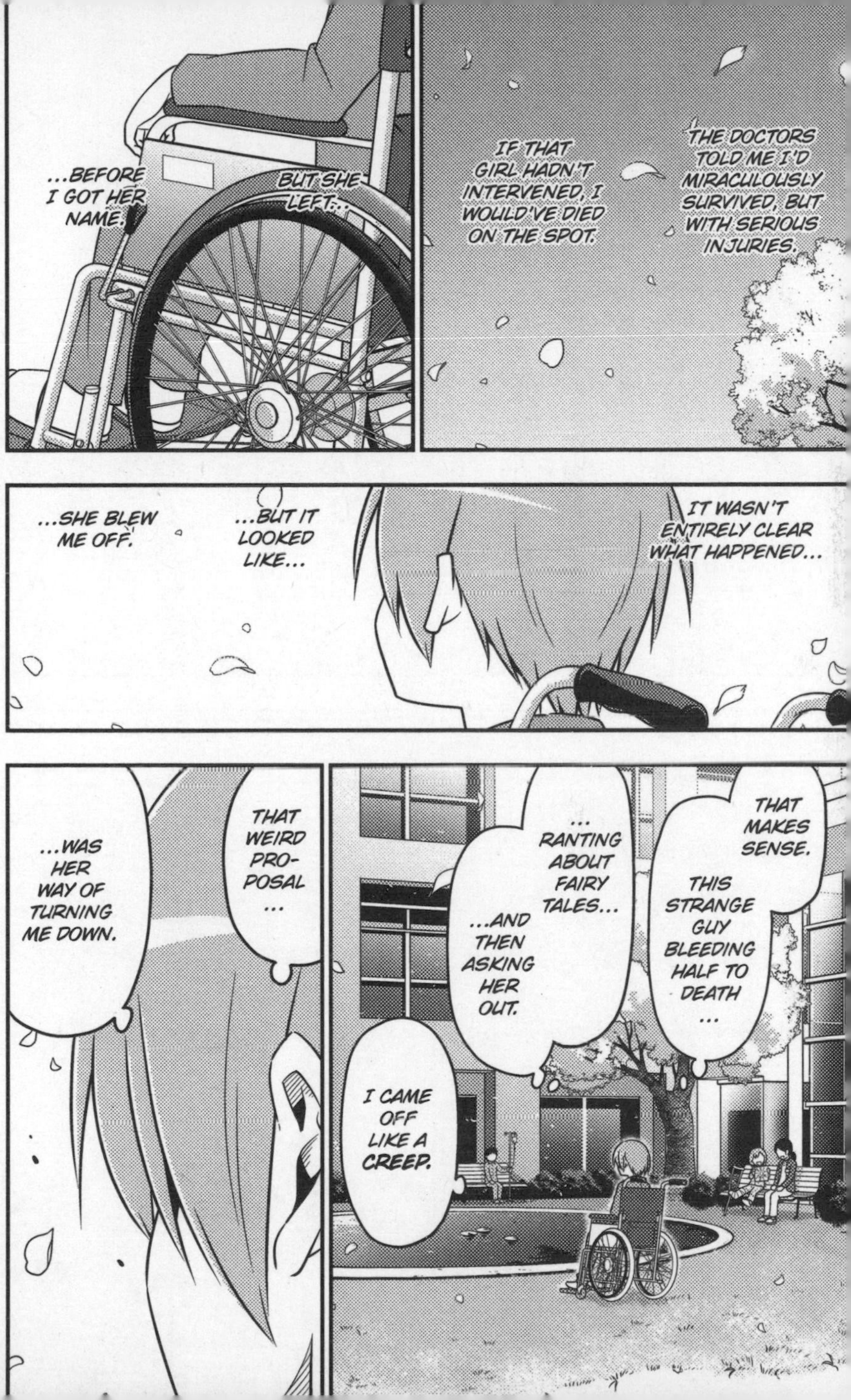
THE DOCTORS TOLD ME I'D MIRACULOUSLY SURVIVED, BUT WITH SERIOUS INJURIES.
IF THAT GIRL HADN'T INTERVENED, I WOULD'VE DIED ON THE SPOT.
BUT SHE LEFT...
...BEFORE I GOT HER NAME.
IT WASN'T ENTIRELY CLEAR WHAT HAPPENED...
...BUT IT LOOKED LIKE...
...SHE BLEW ME OFF.
THAT MAKES SENSE.
THIS STRANGE GUY BLEEDING HALF TO DEATH...
...RANTING ABOUT FAIRY TALES...
...AND THEN ASKING HER OUT.
I CAME OFF LIKE A CREEP.
THAT WEIRD PRO-POSAL...
...WAS HER WAY OF TURNING ME DOWN.

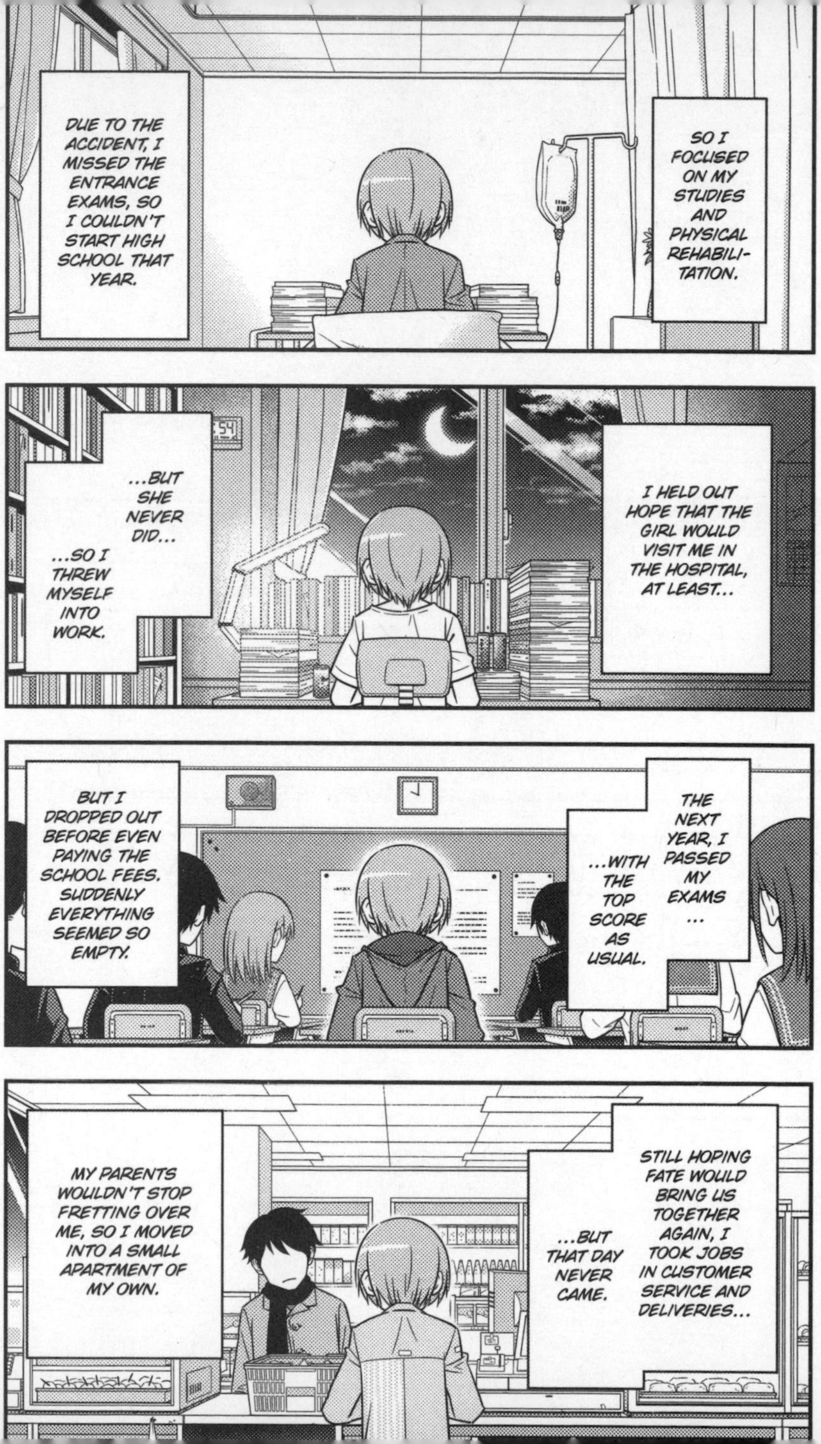
SO I FOCUSED ON MY STUDIES AND PHYSICAL REHABILITATION.
DUE TO THE ACCIDENT, I MISSED THE ENTRANCE EXAMS, SO I COULDN'T START HIGH SCHOOL THAT YEAR.
I HELD OUT HOPE THAT THE GIRL WOULD VISIT ME IN THE HOSPITAL, AT LEAST...
...BUT SHE NEVER DID...
...SO I THREW MYSELF INTO WORK.
THE NEXT YEAR, I PASSED MY EXAMS...
...WITH THE TOP SCORE AS USUAL.
BUT I DROPPED OUT BEFORE EVEN PAYING THE SCHOOL FEES. SUDDENLY EVERYTHING SEEMED SO EMPTY.
STILL HOPING FATE WOULD BRING US TOGETHER AGAIN, I TOOK JOBS IN CUSTOMER SERVICE AND DELIVERIES...
...BUT THAT DAY NEVER CAME.
MY PARENTS WOULDN'T STOP FRETTING OVER ME, SO I MOVED INTO A SMALL APARTMENT OF MY OWN.

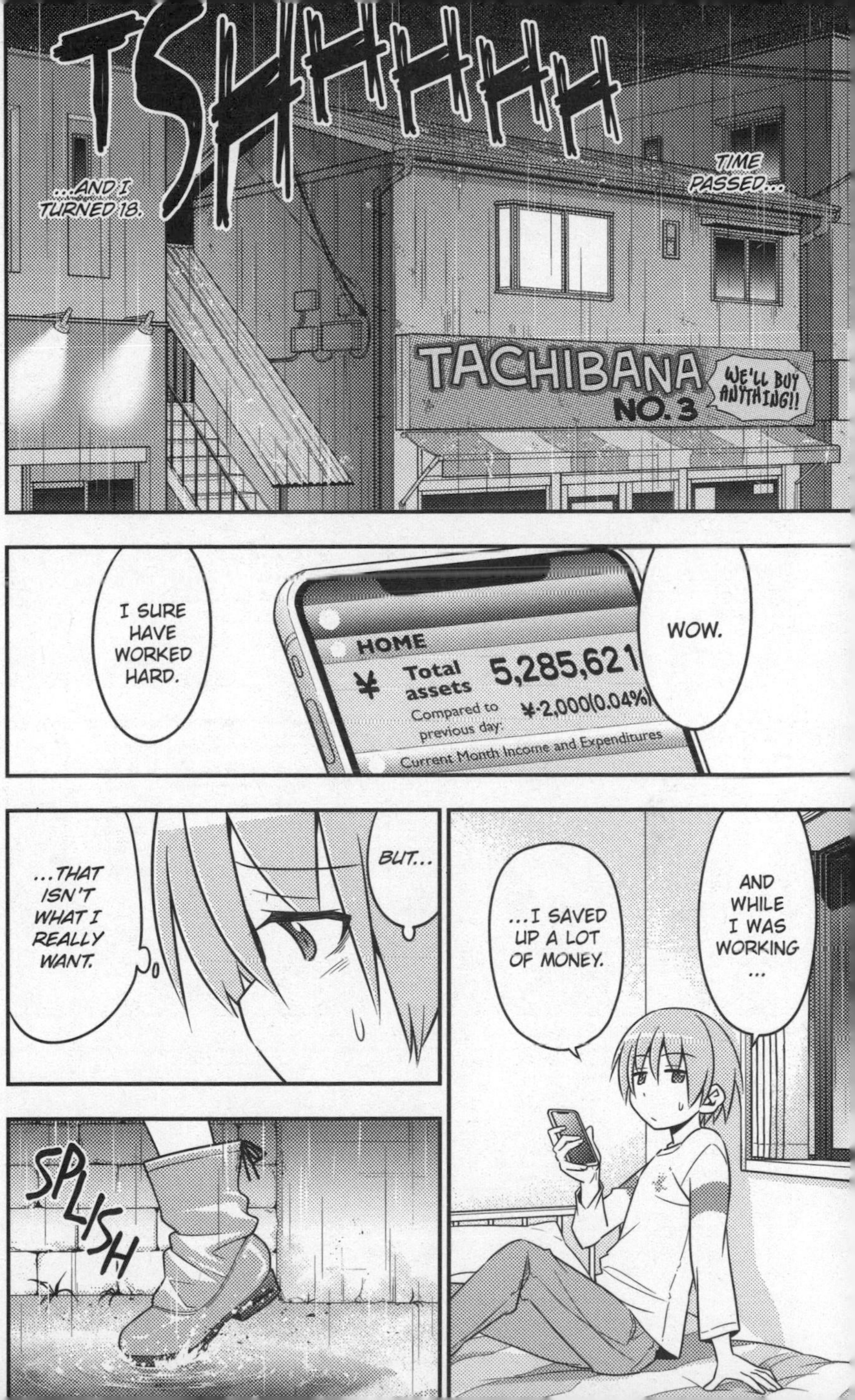
TSHHHHHH
TIME PASSED...
...AND I TURNED 18.
TACHIBANA NO. 3
WE'LL BUY ANYTHING!!
WOW.
HOME
¥ Total assets 5,285,621
Compared to previous day: ¥-2,000(0.04%)
Current Month Income and Expenditures
I SURE HAVE WORKED HARD.
AND WHILE I WAS WORKING...
...I SAVED UP A LOT OF MONEY.
BUT...
...THAT ISN'T WHAT I REALLY WANT.
SPLISH

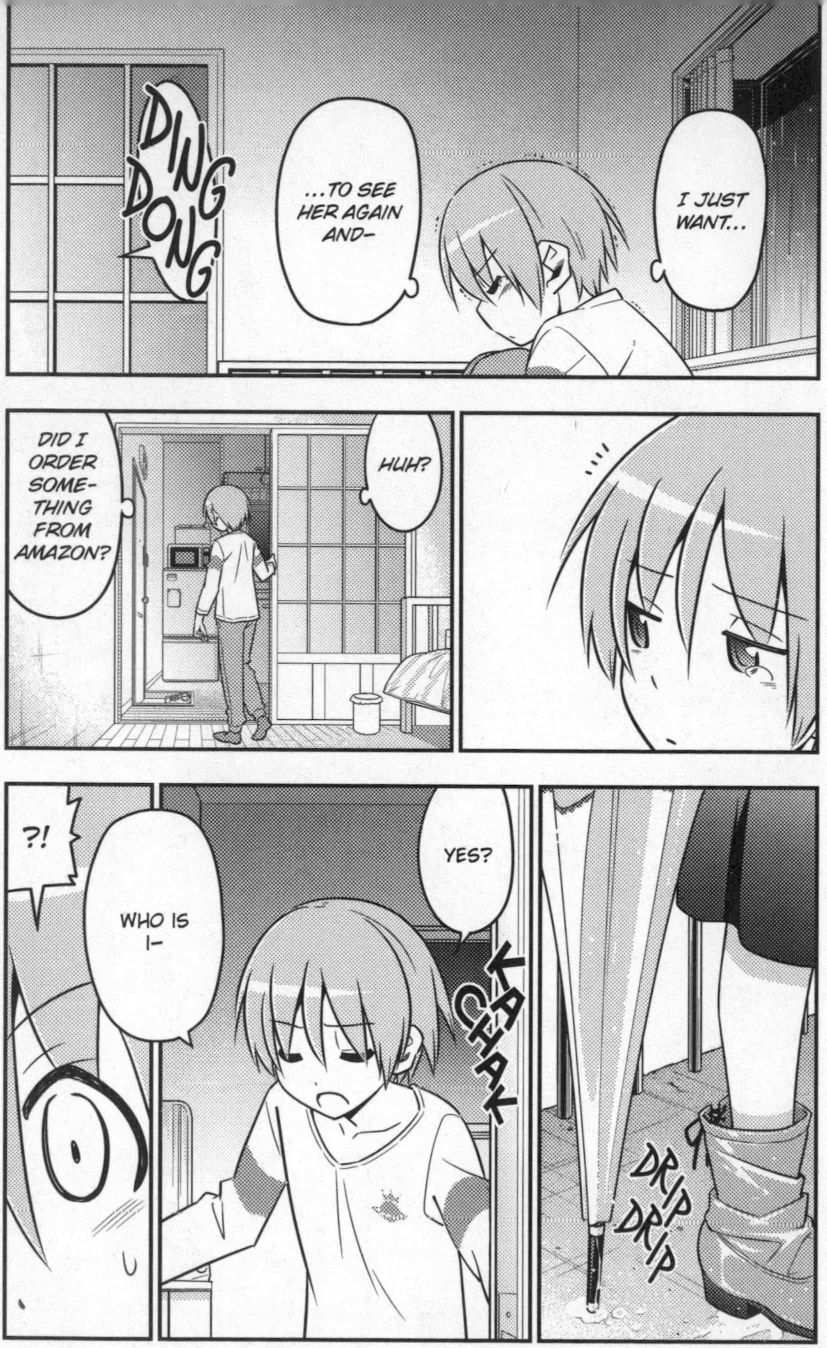
I JUST WANT...
...TO SEE HER AGAIN AND-
DING DONG
HUH?
DID I ORDER SOME-THING FROM AMAZON?
DRIP DRIP
YES?
KACHAK
WHO IS I-
?!

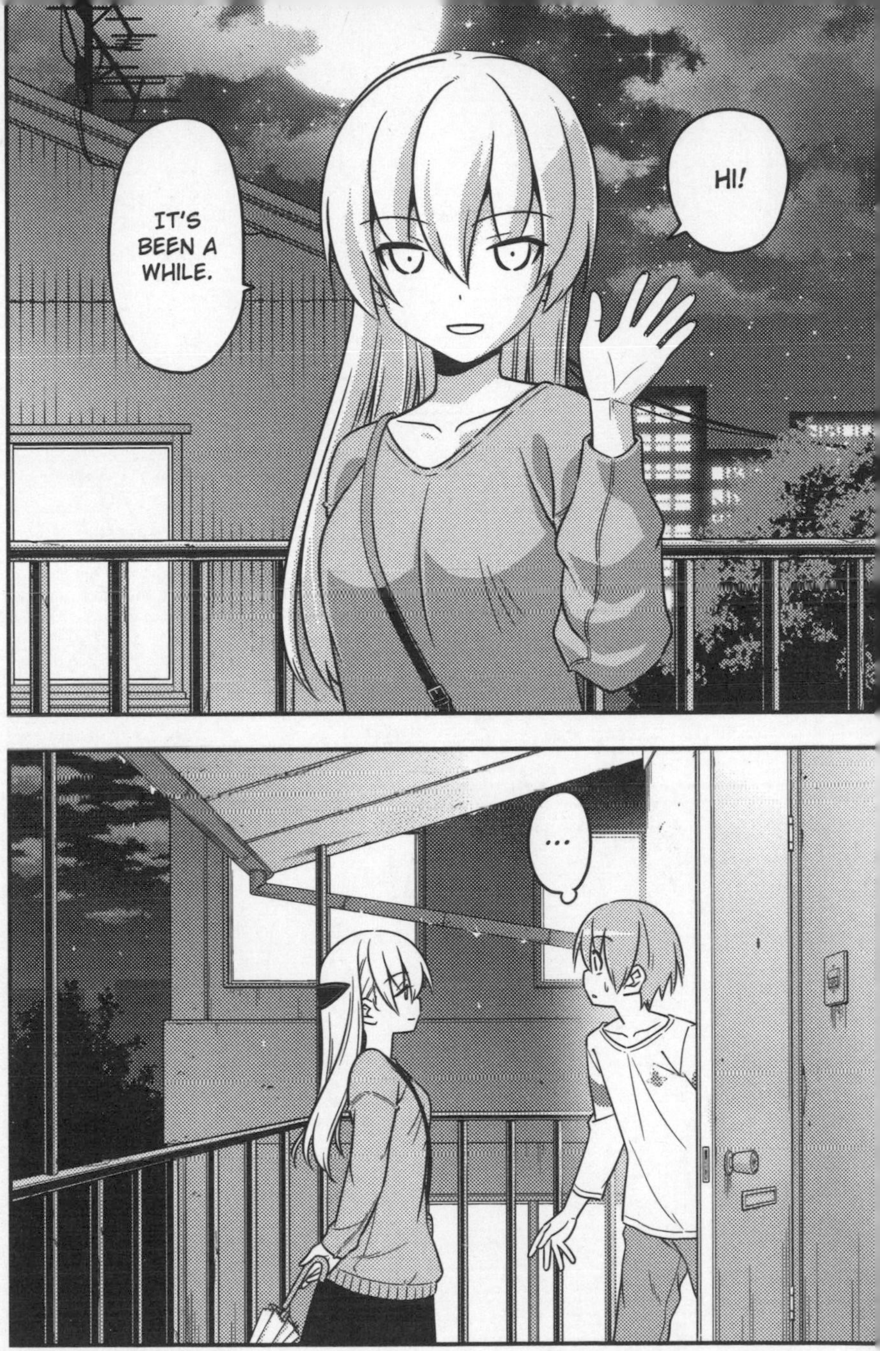
HI!
IT'S BEEN A WHILE.
...

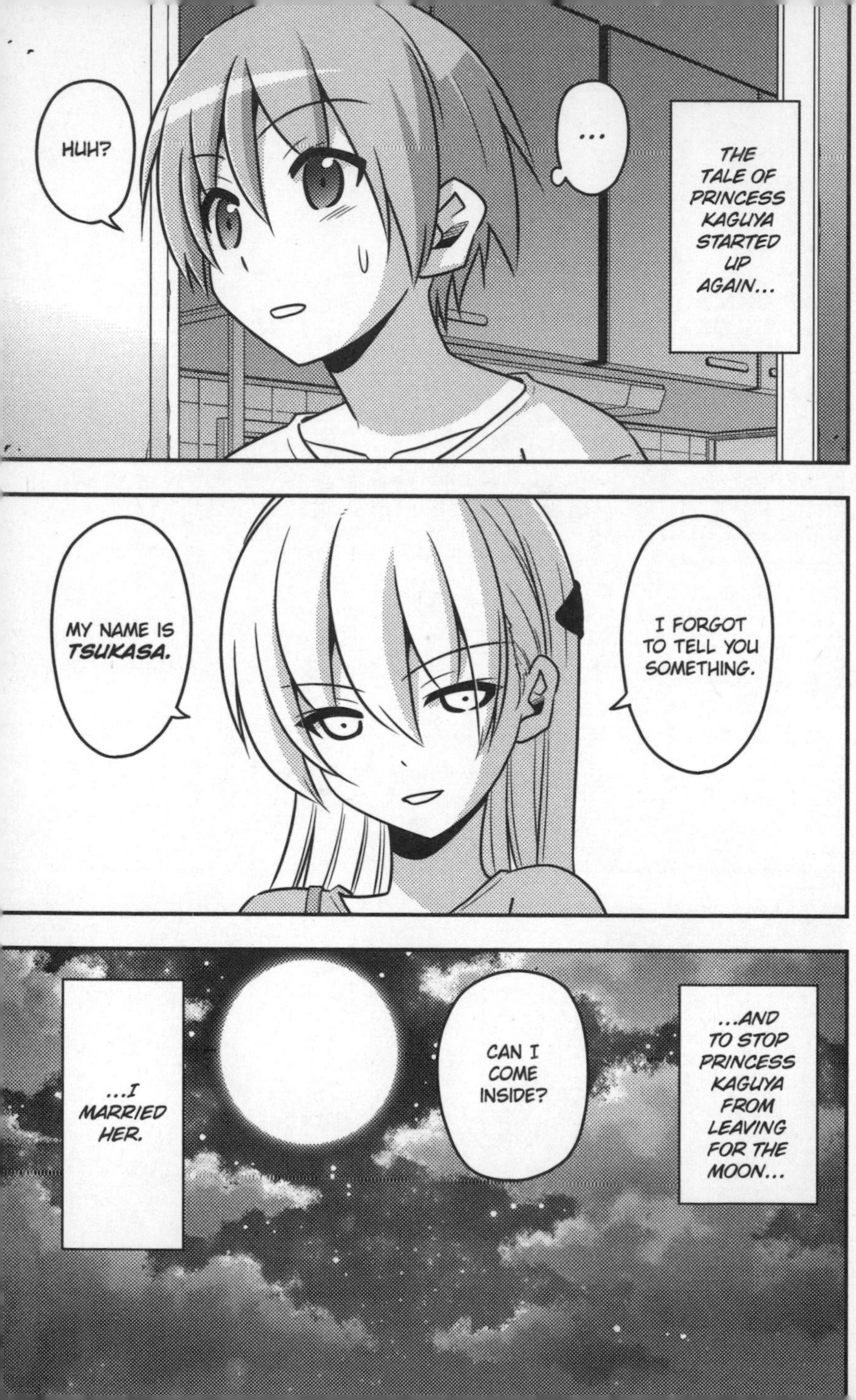
THE TALE OF PRINCESS KAGUYA STARTED UP AGAIN…
…
HUH?
I FORGOT TO TELL YOU SOMETHING.
MY NAME IS *TSUKASA.*
…AND TO STOP PRINCESS KAGUYA FROM LEAVING FOR THE MOON…
CAN I COME INSIDE?
…I MARRIED HER.

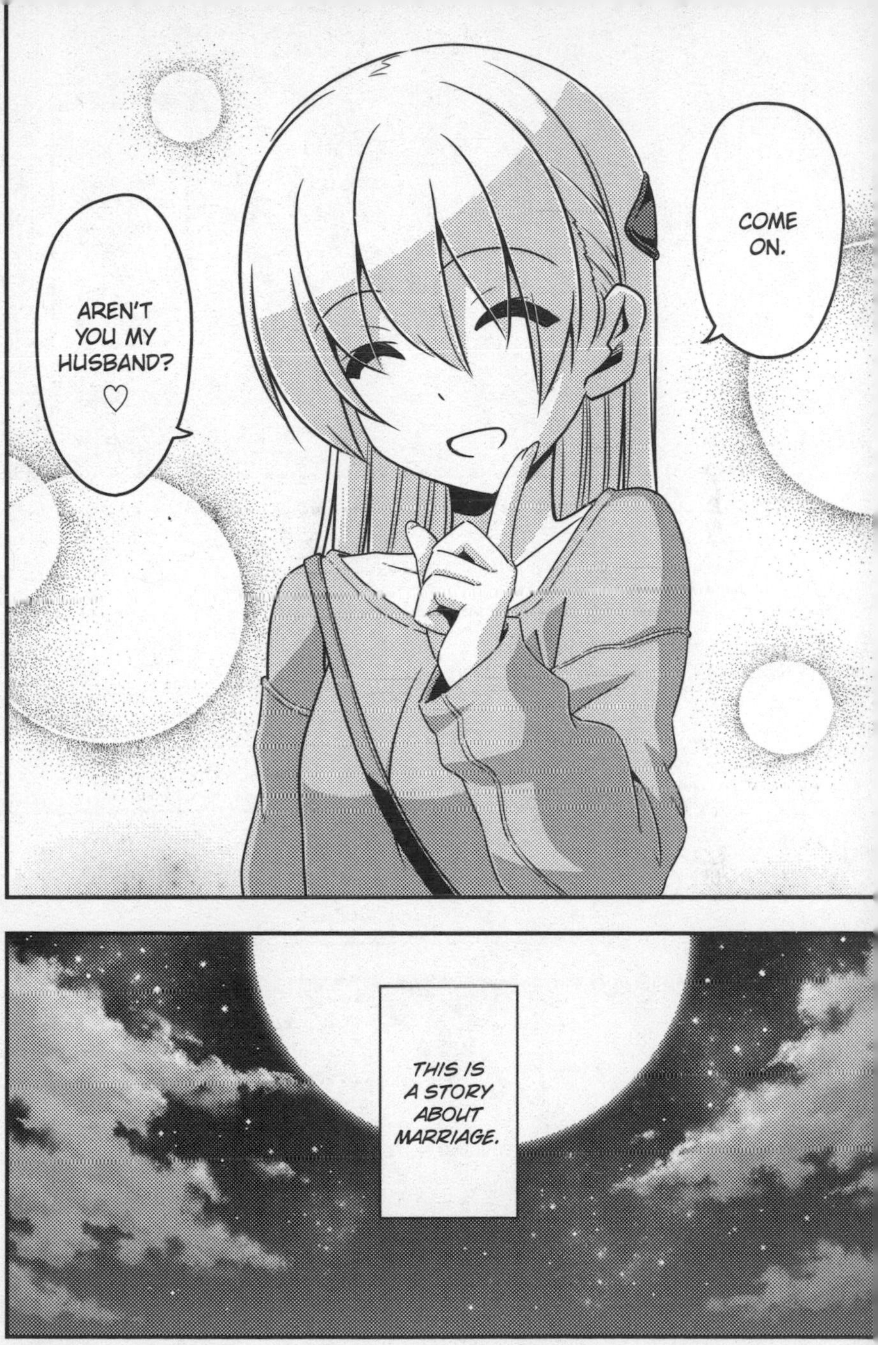
COME ON.
AREN'T YOU MY HUSBAND? ♡
THIS IS A STORY ABOUT MARRIAGE.

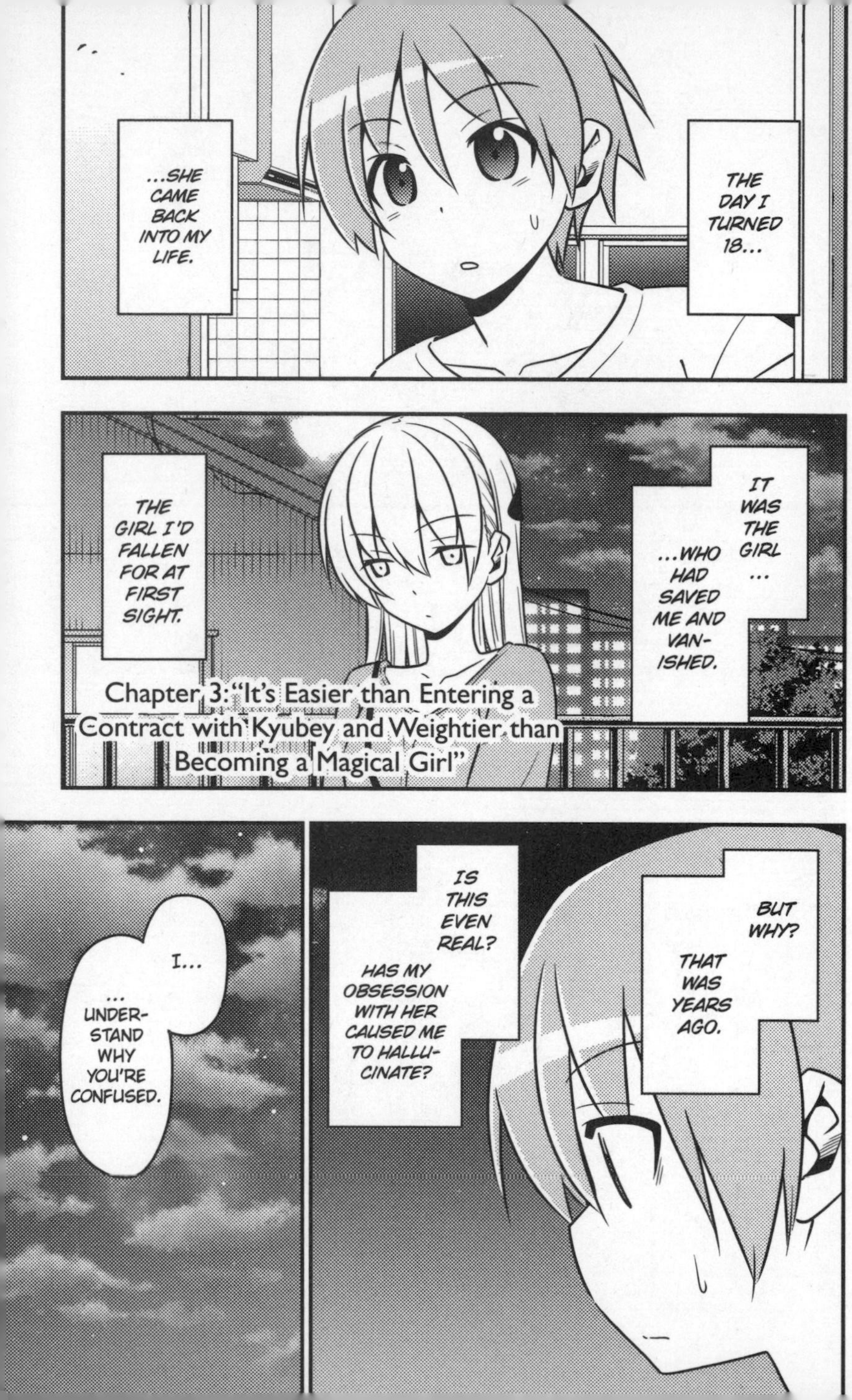
THE DAY I TURNED 18...
...SHE CAME BACK INTO MY LIFE.
IT WAS THE GIRL ...
...WHO HAD SAVED ME AND VAN-ISHED.
THE GIRL I'D FALLEN FOR AT FIRST SIGHT.
Chapter 3: "It's Easier than Entering a Contract with Kyubey and Weightier than Becoming a Magical Girl"
BUT WHY?
THAT WAS YEARS AGO.
IS THIS EVEN REAL?
HAS MY OBSESSION WITH HER CAUSED ME TO HALLUCINATE?
I...
...UNDERSTAND WHY YOU'RE CONFUSED.

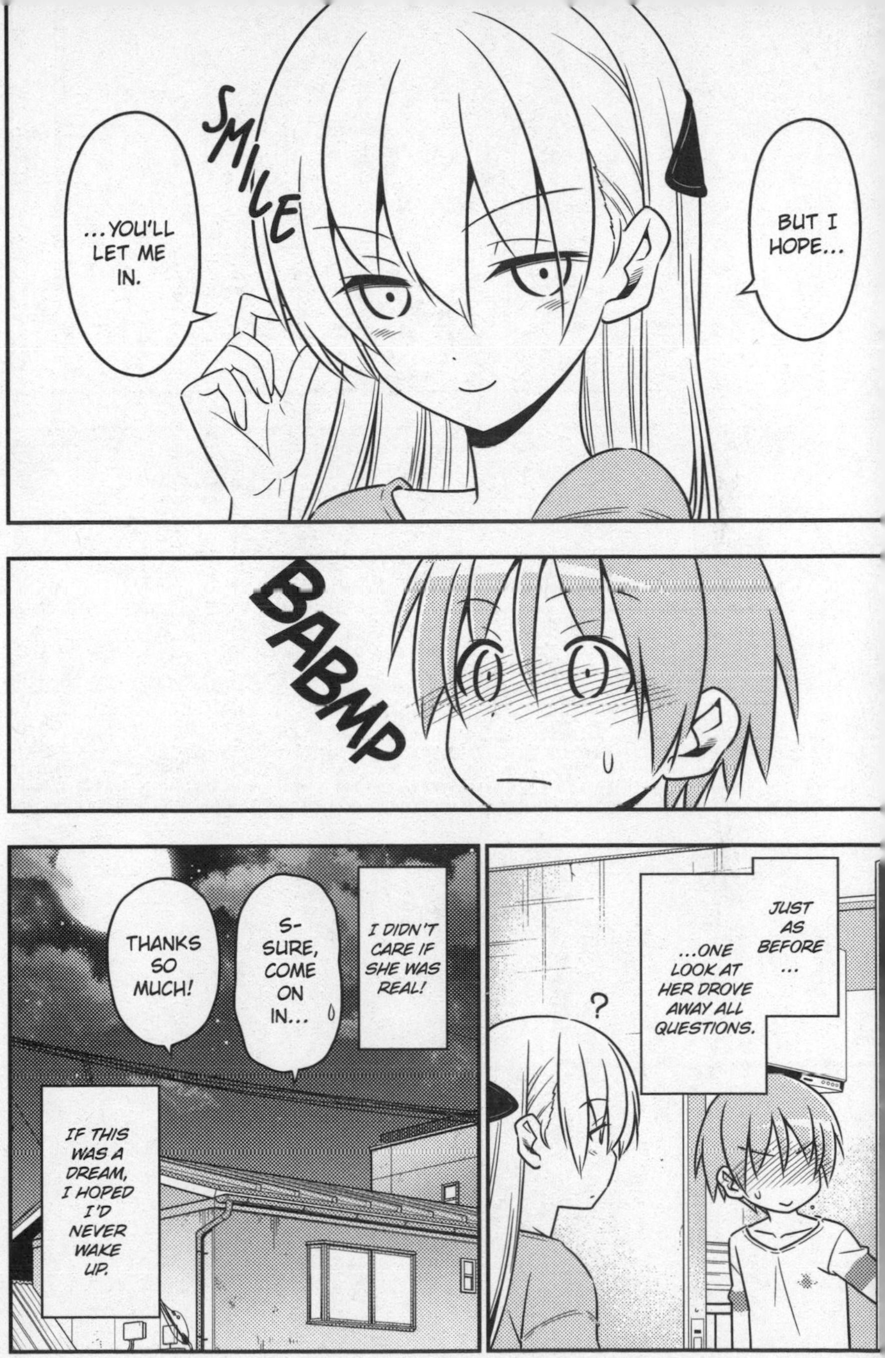
BUT I HOPE...
SMILE
...YOU'LL LET ME IN.
BABMP
JUST AS BEFORE...
...ONE LOOK AT HER DROVE AWAY ALL QUESTIONS.
?
I DIDN'T CARE IF SHE WAS REAL!
S-SURE, COME ON IN...
THANKS SO MUCH!
IF THIS WAS A DREAM, I HOPED I'D NEVER WAKE UP.

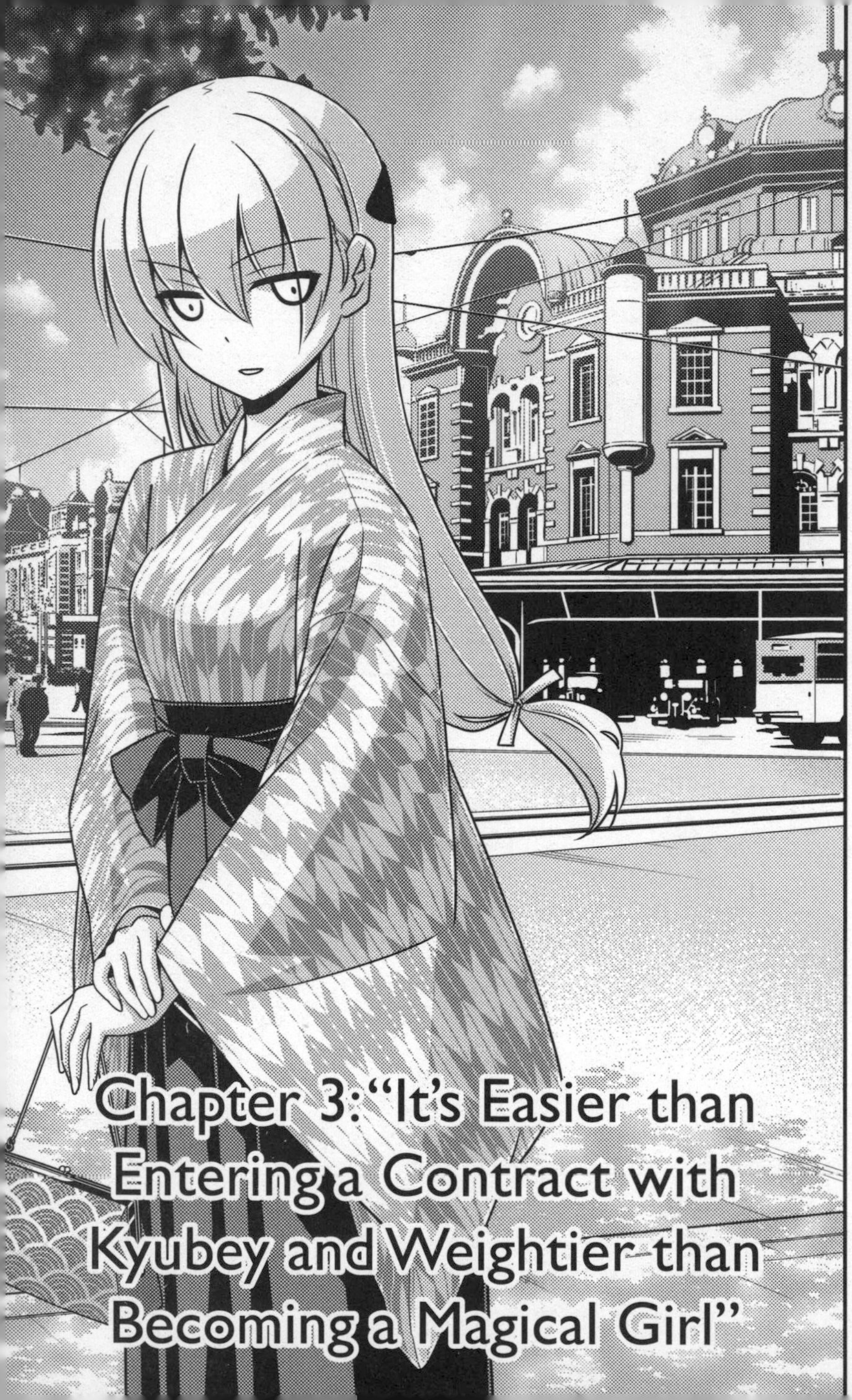
Chapter 3: "It's Easier than Entering a Contract with Kyubey and Weightier than Becoming a Magical Girl"

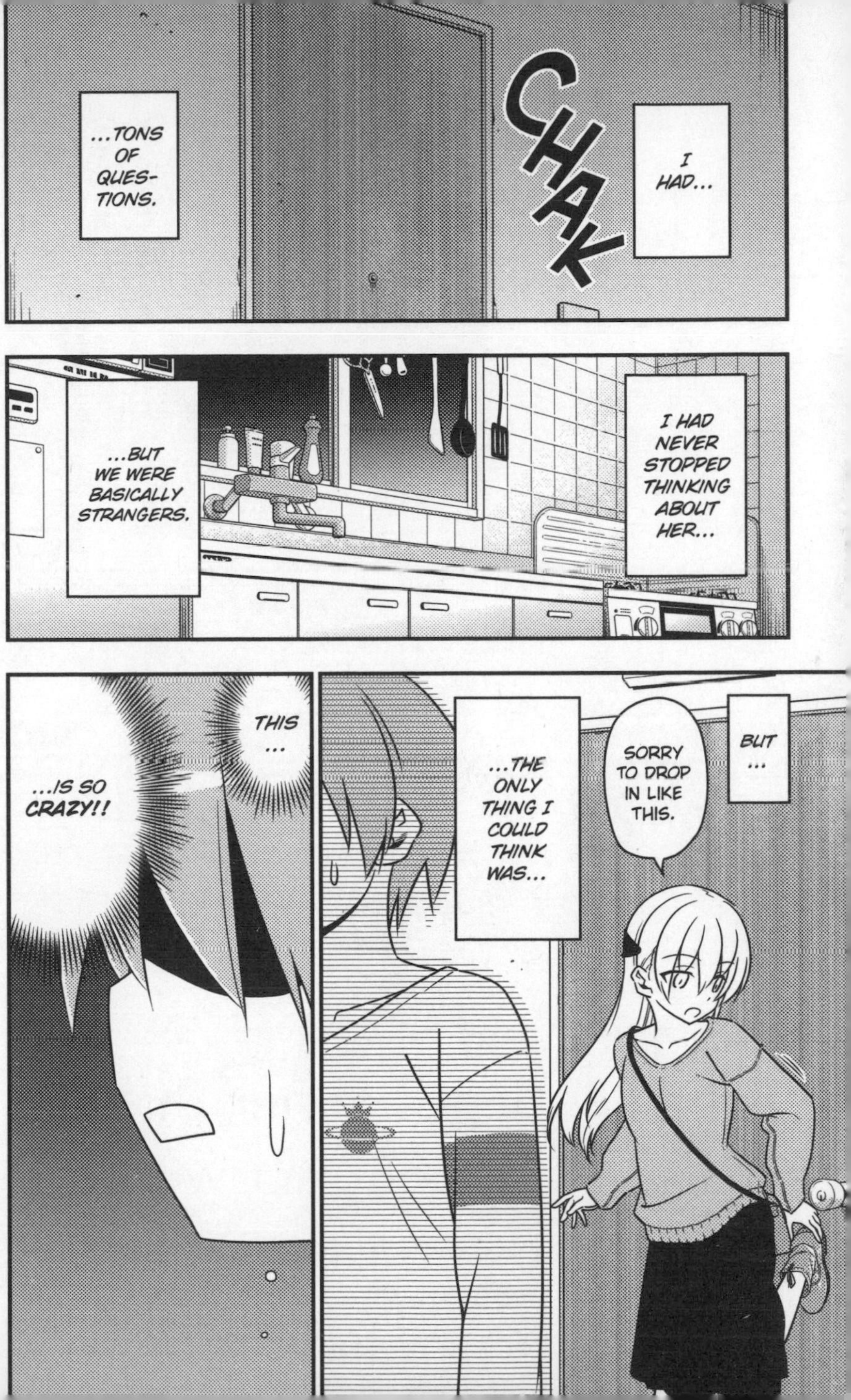
I HAD...
CHAK
...TONS OF QUES-TIONS.
I HAD NEVER STOPPED THINKING ABOUT HER...
...BUT WE WERE BASICALLY STRANGERS.
BUT ...
SORRY TO DROP IN LIKE THIS.
...THE ONLY THING I COULD THINK WAS...
THIS ...
...IS SO CRAZY!!

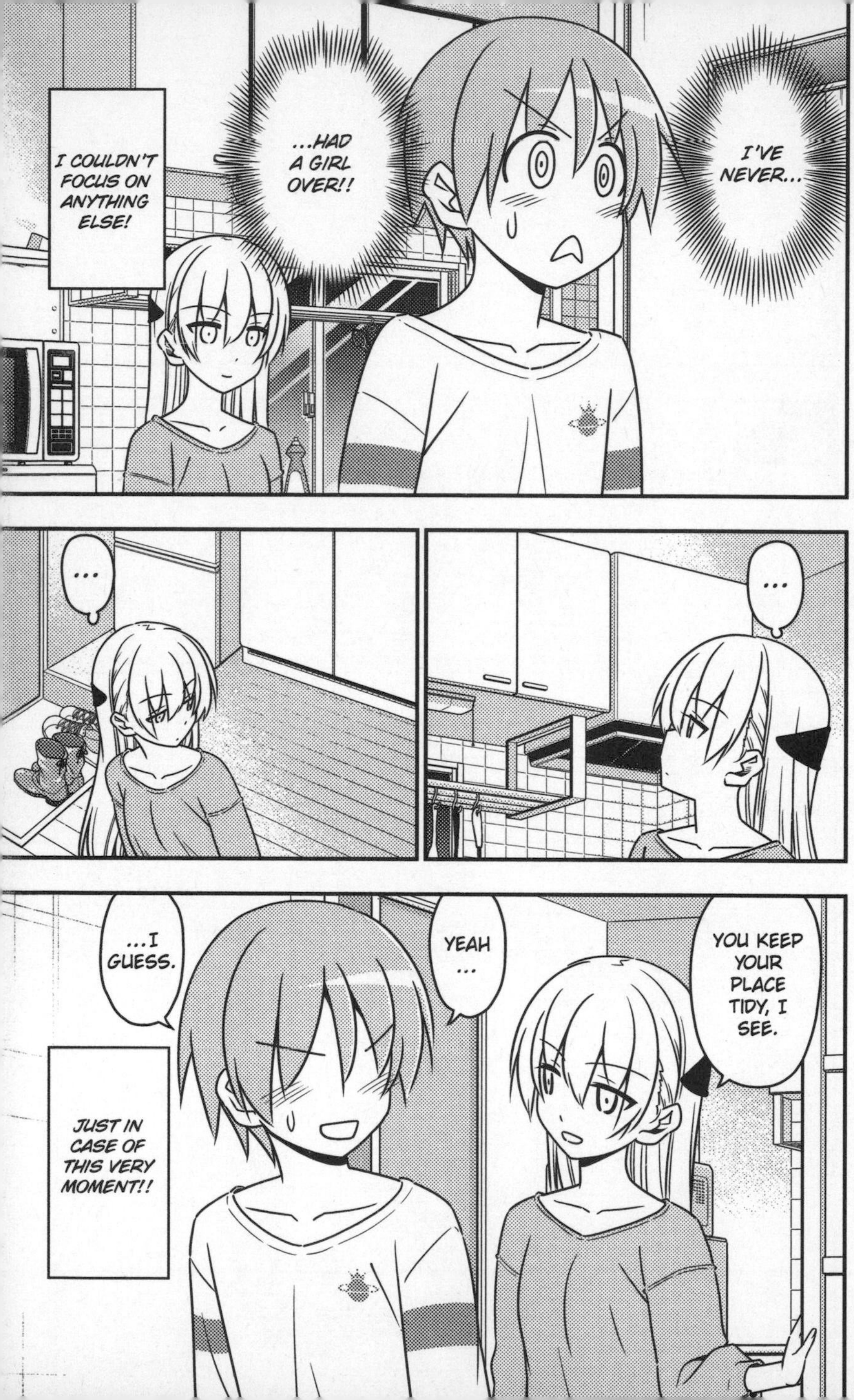
I'VE NEVER...
...HAD A GIRL OVER!!
I COULDN'T FOCUS ON ANYTHING ELSE!
...
...
YOU KEEP YOUR PLACE TIDY, I SEE.
YEAH ...
...I GUESS.
JUST IN CASE OF THIS VERY MOMENT!!

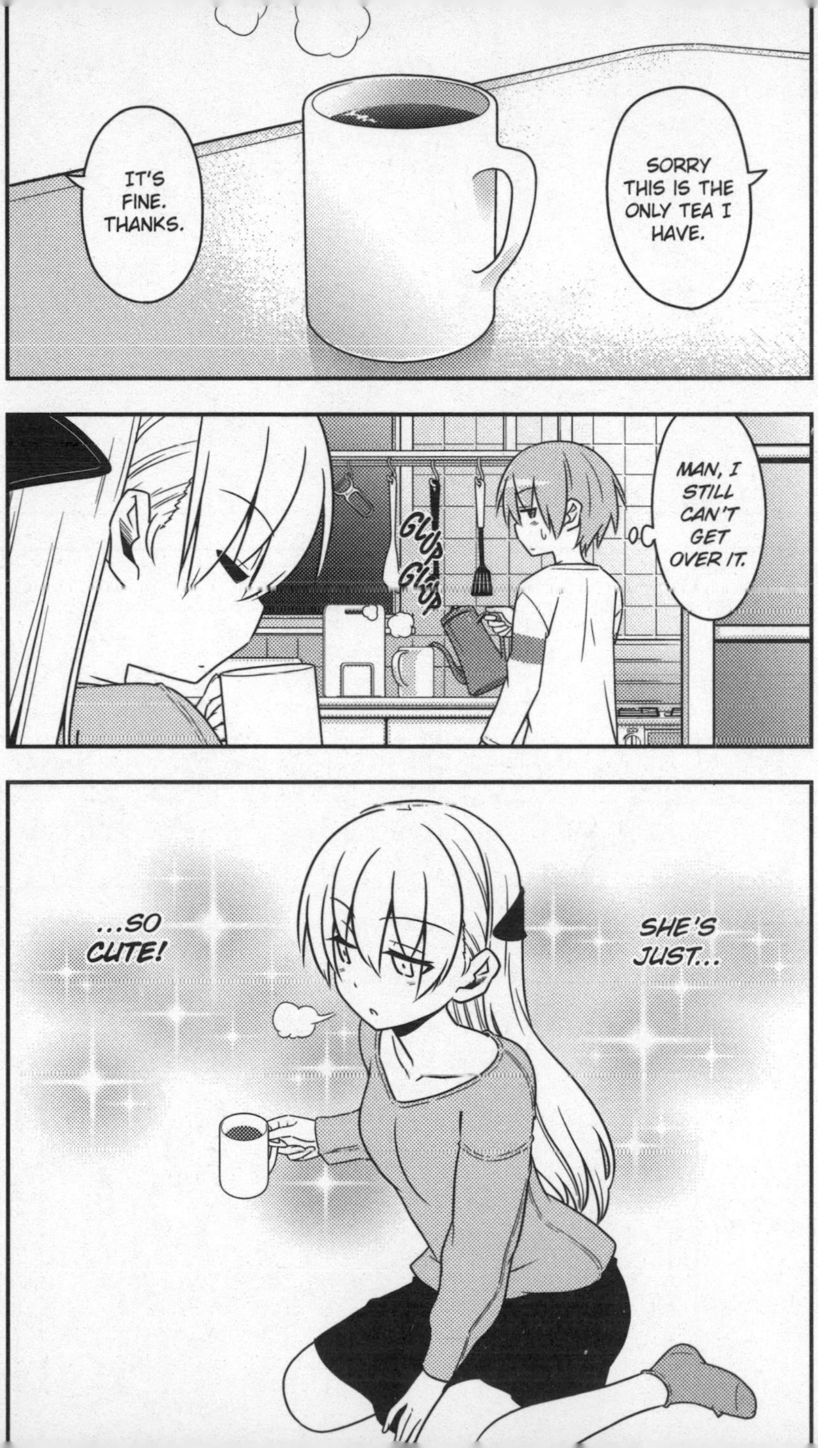
SORRY THIS IS THE ONLY TEA I HAVE.
IT'S FINE. THANKS.
MAN, I STILL CAN'T GET OVER IT.
GLUP GLUP
SHE'S JUST...
...SO CUTE!

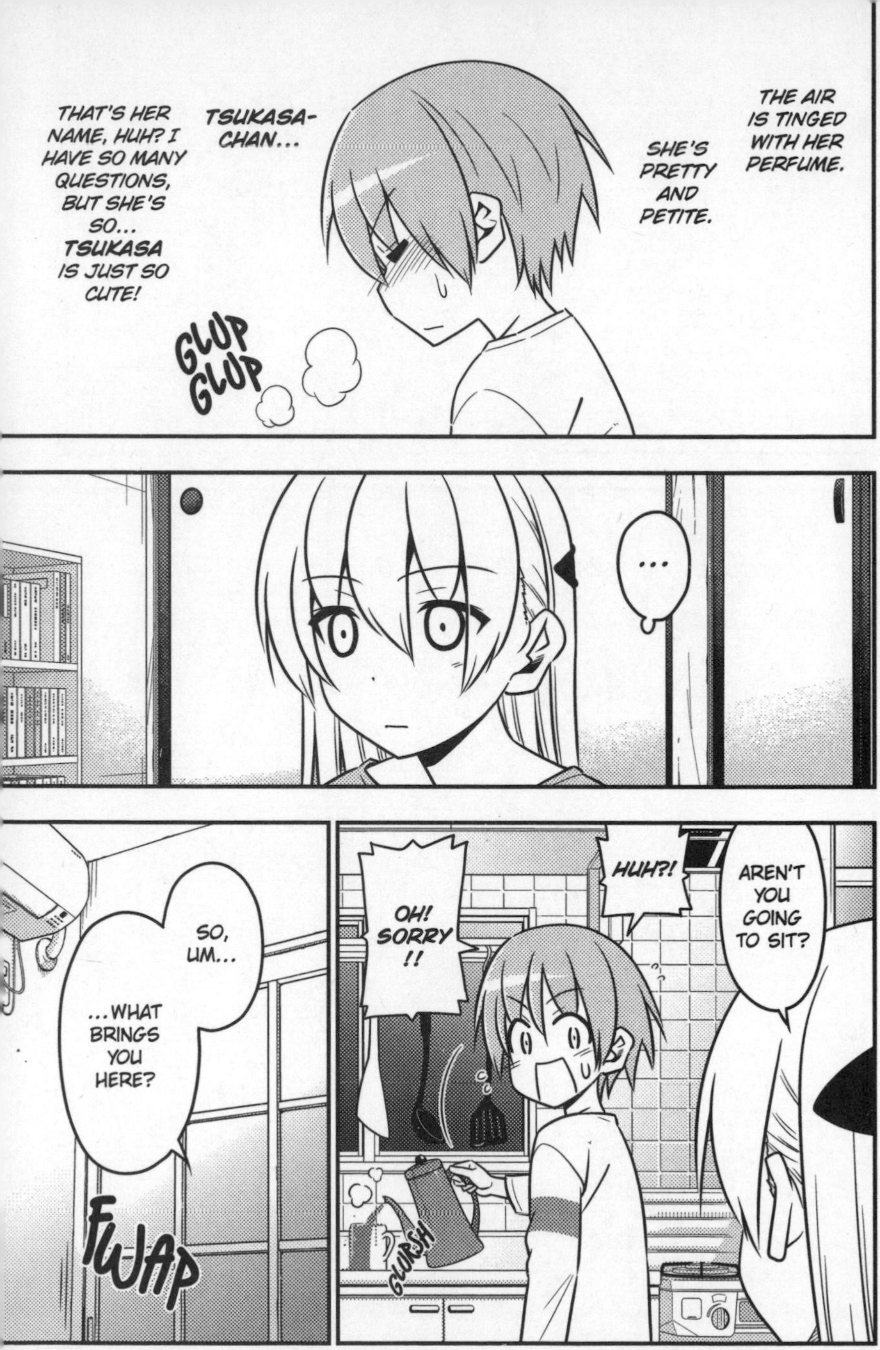
THE AIR IS TINGED WITH HER PERFUME.
SHE'S PRETTY AND PETITE.
TSUKASA-CHAN...
THAT'S HER NAME, HUH? I HAVE SO MANY QUESTIONS, BUT SHE'S SO... TSUKASA IS JUST SO CUTE!
GLUP GLUP
...
AREN'T YOU GOING TO SIT?
HUH?!
OH! SORRY!!
GLORSH
SO, UM...
...WHAT BRINGS YOU HERE?
FWAP

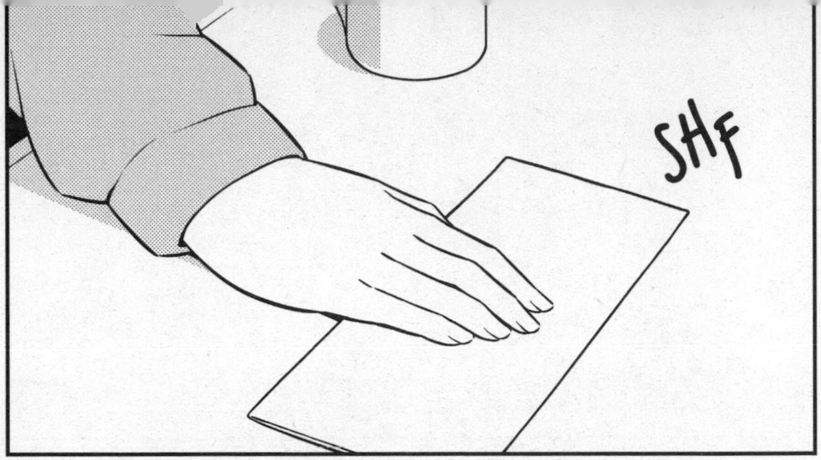
SHF

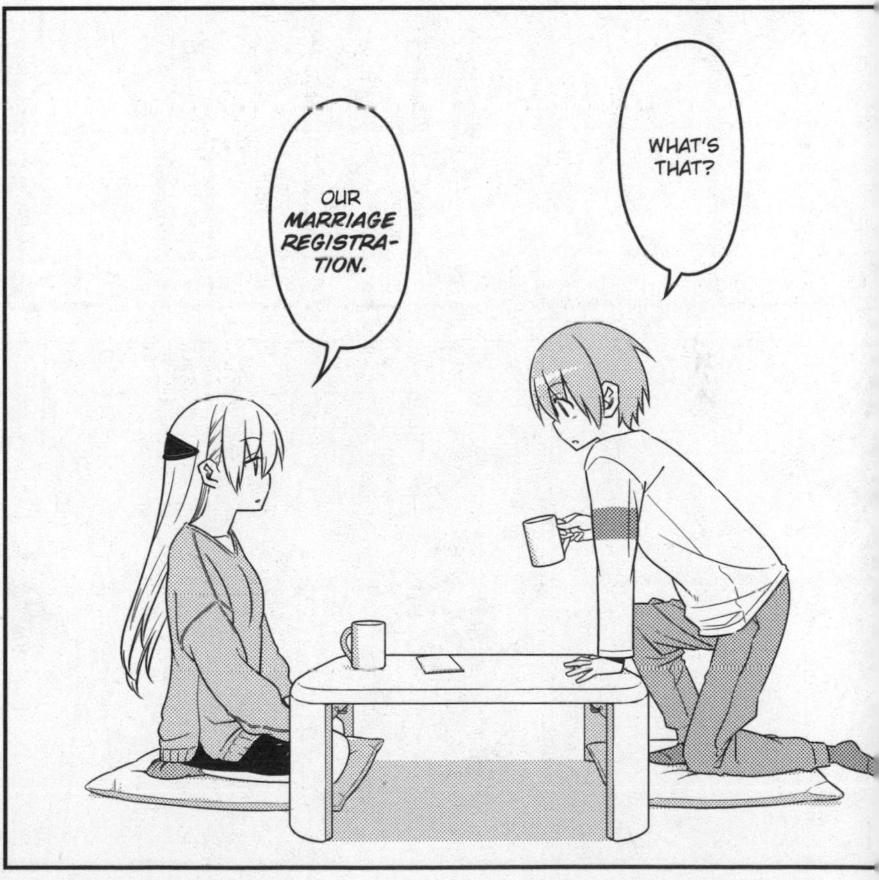
WHAT'S THAT?
OUR MARRIAGE REGISTRATION.

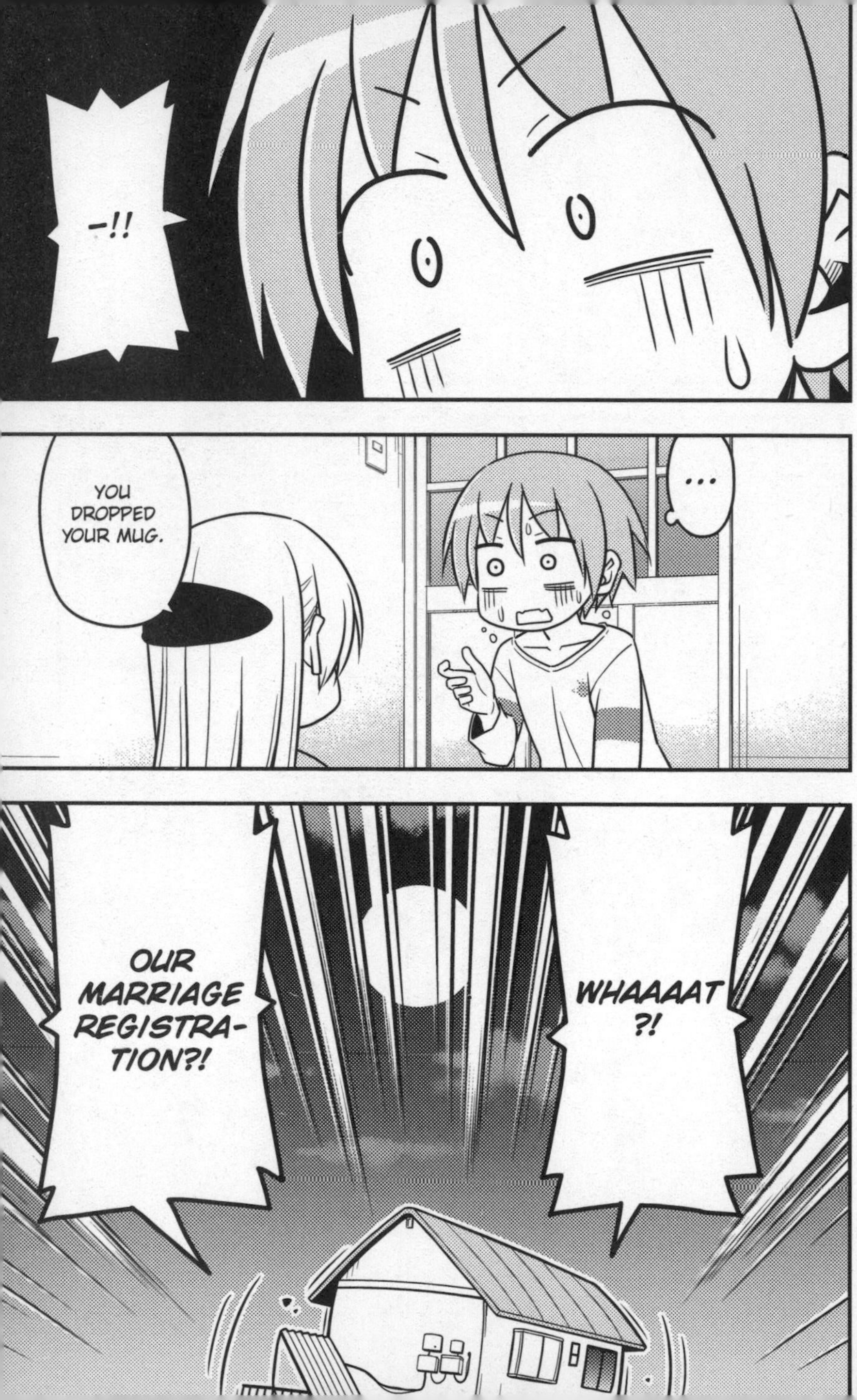
–!!
...
YOU DROPPED YOUR MUG.
WHAAAAT ?!
OUR MARRIAGE REGISTRA- TION?!

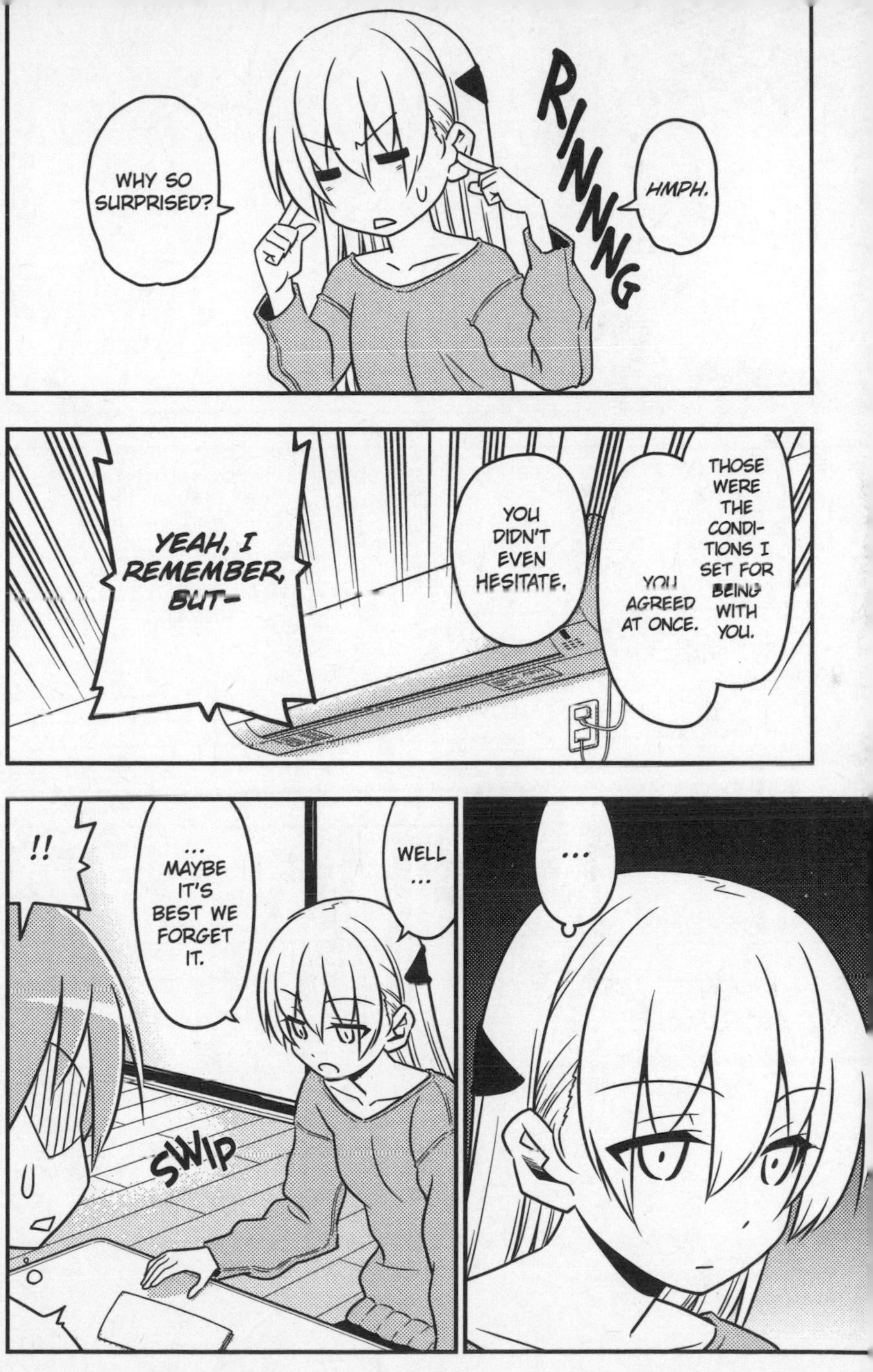
HMPH.
RINNNG
WHY SO SURPRISED?
THOSE WERE THE CONDITIONS I SET FOR BEING WITH YOU.
YOU AGREED AT ONCE.
YOU DIDN'T EVEN HESITATE.
YEAH, I REMEMBER, BUT–
...
WELL ...
... MAYBE IT'S BEST WE FORGET IT.
!!
SWIP

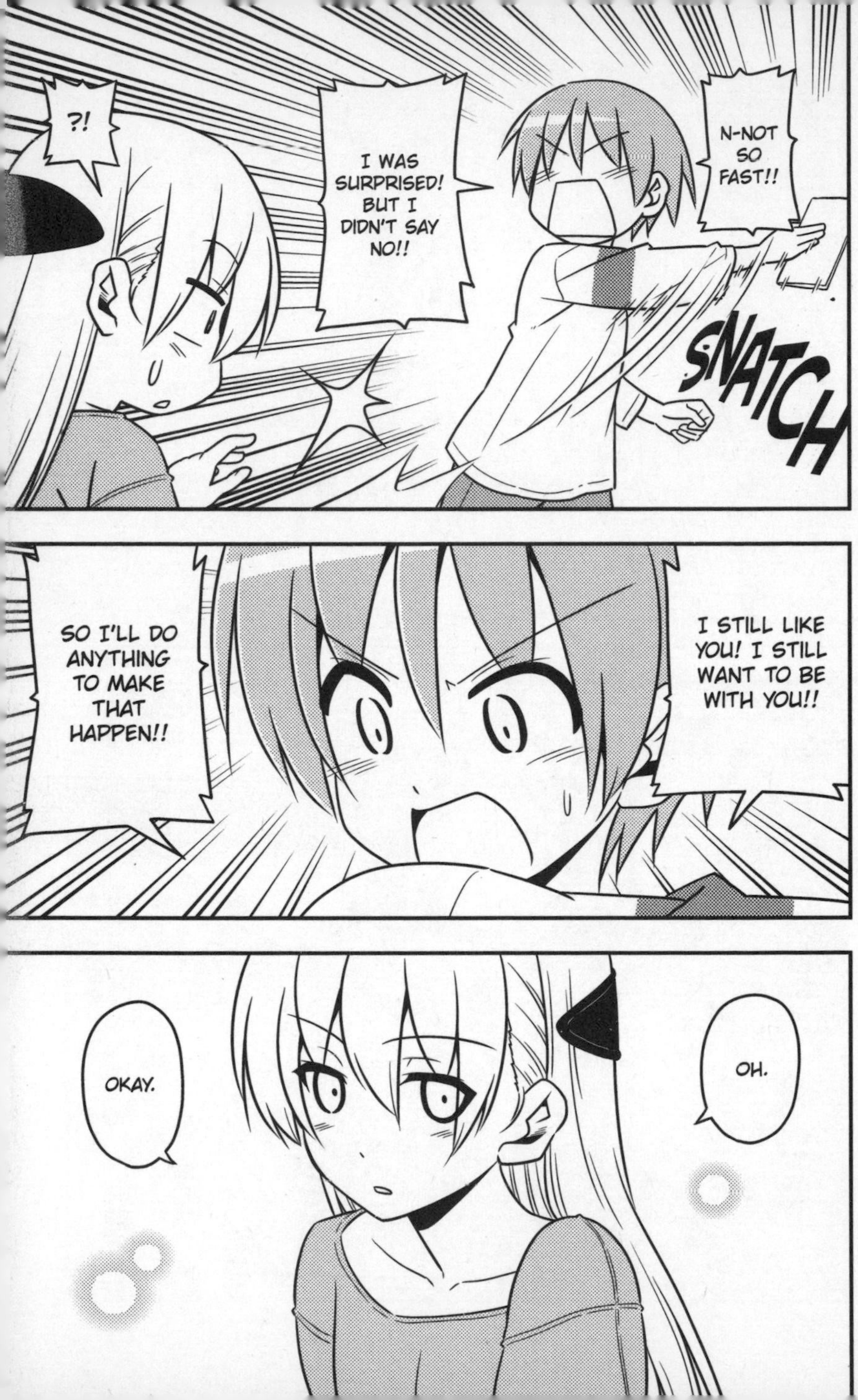
N-NOT SO FAST!!
SNATCH
I WAS SURPRISED! BUT I DIDN'T SAY NO!!
?!
I STILL LIKE YOU! I STILL WANT TO BE WITH YOU!!
SO I'LL DO ANYTHING TO MAKE THAT HAPPEN!!
OH.
OKAY.

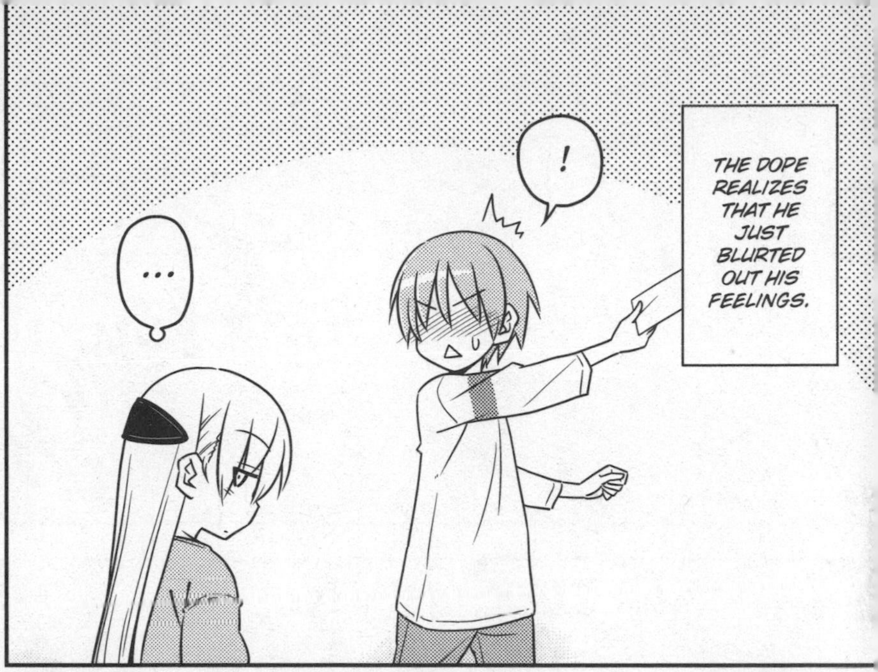
THE DOPE REALIZES THAT HE JUST BLURTED OUT HIS FEELINGS.
!
...

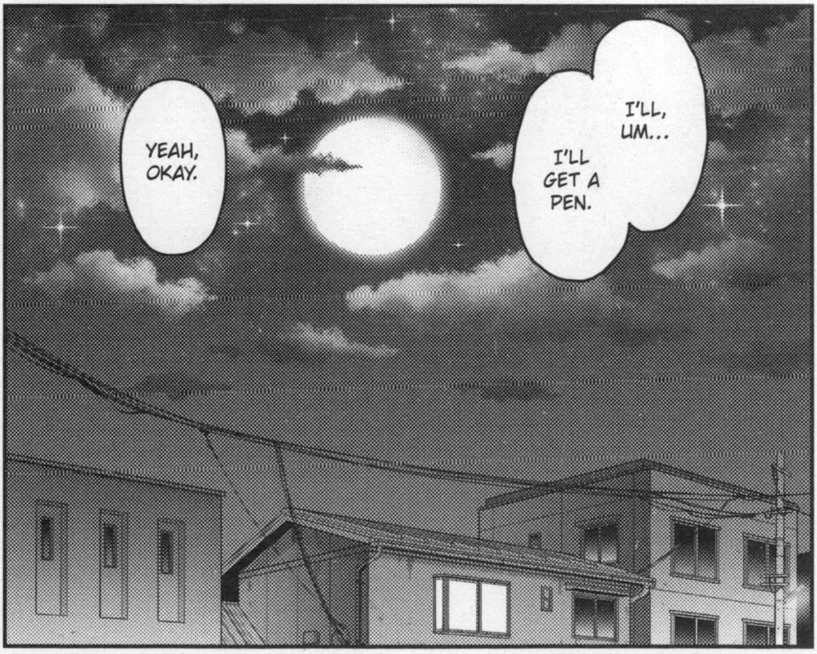
I'LL, UM... I'LL GET A PEN.
YEAH, OKAY.

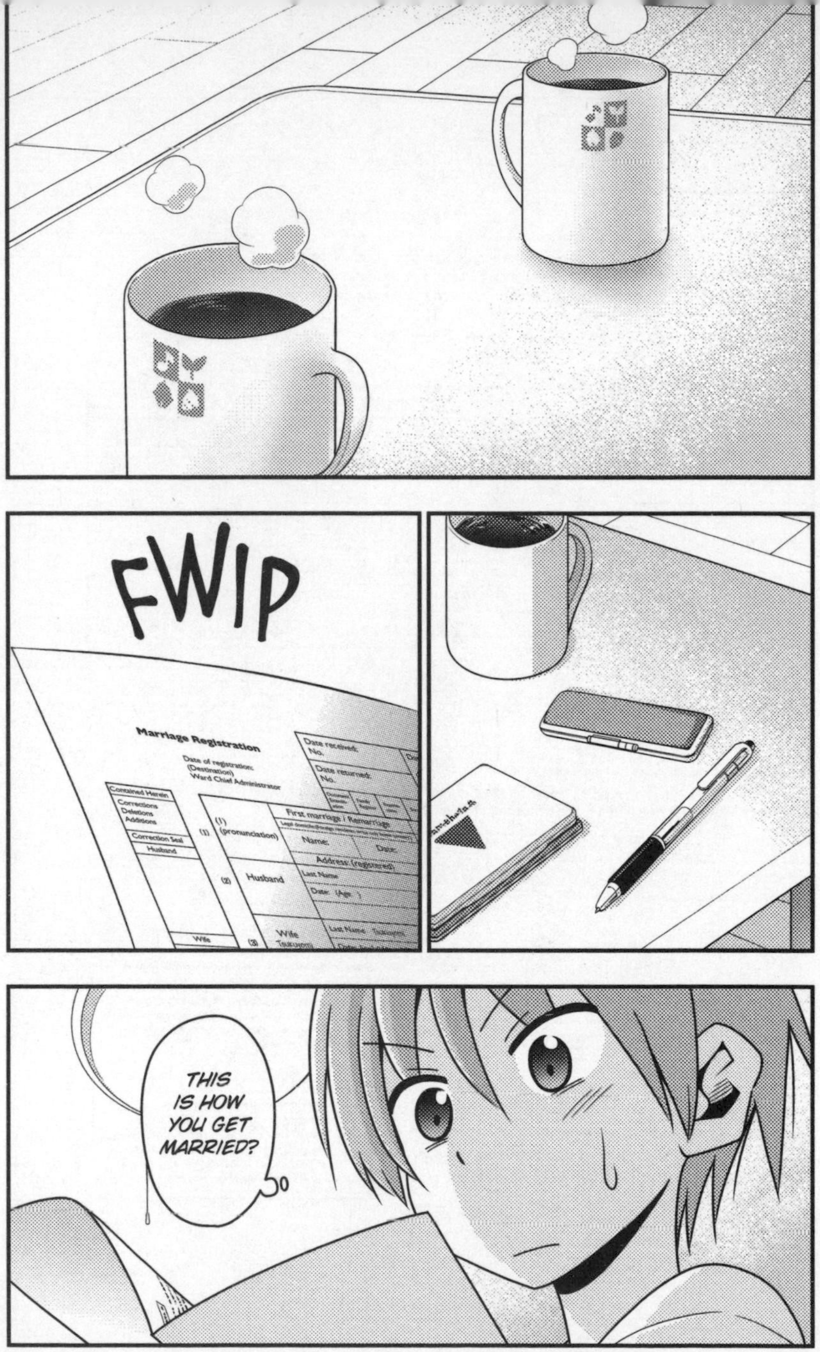
FWIP
Marriage Registration
Date of registration:
(Destination)
Ward Chief Administrator
Date received:
No.
Date returned:
No.
Contained Herein
Corrections
Deletions
Additions
Correction Seal
Husband
(1)
(1) (pronunciation)
First marriage / Remarriage
Name:
Date:
Address (registered)
(2)
Husband
Last Name
Date: (Age)
Wife
(3)
Wife
Last Name
THIS IS HOW YOU GET MARRIED?

Notes:

Do not write with pencil or easily erasable ink.
Registrants complete this section beforehand for submission on the day of their wedding ceremony or beginning of cohabitation. Reception is available on Sundays and holidays.
At ward offices in the Tokyo Metropolitan Area, submission of only one copy is necessary. (When submitting elsewhere, check with the relevant receiving office.)
When submitting in an area different from the location of their legal domicile, registrants must present a copy of their family registers or equivalent documentation.

Witness		
Signature / Seal	Tokiko Tsukuyomi 印	Chitose Kaginoji 印
Birthday	April 23 (Age: 81)	October 20 (Age: 44)
Address	Toranomon, Minato Ward	Minami-Aoyama, Minato
	1-28 Block: No.	1-32 Block: No.
Legal domicile	Toranomon, Minato Ward	Minami Aoyama, Minato
	1-28 Block: No.	1-32 Block: No.

→ Write the name of the person recorded first in the family register.

☐ Write a check mark in the appropriate box.
→ ☑ If the checked person is not yet the family head in the family register, a new family register may be prepared, so write the desired legal domicile.

→ In case of remarriage, provide details of most recent previous marriage. Living together outside of legal marriage is not applicable.

Contact information
(husband / wife / other)
Phone ( ) No.
Home / Business [ ] / Mobile [ ]

If the marriage will change a registrant's address or head of household, then the respective forms providing notification of such changes must be submitted.

When submitting such notification on the same occasion as marriage registration, write the address or head of household applicable after those changes. The relevant notifications are not accepted outside ward office hours (Sat., Sun., holidays), so please submit them on a later date.

- **Registrants must sign their own names.**
- **Each registrant must apply his or her own seal.**

Marriage Registration

Date of registration:
(Destination)
Ward Chief Administrator

Date received: No.	Date approved:
Date returned: No.	Chief Administrator Seal

Document Examination	Family Register	Examination	Survey	Approval	Attachment	Residence Certificate	Notification

Contained Herein
Corrections Deletions Additions
Correction Seal
Husband
Wife

(1)	(I) (pronunciation)	First marriage / Remarriage Legal domicile: (Foreign residents write only home country.) Name: Date: Address: (registered)	Beginning of cohabitation: Parents' names and relationship to them: (Write non-birth parents in "Other" below.) Principal occupations of both husband and wife's households before cohabitation and husband and wife's occupations:
(2)	Husband	Last Name Date: (Age:) Name of head of household:	First Name Block No. Relationship:
(3)	Wife Tsukasa Tsukuyomi	Last Name Tsukuyomi Date: April 3 (Age: 16) Name of head of household: Taro	First Name Tsukasa Block No. Relationship: Eldest daughter
(4)		☑ Husband's ☐ Wife's	New legal domicile (Do not complete if individual checked at left is already family head in family register.) Block No.
(5)		Date: (Write date of wedding ceremony or beginning of cohabitation, whichever came first.)	
(6)		☐ Remarriage (☐ Death ☐ Divorce Date:)	☑ First marriage (☐ ☐)
(7)		Husband Wife 1. Household involved in only agriculture or agriculture and other occupation. Husband Wife 2. Household in which an individual is engaged in a freelance profession, commerce and industry, service, etc. Husband Wife 3. Household of regular employee at a company or private business, etc. (nongovernmental) whose place of work has 1 to 99 employees. (For employee with daily or less than one-year contract: 5.) Husband Wife 4. Household of regular employee to whom 3 does not apply or household of a company or group executive. Husband Wife 5. Household with individual involved in other occupation to whom 1 through 4 do not apply. Husband Wife 6. Household without an employed individual.	
(8)			
	Other		
	Registrants Signature and seal	Husband Seal	Wife Seal
	Registration No.		

Date: A.M. P.M. Time received:	
Husband	☐ License ☐ Passport ☐ Other ☐ Residence Certificate ☐ ( )
Nonacceptance	☐ Yes ☐ No
Notification	☐ Necessary ☐ Unnecessary
Wife	☐ License ☐ Passport ☐ Other ☐ Residence Certificate ☐ ( )
Nonacceptance	☐ Yes ☐ No
Notification	☐ Necessary ☐ Unnecessary
Proxy	☐ License ☐ Passport ☐ Other ☐ Residence Certificate ☐ ( )
Returned	Date:

Confirmation	Notification

Permanent residence	date	Husband	date	Wife

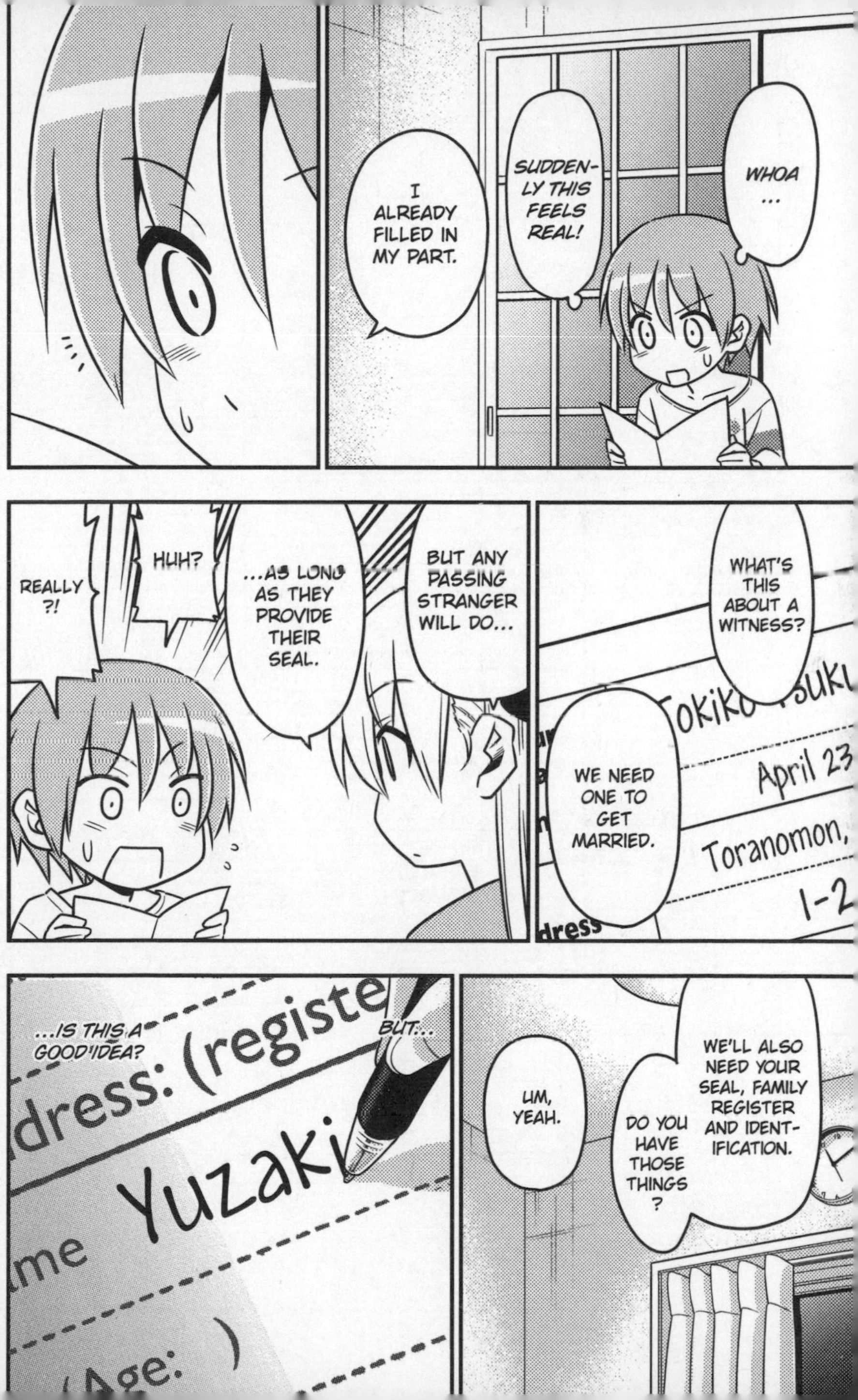
WHOA...
SUDDENLY THIS FEELS REAL!
I ALREADY FILLED IN MY PART.
WHAT'S THIS ABOUT A WITNESS?
WE NEED ONE TO GET MARRIED.
April 23
Toranomon,
BUT ANY PASSING STRANGER WILL DO...
...AS LONG AS THEY PROVIDE THEIR SEAL.
HUH?
REALLY?!
WE'LL ALSO NEED YOUR SEAL, FAMILY REGISTER AND IDENTIFICATION.
DO YOU HAVE THOSE THINGS?
UM, YEAH.
BUT...
...IS THIS A GOOD IDEA?
Yuzaki

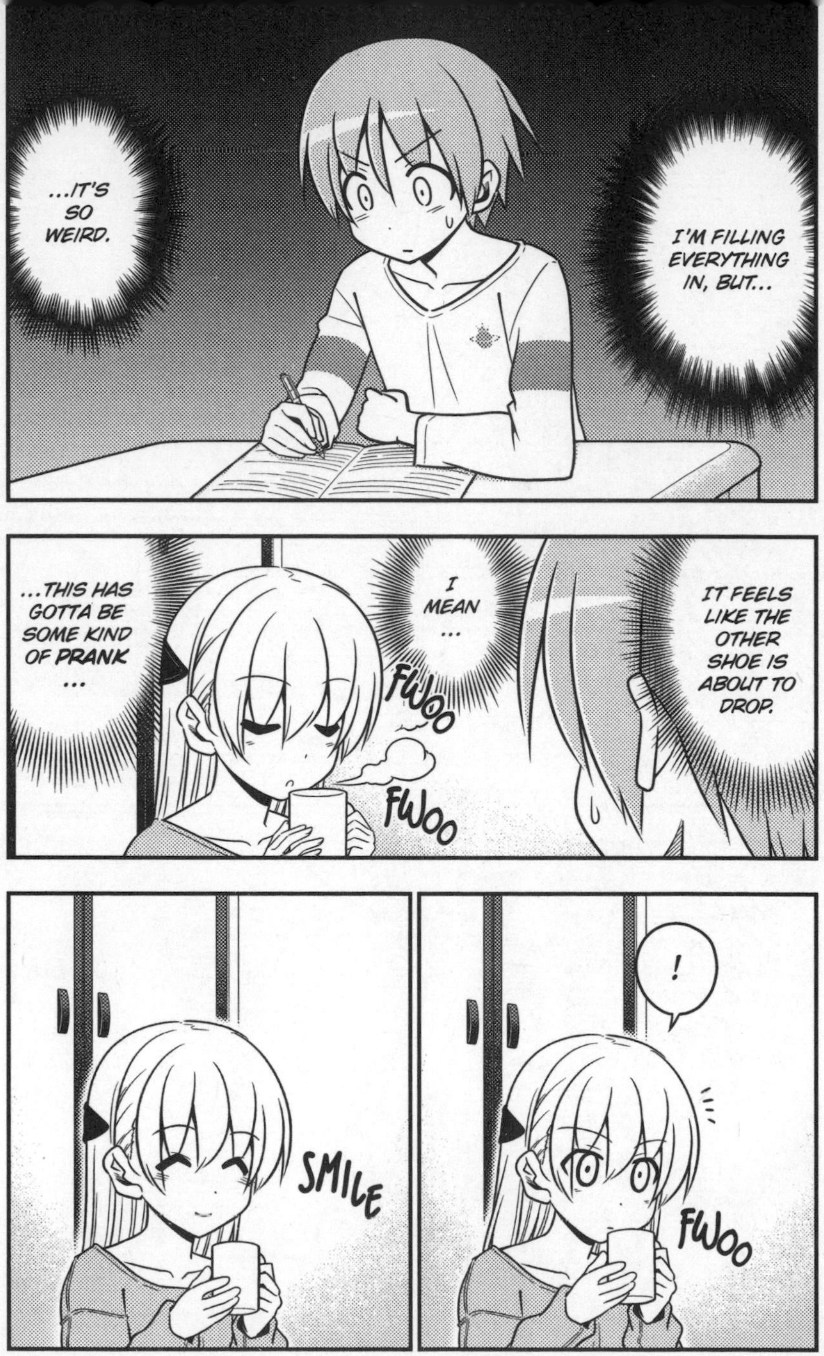
I'M FILLING EVERYTHING IN, BUT...
...IT'S SO WEIRD.
IT FEELS LIKE THE OTHER SHOE IS ABOUT TO DROP.
I MEAN ...
FWOO
FWOO
...THIS HAS GOTTA BE SOME KIND OF PRANK ...
!
FWOO
SMILE

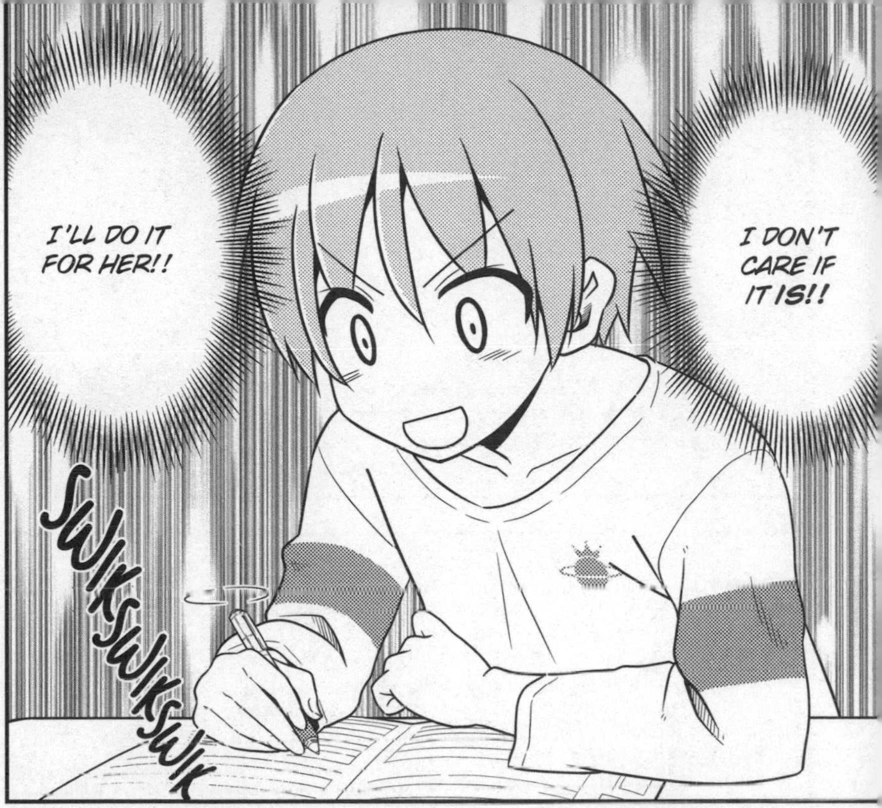
I DON'T CARE IF IT IS!!
I'LL DO IT FOR HER!!
SWIKSWIKSWIK

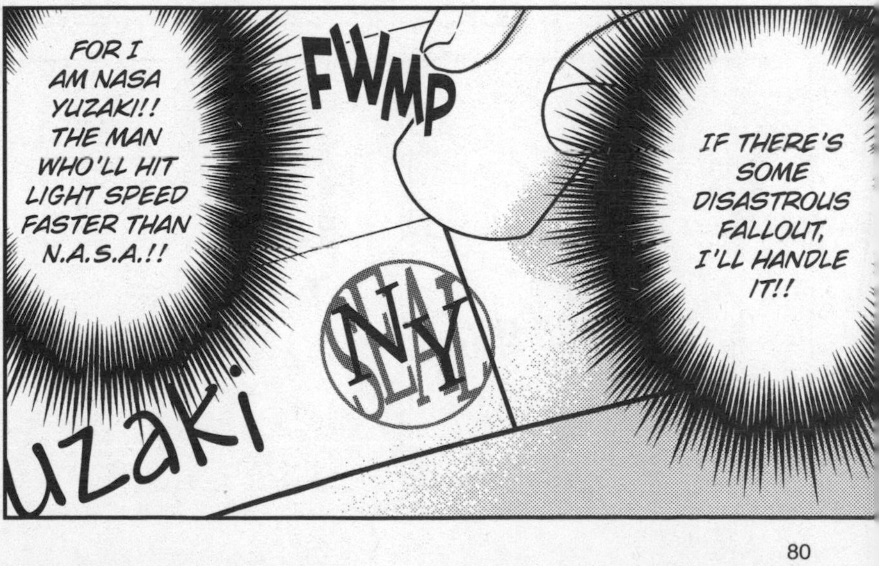
IF THERE'S SOME DISASTROUS FALLOUT, I'LL HANDLE IT!!
FWMP
FOR I AM NASA YUZAKI!! THE MAN WHO'LL HIT LIGHT SPEED FASTER THAN N.A.S.A.!!
NY
uzaki

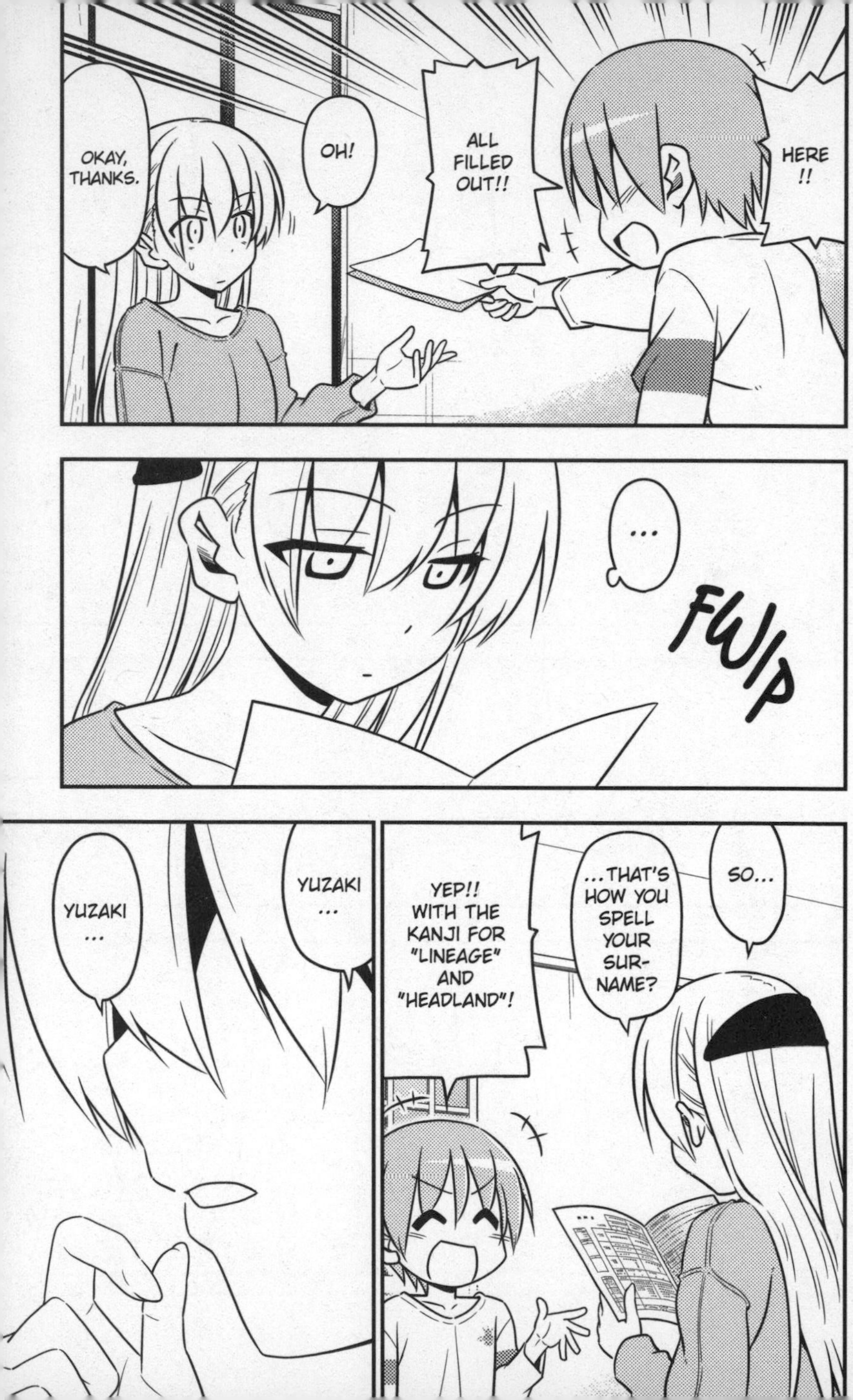
HERE !!
ALL FILLED OUT!!
OH!
OKAY, THANKS.
...
FWIP
SO...
...THAT'S HOW YOU SPELL YOUR SUR-NAME?
YEP!! WITH THE KANJI FOR "LINEAGE" AND "HEADLAND"!
YUZAKI ...
YUZAKI ...

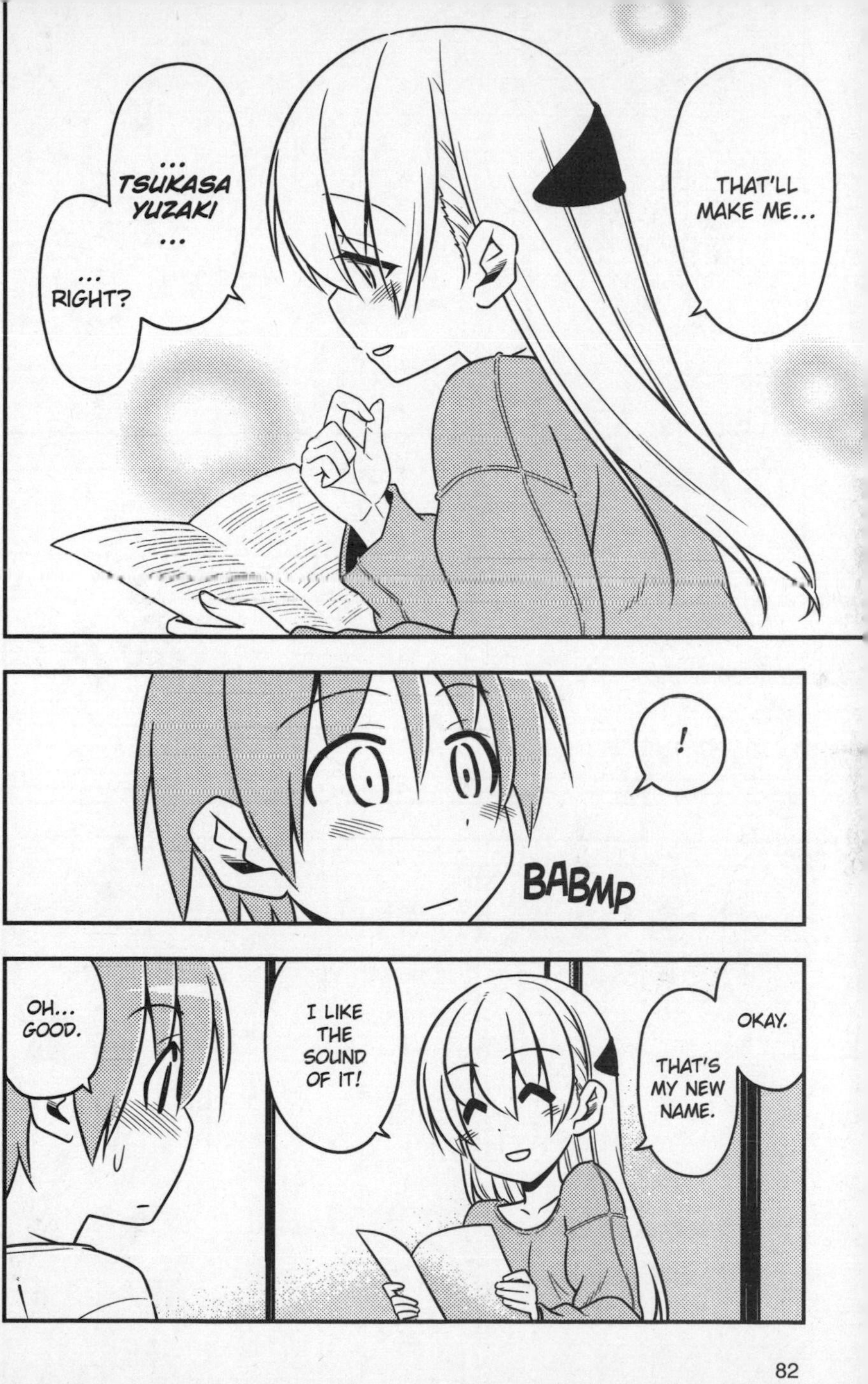
THAT'LL MAKE ME...
... TSUKASA YUZAKI ... ... RIGHT?
!
BABMP
OKAY. THAT'S MY NEW NAME.
I LIKE THE SOUND OF IT!
OH... GOOD.

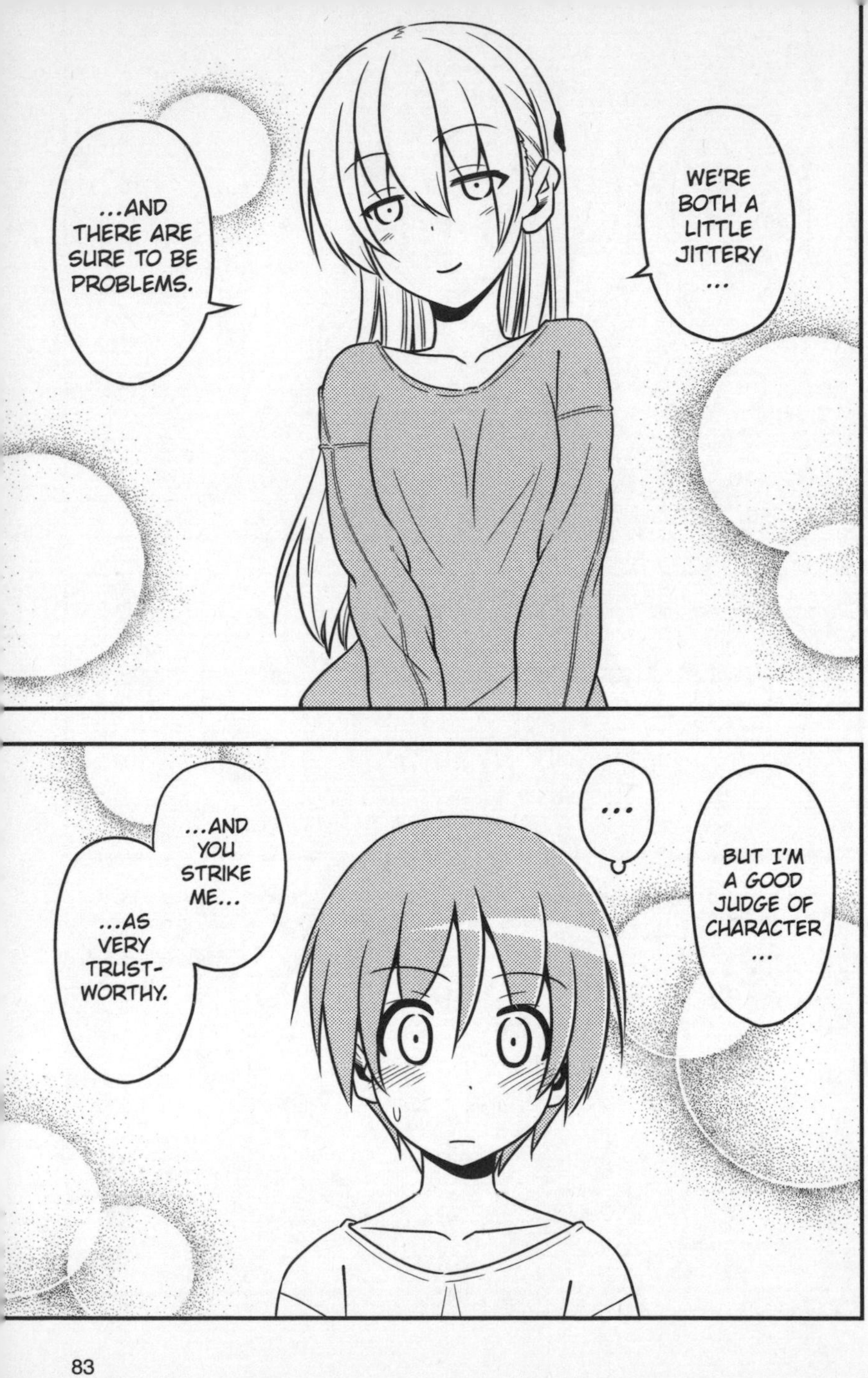
WE'RE BOTH A LITTLE JITTERY ...
...AND THERE ARE SURE TO BE PROBLEMS.
BUT I'M A GOOD JUDGE OF CHARACTER ...
...
...AND YOU STRIKE ME...
...AS VERY TRUST-WORTHY.

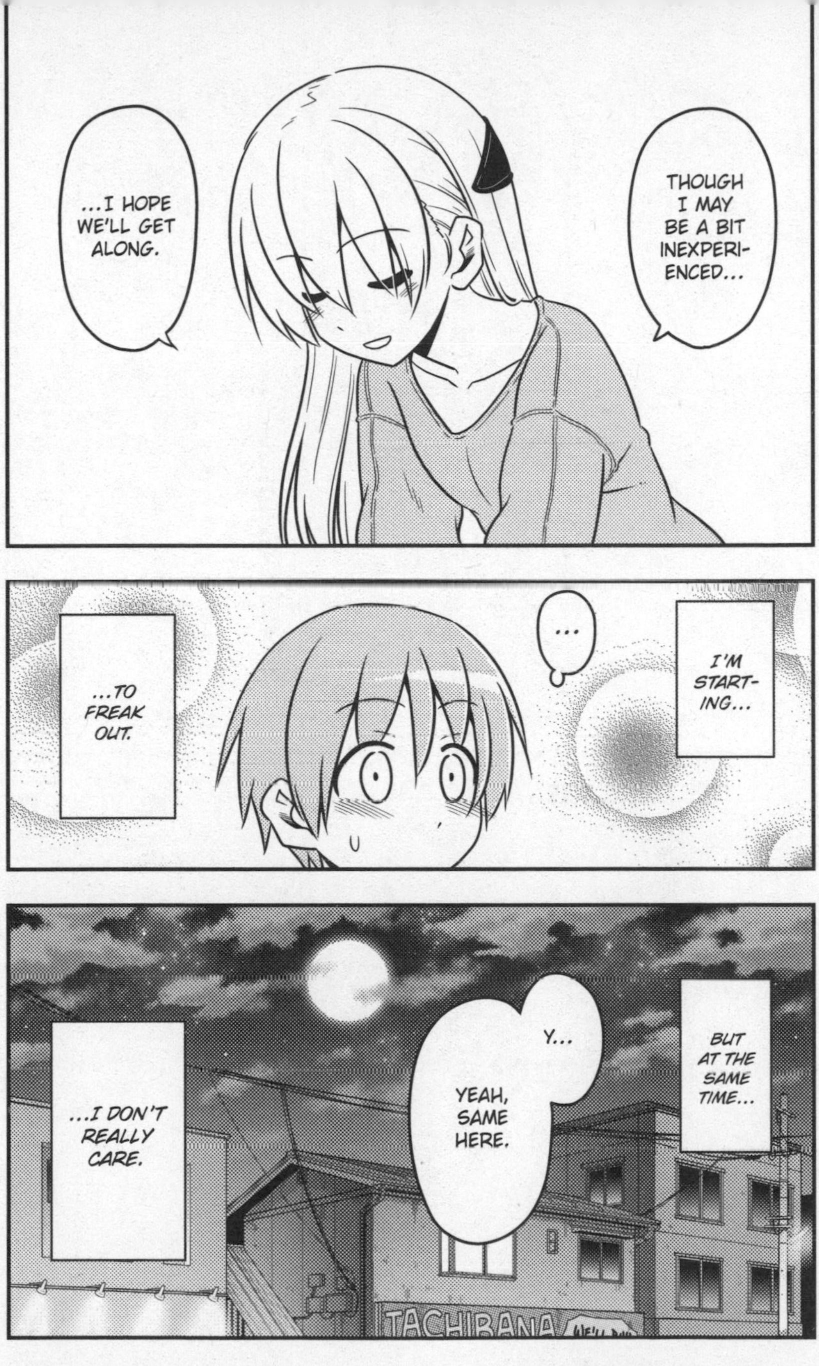
THOUGH I MAY BE A BIT INEXPERIENCED...
...I HOPE WE'LL GET ALONG.
I'M STARTING...
...
...TO FREAK OUT.
BUT AT THE SAME TIME...
Y...
YEAH, SAME HERE.
...I DON'T REALLY CARE.
TACHIBANA

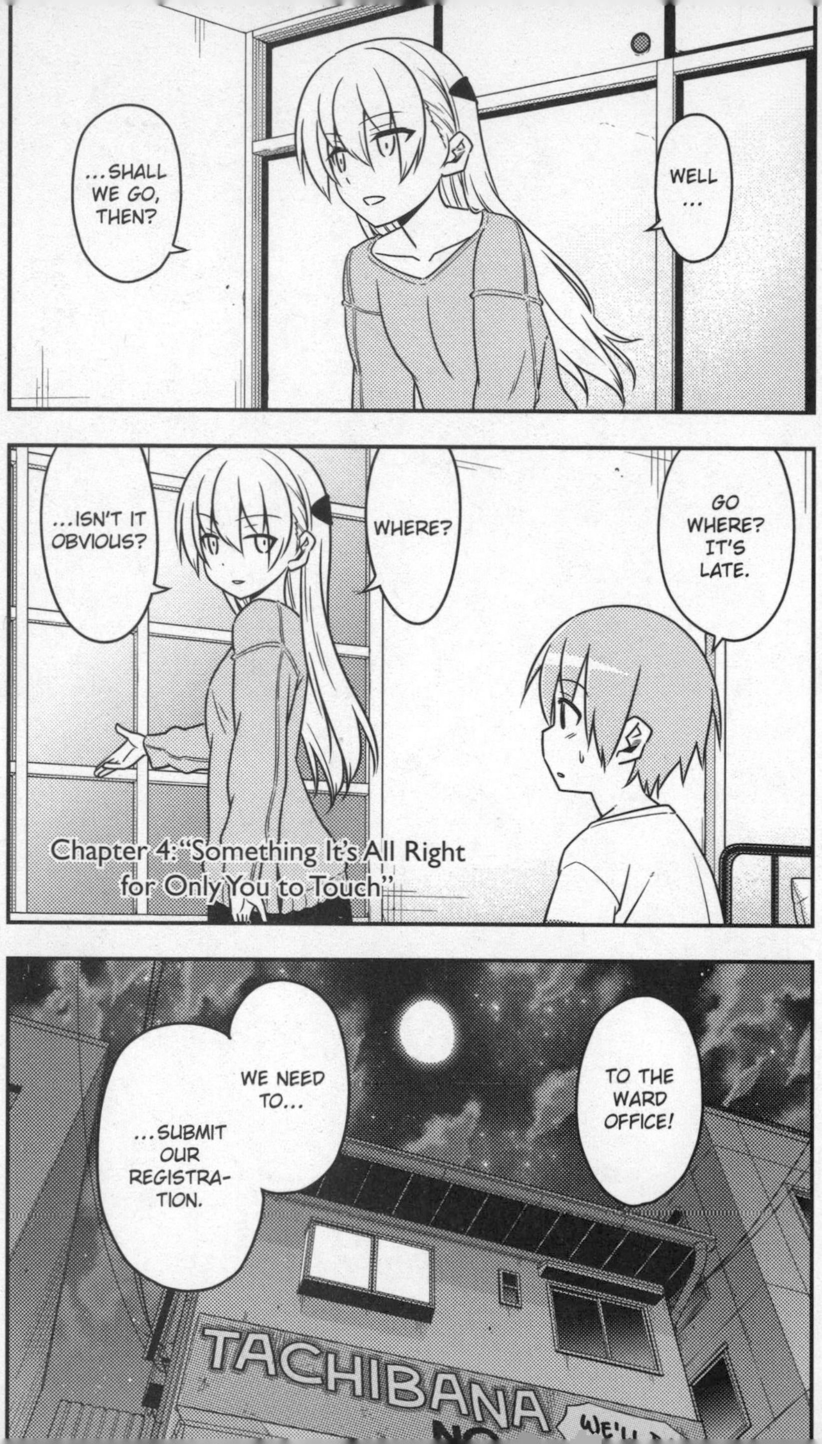
WELL ...
...SHALL WE GO, THEN?
GO WHERE? IT'S LATE.
WHERE?
...ISN'T IT OBVIOUS?
Chapter 4: "Something It's All Right for Only You to Touch"
TO THE WARD OFFICE!
WE NEED TO...
...SUBMIT OUR REGISTRATION.
TACHIBANA

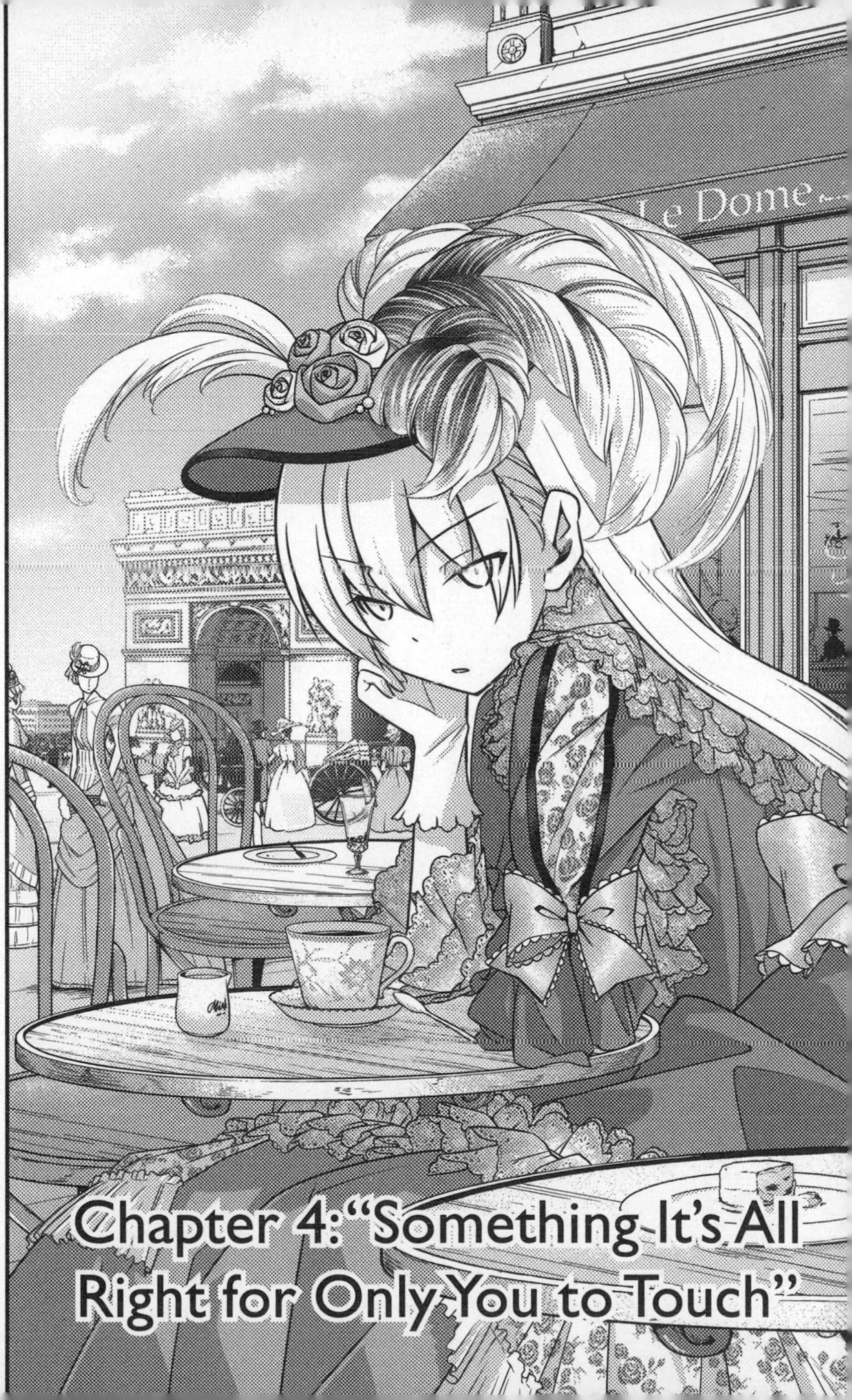
Le Dome
Chapter 4: "Something It's All Right for Only You to Touch"

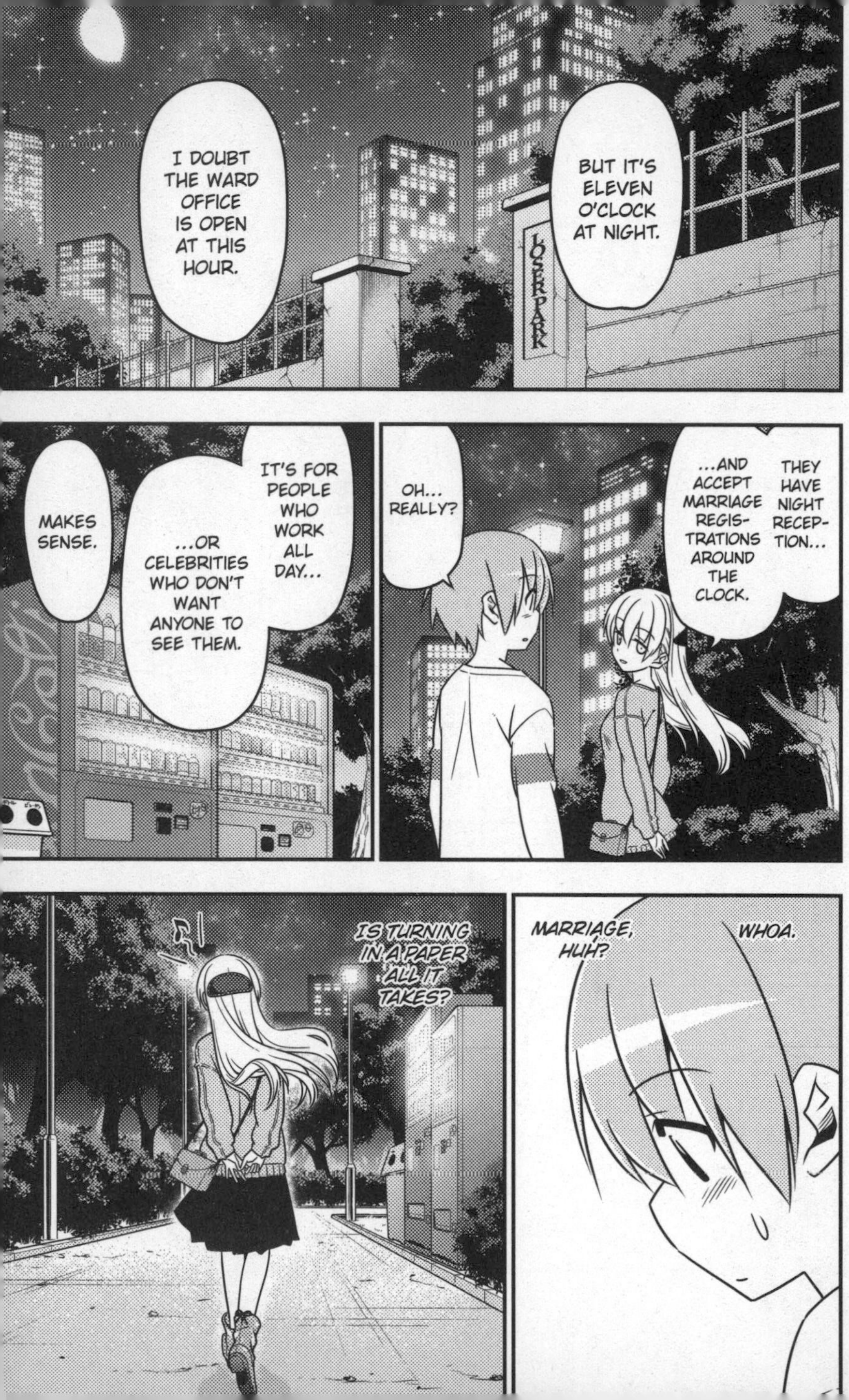
BUT IT'S ELEVEN O'CLOCK AT NIGHT.
LOSERPARK
I DOUBT THE WARD OFFICE IS OPEN AT THIS HOUR.
THEY HAVE NIGHT RECEPTION...
...AND ACCEPT MARRIAGE REGISTRATIONS AROUND THE CLOCK.
OH... REALLY?
IT'S FOR PEOPLE WHO WORK ALL DAY...
...OR CELEBRITIES WHO DON'T WANT ANYONE TO SEE THEM.
MAKES SENSE.
WHOA.
MARRIAGE, HUH?
IS TURNING IN A PAPER ALL IT TAKES?

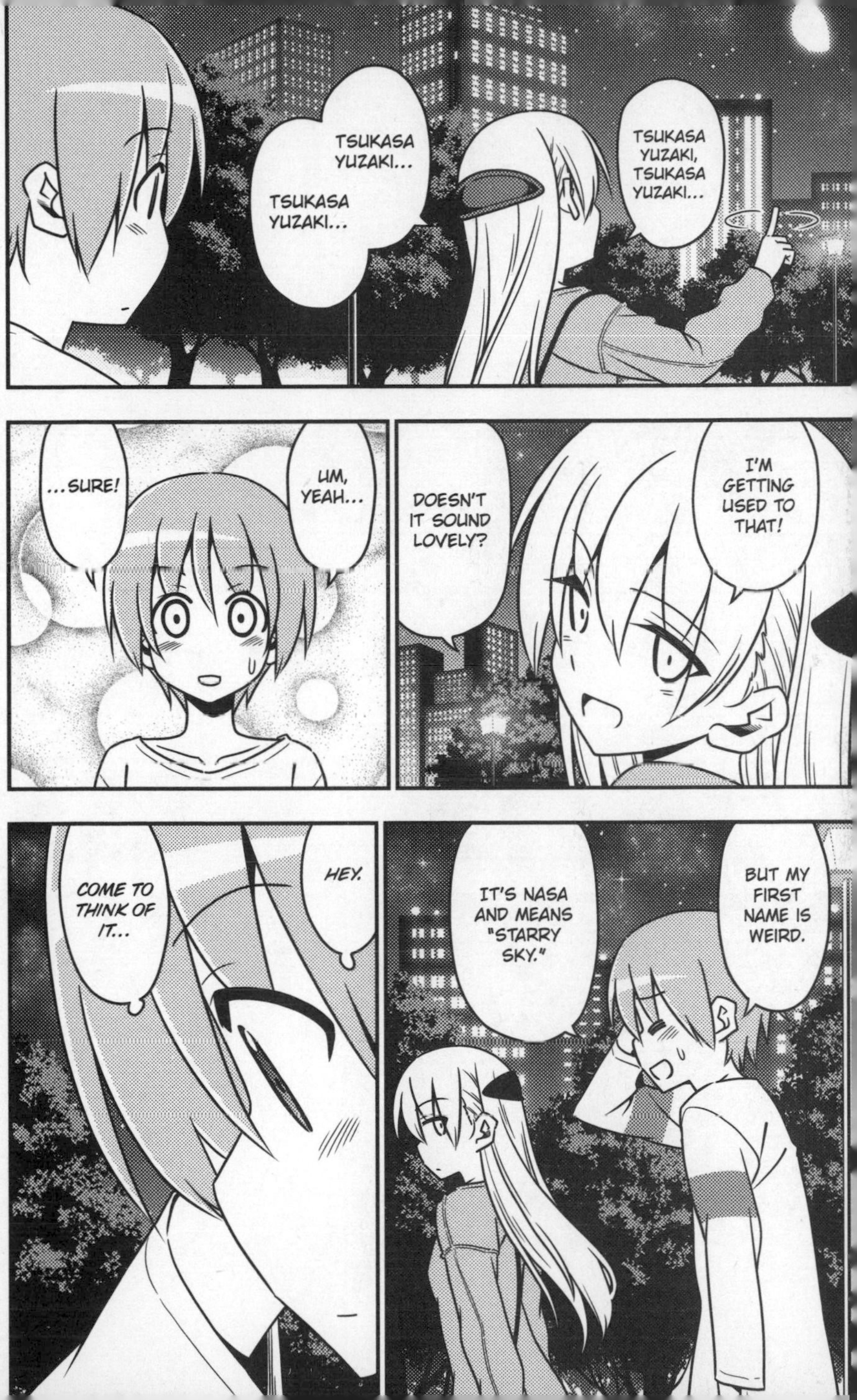
TSUKASA YUZAKI, TSUKASA YUZAKI...
TSUKASA YUZAKI...
TSUKASA YUZAKI...
I'M GETTING USED TO THAT!
DOESN'T IT SOUND LOVELY?
UM, YEAH...
...SURE!
BUT MY FIRST NAME IS WEIRD.
IT'S NASA AND MEANS "STARRY SKY."
HEY.
COME TO THINK OF IT...

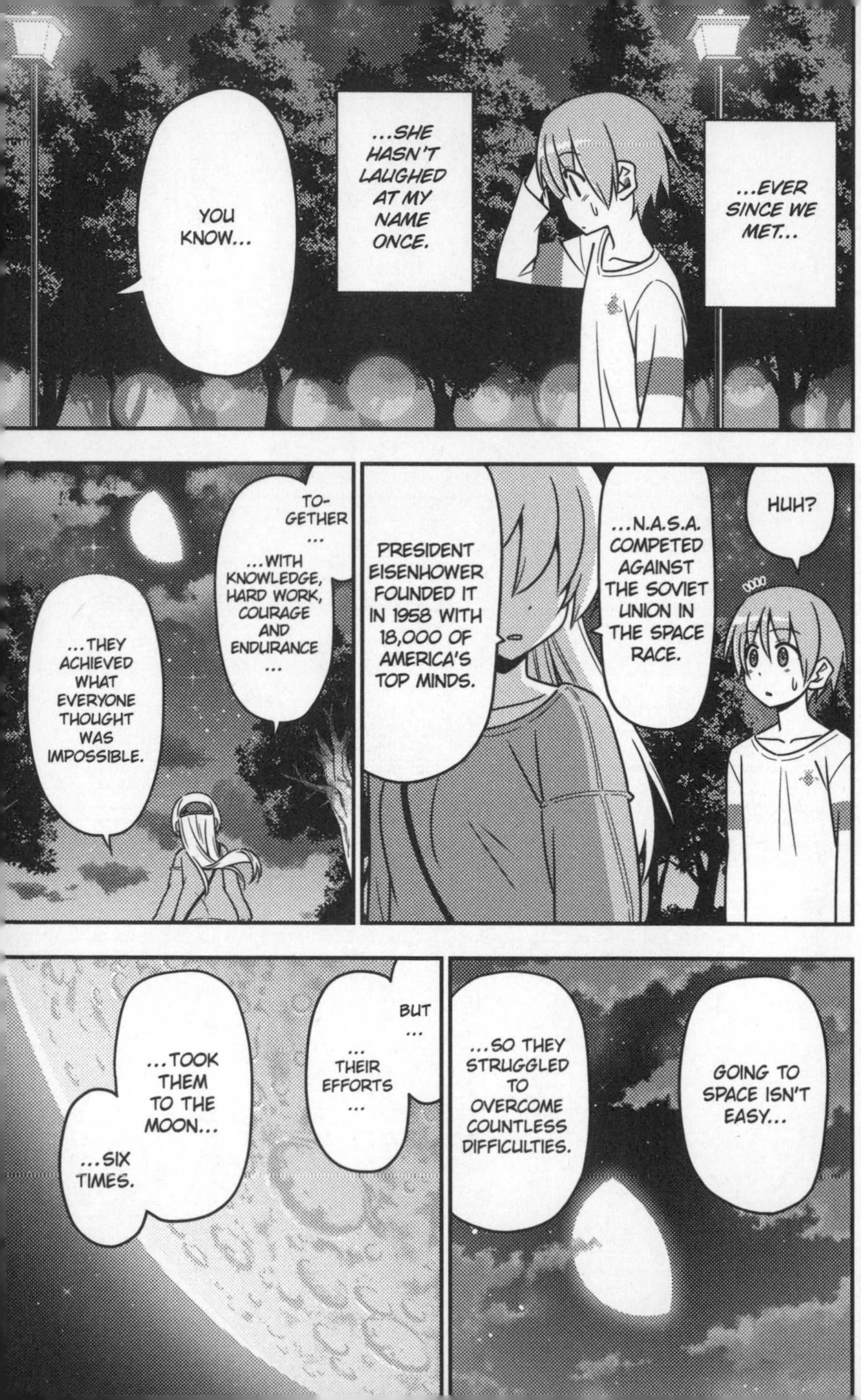
...EVER SINCE WE MET...
...SHE HASN'T LAUGHED AT MY NAME ONCE.
YOU KNOW...
HUH?
...N.A.S.A. COMPETED AGAINST THE SOVIET UNION IN THE SPACE RACE.
PRESIDENT EISENHOWER FOUNDED IT IN 1958 WITH 18,000 OF AMERICA'S TOP MINDS.
TO-GETHER ... ...WITH KNOWLEDGE, HARD WORK, COURAGE AND ENDURANCE ...
...THEY ACHIEVED WHAT EVERYONE THOUGHT WAS IMPOSSIBLE.
GOING TO SPACE ISN'T EASY...
...SO THEY STRUGGLED TO OVERCOME COUNTLESS DIFFICULTIES.
BUT ... ... THEIR EFFORTS ...
...TOOK THEM TO THE MOON... ...SIX TIMES.

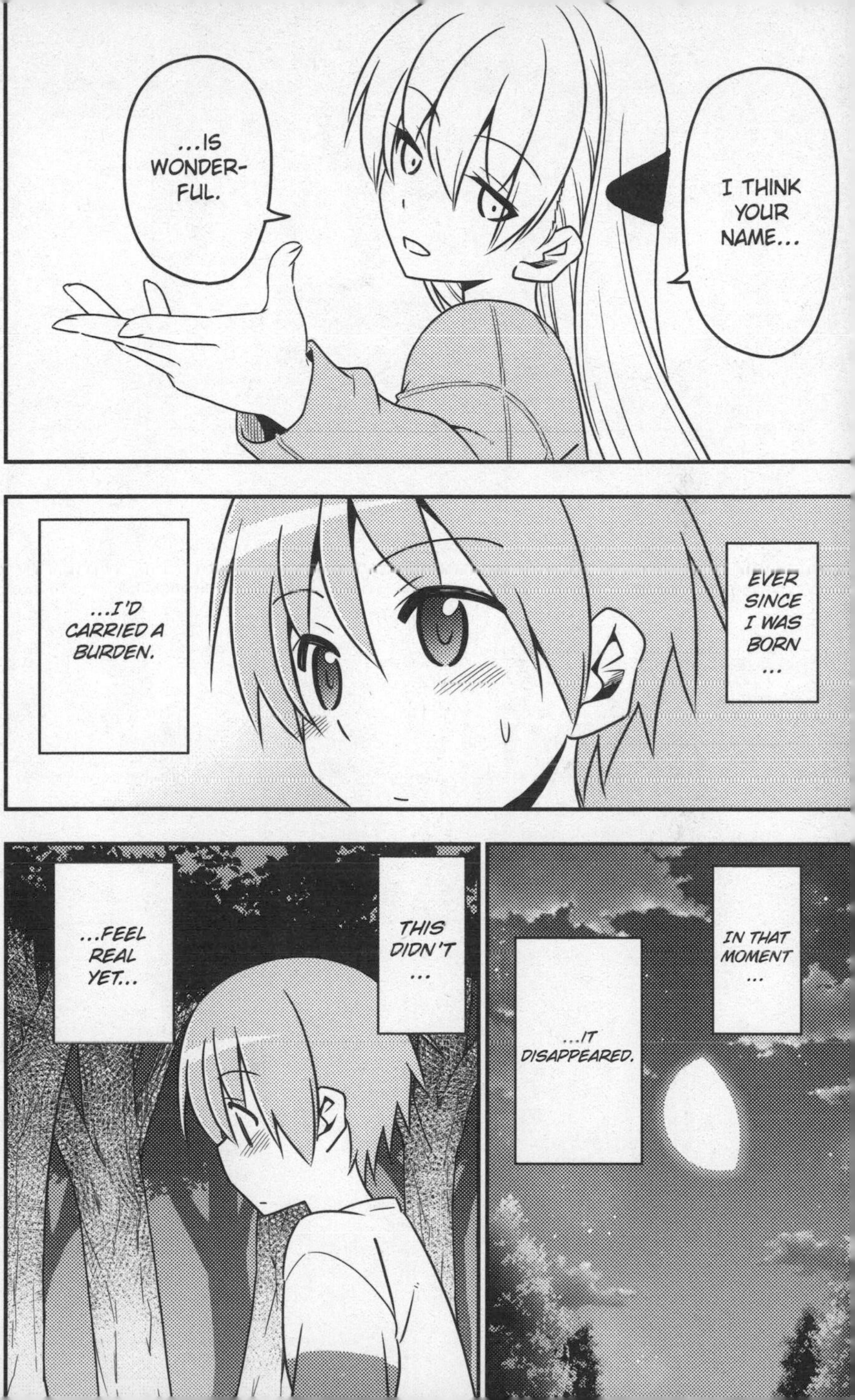
I THINK YOUR NAME...
...IS WONDER-FUL.
EVER SINCE I WAS BORN ...
...I'D CARRIED A BURDEN.
IN THAT MOMENT ...
...IT DISAPPEARED.
THIS DIDN'T ...
...FEEL REAL YET...

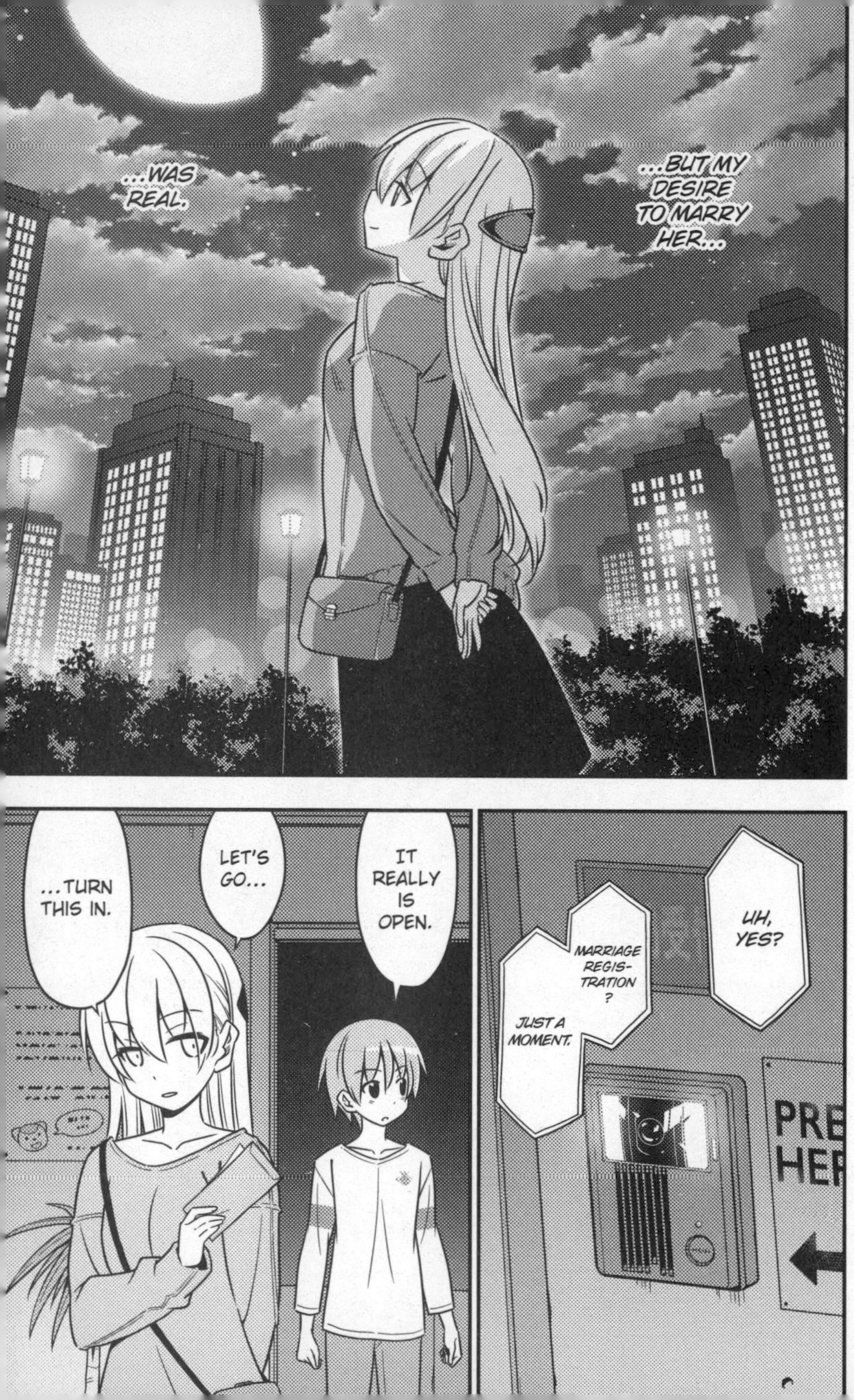
...BUT MY DESIRE TO MARRY HER...
...WAS REAL.
UH, YES?
MARRIAGE REGIS-TRATION?
JUST A MOMENT.
IT REALLY IS OPEN.
LET'S GO...
...TURN THIS IN.

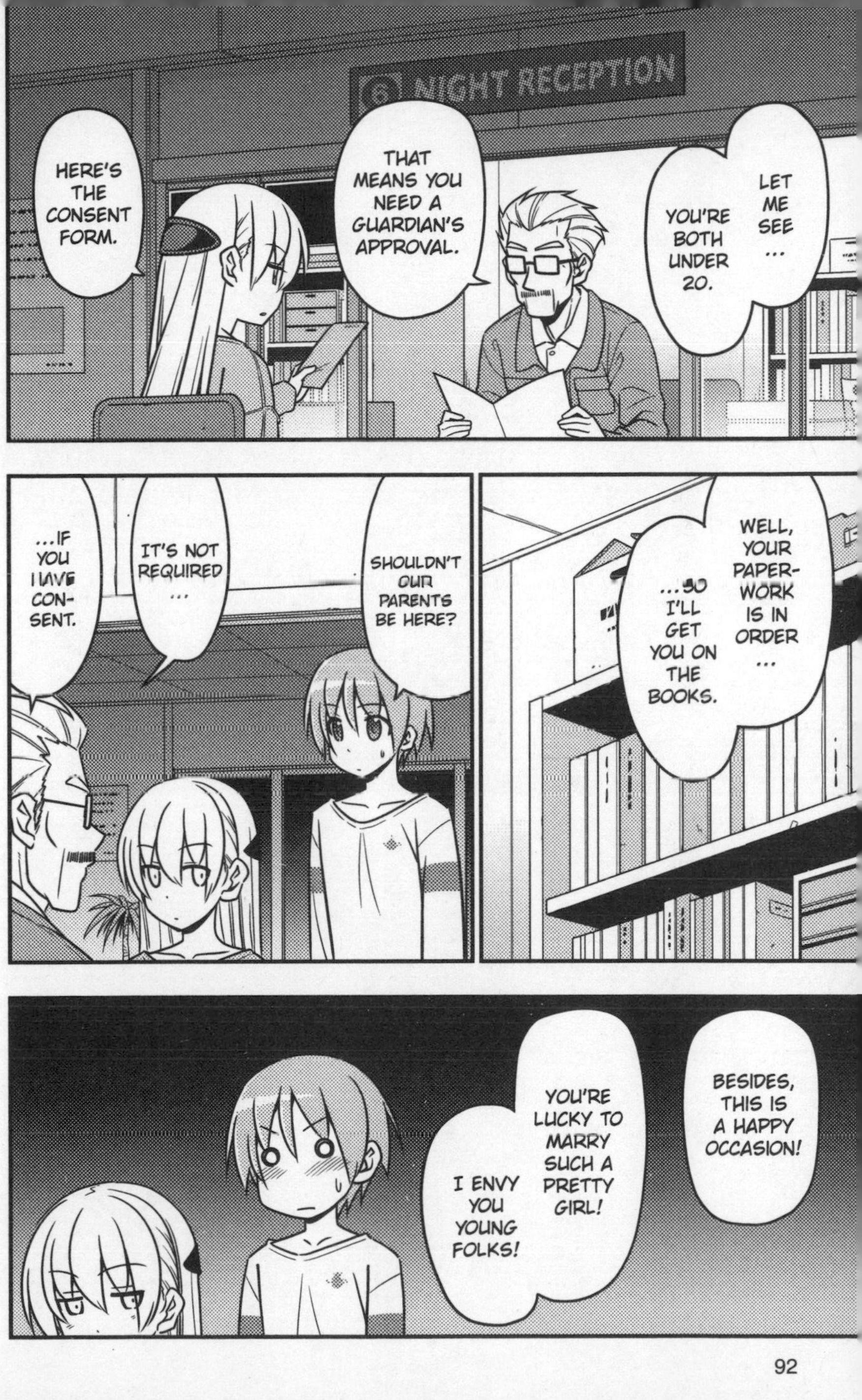
6 NIGHT RECEPTION
LET ME SEE ...
YOU'RE BOTH UNDER 20.
THAT MEANS YOU NEED A GUARDIAN'S APPROVAL.
HERE'S THE CONSENT FORM.
WELL, YOUR PAPER-WORK IS IN ORDER ...
...SO I'LL GET YOU ON THE BOOKS.
SHOULDN'T OUR PARENTS BE HERE?
IT'S NOT REQUIRED ...
...IF YOU HAVE CON-SENT.
BESIDES, THIS IS A HAPPY OCCASION!
YOU'RE LUCKY TO MARRY SUCH A PRETTY GIRL!
I ENVY YOU YOUNG FOLKS!

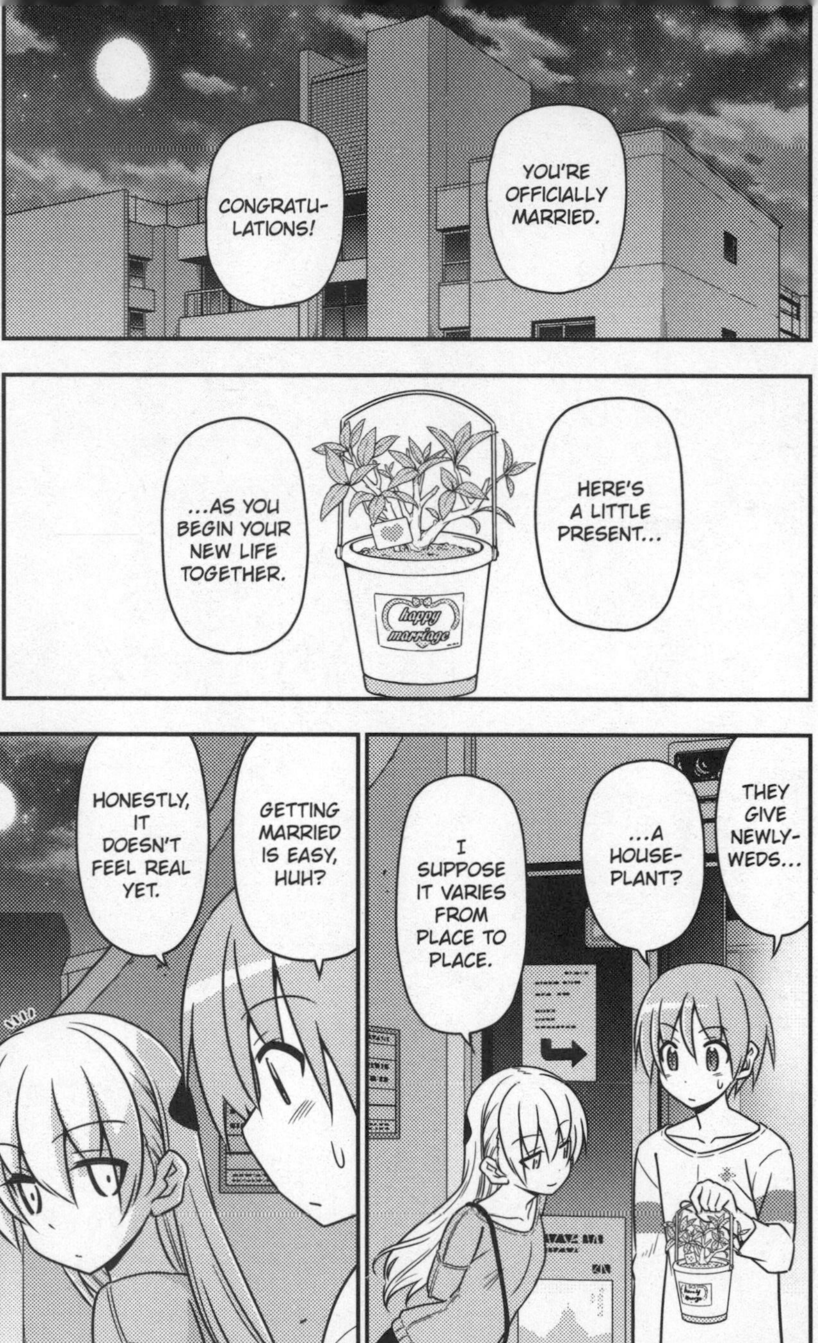
YOU'RE OFFICIALLY MARRIED.
CONGRATU-LATIONS!
HERE'S A LITTLE PRESENT...
...AS YOU BEGIN YOUR NEW LIFE TOGETHER.
happy marriage
THEY GIVE NEWLY-WEDS...
...A HOUSE-PLANT?
I SUPPOSE IT VARIES FROM PLACE TO PLACE.
GETTING MARRIED IS EASY, HUH?
HONESTLY, IT DOESN'T FEEL REAL YET.

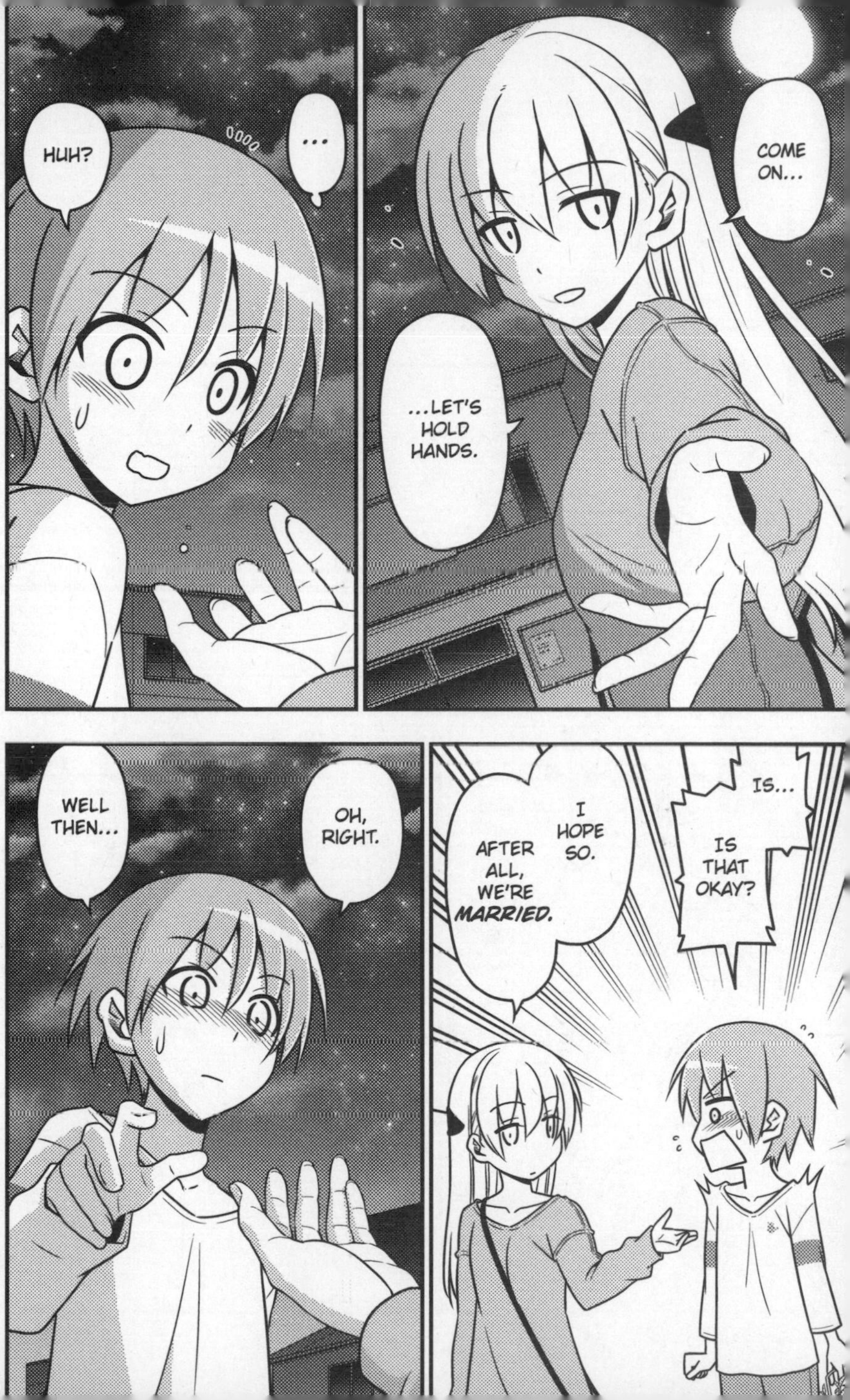
COME ON...
...LET'S HOLD HANDS.
...
HUH?
IS...
IS THAT OKAY?
I HOPE SO.
AFTER ALL, WE'RE *MARRIED.*
OH, RIGHT.
WELL THEN...

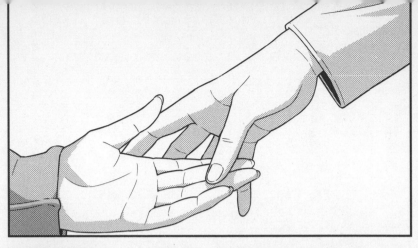

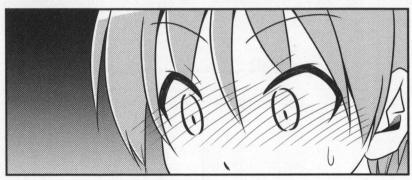

TCH

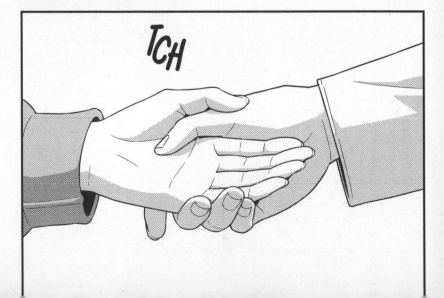

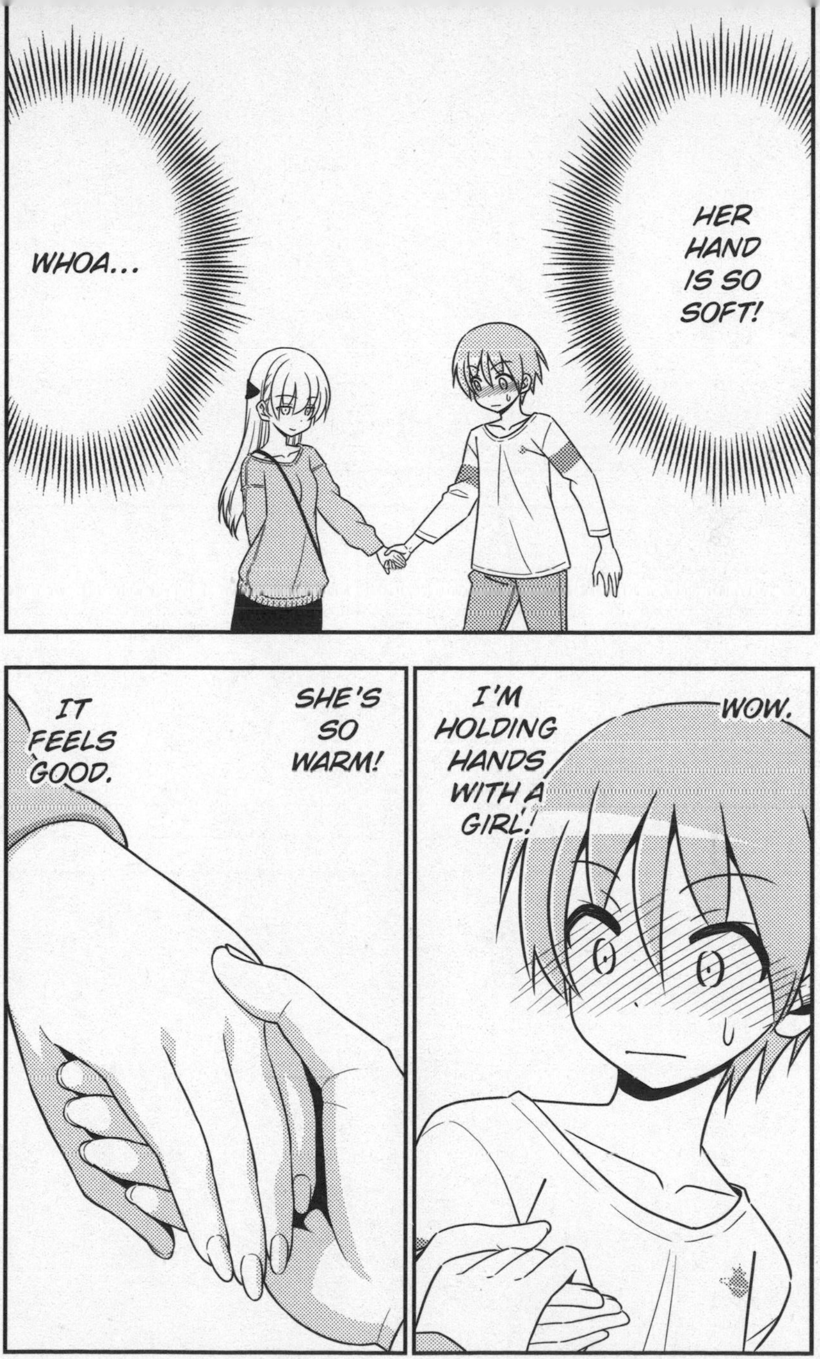
HER HAND IS SO SOFT!
WHOA...
WOW.
I'M HOLDING HANDS WITH A GIRL!
SHE'S SO WARM!
IT FEELS GOOD.

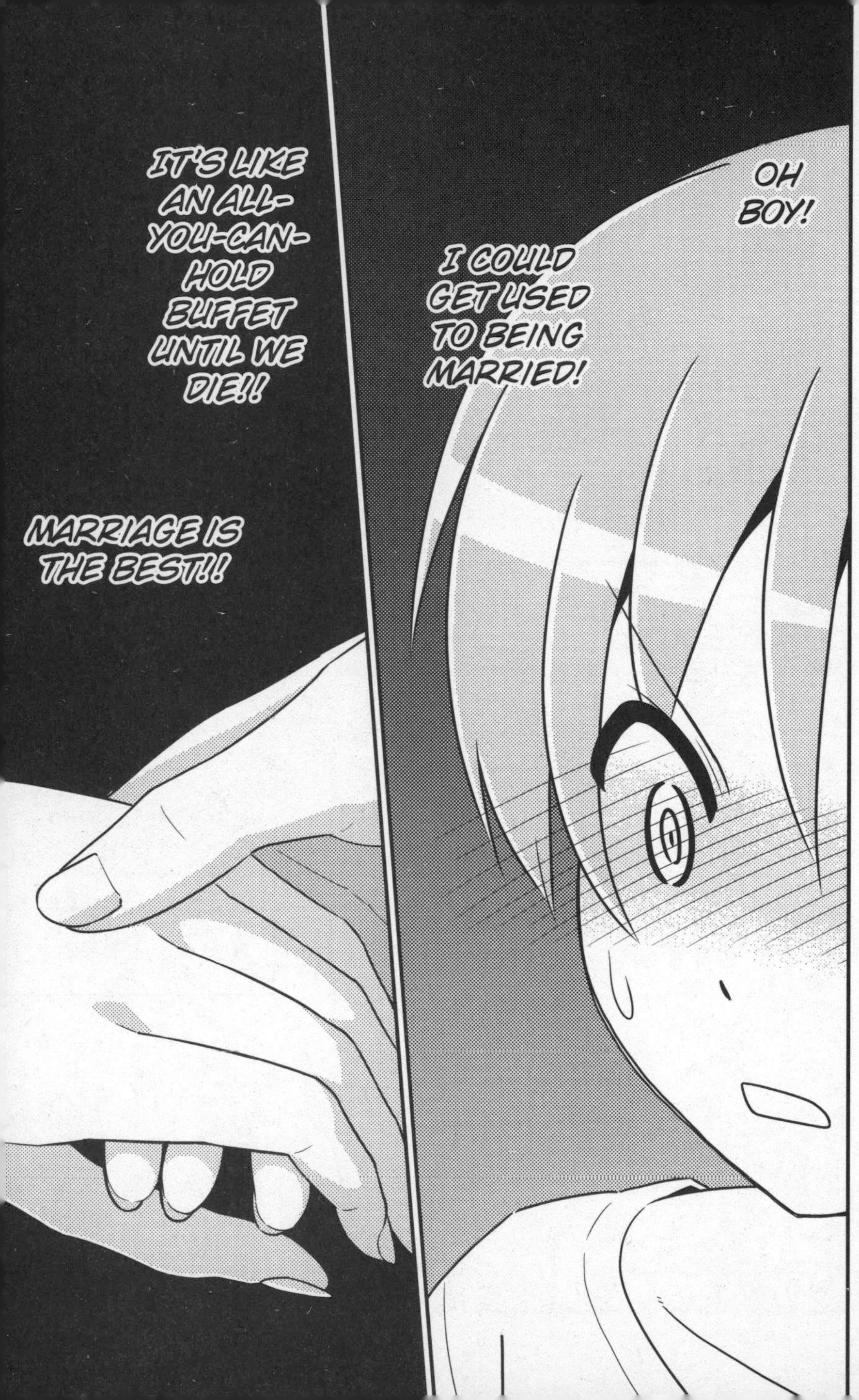
OH BOY!
I COULD GET USED TO BEING MARRIED!
IT'S LIKE AN ALL-YOU-CAN-HOLD BUFFET UNTIL WE DIE!!
MARRIAGE IS THE BEST!!

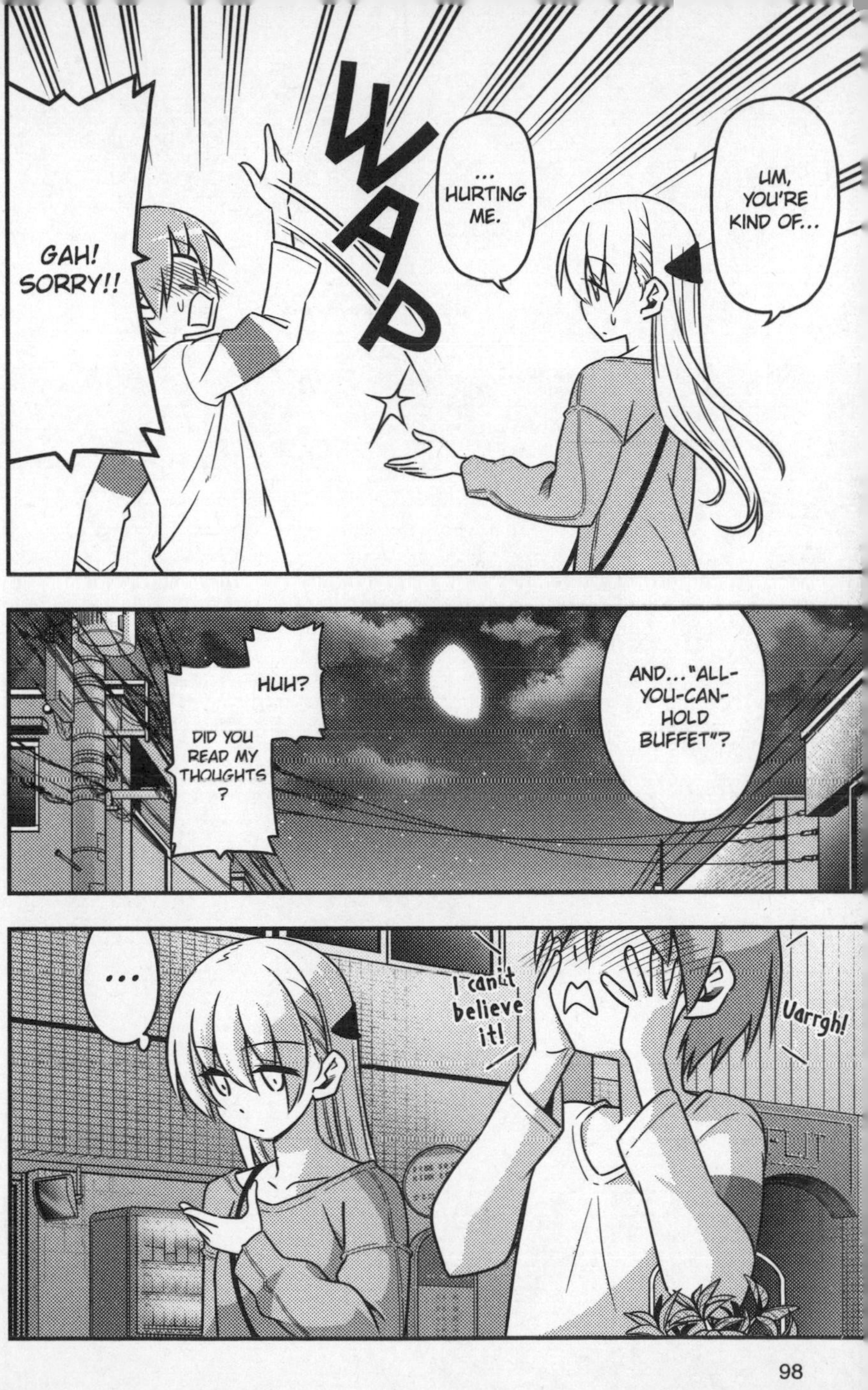
UM, YOU'RE KIND OF...
... HURTING ME.
WAP
GAH! SORRY!!
AND... "ALL-YOU-CAN-HOLD BUFFET"?
HUH?
DID YOU READ MY THOUGHTS?
Uarrgh!
I can't believe it!
...

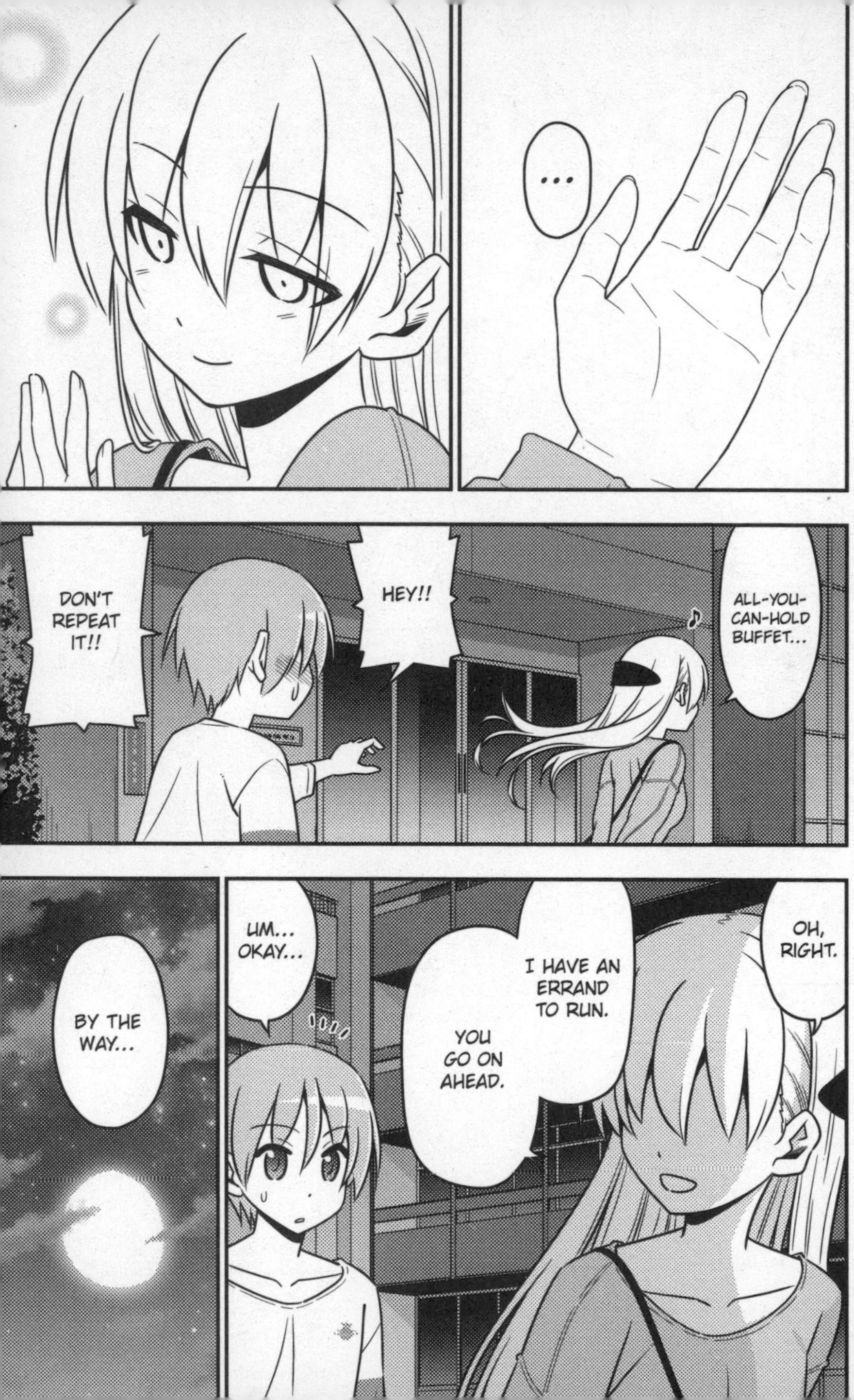
...
ALL-YOU-CAN-HOLD BUFFET...
HEY!!
DON'T REPEAT IT!!
OH, RIGHT.
I HAVE AN ERRAND TO RUN.
YOU GO ON AHEAD.
UM... OKAY...
BY THE WAY...

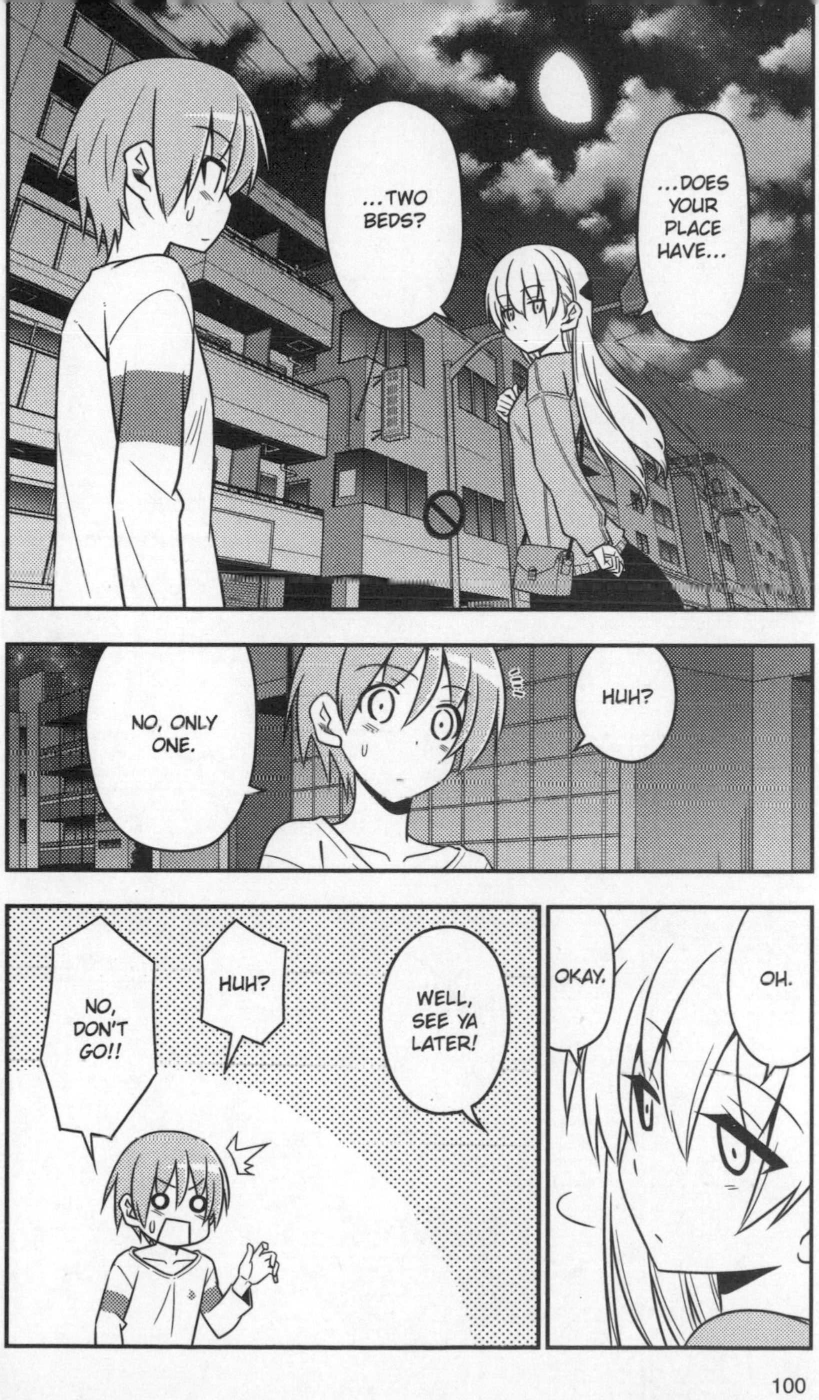
...DOES YOUR PLACE HAVE...
...TWO BEDS?
HUH?
NO, ONLY ONE.
OH.
OKAY.
WELL, SEE YA LATER!
HUH?
NO, DON'T GO!!

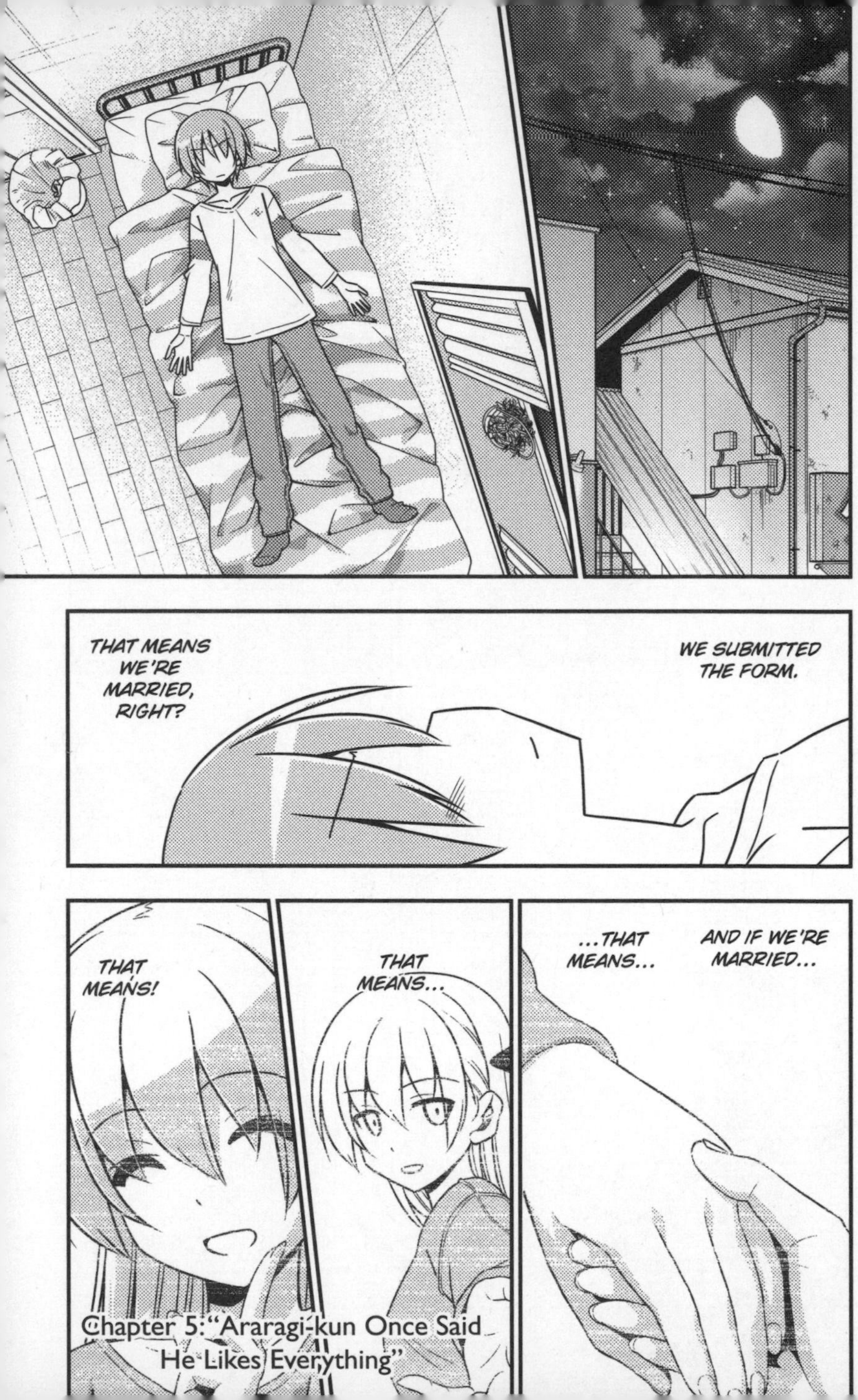
WE SUBMITTED THE FORM.
THAT MEANS WE'RE MARRIED, RIGHT?
AND IF WE'RE MARRIED...
...THAT MEANS...
THAT MEANS...
THAT MEANS!

Chapter 5: "Araragi-kun Once Said He Likes Everything"

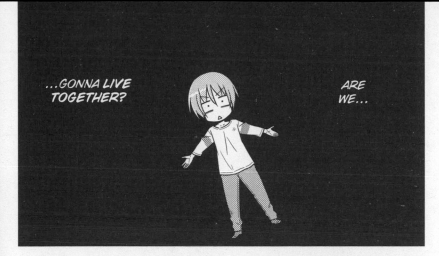

...GONNA LIVE TOGETHER?

ARE WE...

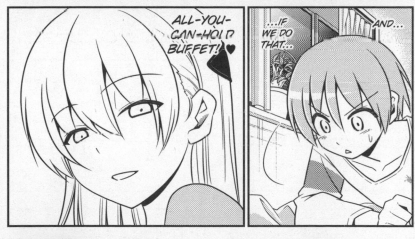

ALL-YOU-CAN-HOLD BUFFET! ♥

...IF WE DO THAT...

AND...

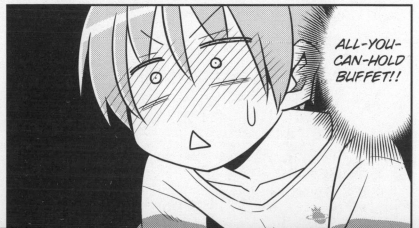

ALL-YOU-CAN-HOLD BUFFET!!

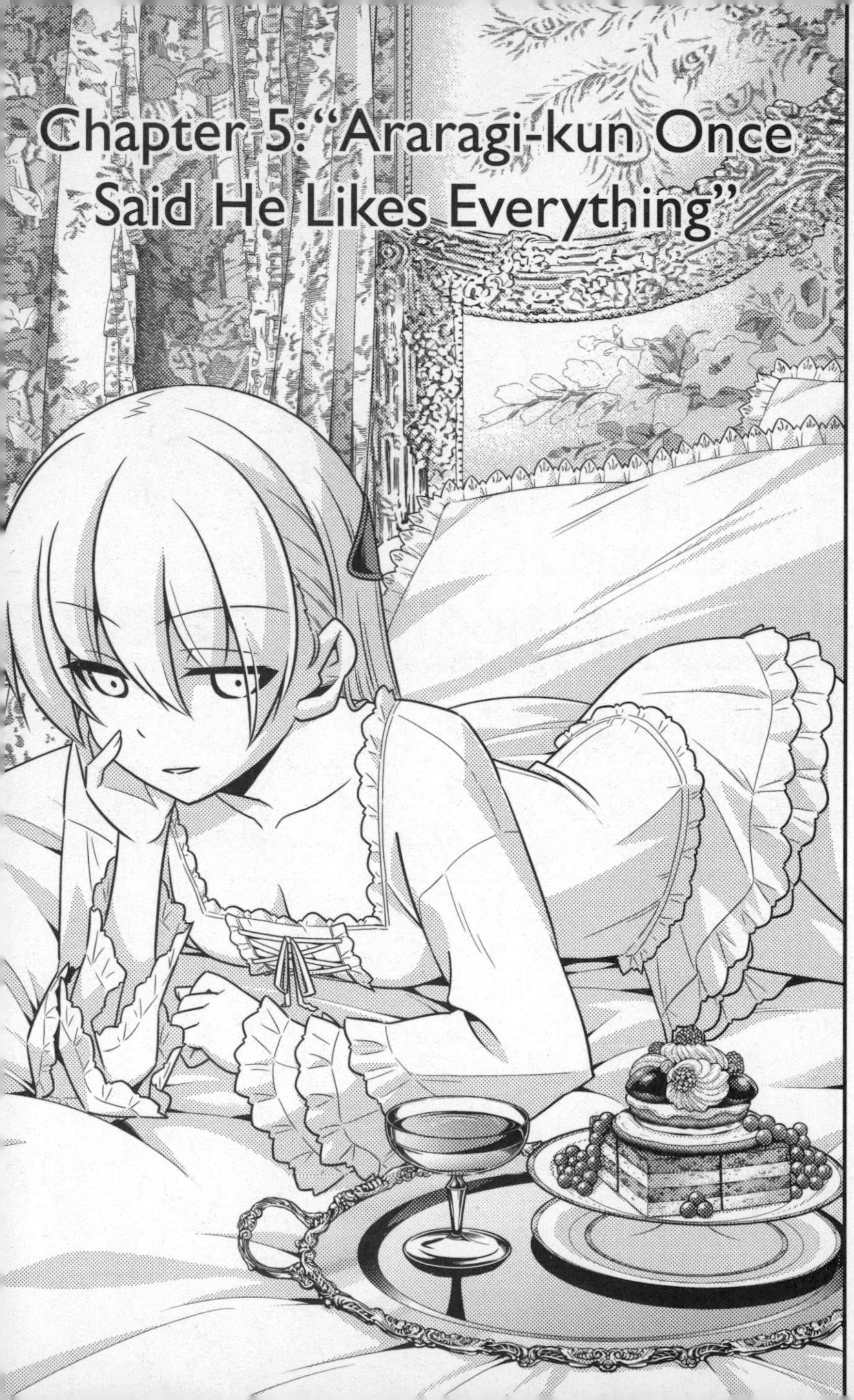
Chapter 5: "Araragi-kun Once Said He Likes Everything"

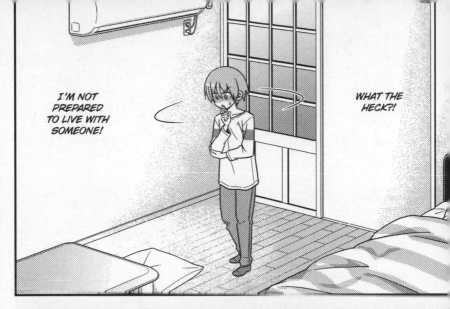

I'M NOT PREPARED TO LIVE WITH SOMEONE!

WHAT THE HECK?!

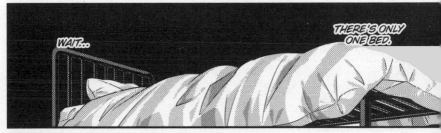

WAIT...

THERE'S ONLY ONE BED.

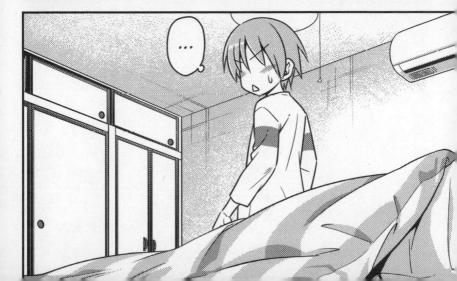

...

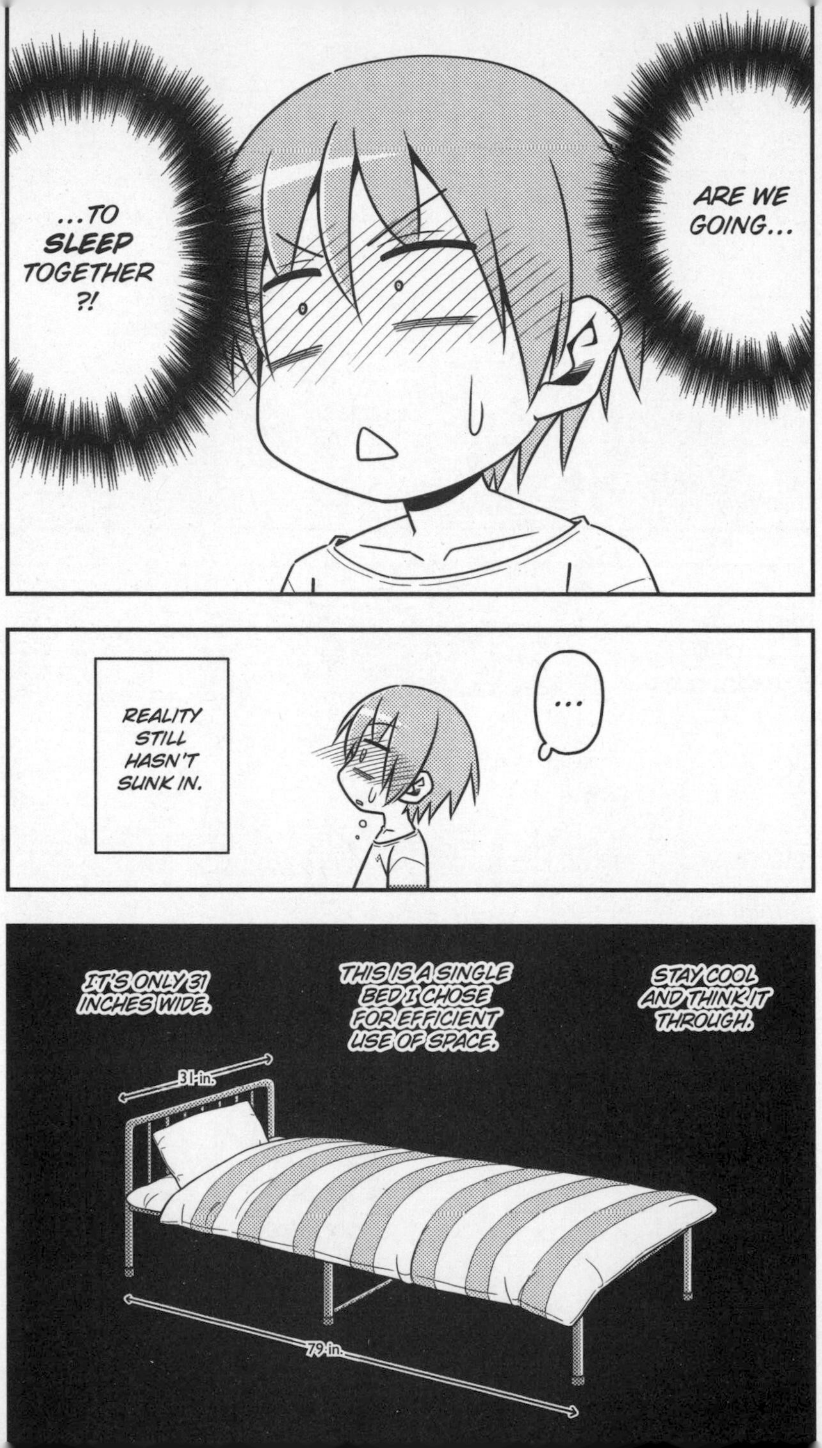
ARE WE GOING...
...TO SLEEP TOGETHER ?!
...
REALITY STILL HASN'T SUNK IN.
STAY COOL AND THINK IT THROUGH.
THIS IS A SINGLE BED I CHOSE FOR EFFICIENT USE OF SPACE.
IT'S ONLY 31 INCHES WIDE.
31 in.
79 in.

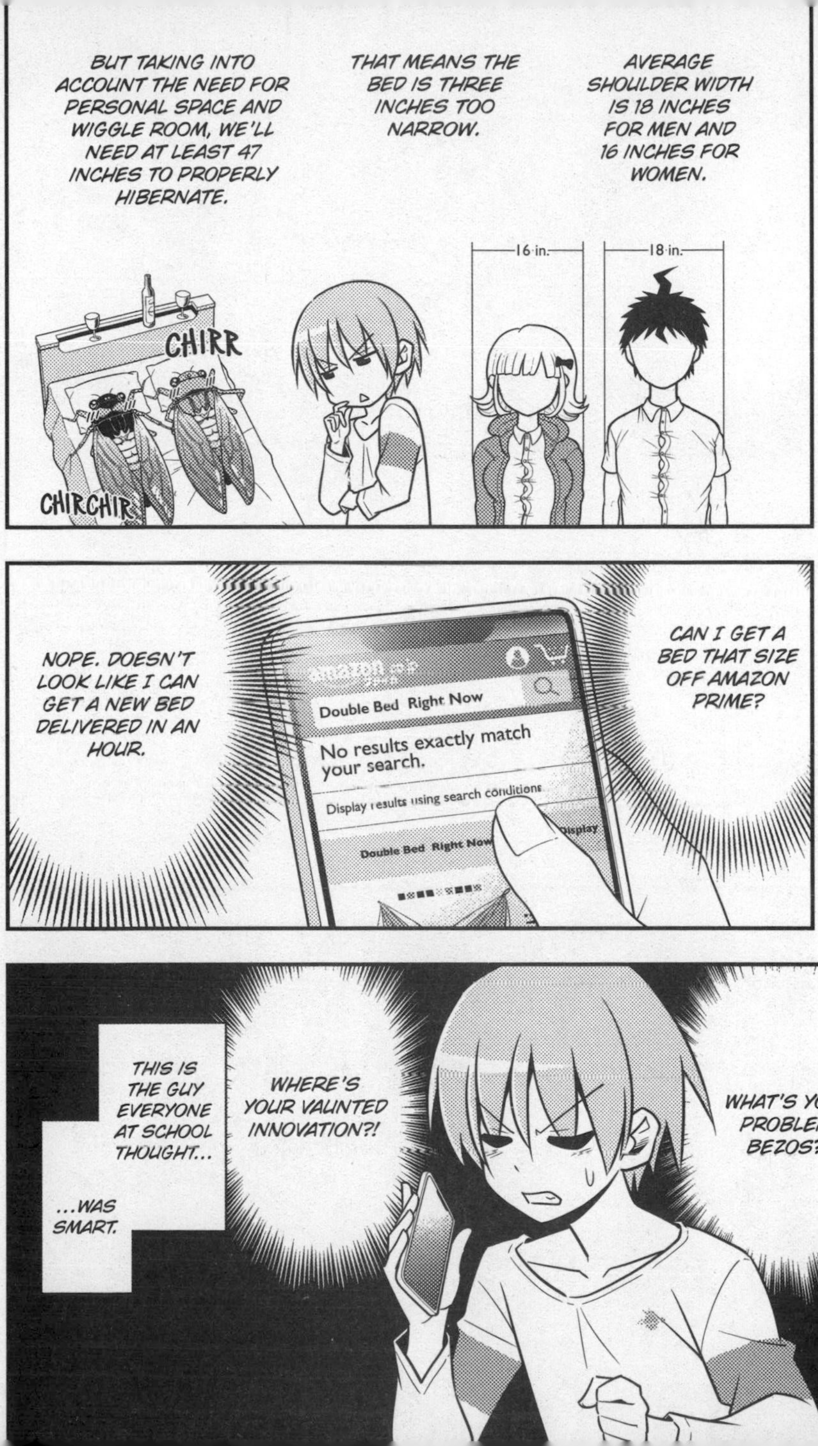
AVERAGE SHOULDER WIDTH IS 18 INCHES FOR MEN AND 16 INCHES FOR WOMEN.
18 in.
16 in.
THAT MEANS THE BED IS THREE INCHES TOO NARROW.
BUT TAKING INTO ACCOUNT THE NEED FOR PERSONAL SPACE AND WIGGLE ROOM, WE'LL NEED AT LEAST 47 INCHES TO PROPERLY HIBERNATE.
CHIRR
CHIRCHIR
CAN I GET A BED THAT SIZE OFF AMAZON PRIME?
Double Bed Right Now
No results exactly match your search.
Display results using search conditions
Display
Double Bed Right Now
NOPE. DOESN'T LOOK LIKE I CAN GET A NEW BED DELIVERED IN AN HOUR.
WHAT'S YOUR PROBLEM, BEZOS?!
WHERE'S YOUR VAUNTED INNOVATION?!
THIS IS THE GUY EVERYONE AT SCHOOL THOUGHT...
...WAS SMART.

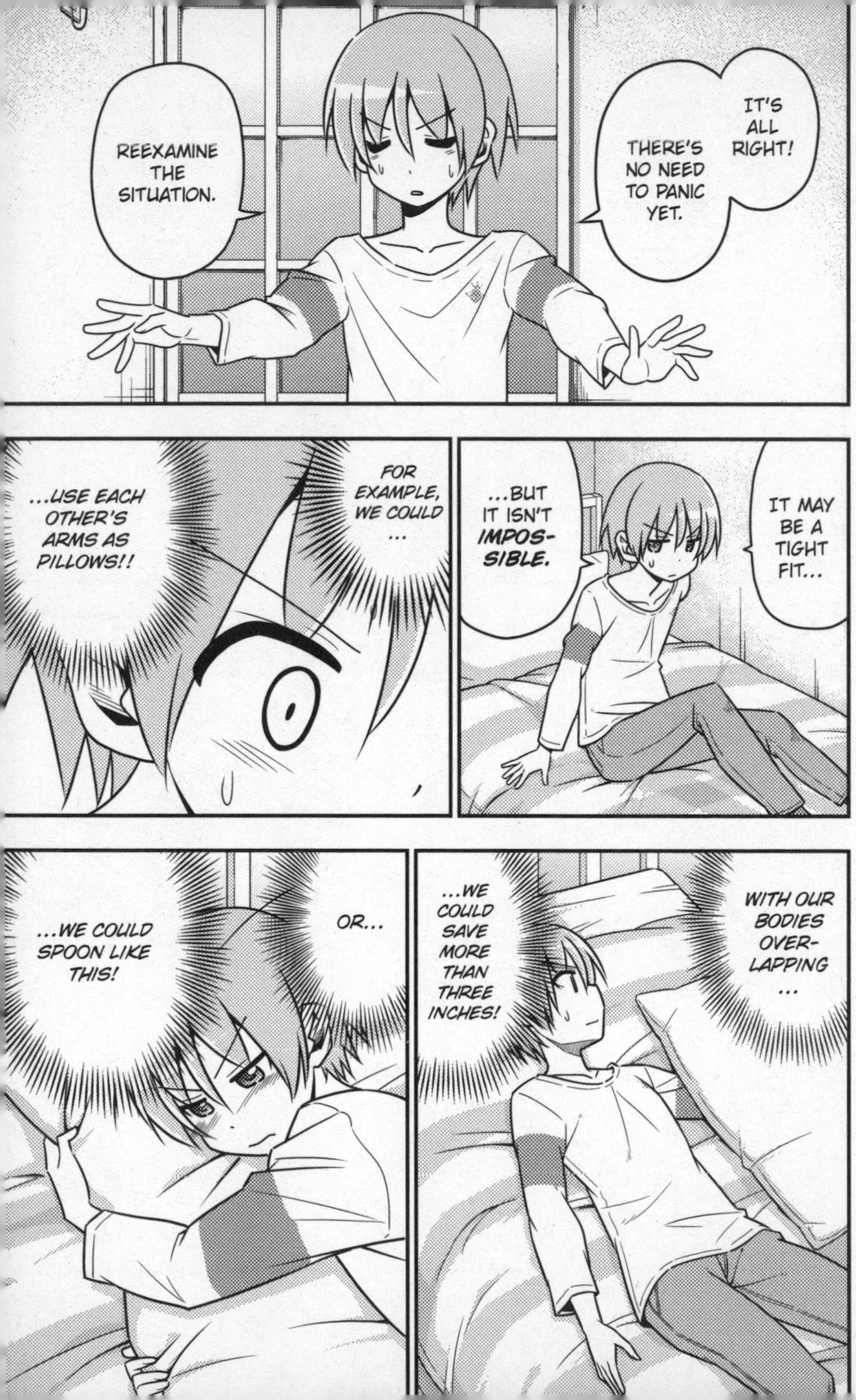
IT'S ALL RIGHT!
THERE'S NO NEED TO PANIC YET.
REEXAMINE THE SITUATION.
IT MAY BE A TIGHT FIT...
...BUT IT ISN'T IMPOSSIBLE.
FOR EXAMPLE, WE COULD ...
...USE EACH OTHER'S ARMS AS PILLOWS!!
WITH OUR BODIES OVERLAPPING ...
...WE COULD SAVE MORE THAN THREE INCHES!
OR...
...WE COULD SPOON LIKE THIS!

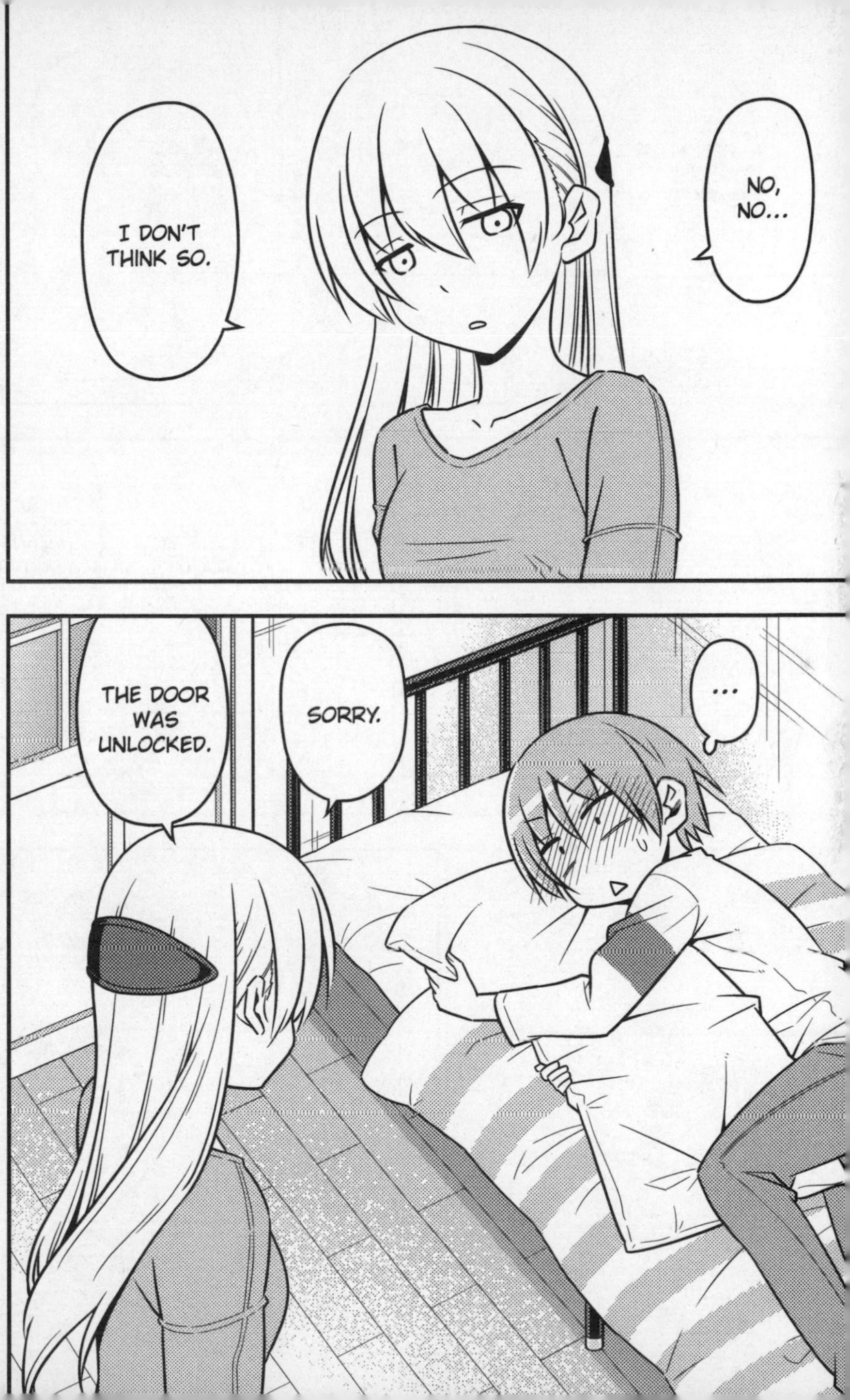
NO, NO...
I DON'T THINK SO.
...
SORRY.
THE DOOR WAS UNLOCKED.

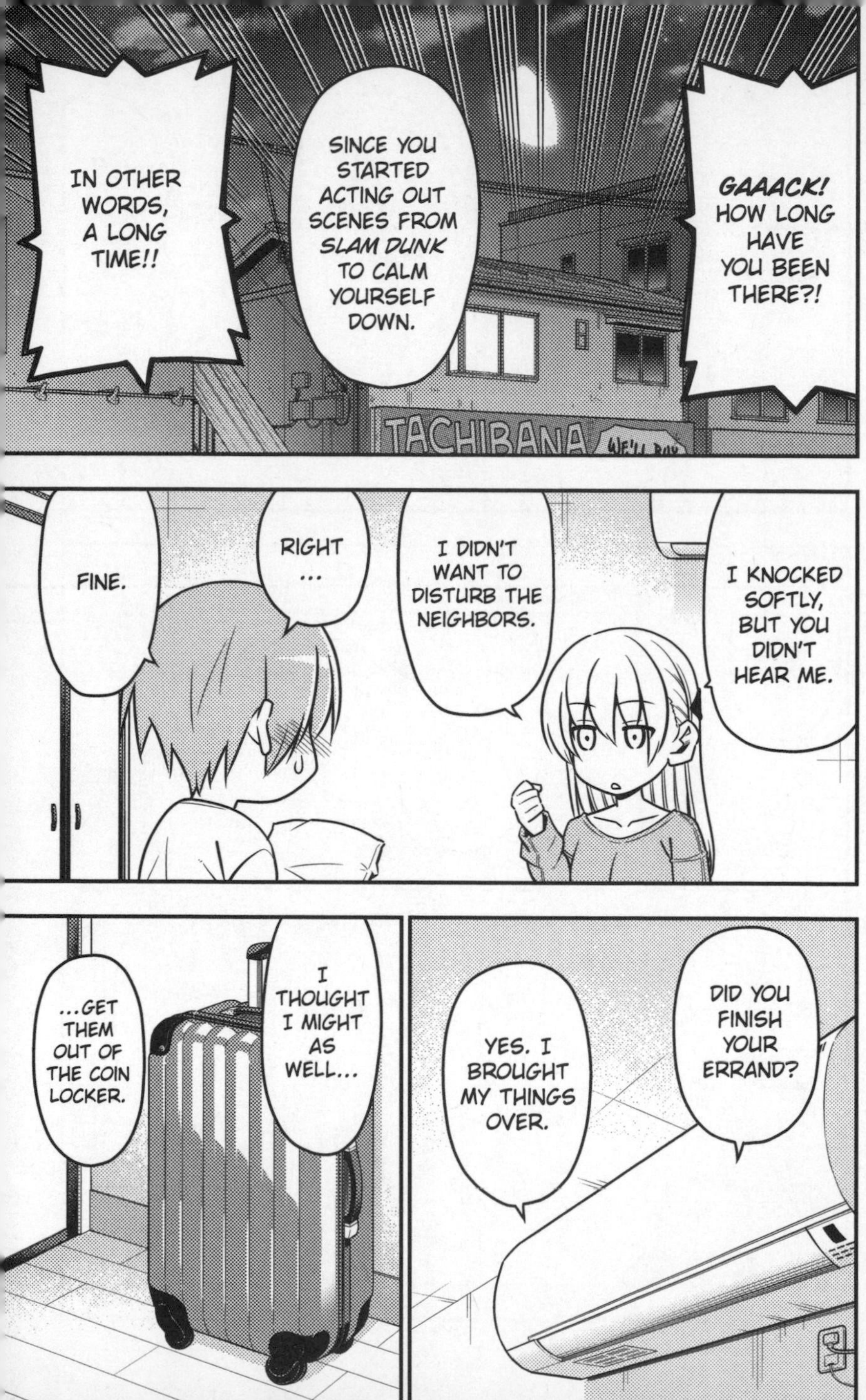
GAAACK! HOW LONG HAVE YOU BEEN THERE?!
SINCE YOU STARTED ACTING OUT SCENES FROM SLAM DUNK TO CALM YOURSELF DOWN.
IN OTHER WORDS, A LONG TIME!!
TACHIBANA
WE'LL BUY
I KNOCKED SOFTLY, BUT YOU DIDN'T HEAR ME.
I DIDN'T WANT TO DISTURB THE NEIGHBORS.
RIGHT...
FINE.
DID YOU FINISH YOUR ERRAND?
YES. I BROUGHT MY THINGS OVER.
I THOUGHT I MIGHT AS WELL...
...GET THEM OUT OF THE COIN LOCKER.

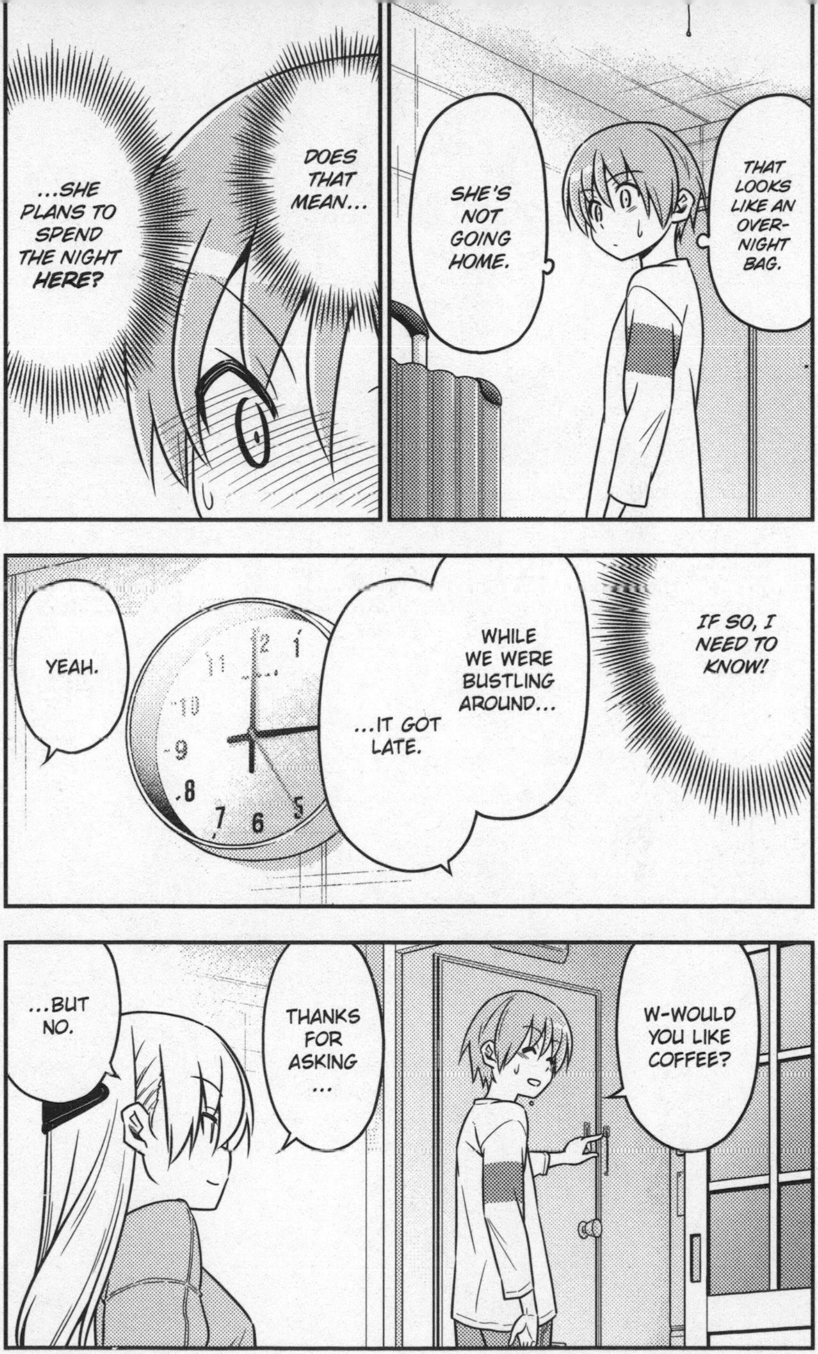
THAT LOOKS LIKE AN OVER-NIGHT BAG.
SHE'S NOT GOING HOME.
DOES THAT MEAN...
...SHE PLANS TO SPEND THE NIGHT HERE?
IF SO, I NEED TO KNOW!
WHILE WE WERE BUSTLING AROUND...
...IT GOT LATE.
YEAH.
W-WOULD YOU LIKE COFFEE?
THANKS FOR ASKING...
...BUT NO.

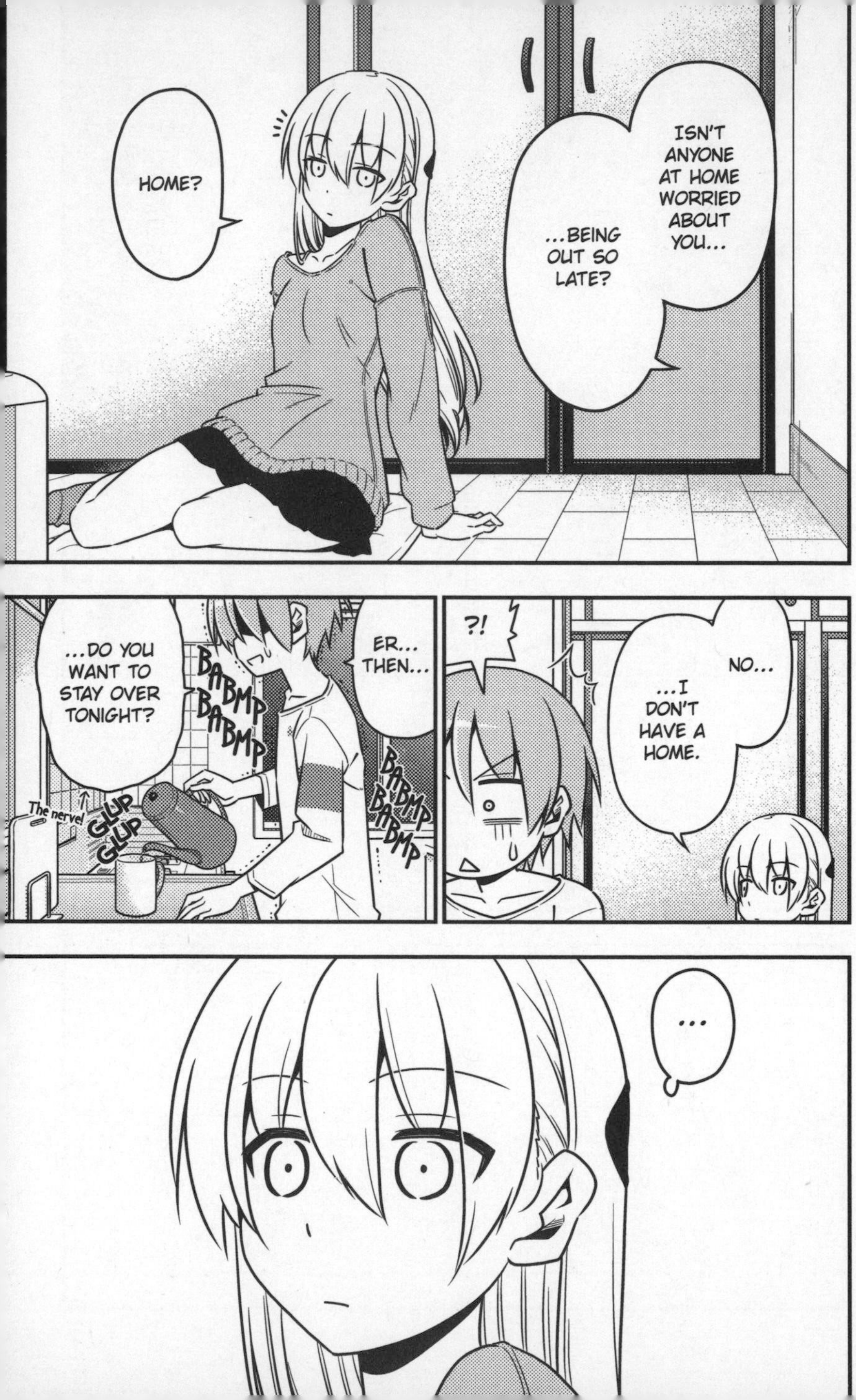
ISN'T ANYONE AT HOME WORRIED ABOUT YOU...
...BEING OUT SO LATE?
HOME?
NO...
...I DON'T HAVE A HOME.
?!
ER... THEN...
BABMP BABMP
BABMP BABMP BABMP
...DO YOU WANT TO STAY OVER TONIGHT?
GLUP GLUP
The nerve!
...

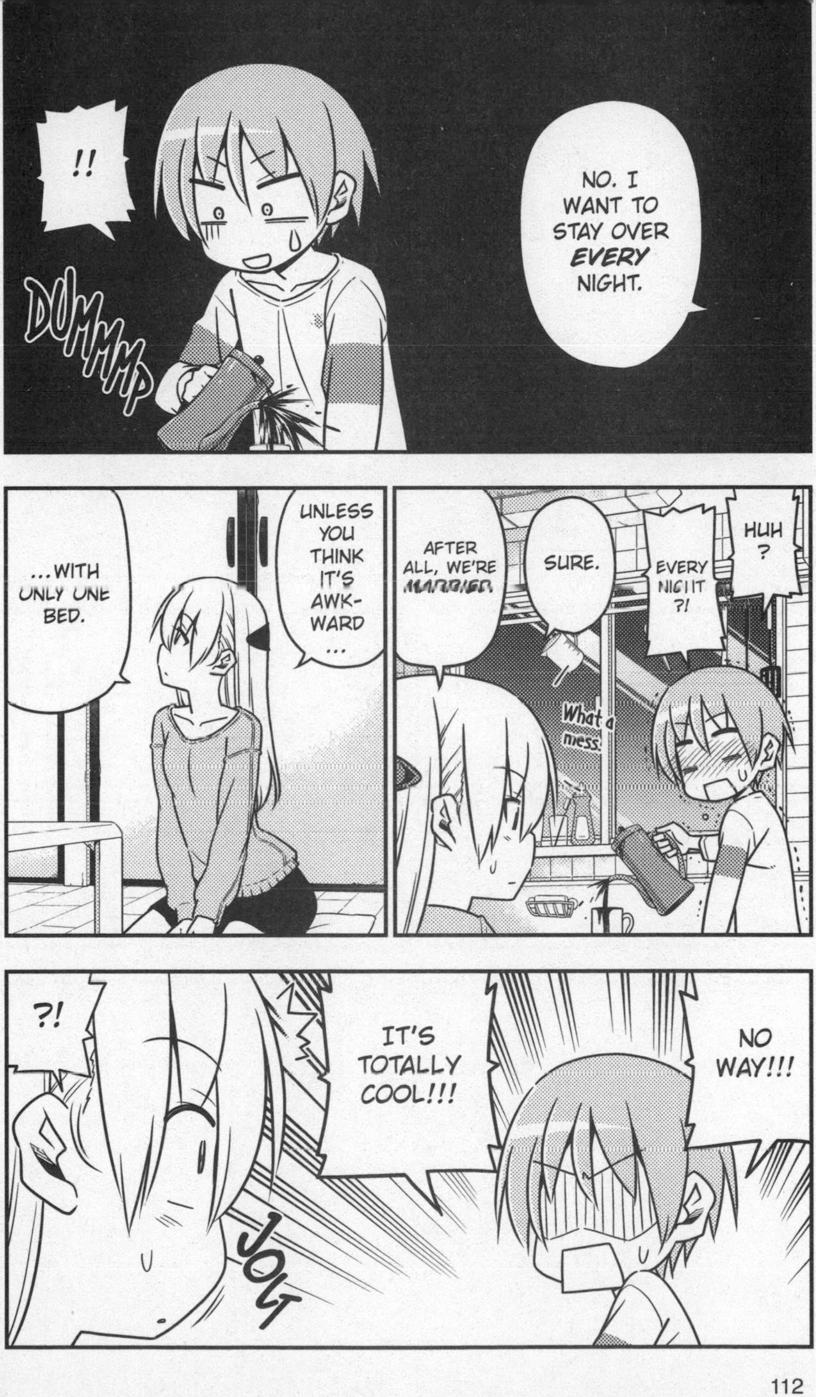
NO. I WANT TO STAY OVER **EVERY** NIGHT.
!!
DUMMMP
HUH?
EVERY NIGHT?!
SURE.
AFTER ALL, WE'RE MARRIED.
What a mess.
UNLESS YOU THINK IT'S AWKWARD...
...WITH ONLY ONE BED.
NO WAY!!!
IT'S TOTALLY COOL!!!
JOLT
?!

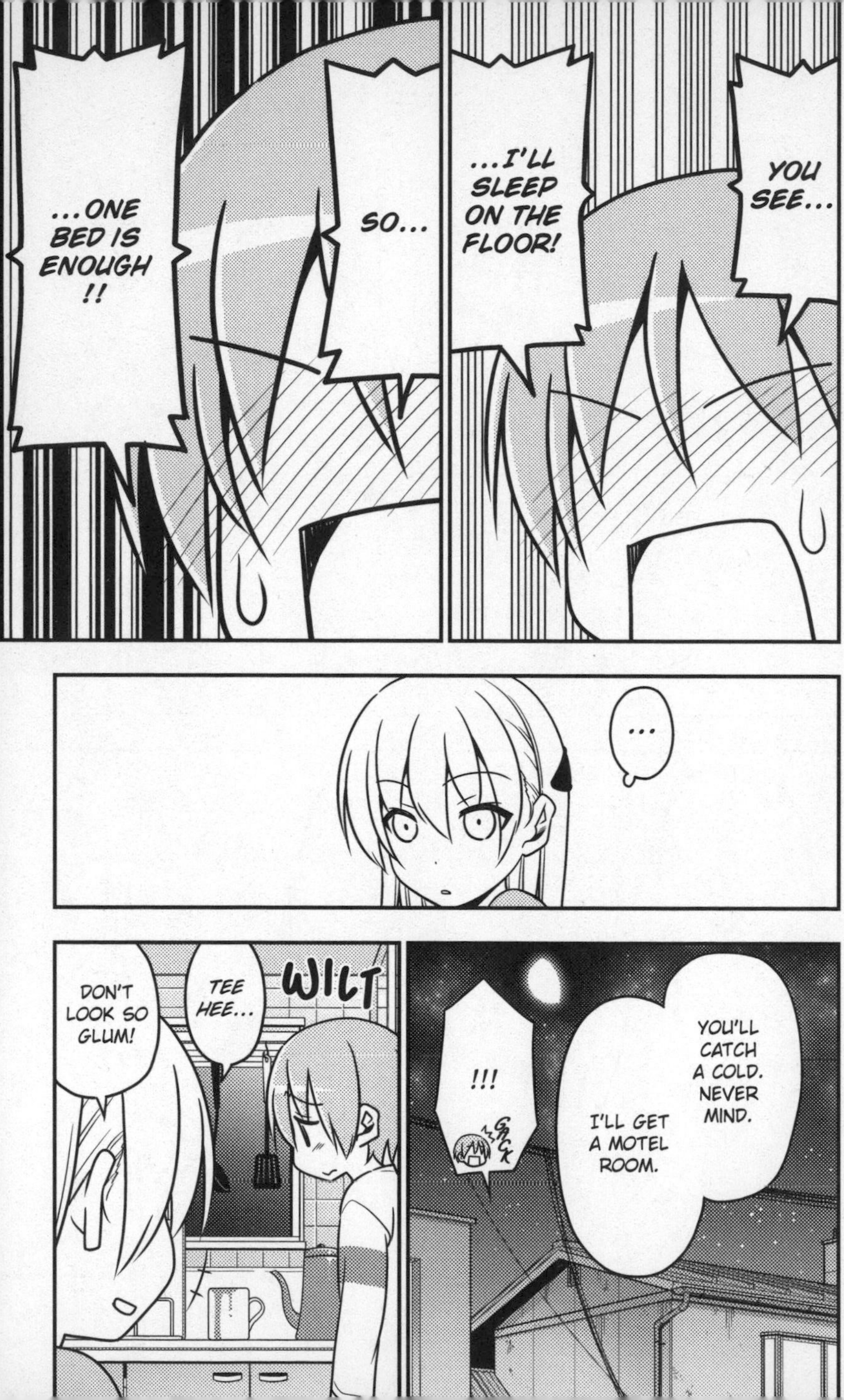
YOU SEE...
...I'LL SLEEP ON THE FLOOR!
SO...
...ONE BED IS ENOUGH !!
...
YOU'LL CATCH A COLD. NEVER MIND.
I'LL GET A MOTEL ROOM.
!!!
GRCK
WILT
TEE HEE...
DON'T LOOK SO GLUM!

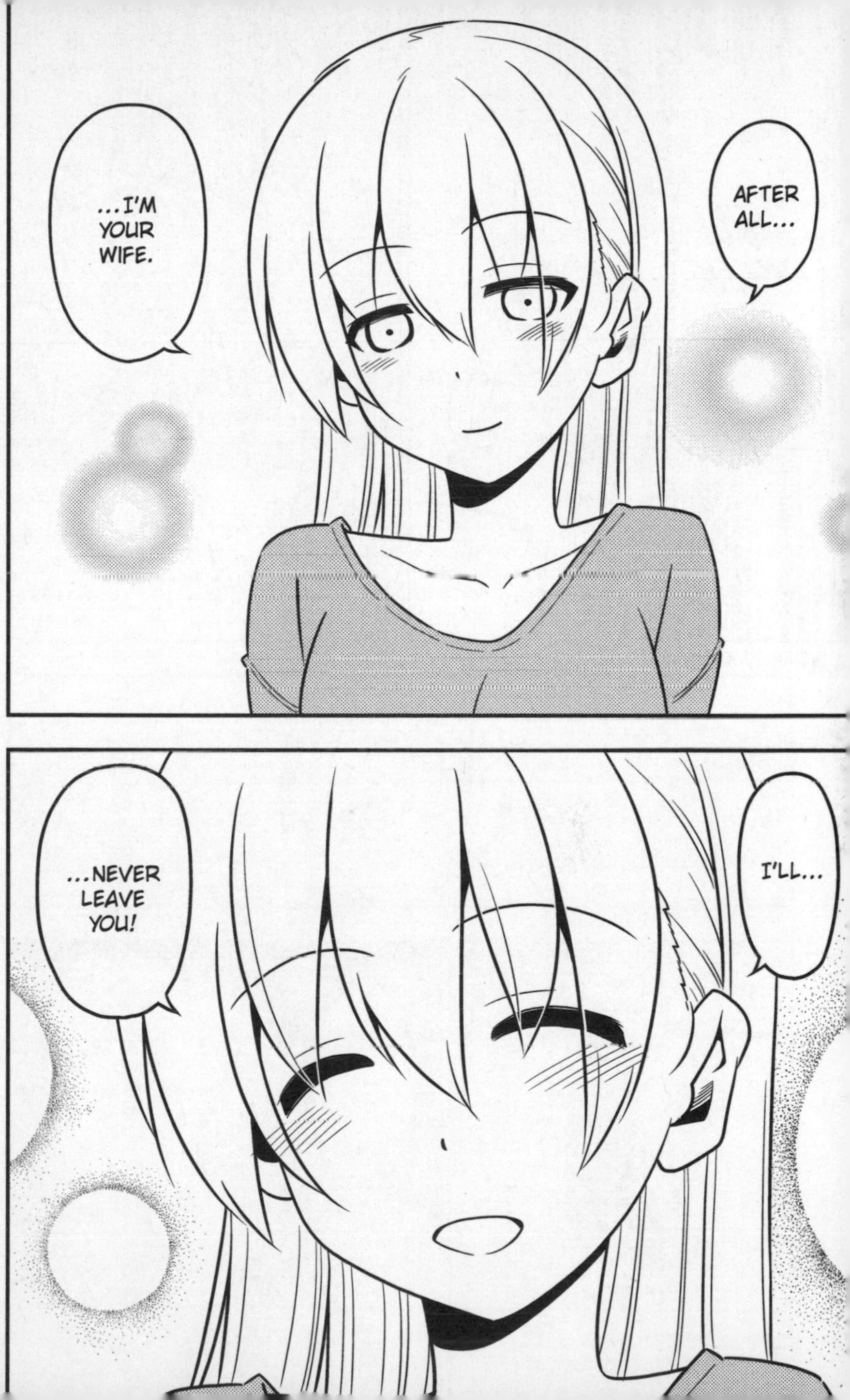
AFTER ALL...
...I'M YOUR WIFE.
I'LL...
...NEVER LEAVE YOU!

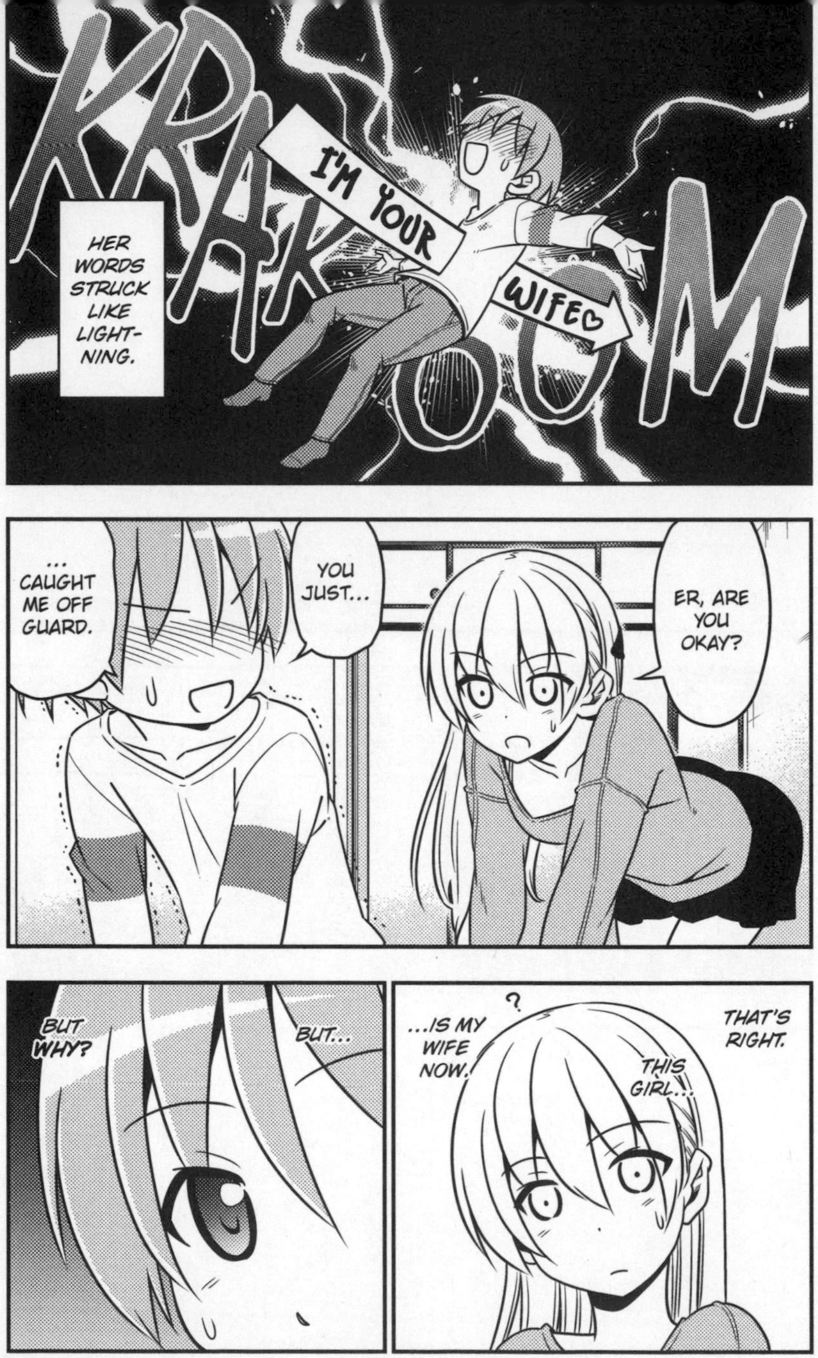
I'M YOUR
WIFE♡
KRAKOOOM
HER WORDS STRUCK LIKE LIGHT-NING.
ER, ARE YOU OKAY?
YOU JUST...
...CAUGHT ME OFF GUARD.
THAT'S RIGHT.
THIS GIRL...
?
...IS MY WIFE NOW.
BUT...
BUT WHY?

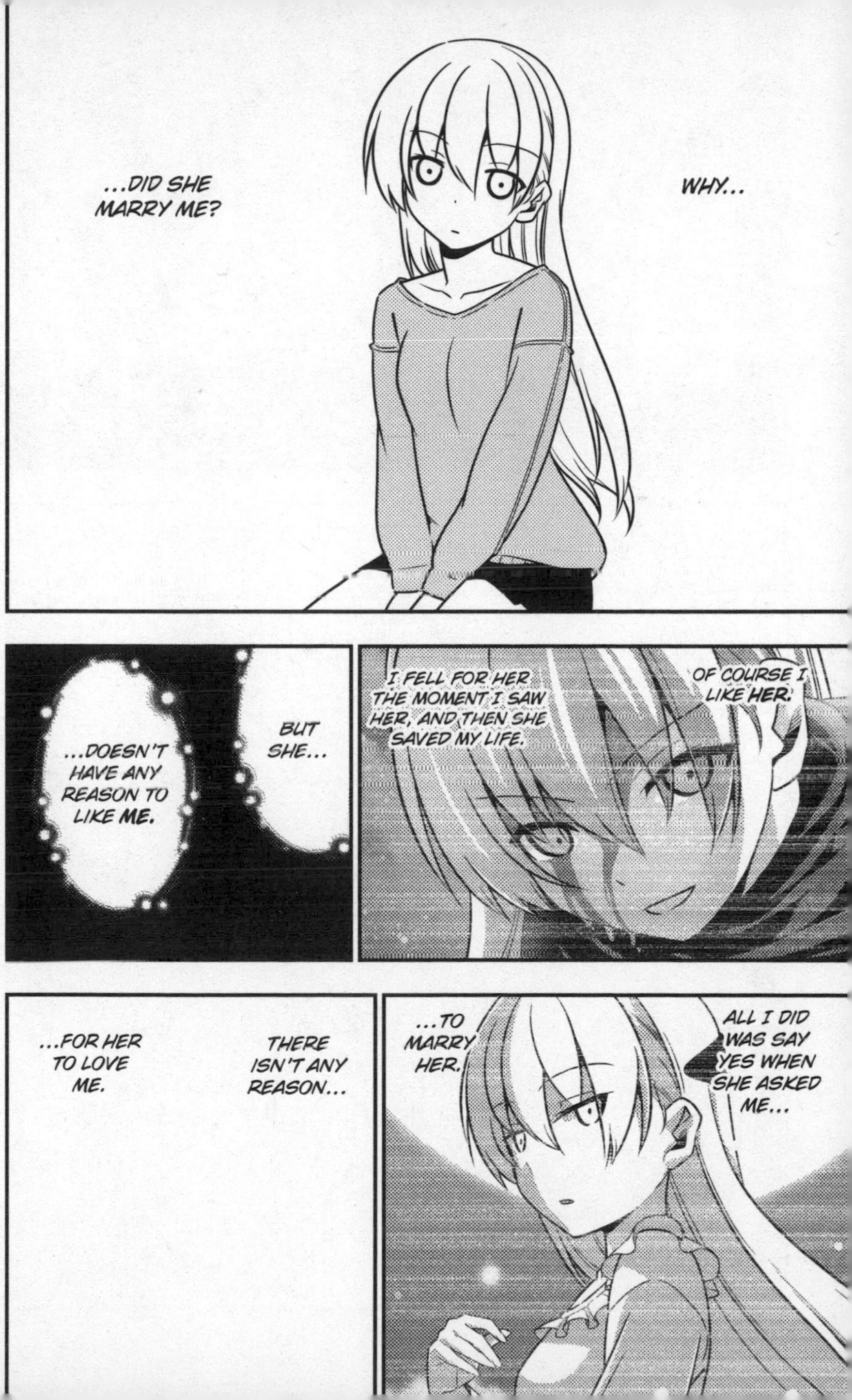
WHY...
...DID SHE MARRY ME?
OF COURSE I LIKE HER.
I FELL FOR HER THE MOMENT I SAW HER, AND THEN SHE SAVED MY LIFE.
BUT SHE...
...DOESN'T HAVE ANY REASON TO LIKE ME.
ALL I DID WAS SAY YES WHEN SHE ASKED ME...
...TO MARRY HER.
THERE ISN'T ANY REASON...
...FOR HER TO LOVE ME.

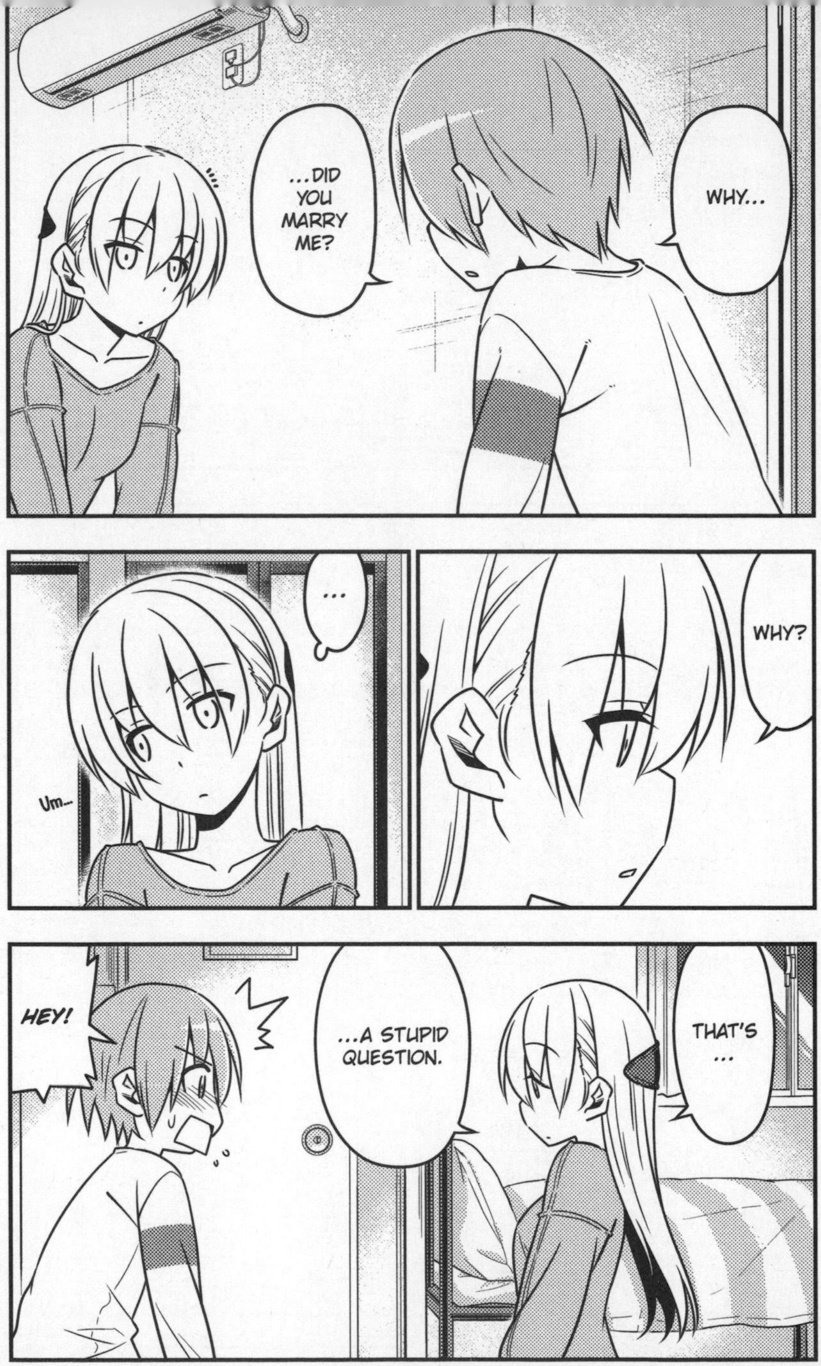
WHY...
...DID YOU MARRY ME?
WHY?
...
Um...
THAT'S ...
...A STUPID QUESTION.
HEY!

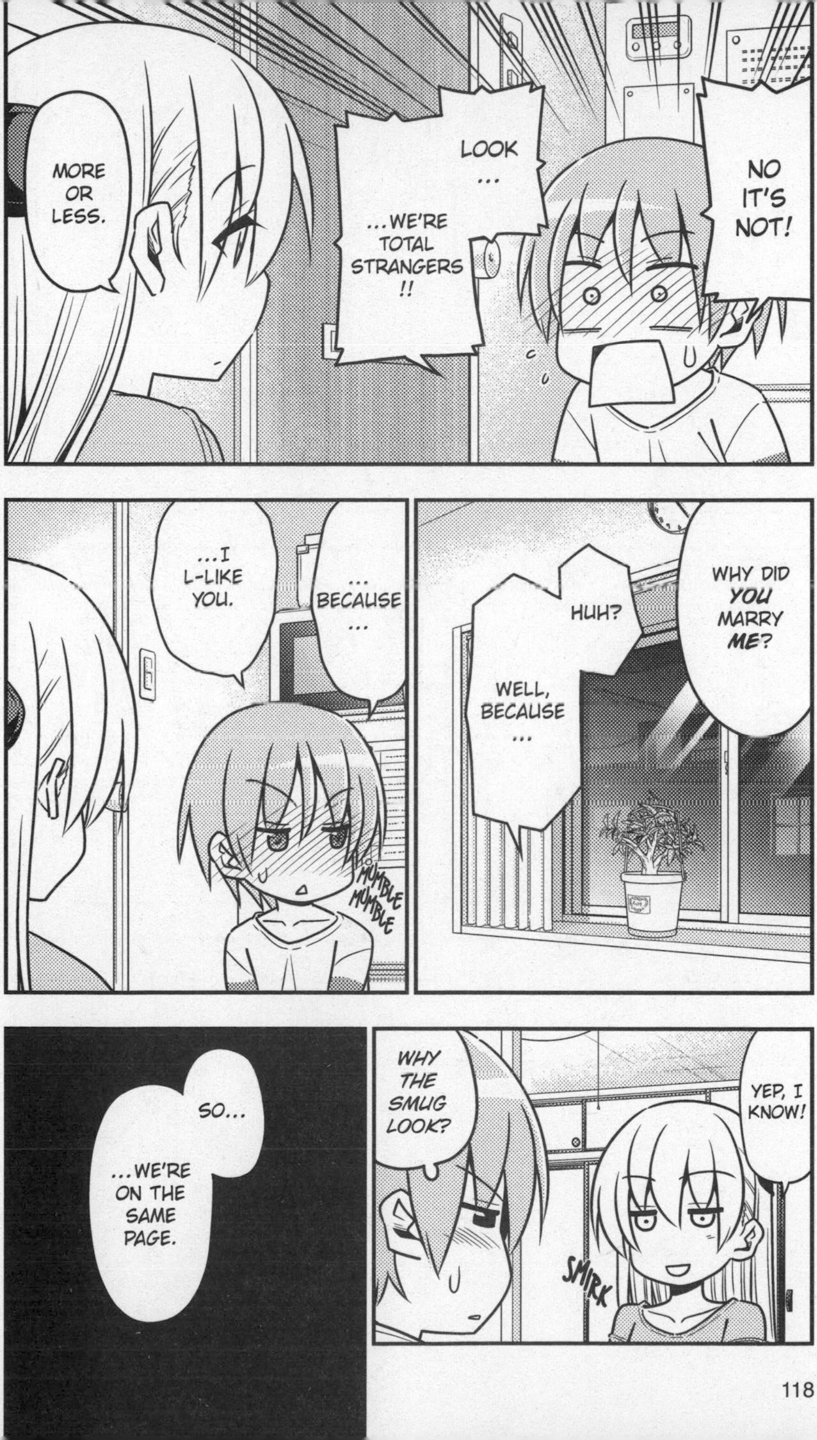
NO IT'S NOT!
LOOK... ...WE'RE TOTAL STRANGERS!!
MORE OR LESS.
WHY DID YOU MARRY ME?
HUH?
WELL, BECAUSE...
...BECAUSE...
...I L-LIKE YOU.
MUMBLE MUMBLE
YEP, I KNOW!
WHY THE SMUG LOOK?
SMIRK
SO...
...WE'RE ON THE SAME PAGE.

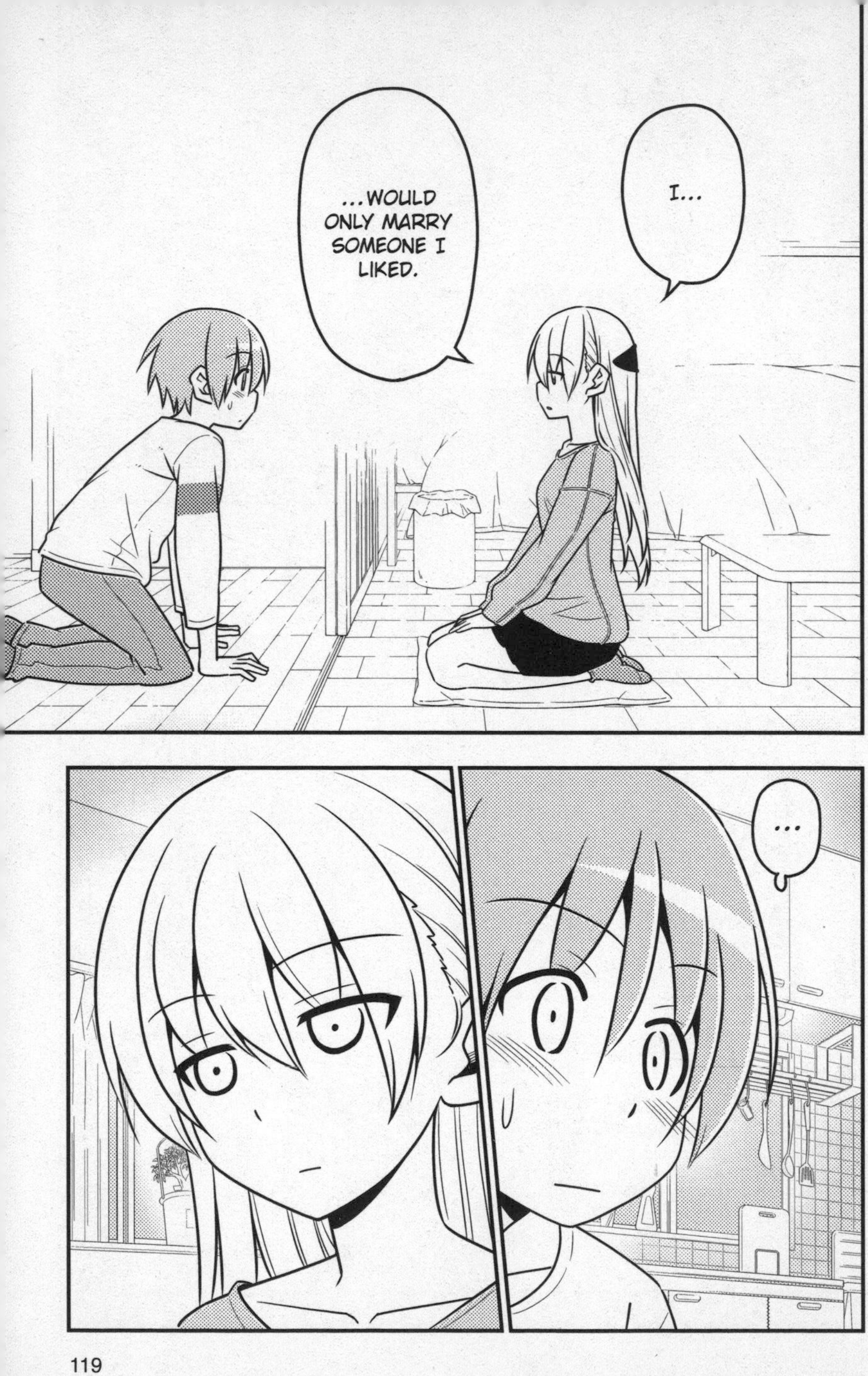
I...
...WOULD ONLY MARRY SOMEONE I LIKED.
...

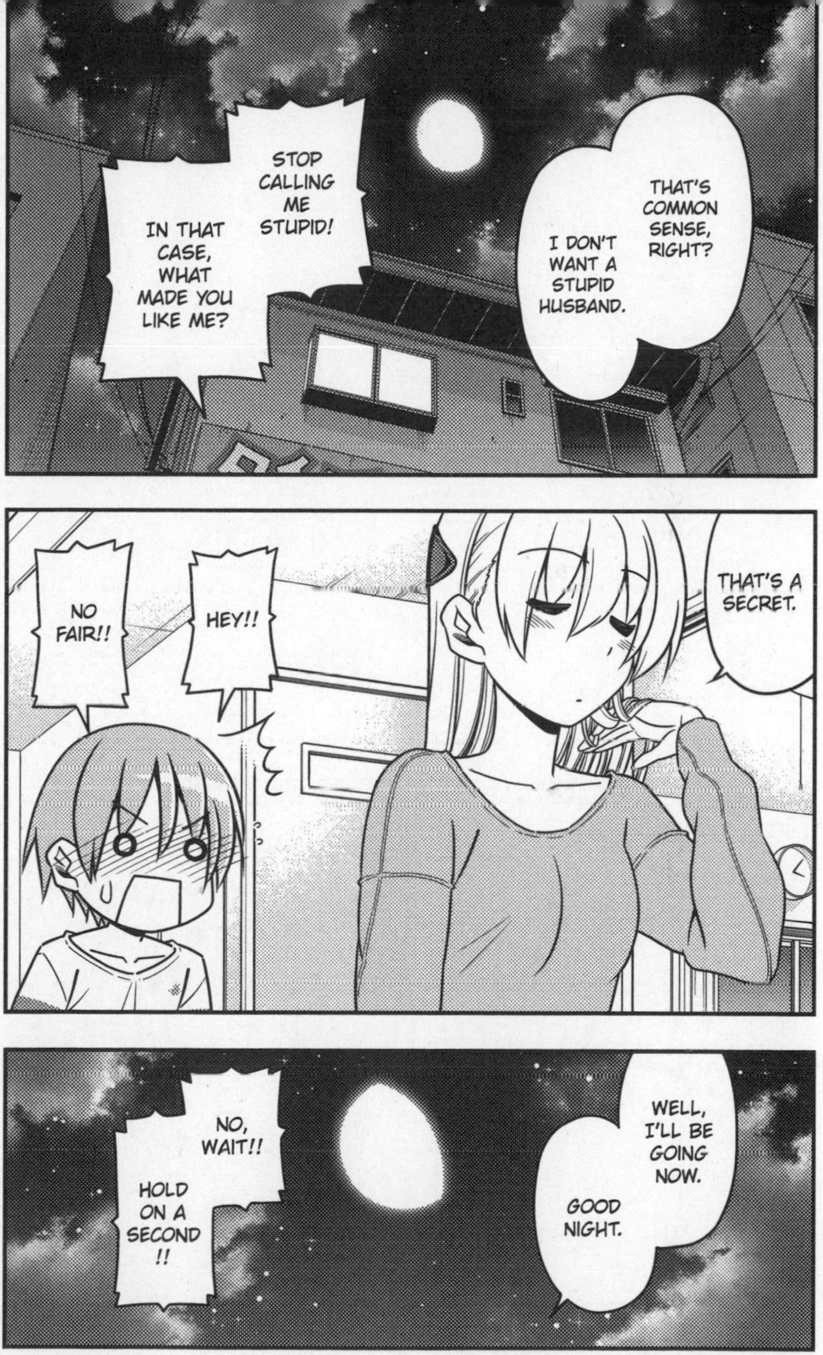
THAT'S COMMON SENSE, RIGHT?
I DON'T WANT A STUPID HUSBAND.
STOP CALLING ME STUPID!
IN THAT CASE, WHAT MADE YOU LIKE ME?
THAT'S A SECRET.
HEY!!
NO FAIR!!
WELL, I'LL BE GOING NOW.
GOOD NIGHT.
NO, WAIT!!
HOLD ON A SECOND !!

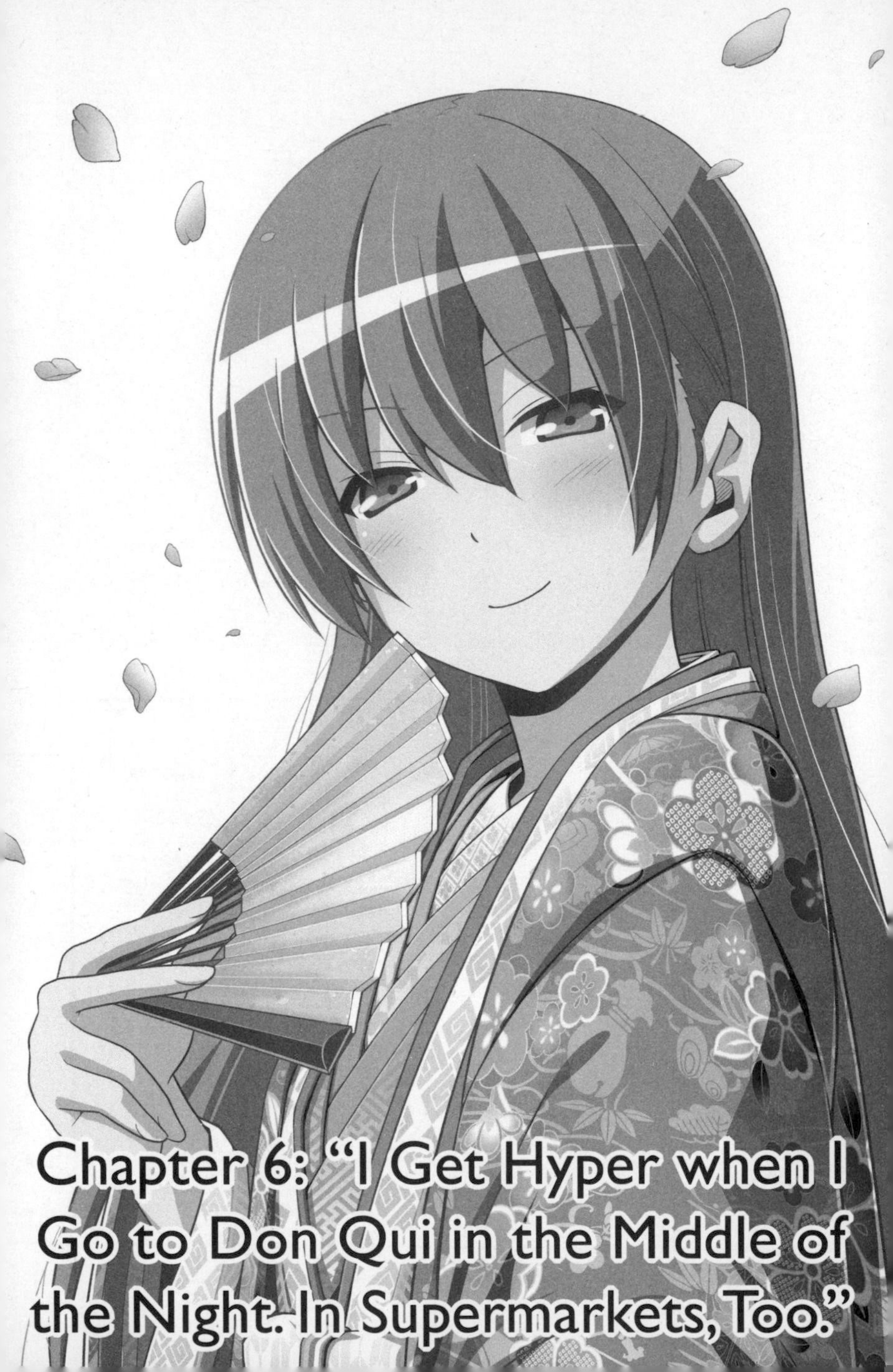

Chapter 6: "I Get Hyper when I Go to Don Qui in the Middle of the Night. In Supermarkets, Too."

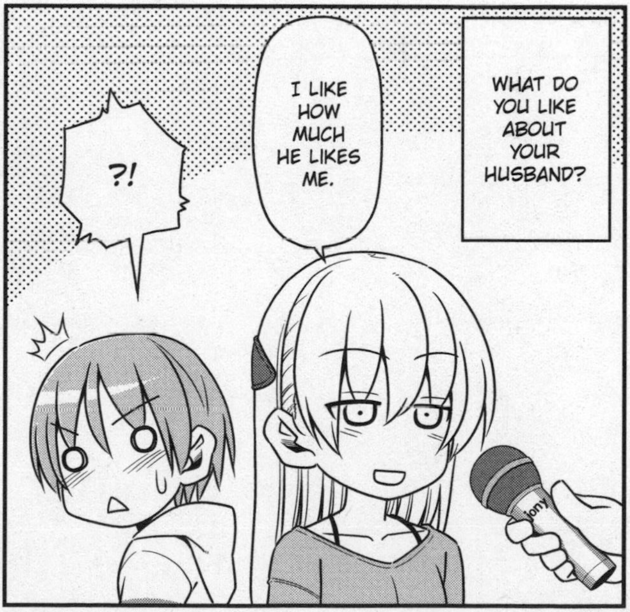
WHAT DO YOU LIKE ABOUT YOUR HUSBAND?
I LIKE HOW MUCH HE LIKES ME.
?!

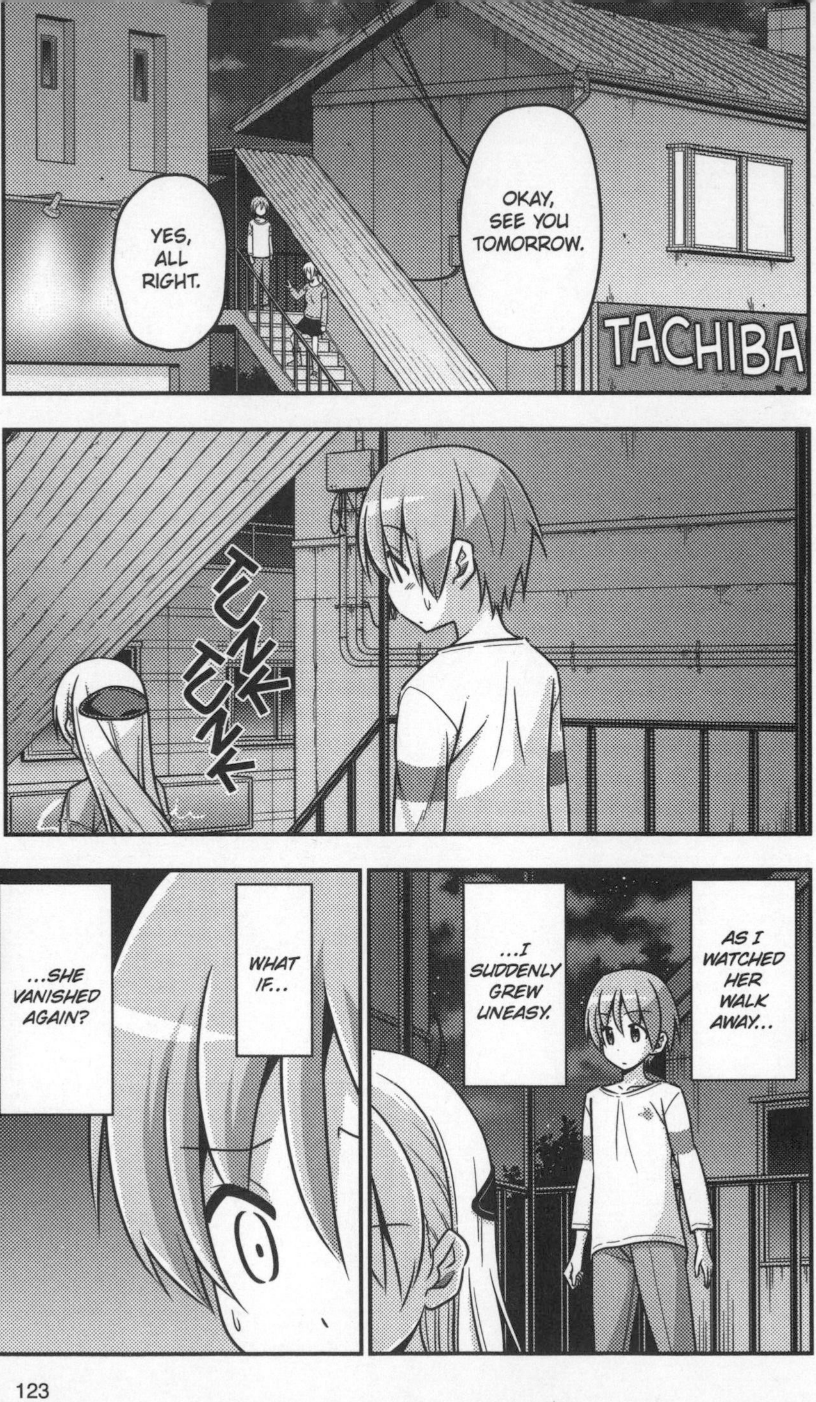
OKAY, SEE YOU TOMORROW.
TACHIBA
YES, ALL RIGHT.
TUNK TUNK
AS I WATCHED HER WALK AWAY...
...I SUDDENLY GREW UNEASY.
WHAT IF...
...SHE VANISHED AGAIN?

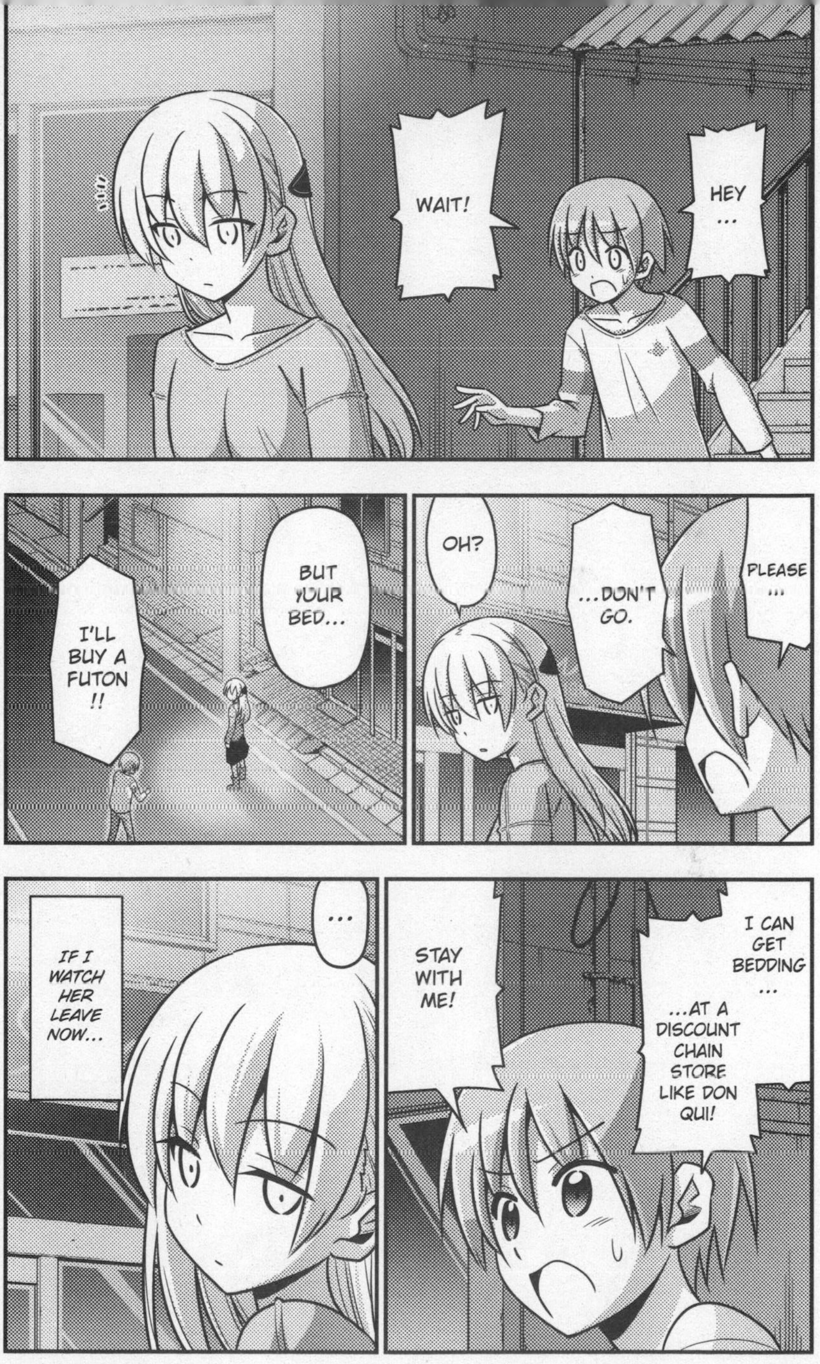
HEY ...
WAIT!
PLEASE ...
...DON'T GO.
OH?
BUT YOUR BED...
I'LL BUY A FUTON !!
I CAN GET BEDDING ...
...AT A DISCOUNT CHAIN STORE LIKE DON QUI!
STAY WITH ME!
...
IF I WATCH HER LEAVE NOW...

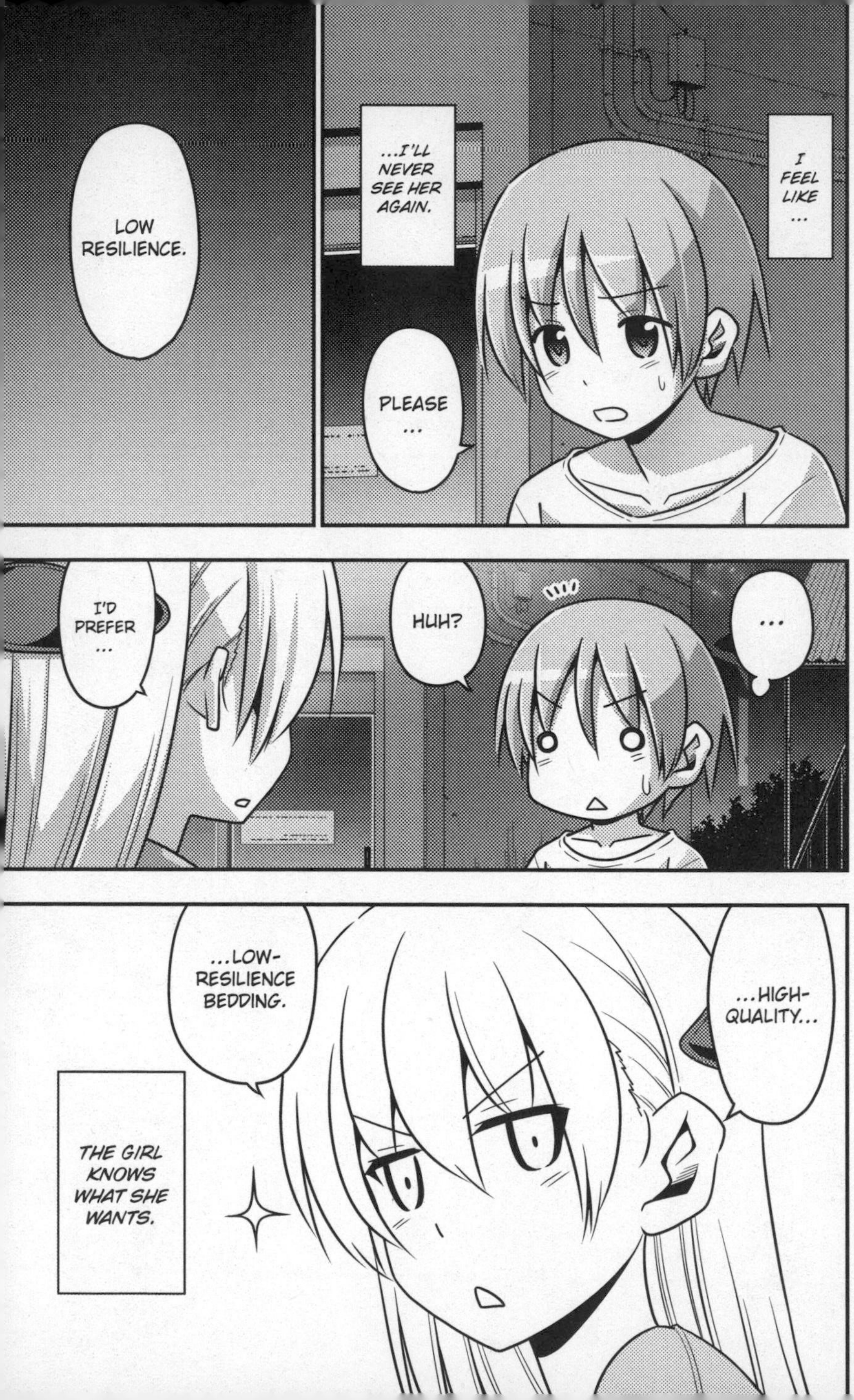
I FEEL LIKE ...
...I'LL NEVER SEE HER AGAIN.
PLEASE ...
LOW RESILIENCE.
...
HUH?
I'D PREFER ...
...HIGH-QUALITY...
...LOW-RESILIENCE BEDDING.
THE GIRL KNOWS WHAT SHE WANTS.

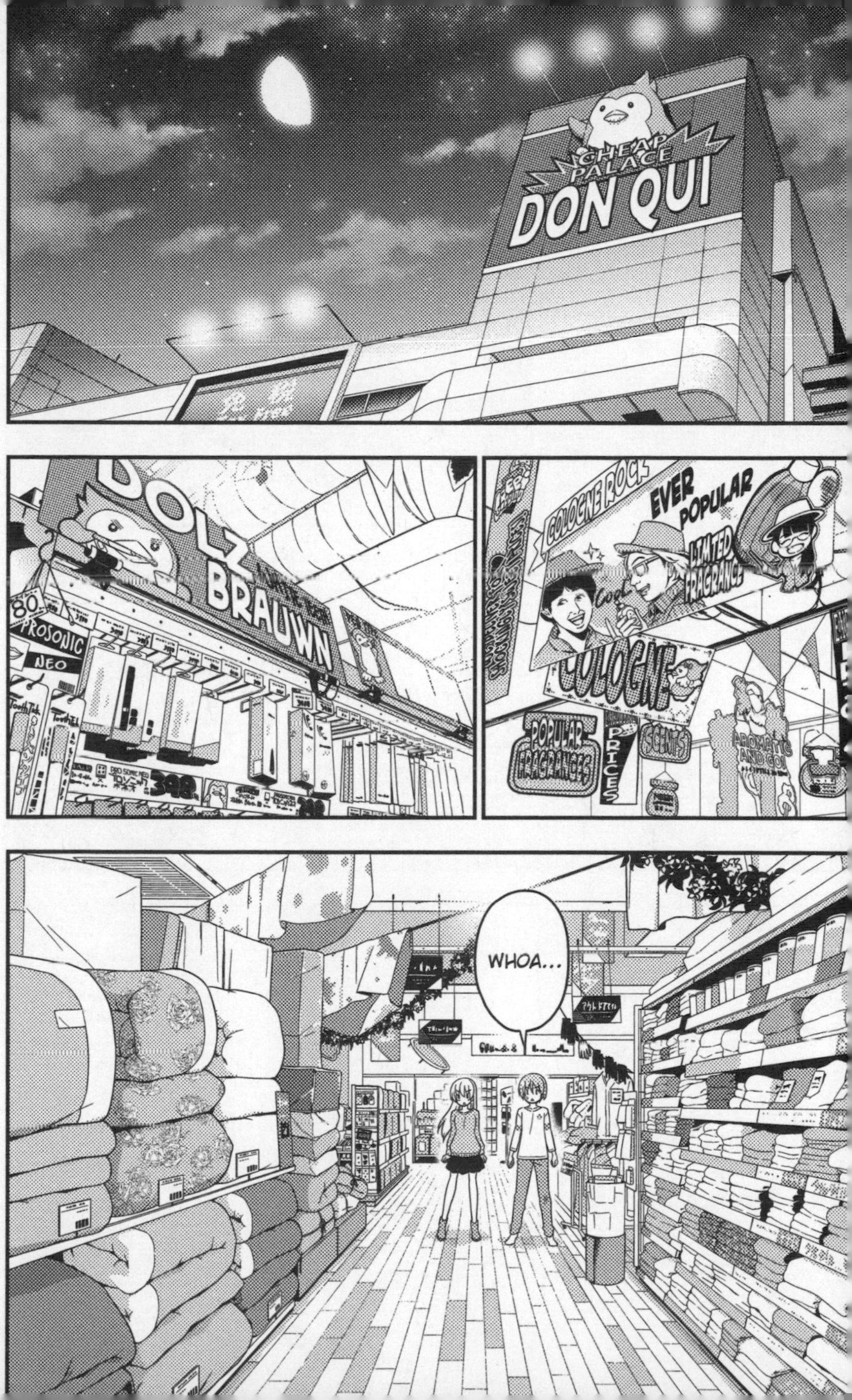
CHEAP PALACE
DON QUI
COLOGNE ROCK
EVER POPULAR
LIMITED FRAGRANCE
Cool
COLOGNE
POPULAR FRAGRANCES
PRICES
SCENTS
AROMATIC AND GO
DOLZ
BRAUWN
80
PROSONIC
NEO
WHOA...

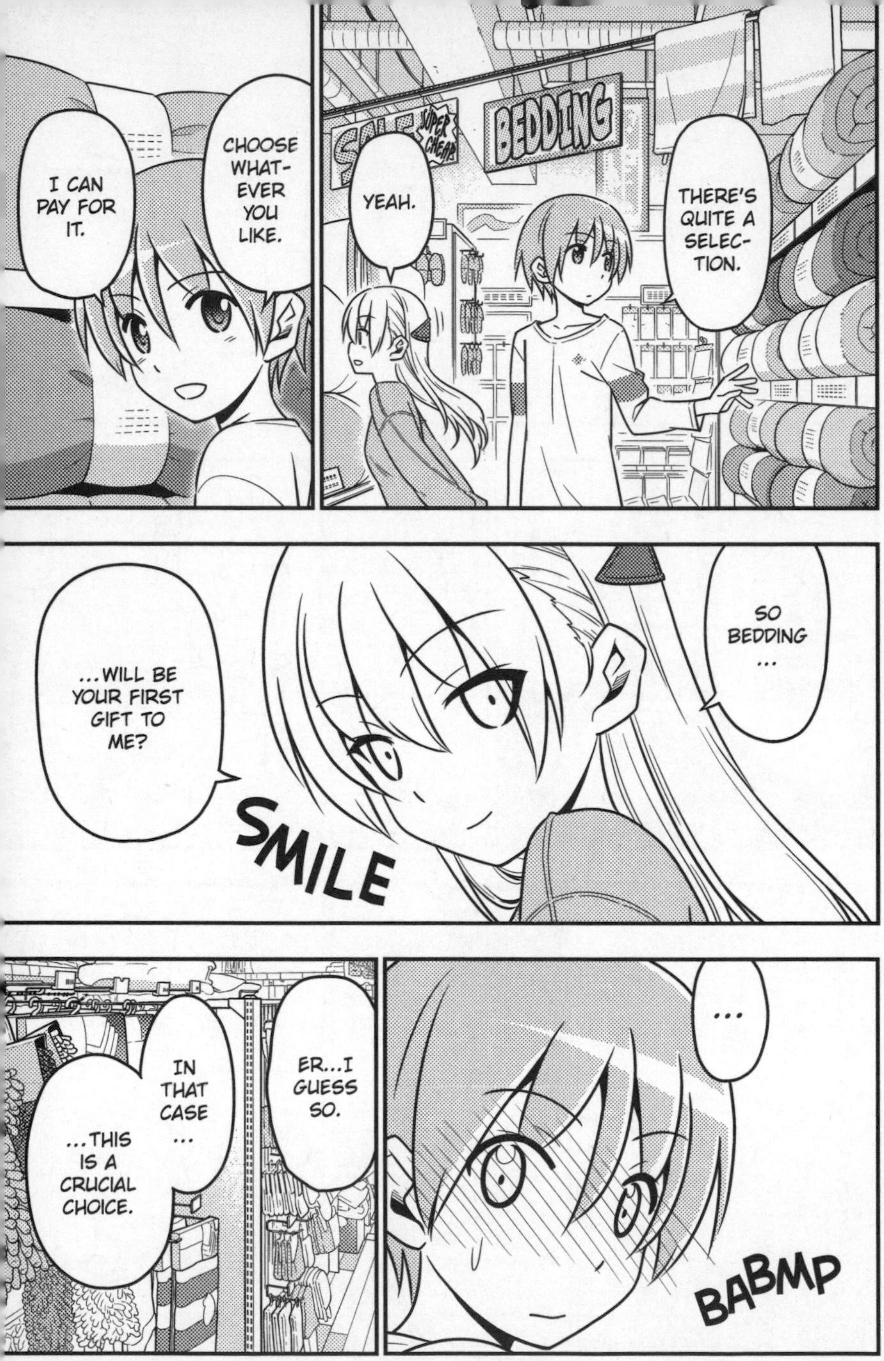
BEDDING
SUPER CHEAP
THERE'S QUITE A SELECTION.
YEAH.
CHOOSE WHATEVER YOU LIKE.
I CAN PAY FOR IT.
SO BEDDING...
...WILL BE YOUR FIRST GIFT TO ME?
SMILE
...
BABMP
ER...I GUESS SO.
IN THAT CASE...
...THIS IS A CRUCIAL CHOICE.

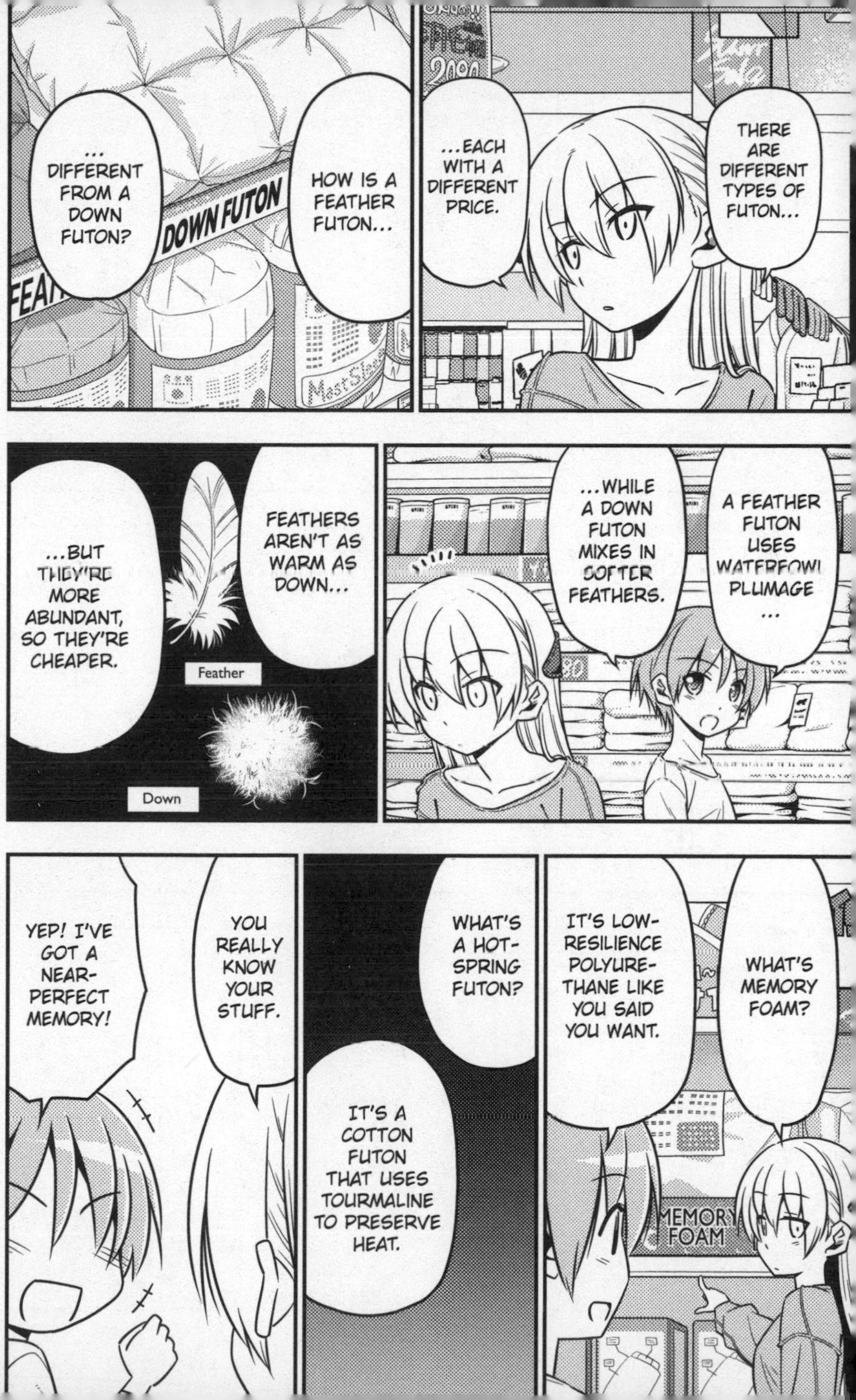
THERE ARE DIFFERENT TYPES OF FUTON...
...EACH WITH A DIFFERENT PRICE.
HOW IS A FEATHER FUTON...
DOWN FUTON
...DIFFERENT FROM A DOWN FUTON?
A FEATHER FUTON USES WATERFOWL PLUMAGE...
...WHILE A DOWN FUTON MIXES IN SOFTER FEATHERS.
FEATHERS AREN'T AS WARM AS DOWN...
...BUT THEY'RE MORE ABUNDANT, SO THEY'RE CHEAPER.
Feather
Down
WHAT'S MEMORY FOAM?
IT'S LOW-RESILIENCE POLYURETHANE LIKE YOU SAID YOU WANT.
MEMORY FOAM
WHAT'S A HOT-SPRING FUTON?
IT'S A COTTON FUTON THAT USES TOURMALINE TO PRESERVE HEAT.
YOU REALLY KNOW YOUR STUFF.
YEP! I'VE GOT A NEAR-PERFECT MEMORY!

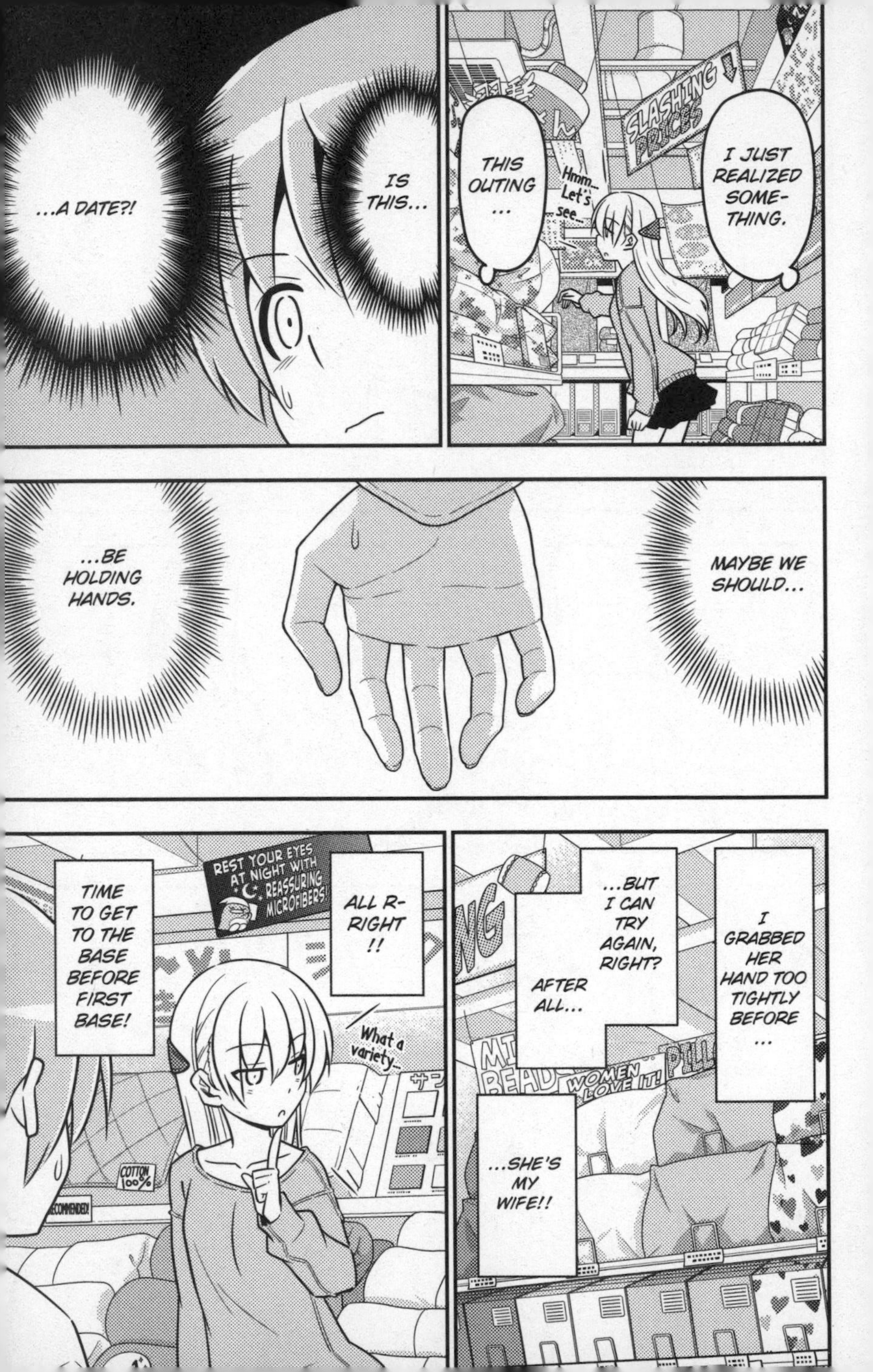

I JUST REALIZED SOMETHING.
SLASHING PRICES
THIS OUTING ...
Hmm... Let's see...
IS THIS...
...A DATE?!
MAYBE WE SHOULD...
...BE HOLDING HANDS.
I GRABBED HER HAND TOO TIGHTLY BEFORE ...
...BUT I CAN TRY AGAIN, RIGHT?
AFTER ALL...
WOMEN LOVE IT!
...SHE'S MY WIFE!!
ALL R-RIGHT !!
REST YOUR EYES AT NIGHT WITH REASSURING MICROFIBERS!
TIME TO GET TO THE BASE BEFORE FIRST BASE!
What a variety...
COTTON 100%
RECOMMENDED!

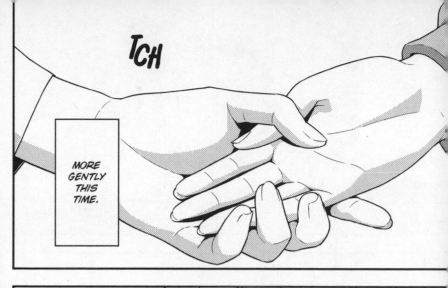

TCH

MORE
GENTLY
THIS
TIME.

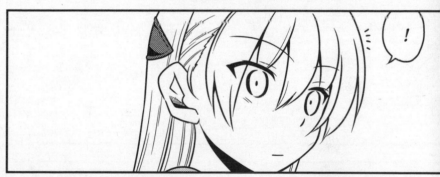

!

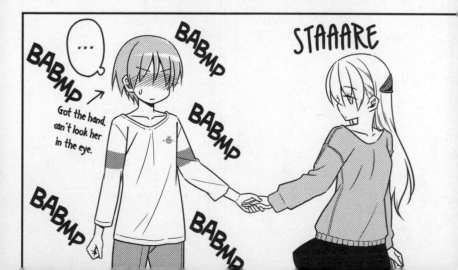

...

BABMP

BABMP

STAAARE

BABMP

BABMP

Got the hand,
can't look her
in the eye.

BABMP

BABMP

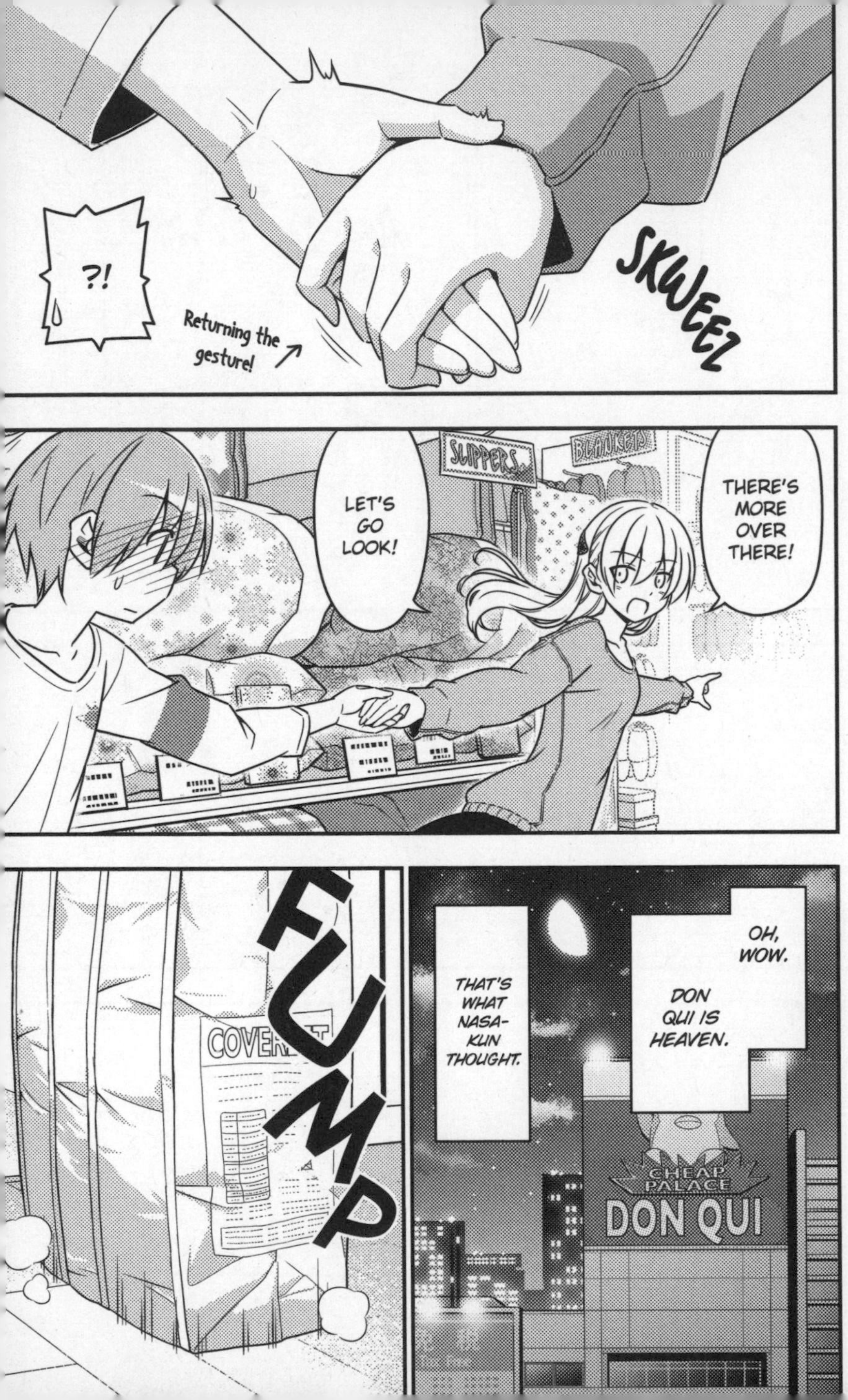
SKWEEZ
Returning the gesture!
?!
BLANKETS
THERE'S MORE OVER THERE!
SLIPPERS
LET'S GO LOOK!
OH, WOW.
DON QUI IS HEAVEN.
THAT'S WHAT NASA-KUN THOUGHT.
CHEAP PALACE
DON QUI
FUMP

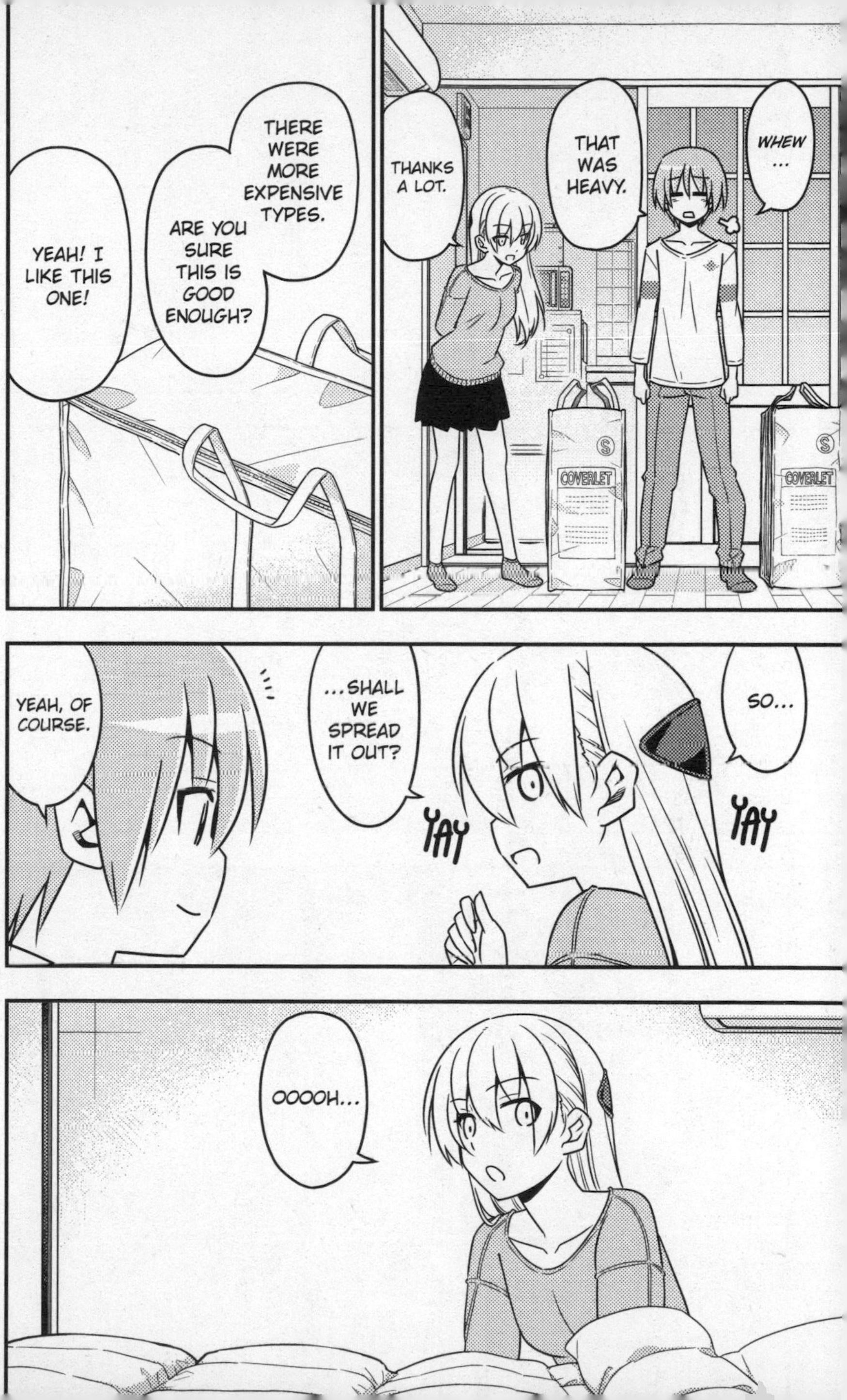
WHEW ...
THAT WAS HEAVY.
THANKS A LOT.
S
COVERLET
S
COVERLET
THERE WERE MORE EXPENSIVE TYPES.
ARE YOU SURE THIS IS GOOD ENOUGH?
YEAH! I LIKE THIS ONE!
SO...
YAY
YAY
...SHALL WE SPREAD IT OUT?
YEAH, OF COURSE.
OOOOH...

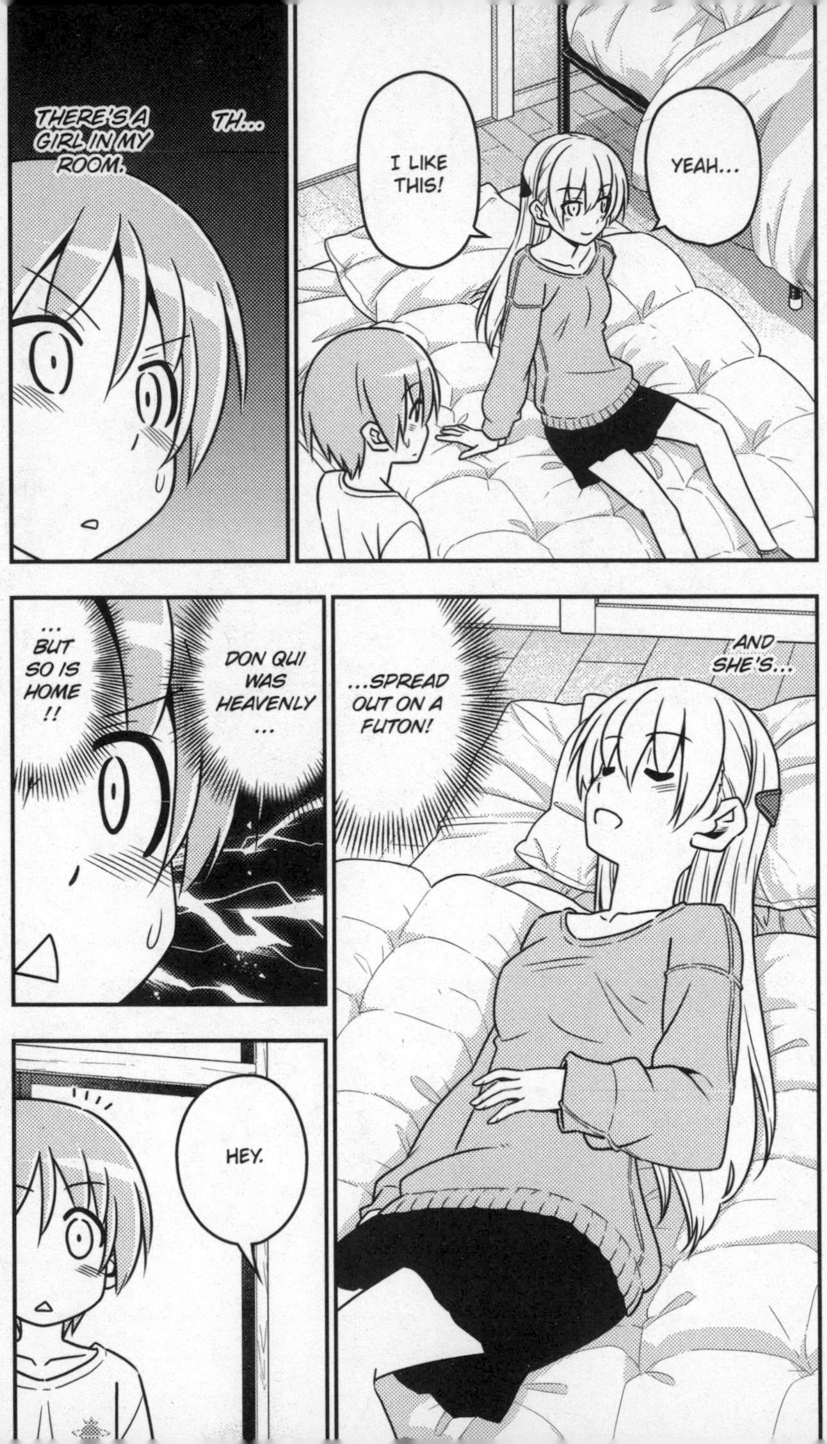
YEAH...
I LIKE THIS!
TH...
THERE'S A GIRL IN MY ROOM.
AND SHE'S...
...SPREAD OUT ON A FUTON!
DON QUI WAS HEAVENLY ...
... BUT SO IS HOME !!
HEY.

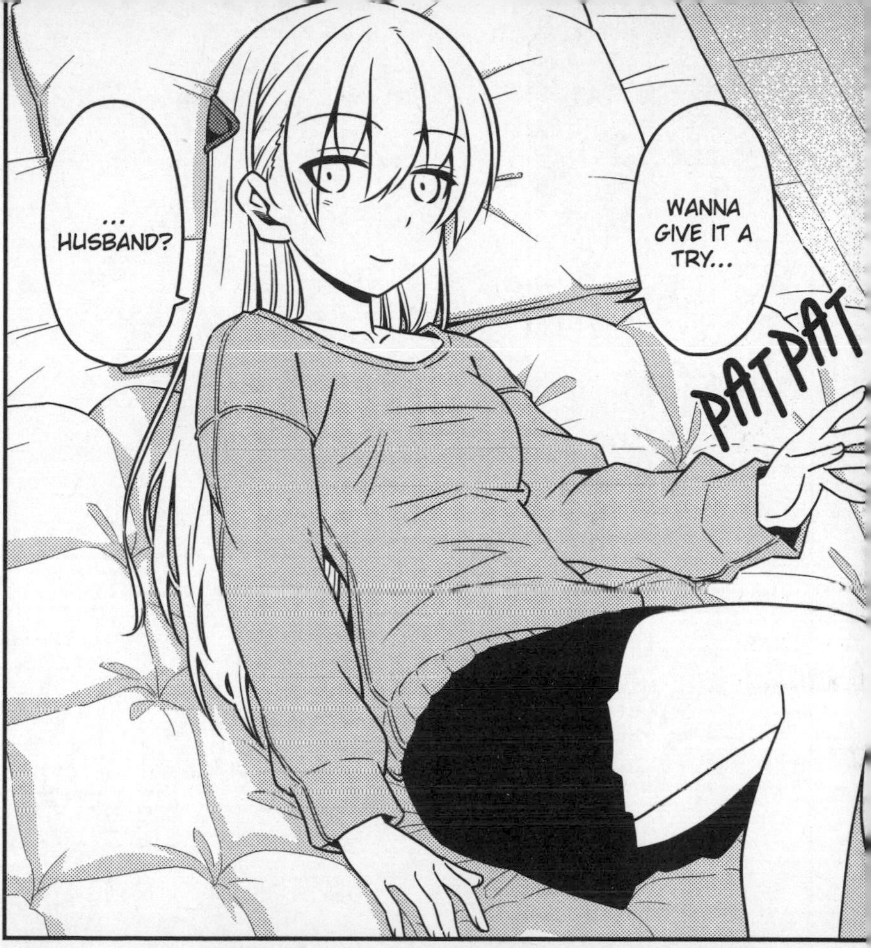
WANNA GIVE IT A TRY...
... HUSBAND?
PATPAT

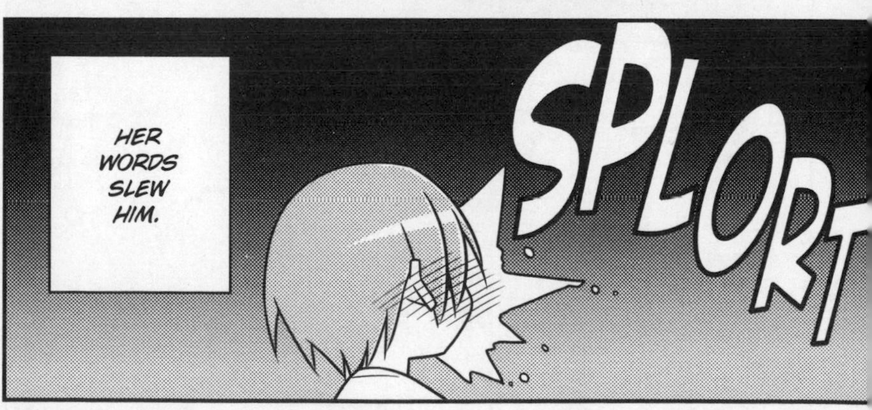
SPLORT
HER WORDS SLEW HIM.

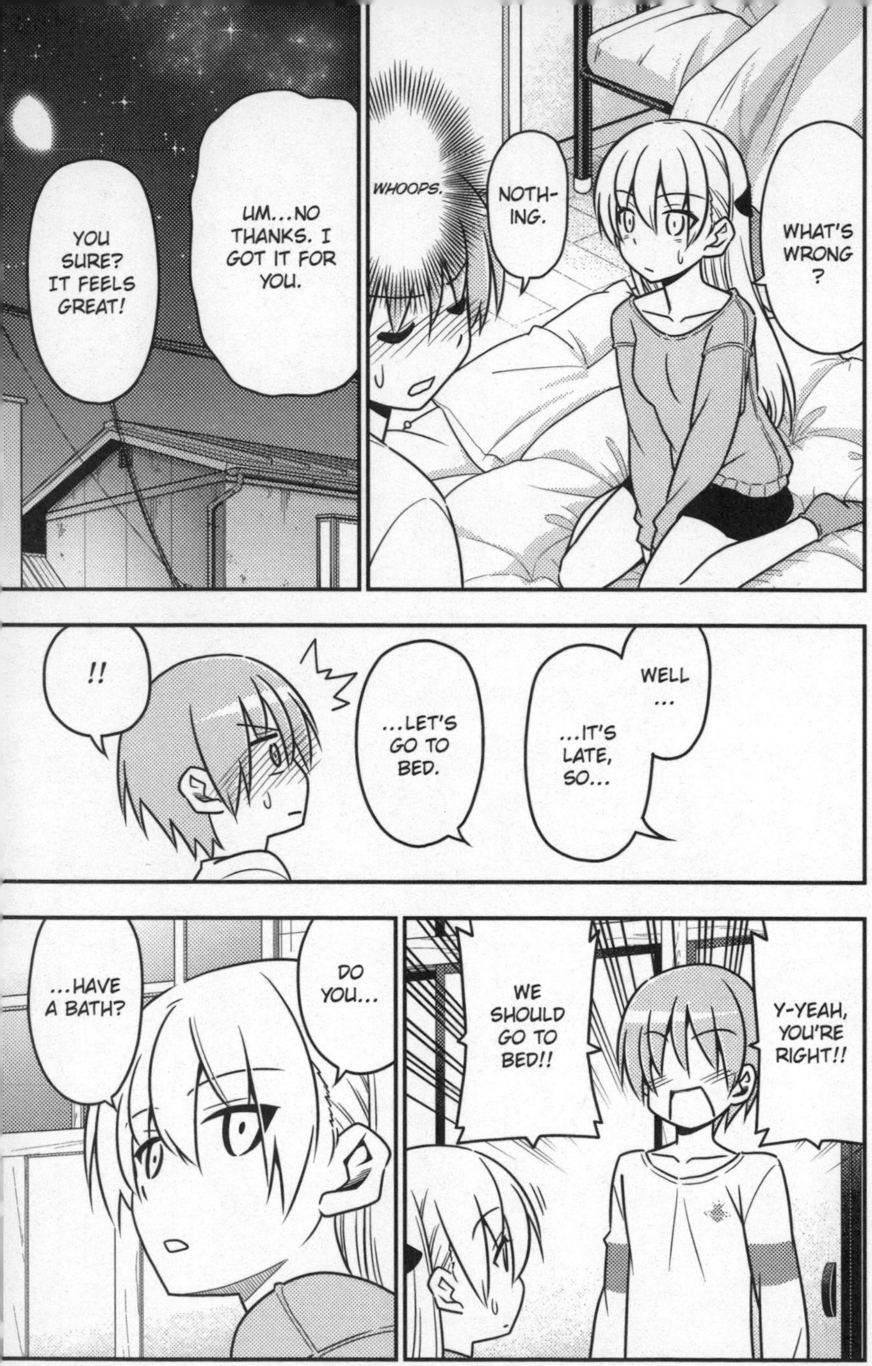
WHAT'S WRONG?
NOTH-ING.
WHOOPS.
UM...NO THANKS. I GOT IT FOR YOU.
YOU SURE? IT FEELS GREAT!
WELL...
...IT'S LATE, SO...
...LET'S GO TO BED.
!!
Y-YEAH, YOU'RE RIGHT!!
WE SHOULD GO TO BED!!
DO YOU...
...HAVE A BATH?

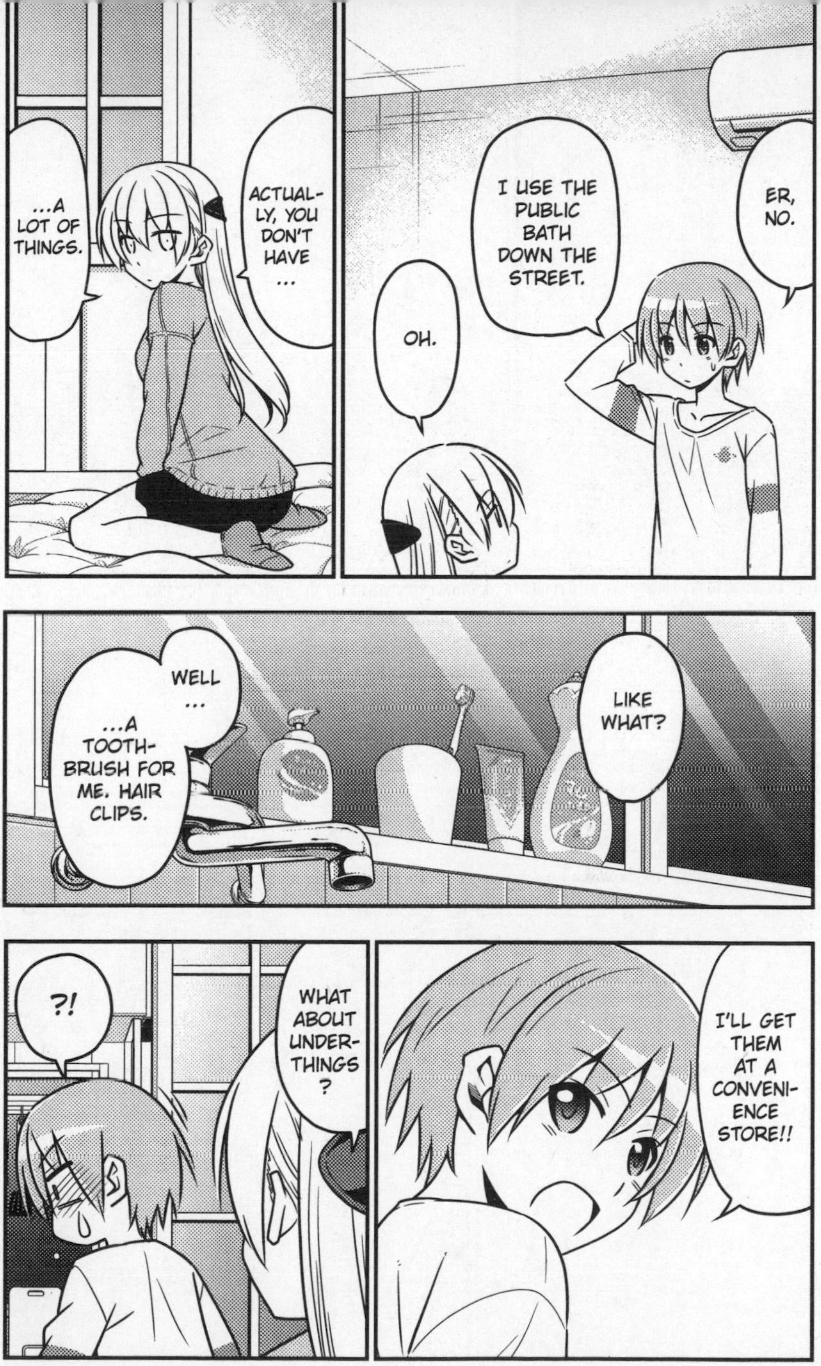
ER, NO.
I USE THE PUBLIC BATH DOWN THE STREET.
OH.
ACTUAL-LY, YOU DON'T HAVE ...
...A LOT OF THINGS.
LIKE WHAT?
WELL ...
...A TOOTH-BRUSH FOR ME. HAIR CLIPS.
I'LL GET THEM AT A CONVENI-ENCE STORE!!
WHAT ABOUT UNDER-THINGS?
?!

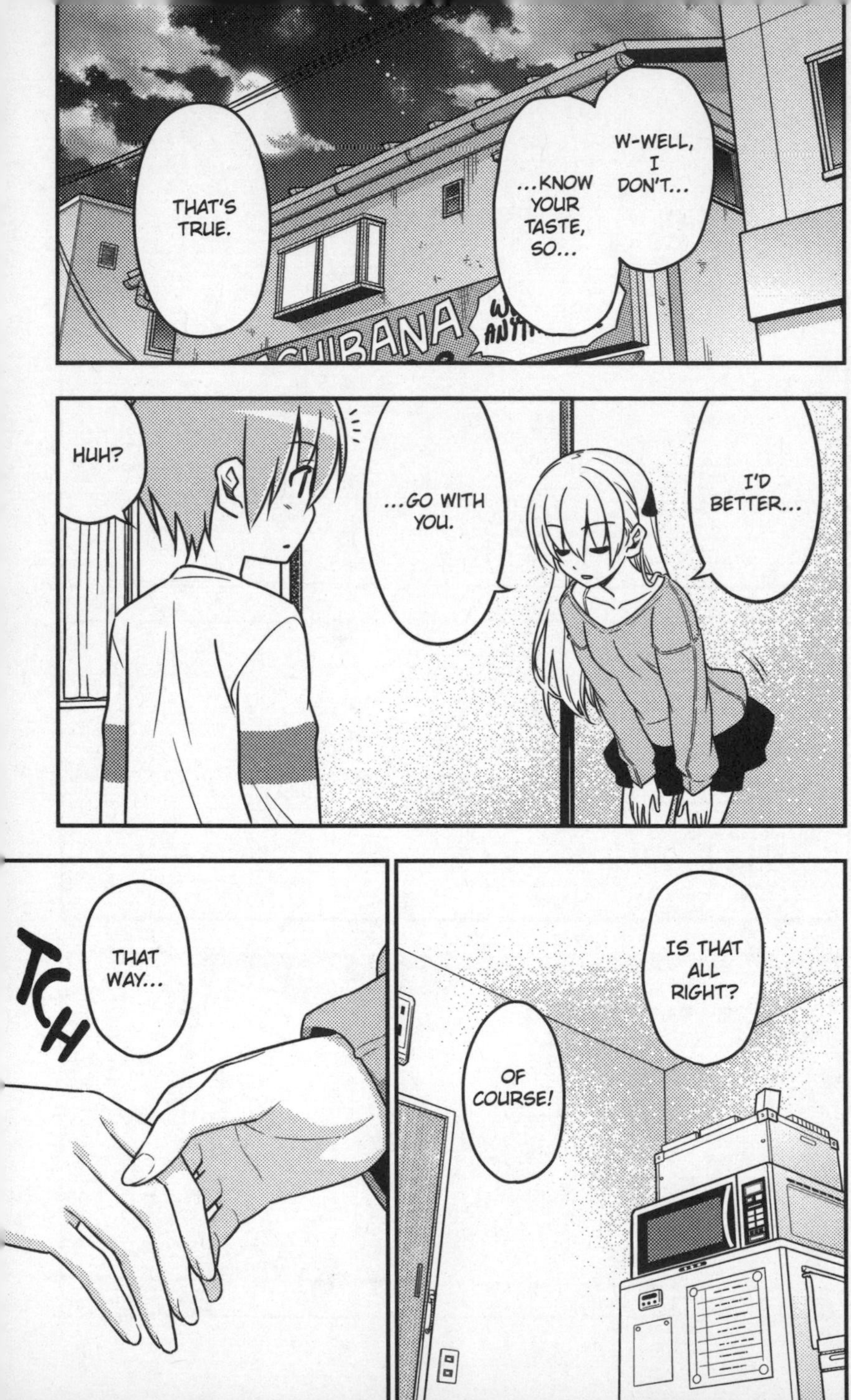
W-WELL, I DON'T...
...KNOW YOUR TASTE, SO...
THAT'S TRUE.
I'D BETTER...
...GO WITH YOU.
HUH?
IS THAT ALL RIGHT?
OF COURSE!
THAT WAY...
TCH

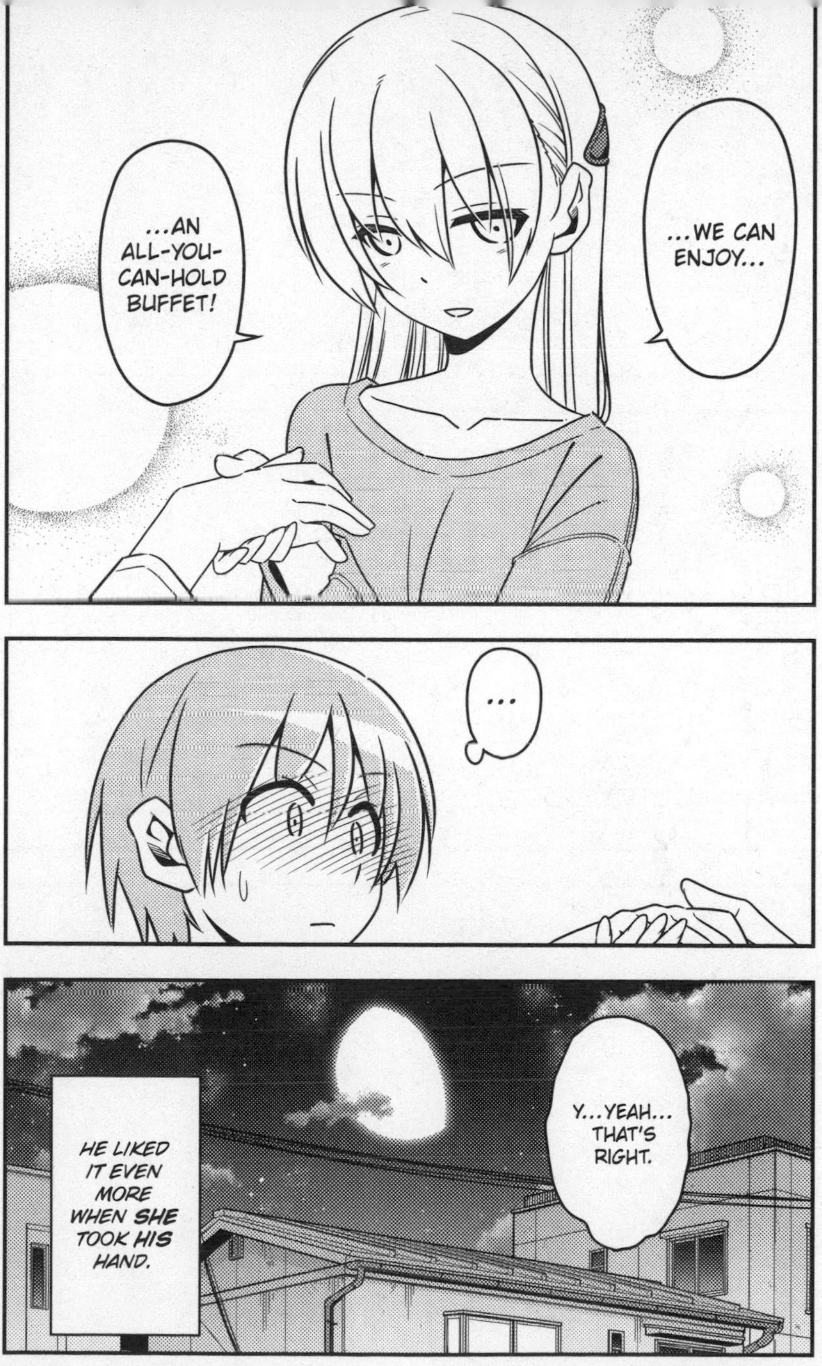
...WE CAN ENJOY...
...AN ALL-YOU-CAN-HOLD BUFFET!
...
Y...YEAH... THAT'S RIGHT.
HE LIKED IT EVEN MORE WHEN SHE TOOK HIS HAND.

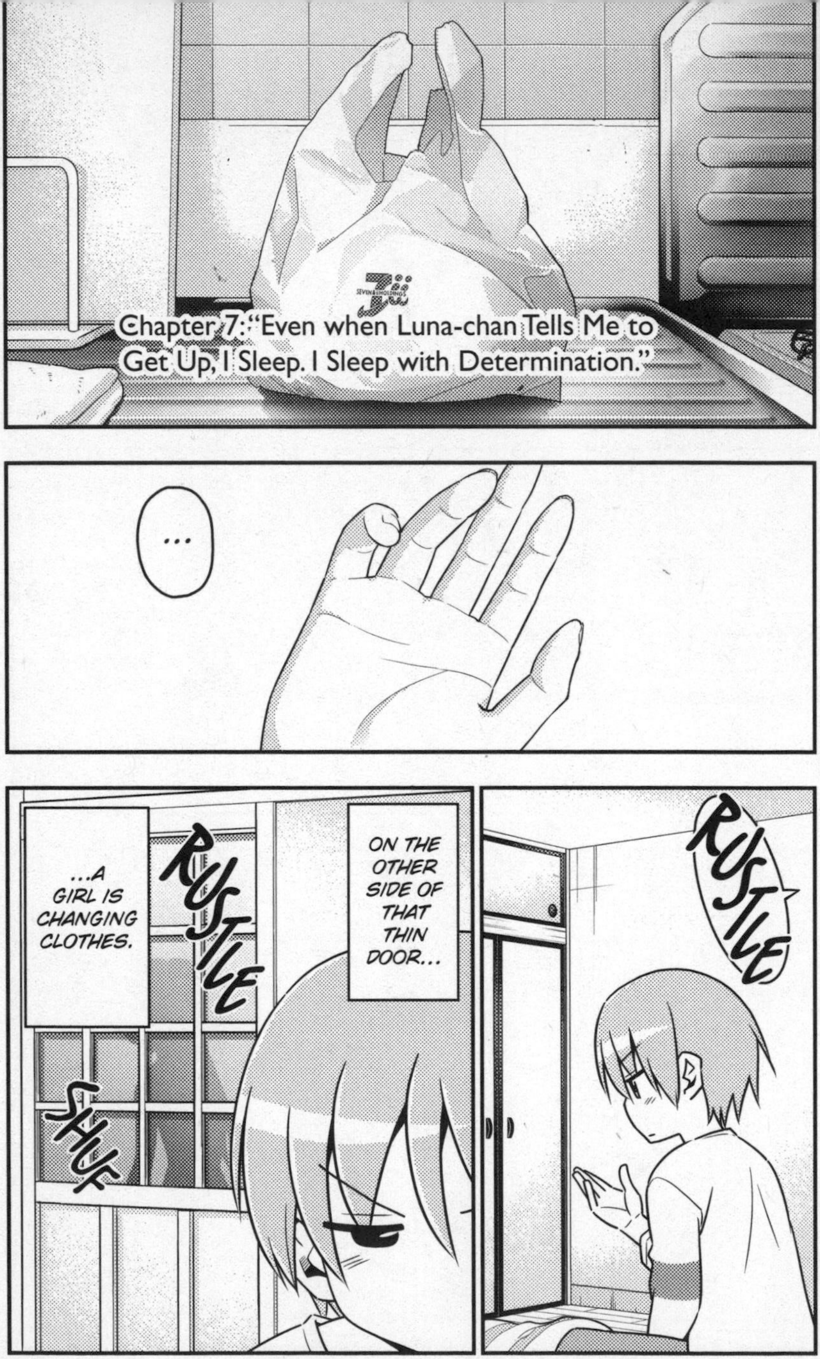
Chapter 7: "Even when Luna-chan Tells Me to Get Up, I Sleep. I Sleep with Determination."
...
RUSTLE
ON THE OTHER SIDE OF THAT THIN DOOR...
...A GIRL IS CHANGING CLOTHES.
RUSTLE
SHUF

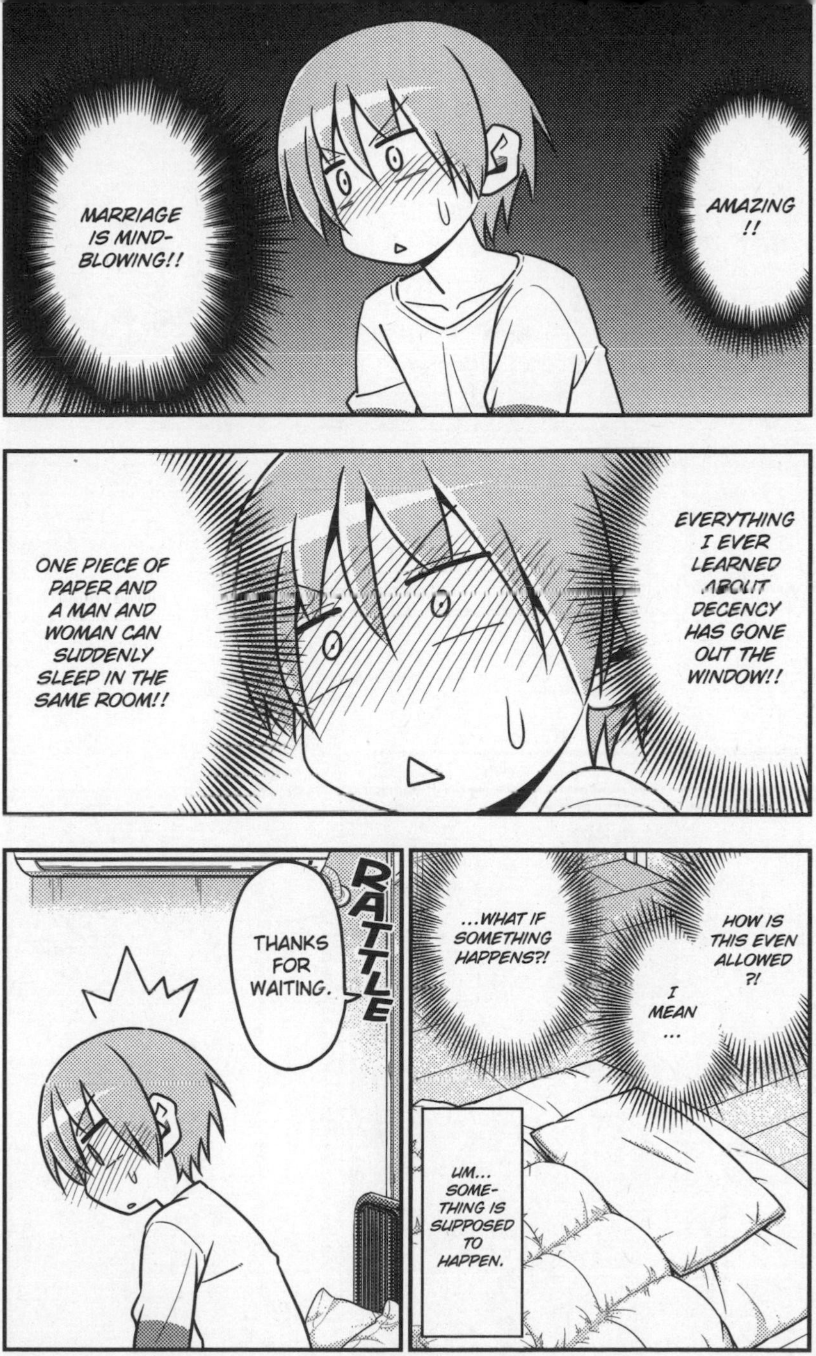
AMAZING!!
MARRIAGE IS MIND-BLOWING!!
EVERYTHING I EVER LEARNED ABOUT DECENCY HAS GONE OUT THE WINDOW!!
ONE PIECE OF PAPER AND A MAN AND WOMAN CAN SUDDENLY SLEEP IN THE SAME ROOM!!
HOW IS THIS EVEN ALLOWED?!
I MEAN...
...WHAT IF SOMETHING HAPPENS?!
UM... SOMETHING IS SUPPOSED TO HAPPEN.
RATTLE
THANKS FOR WAITING.

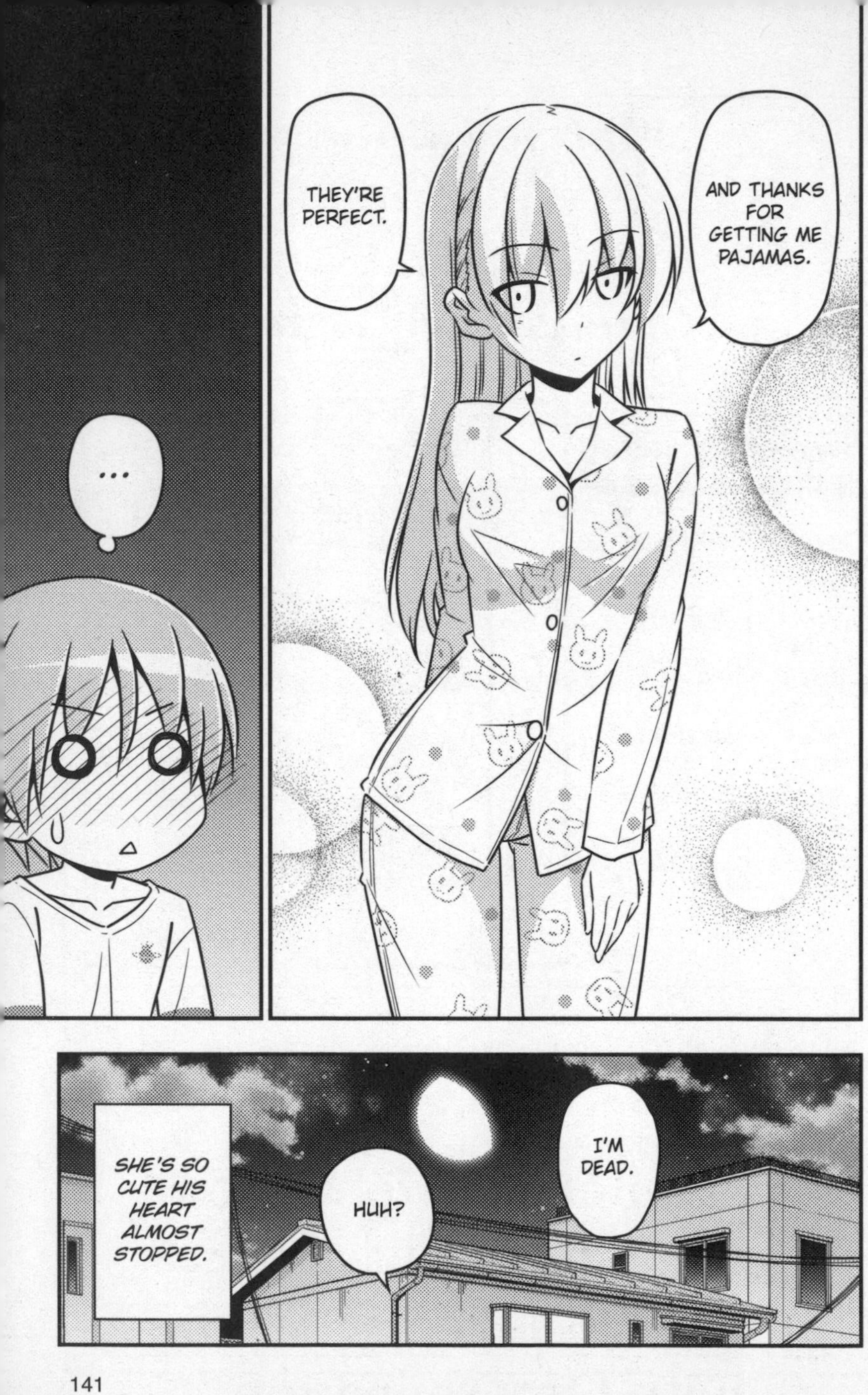
AND THANKS FOR GETTING ME PAJAMAS.
THEY'RE PERFECT.
...
I'M DEAD.
HUH?
SHE'S SO CUTE HIS HEART ALMOST STOPPED.

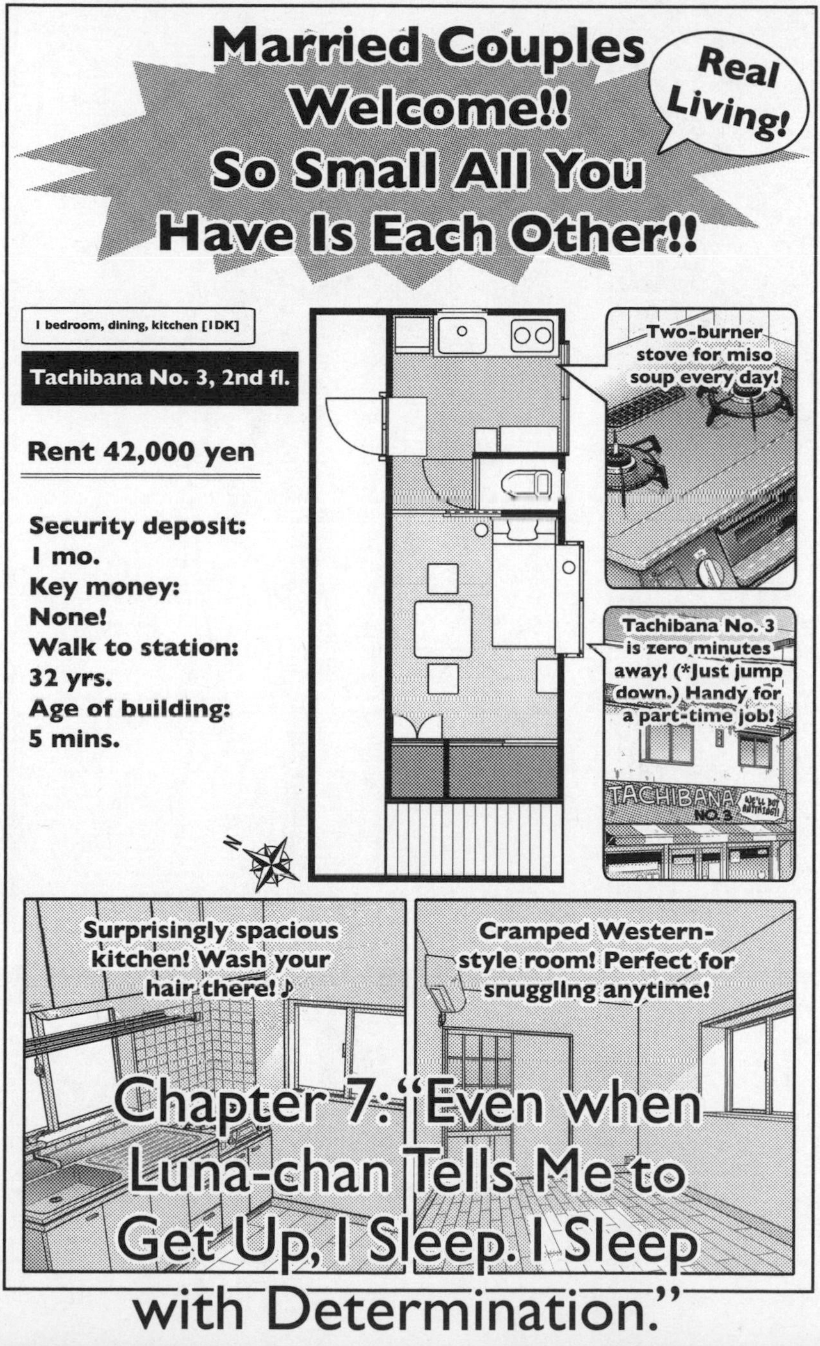
Married Couples Welcome!! So Small All You Have Is Each Other!!
Real Living!
Two-burner stove for miso soup every day!
Tachibana No. 3 is zero minutes away! (*Just jump down.) Handy for a part-time job!
TACHIBANA NO. 3
I bedroom, dining, kitchen [IDK]
Tachibana No. 3, 2nd fl.
Rent 42,000 yen
Security deposit: I mo.
Key money: None!
Walk to station: 32 yrs.
Age of building: 5 mins.
Cramped Western-style room! Perfect for snuggling anytime!
Surprisingly spacious kitchen! Wash your hair there! ♪
Chapter 7: "Even when Luna-chan Tells Me to Get Up, I Sleep. I Sleep with Determination."

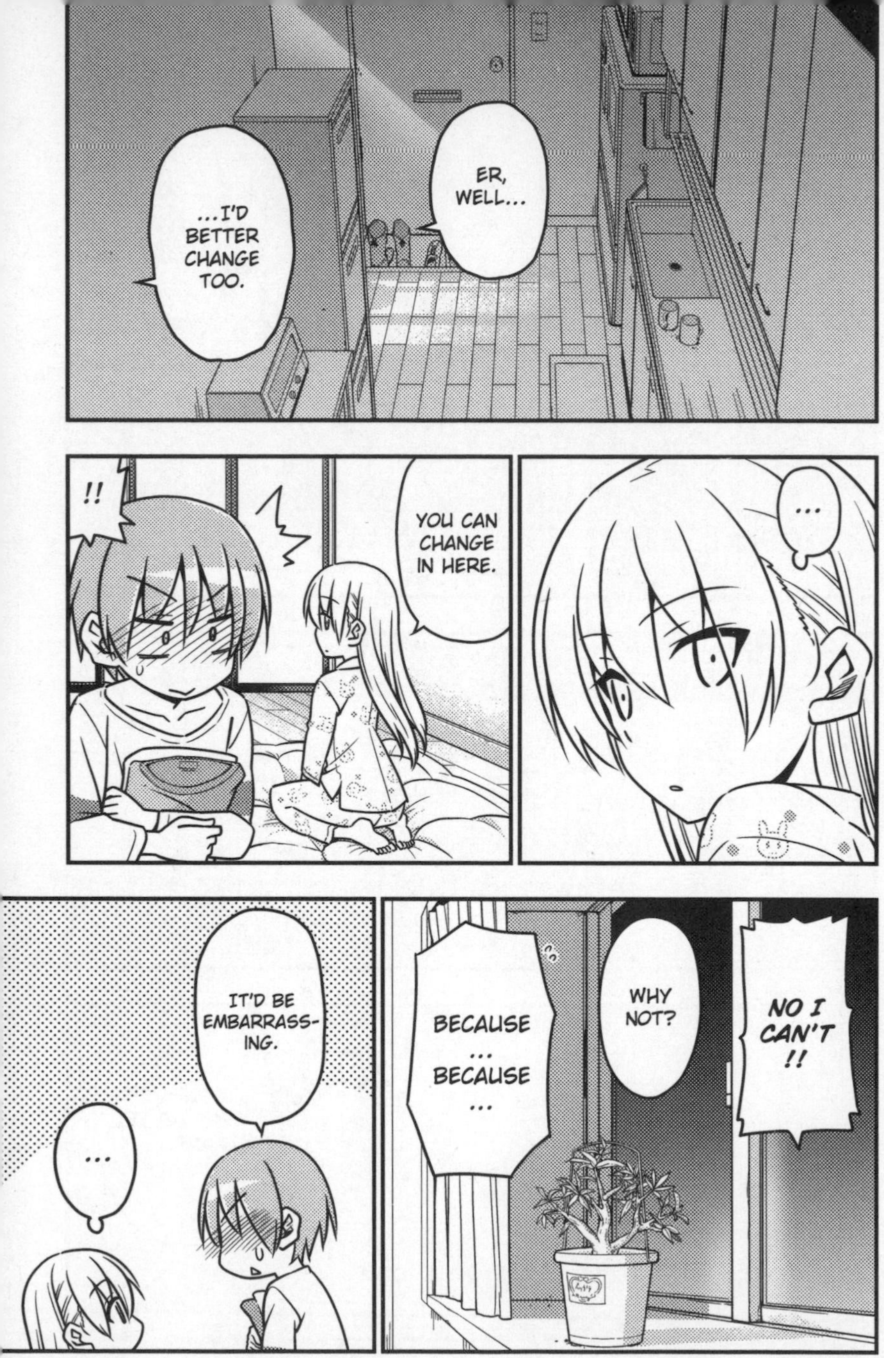
ER, WELL...
...I'D BETTER CHANGE TOO.
...
YOU CAN CHANGE IN HERE.
!!
NO I CAN'T !!
WHY NOT?
BECAUSE ... BECAUSE ...
IT'D BE EMBARRASS-ING.
...

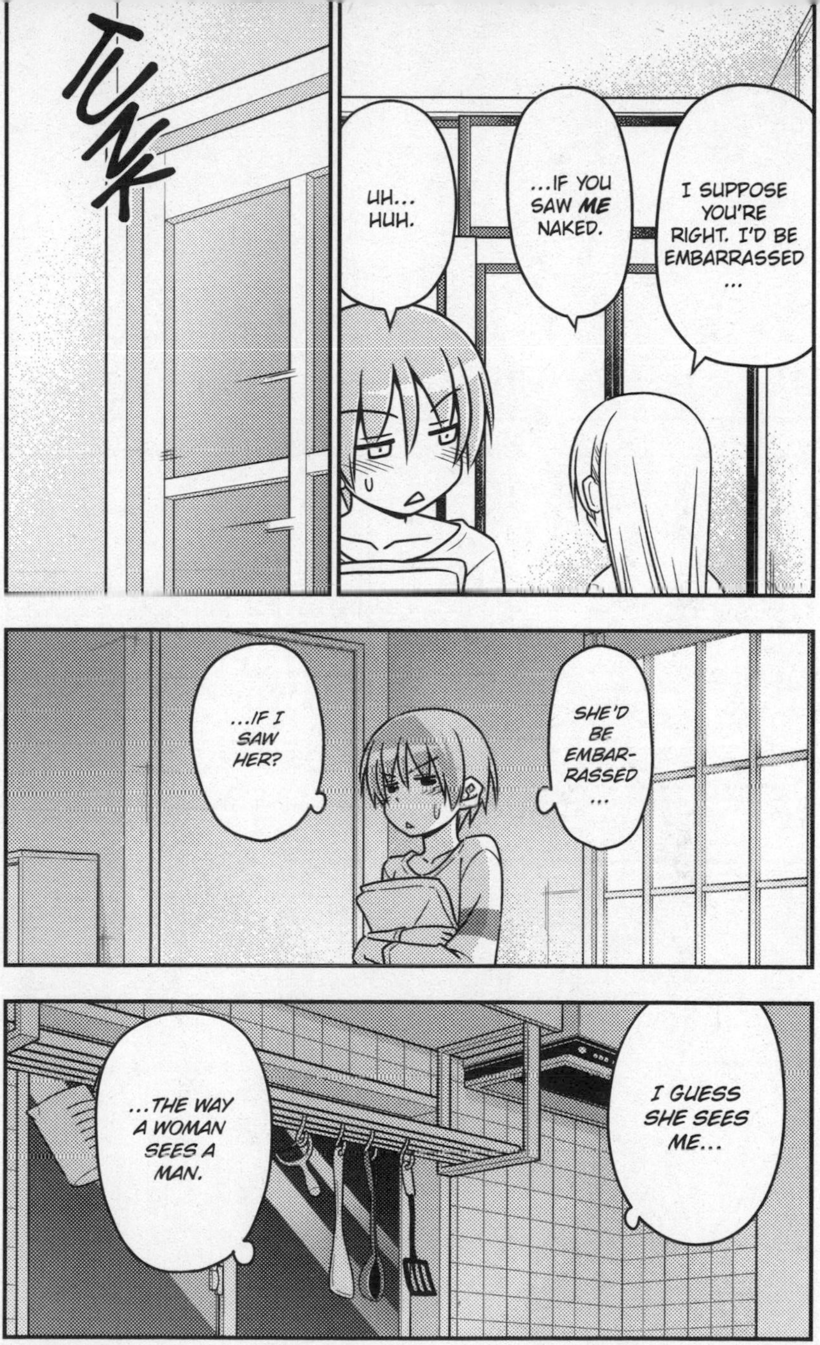
I SUPPOSE YOU'RE RIGHT. I'D BE EMBARRASSED ...
...IF YOU SAW ME NAKED.
UH... HUH.
TUNK
SHE'D BE EMBARRASSED ...
...IF I SAW HER?
I GUESS SHE SEES ME...
...THE WAY A WOMAN SEES A MAN.

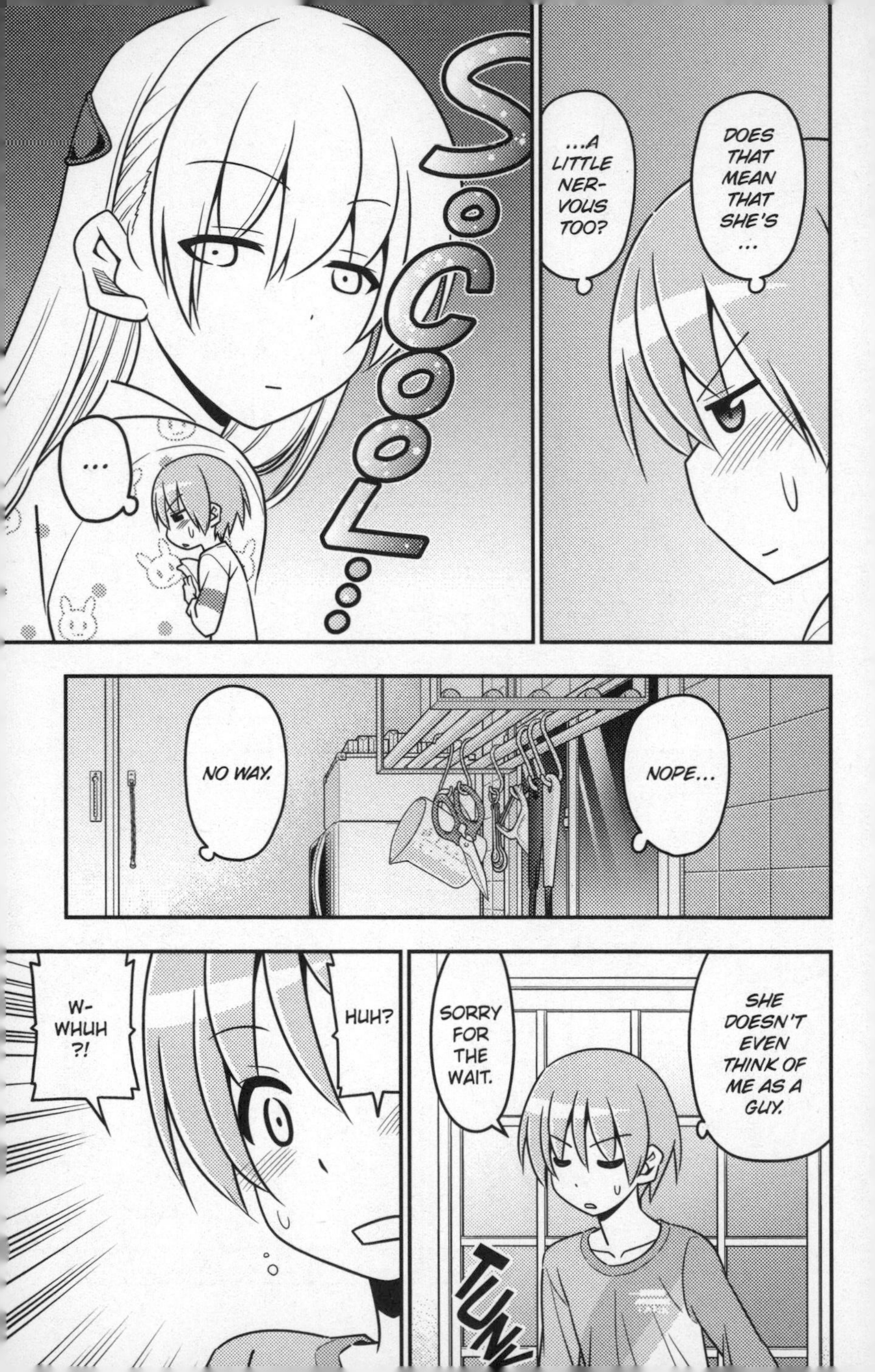
DOES THAT MEAN THAT SHE'S ...
...A LITTLE NER-VOUS TOO?
SooCooL...
...
NOPE...
NO WAY.
SHE DOESN'T EVEN THINK OF ME AS A GUY.
SORRY FOR THE WAIT.
TUNK
HUH?
W-WHUH ?!

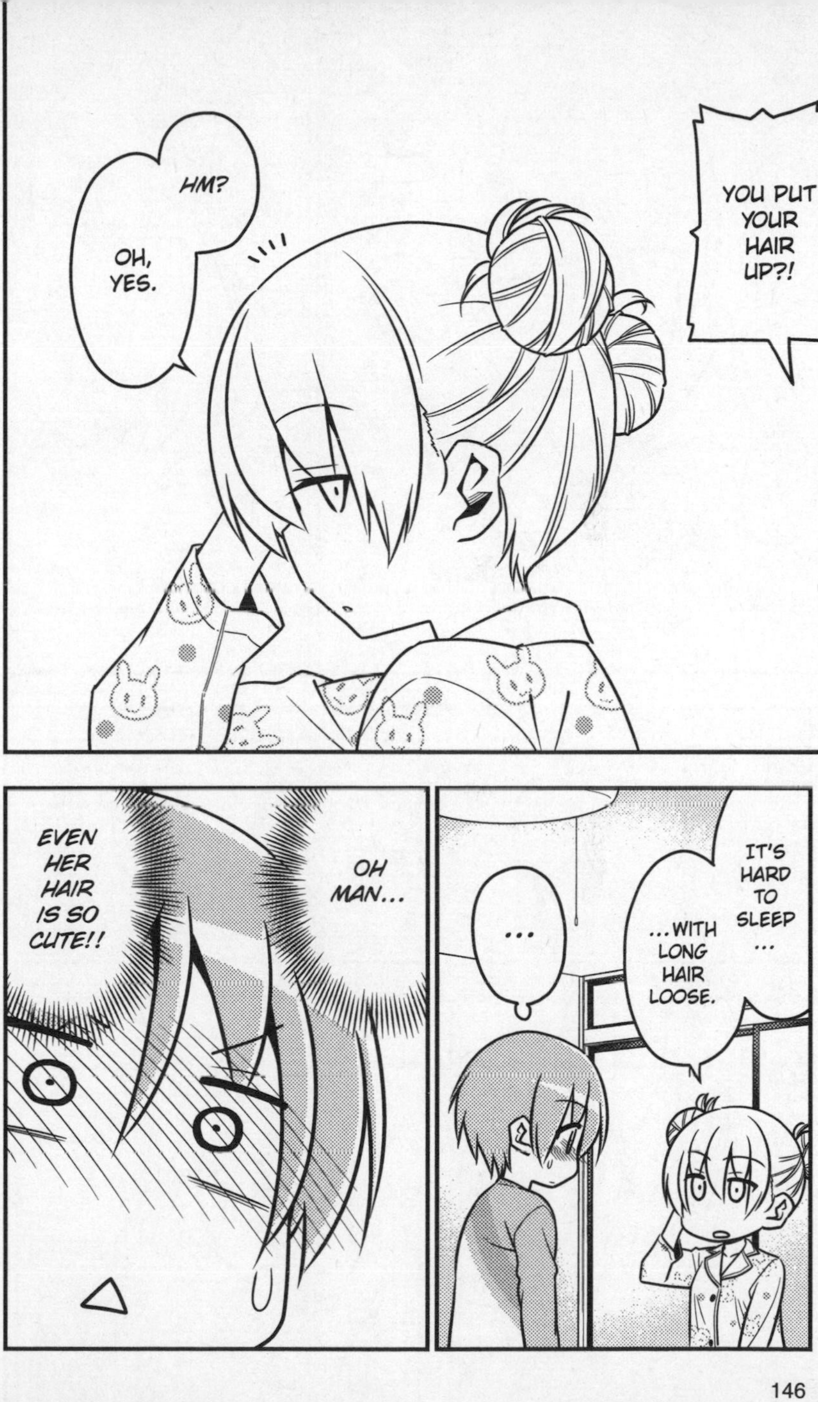
YOU PUT YOUR HAIR UP?!
HM?
OH, YES.
IT'S HARD TO SLEEP ...
...WITH LONG HAIR LOOSE.
...
OH MAN...
EVEN HER HAIR IS SO CUTE!!

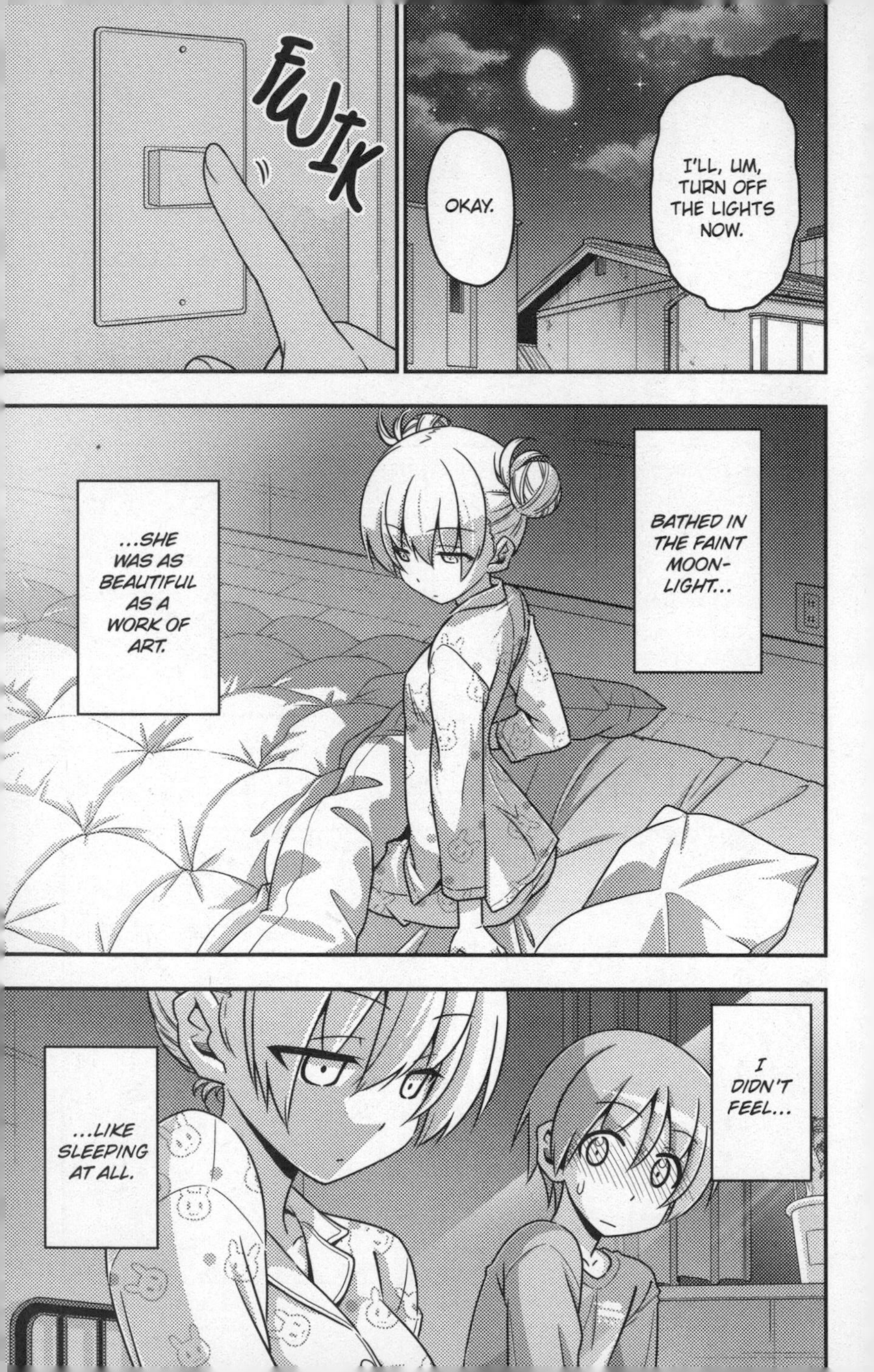
I'LL, UM, TURN OFF THE LIGHTS NOW.
OKAY.
FWIK
BATHED IN THE FAINT MOON-LIGHT...
...SHE WAS AS BEAUTIFUL AS A WORK OF ART.
I DIDN'T FEEL...
...LIKE SLEEPING AT ALL.

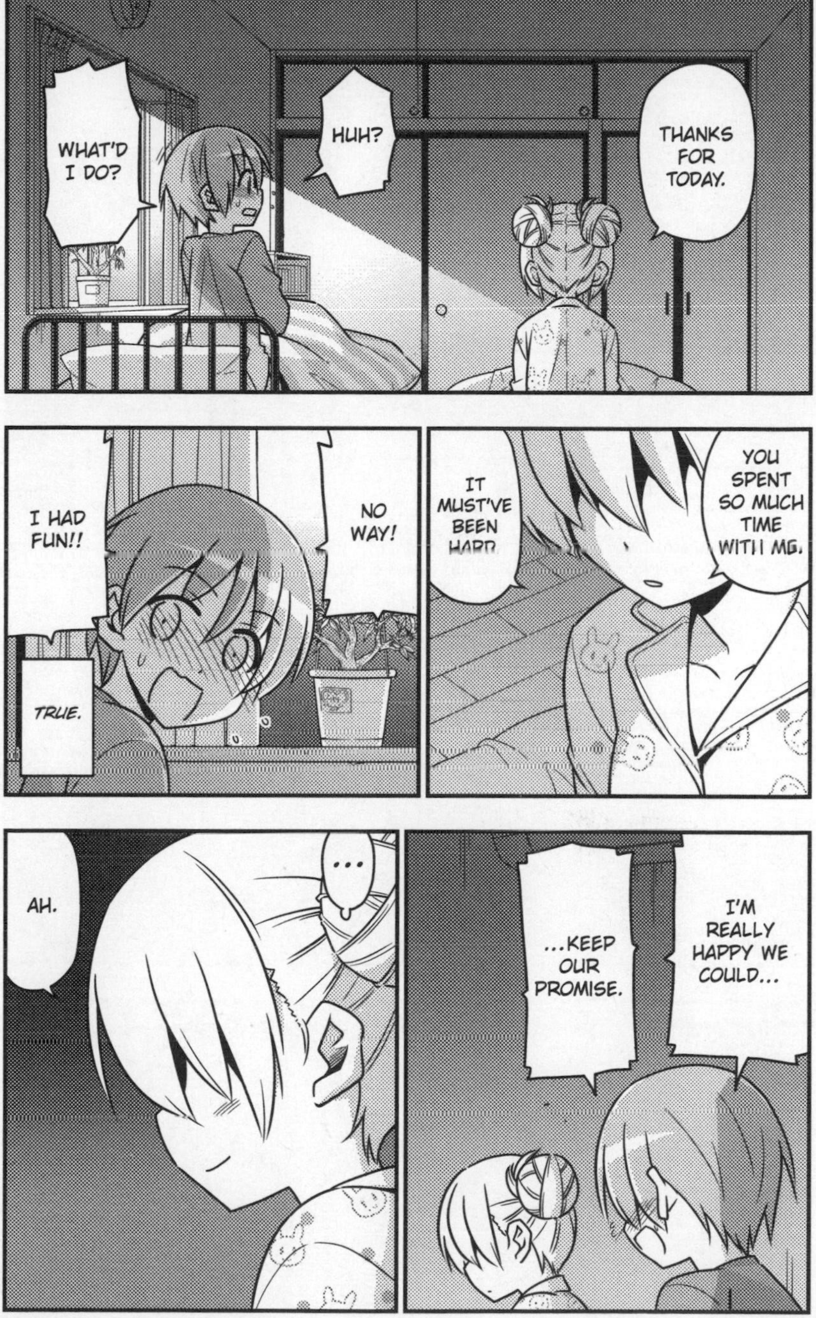
THANKS FOR TODAY.
HUH?
WHAT'D I DO?
YOU SPENT SO MUCH TIME WITH ME.
IT MUST'VE BEEN HARD.
NO WAY!
I HAD FUN!!
TRUE.
I'M REALLY HAPPY WE COULD...
...KEEP OUR PROMISE.
...
AH.

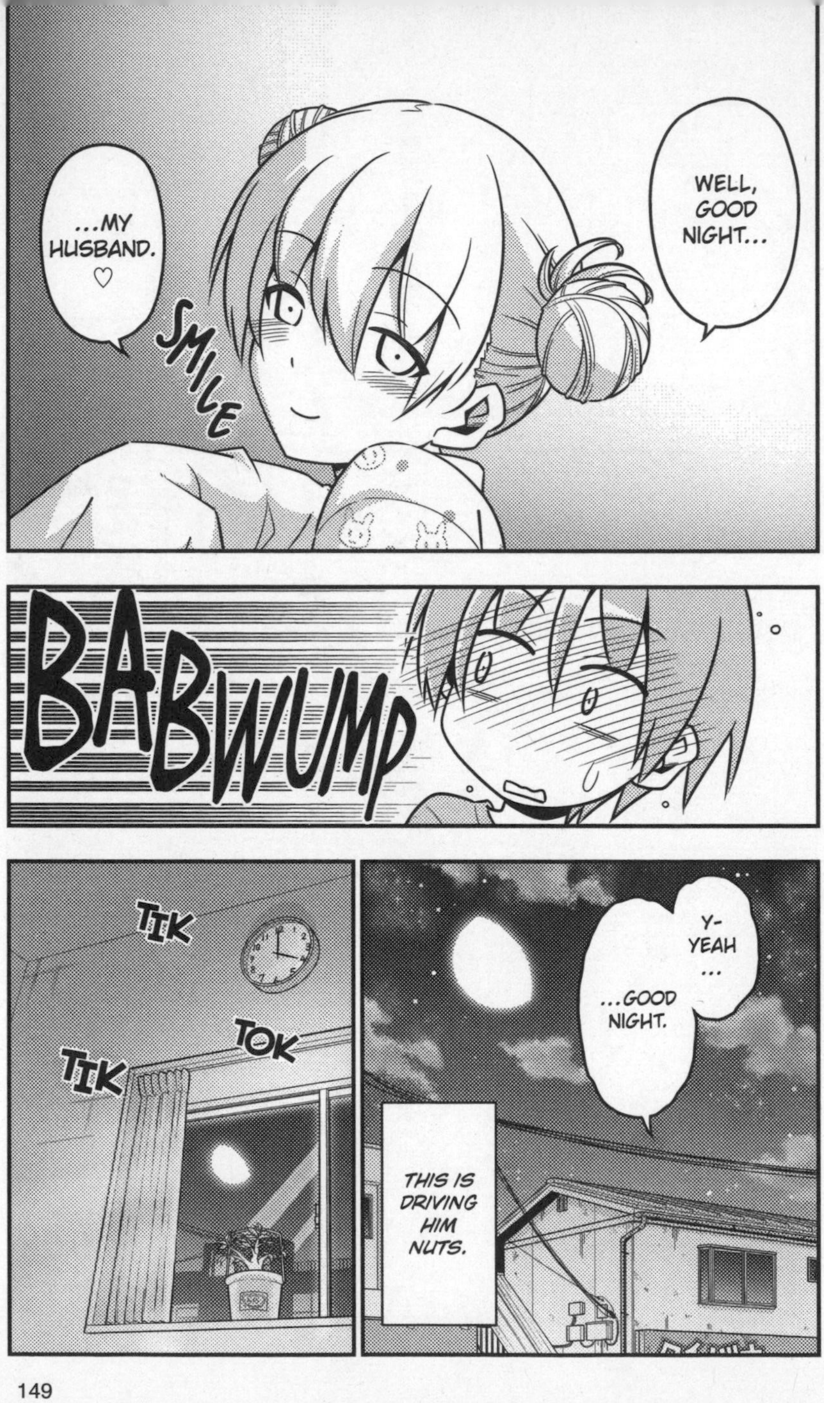
WELL, GOOD NIGHT...
SMILE
...MY HUSBAND. ♡
BABWUMP
Y-YEAH ...
...GOOD NIGHT.
THIS IS DRIVING HIM NUTS.
TIK
TOK
TIK

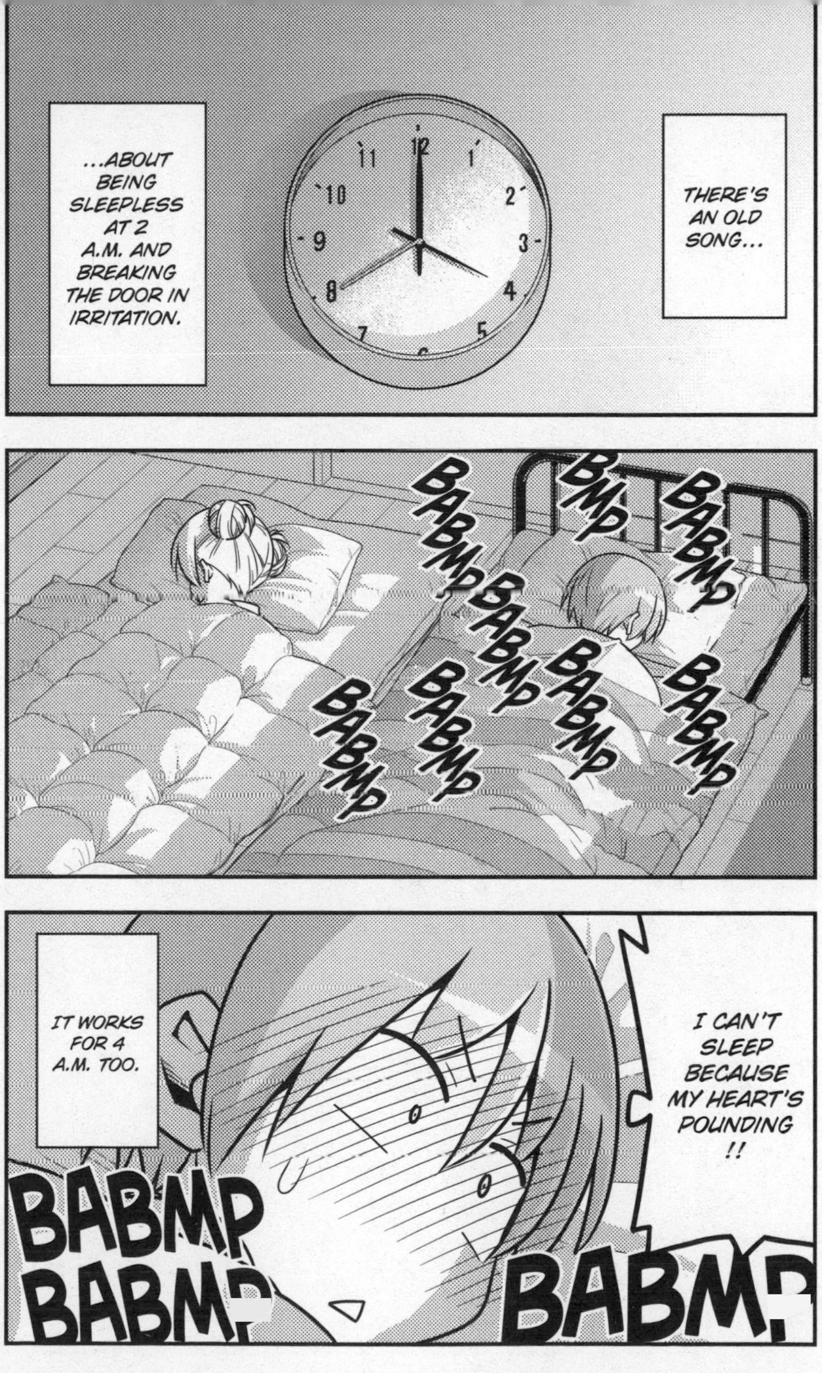
THERE'S AN OLD SONG...
...ABOUT BEING SLEEPLESS AT 2 A.M. AND BREAKING THE DOOR IN IRRITATION.
BABMP
BMP
BABMP
BABMP
BABMP
BABMP
BABMP
BABMP
I CAN'T SLEEP BECAUSE MY HEART'S POUNDING !!
BABMP
IT WORKS FOR 4 A.M. TOO.
BABMP BABMP

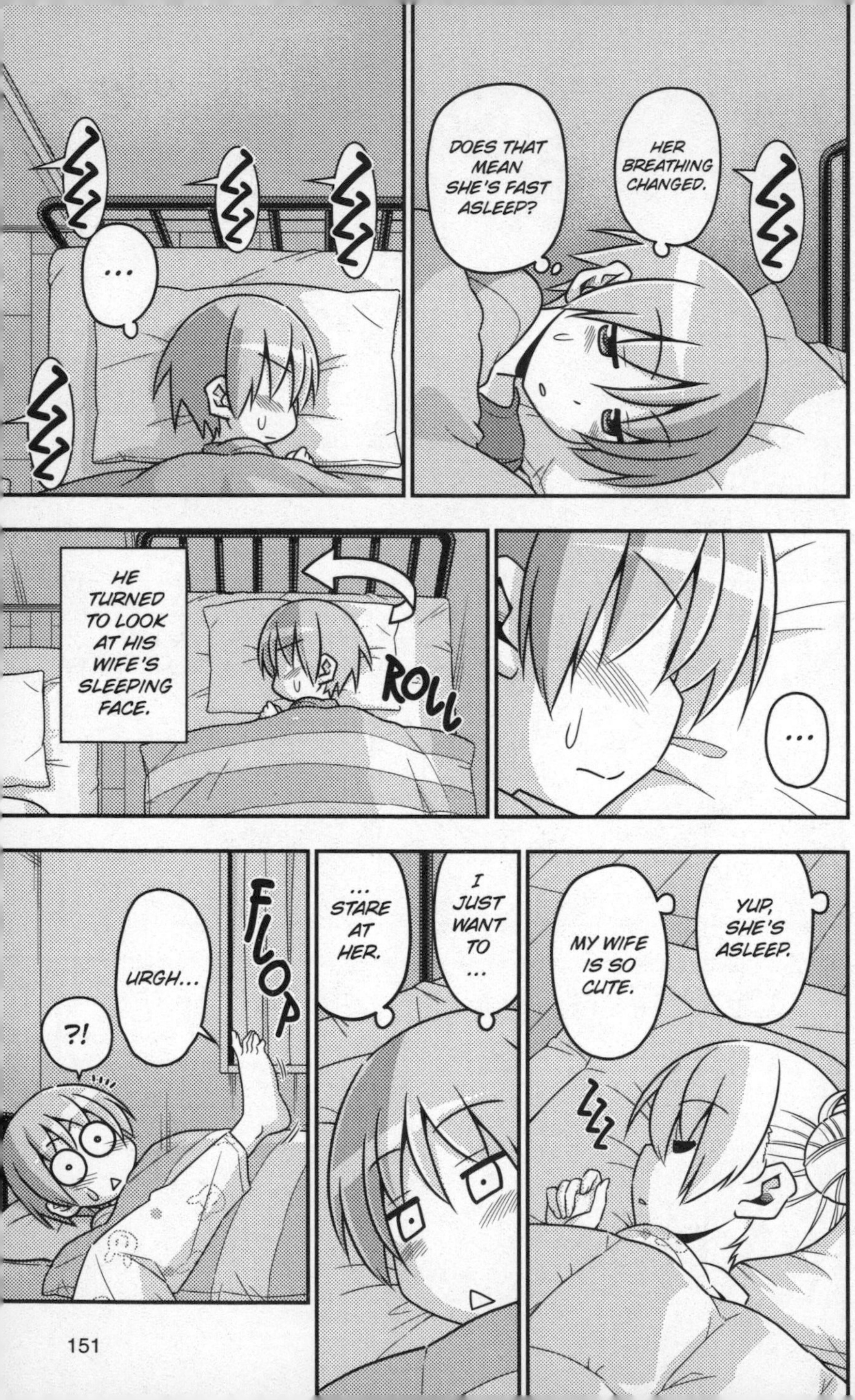
ZZZ
HER BREATHING CHANGED.
DOES THAT MEAN SHE'S FAST ASLEEP?
ZZZ
ZZZ
ZZZ
...
ZZZ
...
HE TURNED TO LOOK AT HIS WIFE'S SLEEPING FACE.
ROLL
YUP, SHE'S ASLEEP.
MY WIFE IS SO CUTE.
ZZZ
I JUST WANT TO ...
... STARE AT HER.
FLOP
URGH...
?!

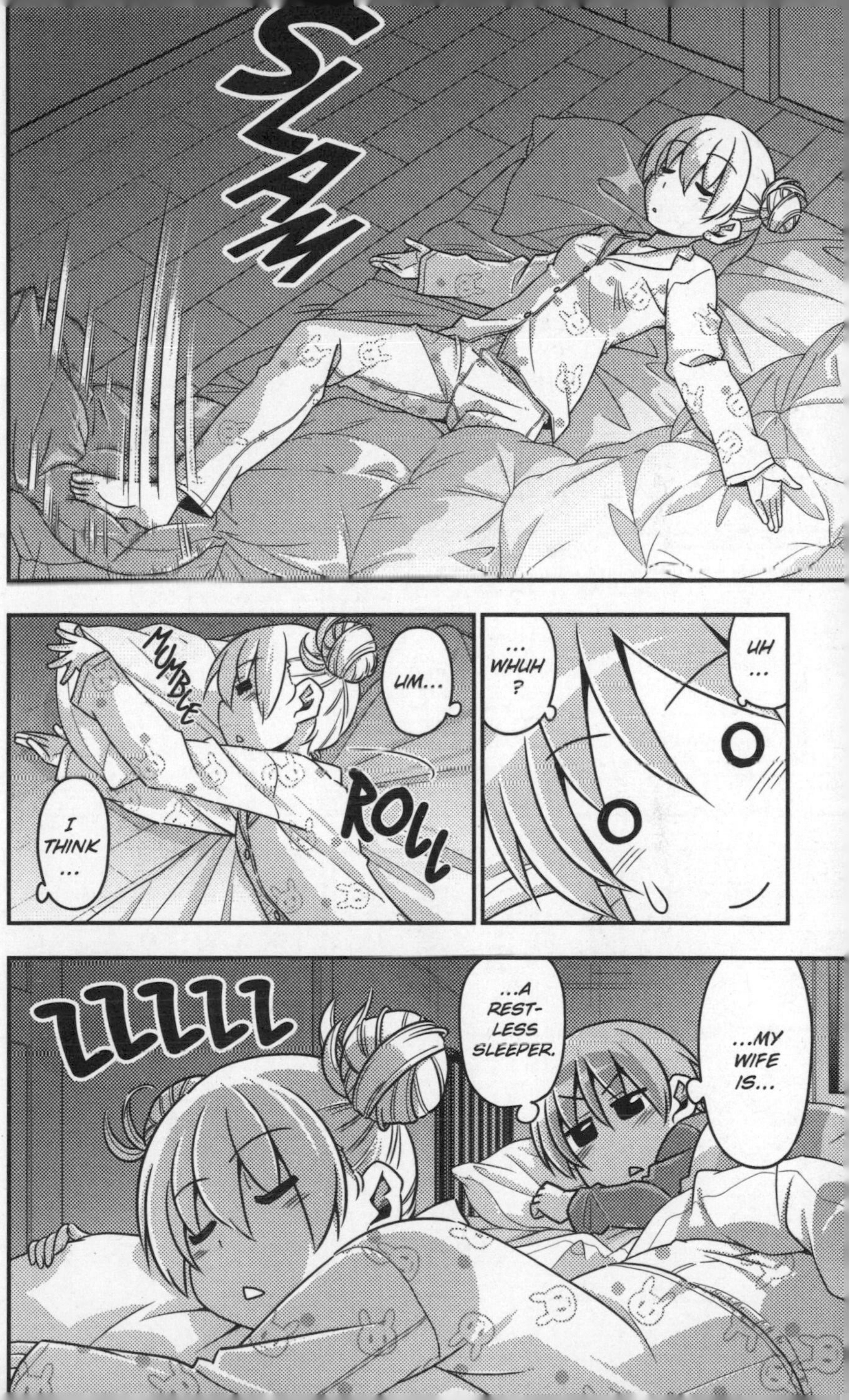
SLAM
UH ...
... WHUH ?
UM...
MUMBLE
ROLL
I THINK ...
...MY WIFE IS...
...A REST-LESS SLEEPER.
ZZZZZZ

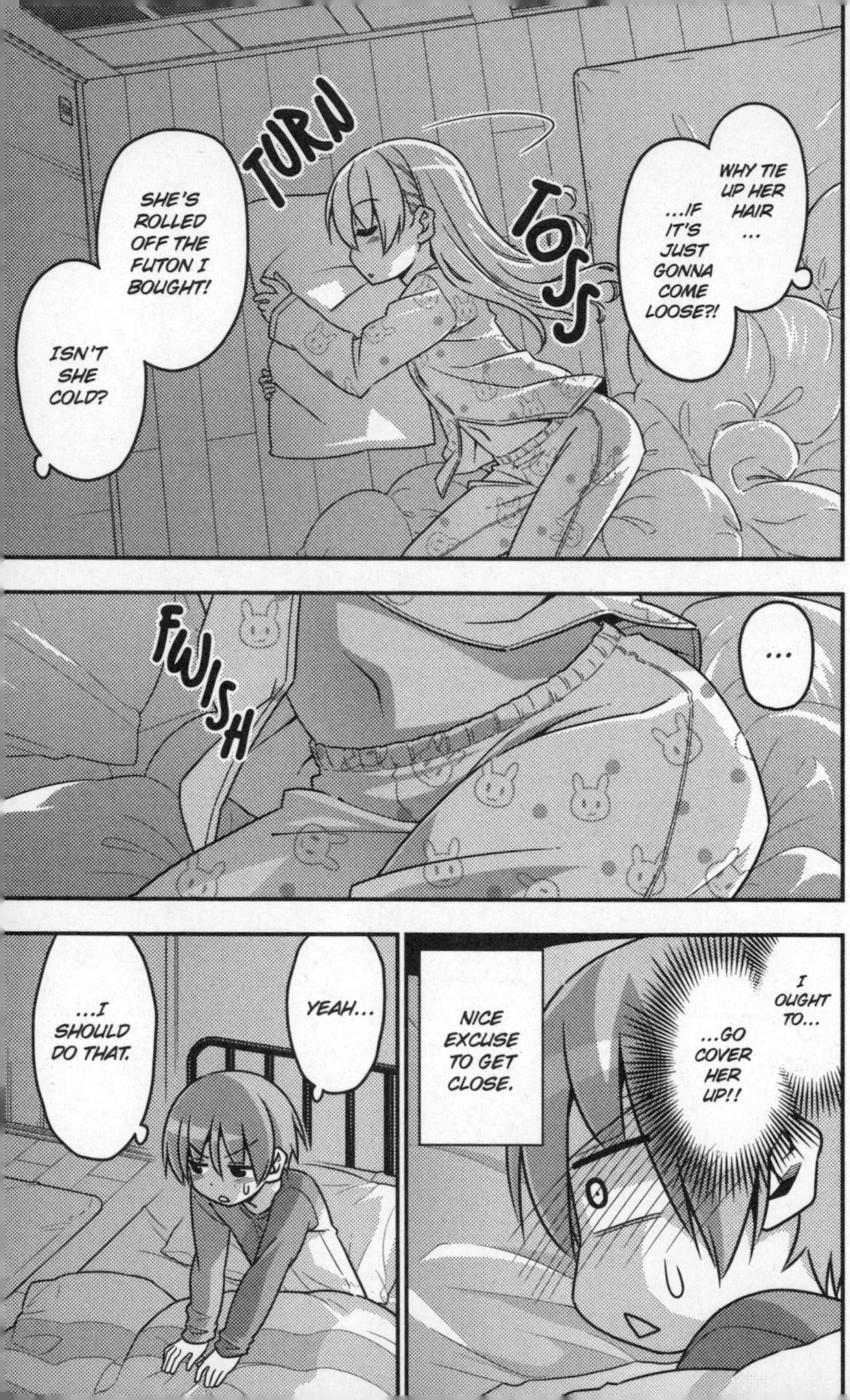
WHY TIE UP HER HAIR ...
...IF IT'S JUST GONNA COME LOOSE?!
TOSS
TURN
SHE'S ROLLED OFF THE FUTON I BOUGHT!
ISN'T SHE COLD?
...
FWISH
I OUGHT TO...
...GO COVER HER UP!!
NICE EXCUSE TO GET CLOSE.
YEAH...
...I SHOULD DO THAT.

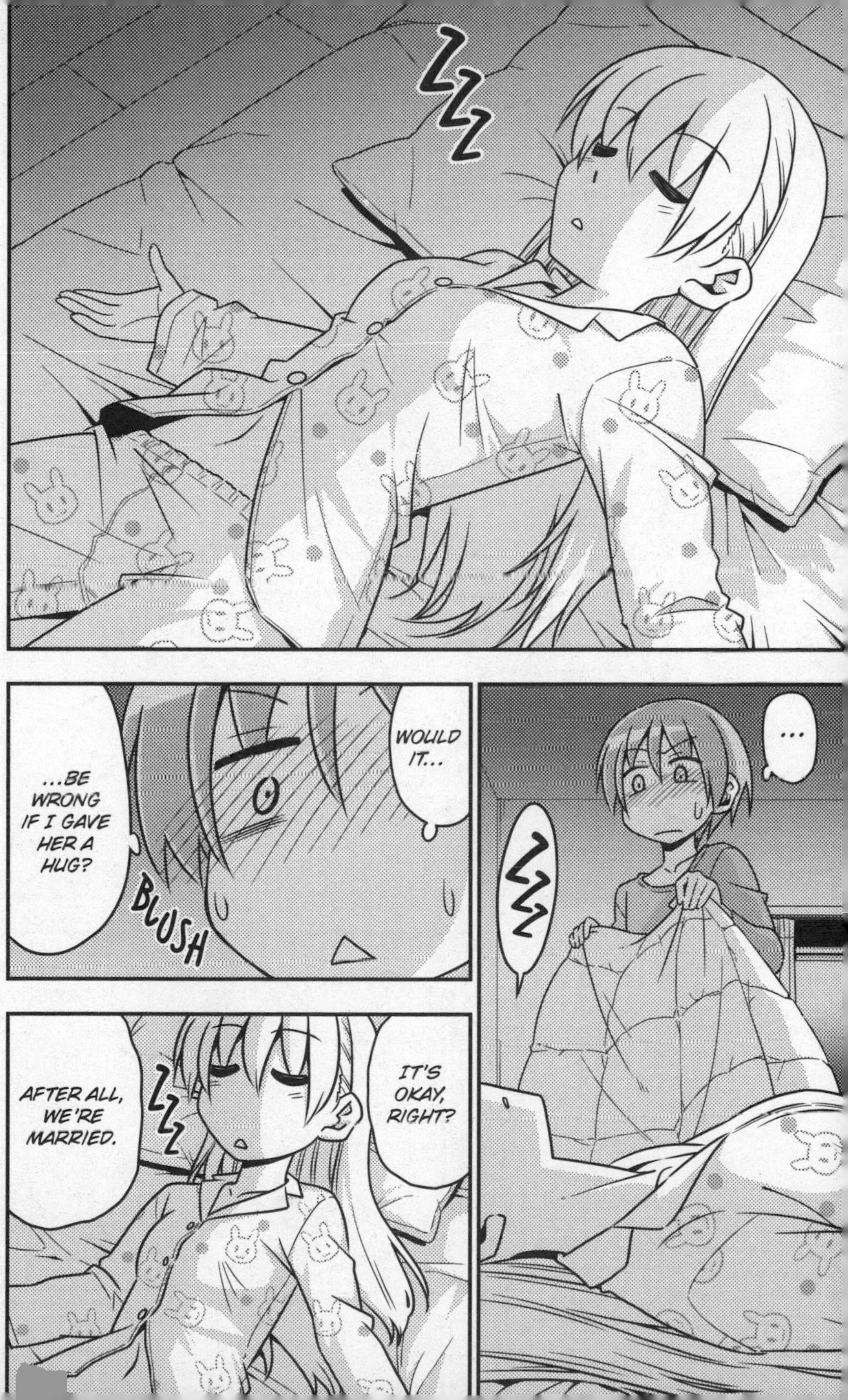
ZZZ
...
ZZZ
WOULD IT...
...BE WRONG IF I GAVE HER A HUG?
BLUSH
IT'S OKAY, RIGHT?
ZZZ
AFTER ALL, WE'RE MARRIED.

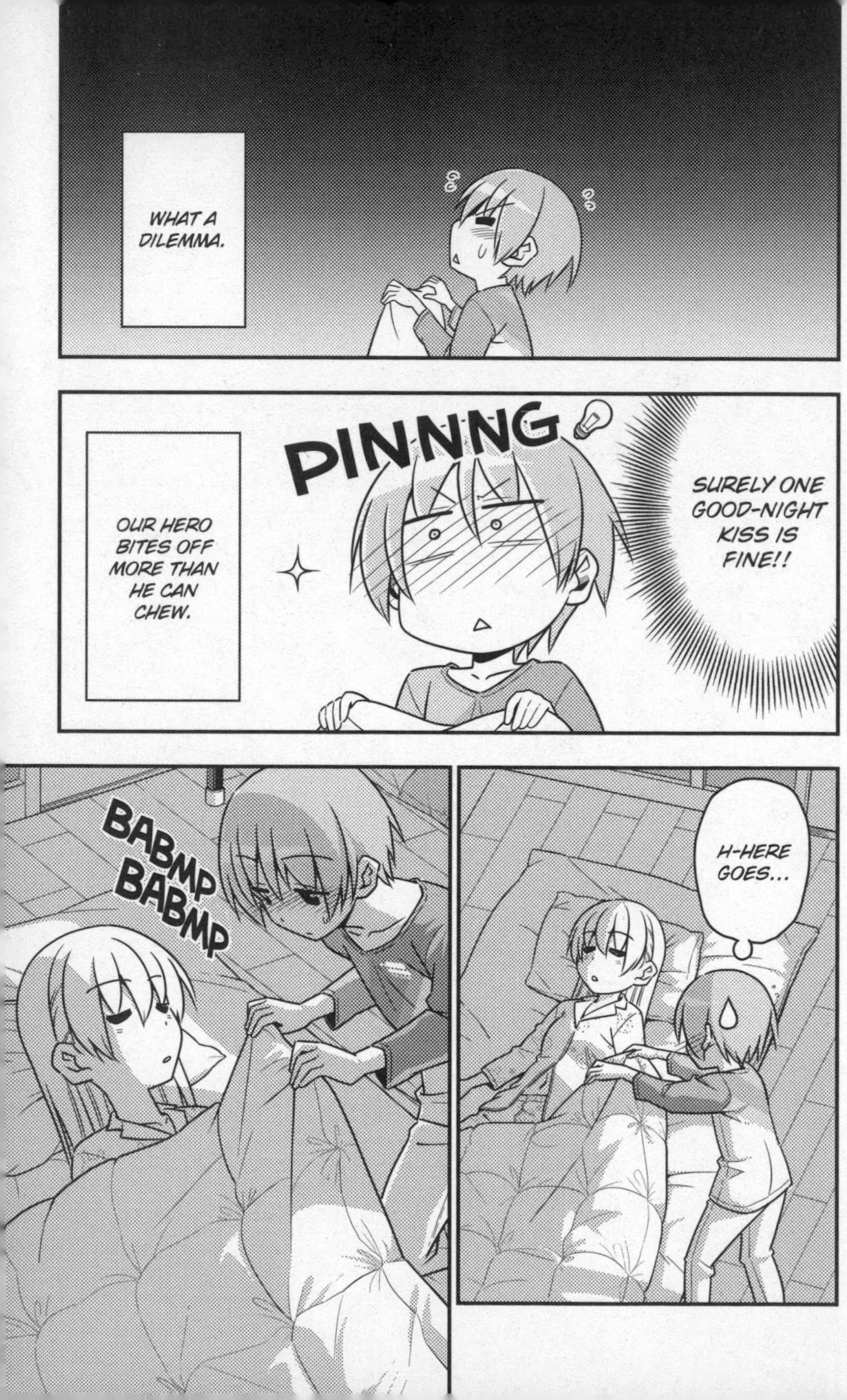
WHAT A DILEMMA.
SURELY ONE GOOD-NIGHT KISS IS FINE!!
PINNNG
OUR HERO BITES OFF MORE THAN HE CAN CHEW.
H-HERE GOES...
BABMP BABMP BABMP

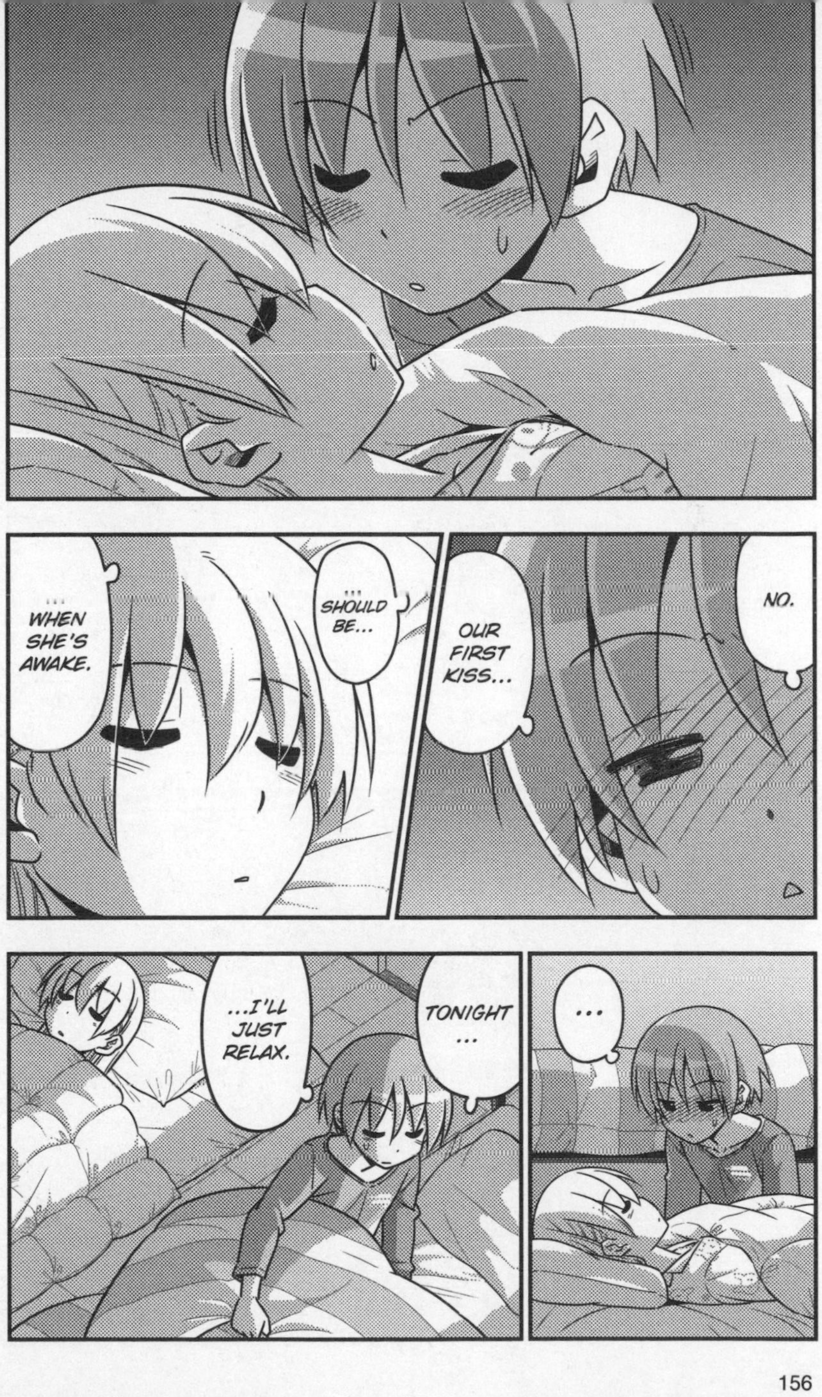
NO.
OUR FIRST KISS...
... SHOULD BE...
... WHEN SHE'S AWAKE.
...
TONIGHT ...
...I'LL JUST RELAX.

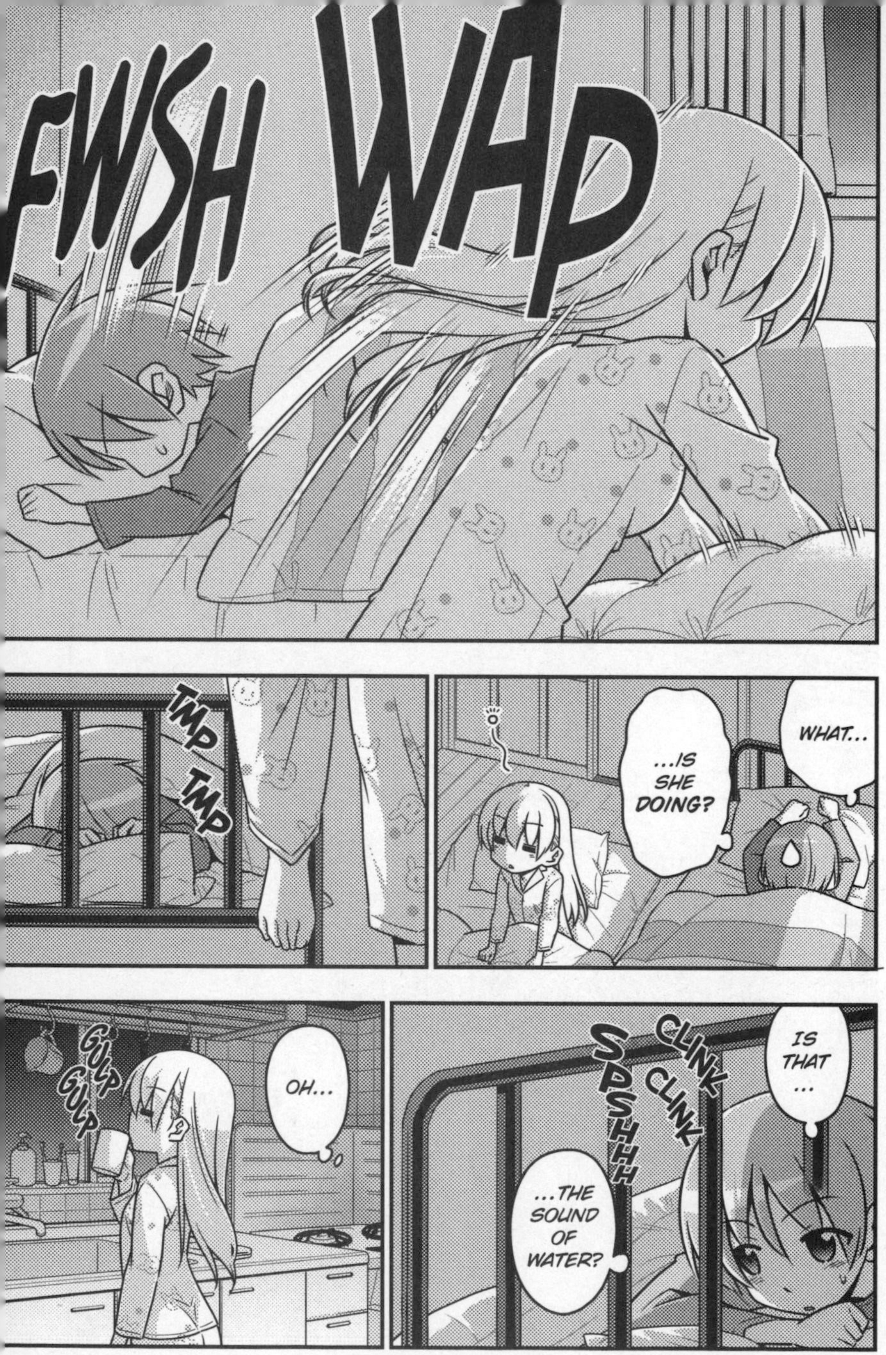
WAP
FWSH
WHAT...
...IS SHE DOING?
TMP TMP
IS THAT ...
CLINK CLINK
SPSHHH
...THE SOUND OF WATER?
OH...
GULP GULP

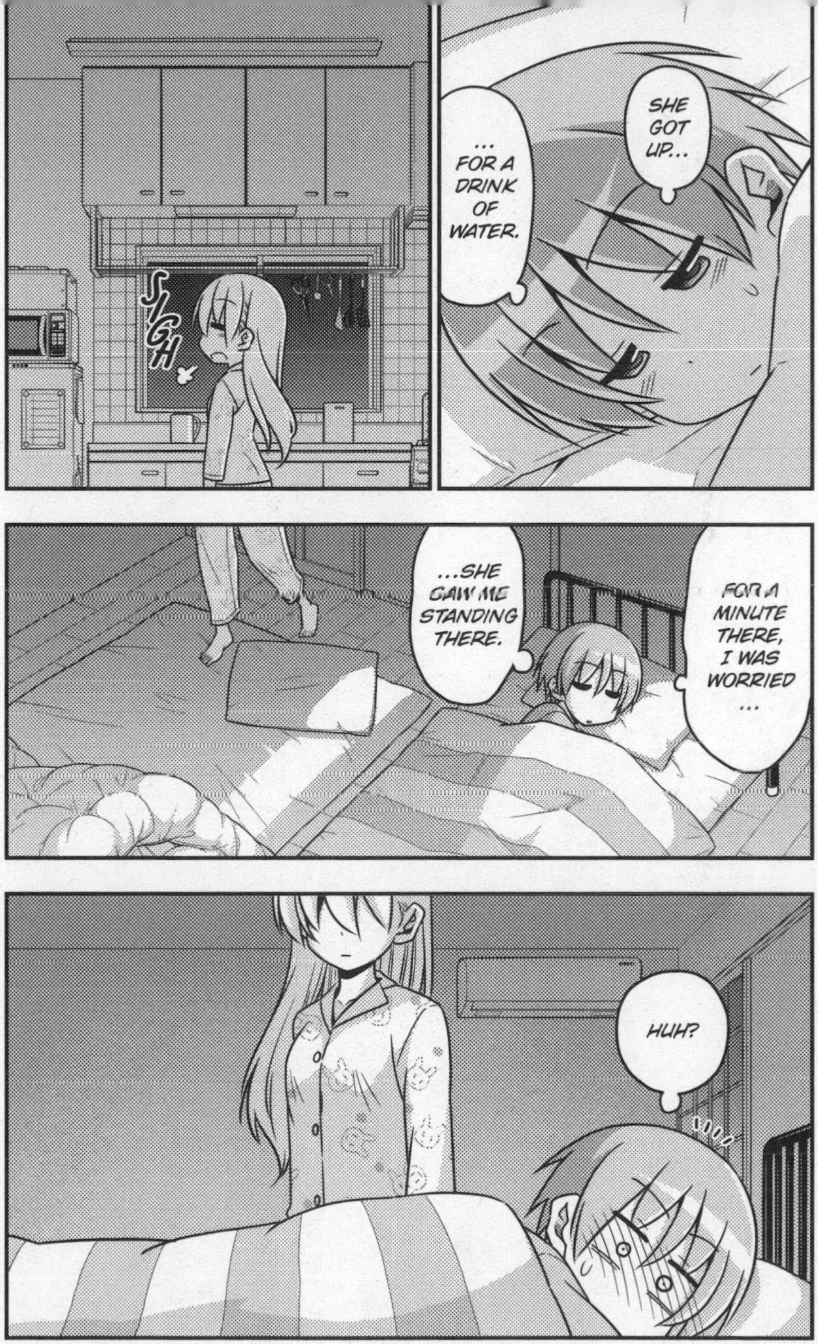
SHE GOT UP...
...FOR A DRINK OF WATER.
SIGH
FOR A MINUTE THERE, I WAS WORRIED ...
...SHE SAW ME STANDING THERE.
HUH?

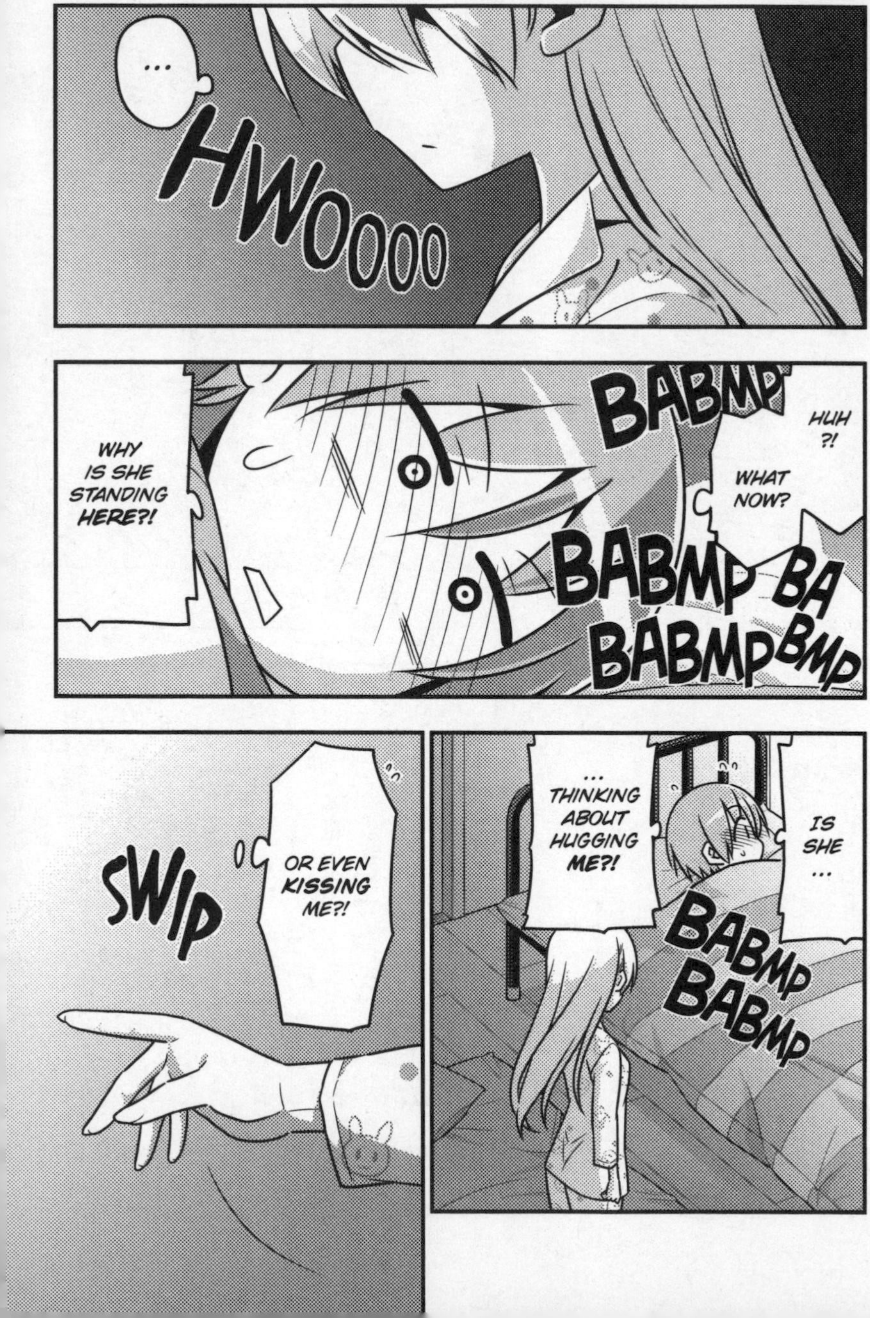
...
HWOOOO
BABMP
HUH ?!
WHAT NOW?
BABMP BA
BABMP BMP
WHY IS SHE STANDING HERE?!
IS SHE ...
... THINKING ABOUT HUGGING ME?!
BABMP BABMP
OR EVEN KISSING ME?!
SWIP

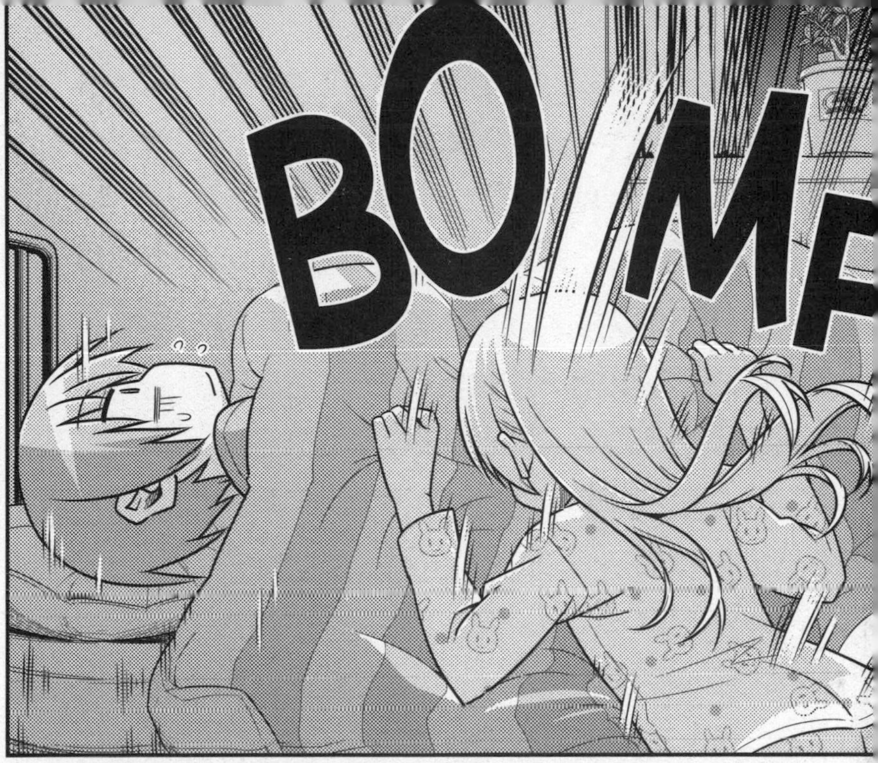
BOM

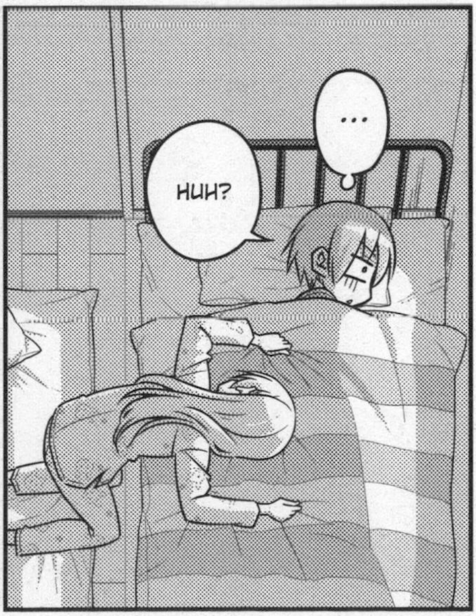
HUH?
...

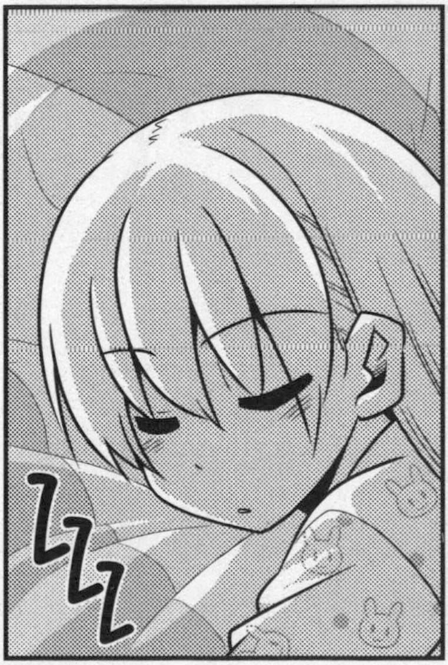
ZZZ

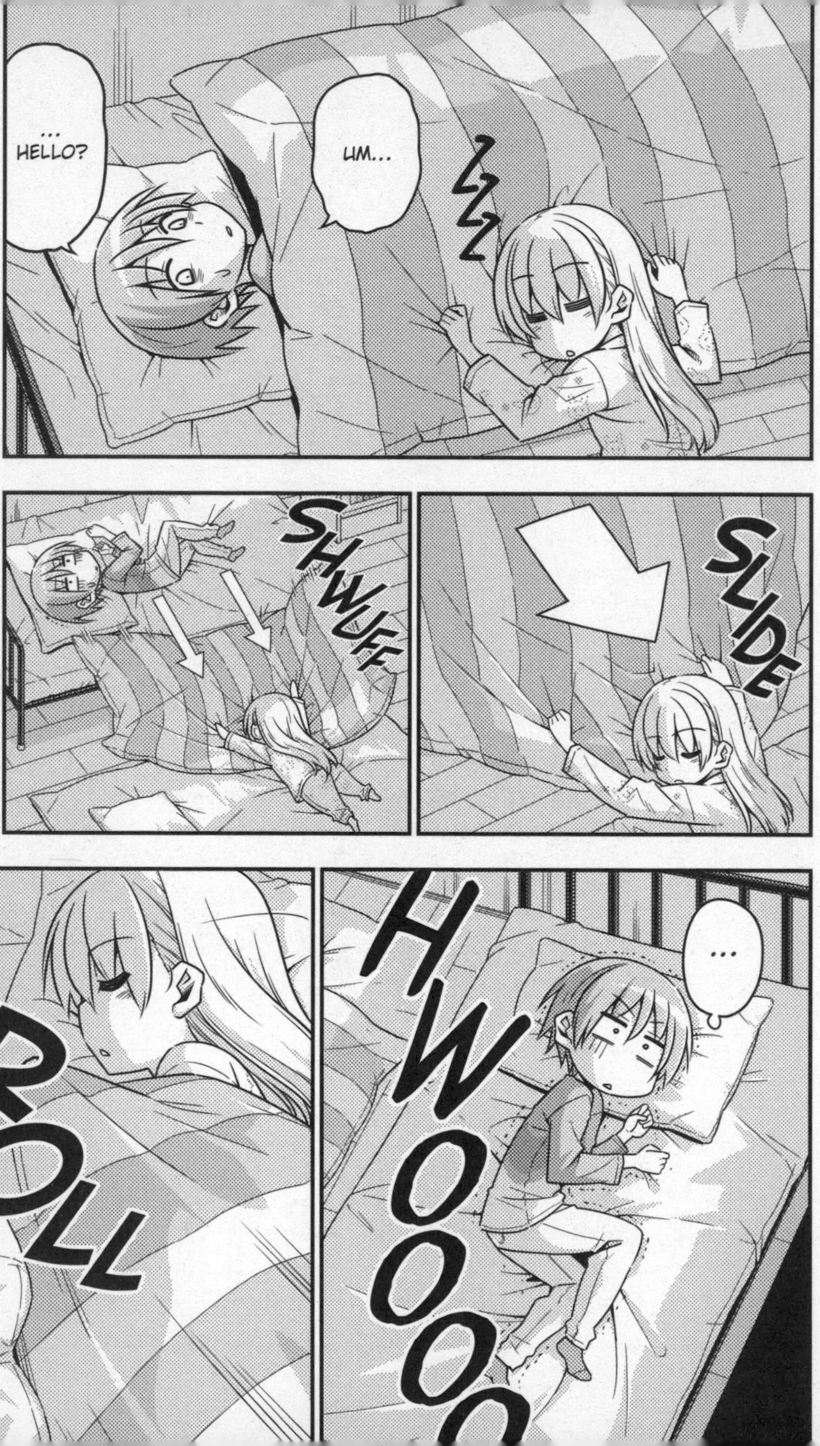
ZZZ
UM...
... HELLO?
SLIDE
SHWUFF
...
HWOOO
ROLL

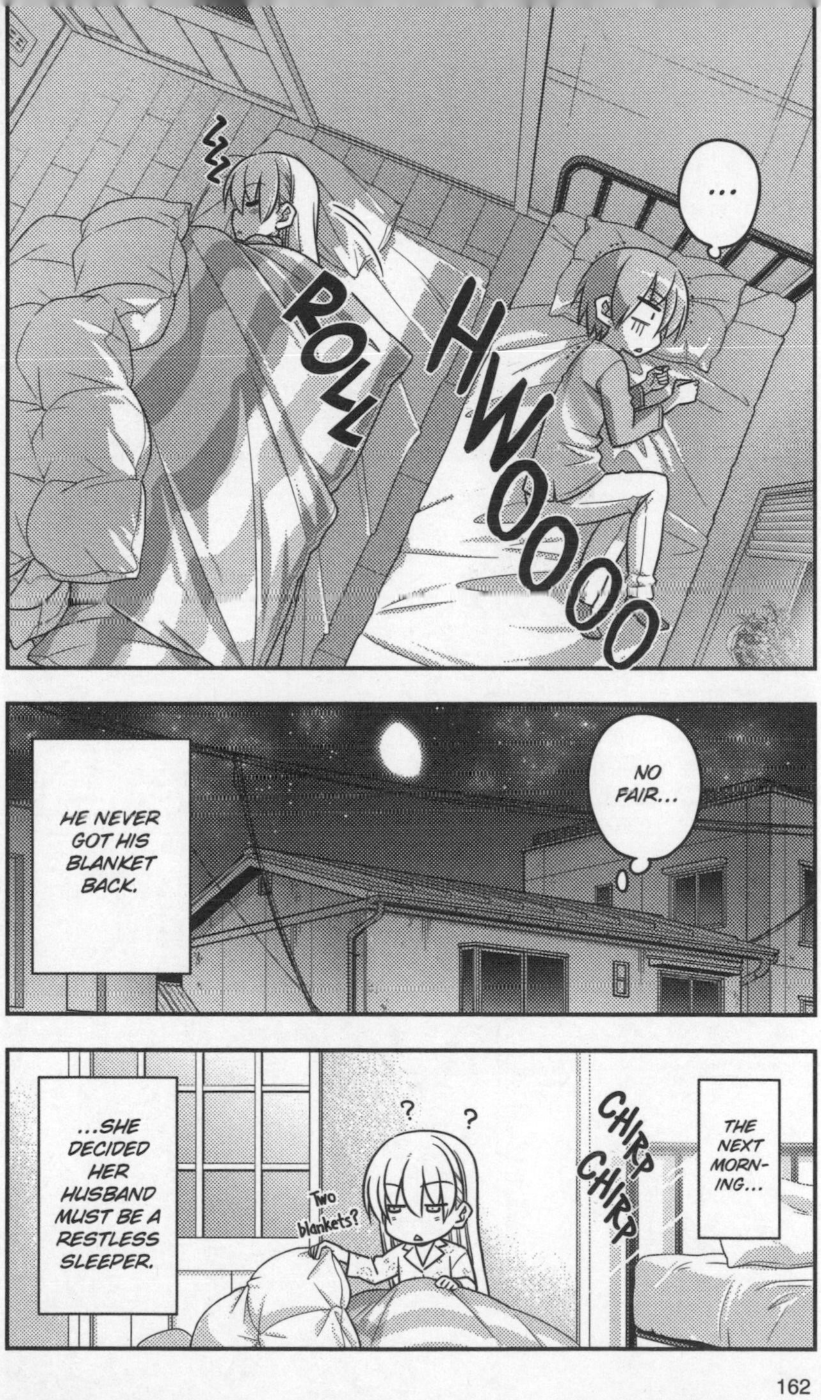
…
HWOOOO
ROLL
ZZZ
NO FAIR…
HE NEVER GOT HIS BLANKET BACK.
THE NEXT MORN-ING…
CHIRP CHIRP
? ?
Two blankets?
…SHE DECIDED HER HUSBAND MUST BE A RESTLESS SLEEPER.

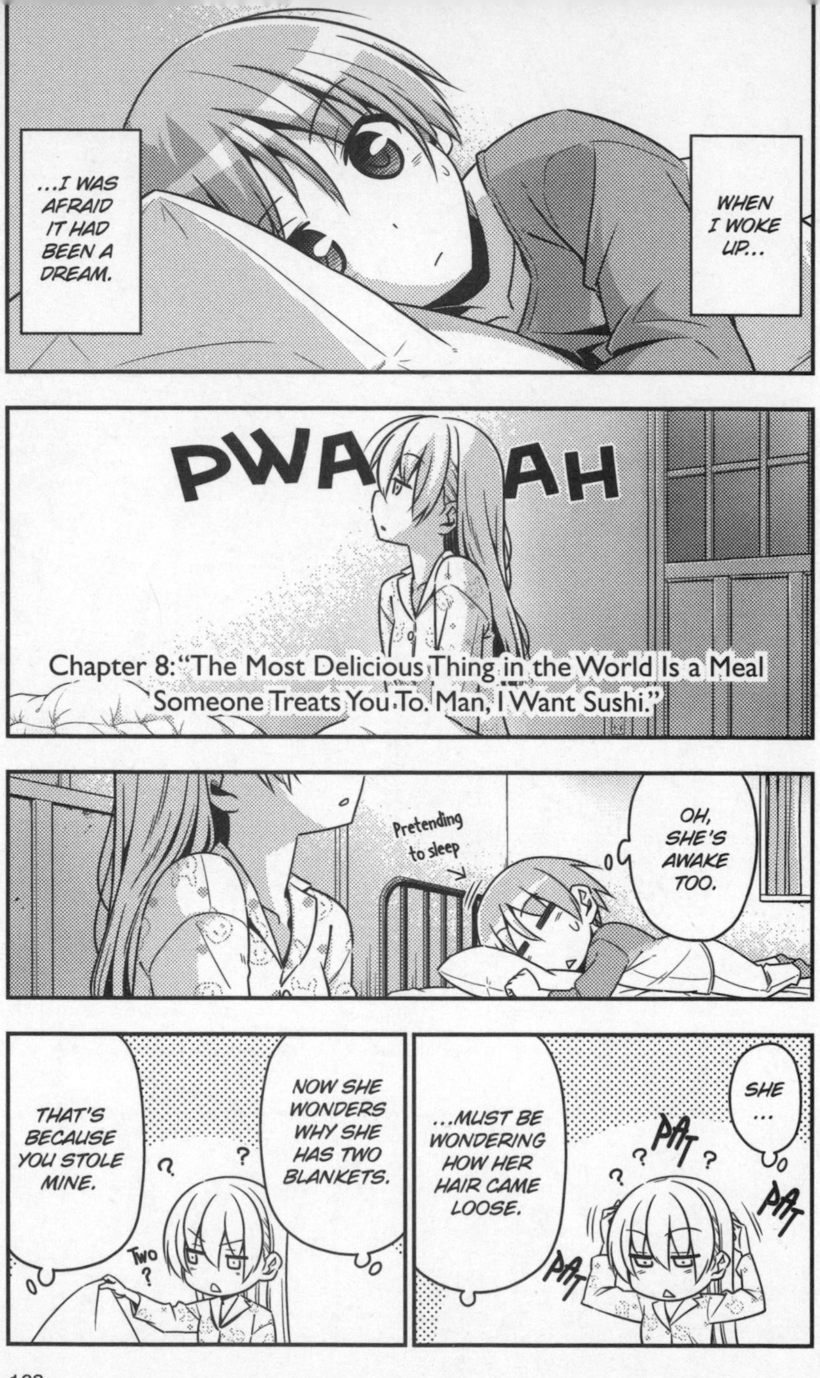
WHEN I WOKE UP...
...I WAS AFRAID IT HAD BEEN A DREAM.
PWAAAH
Chapter 8: "The Most Delicious Thing in the World Is a Meal Someone Treats You To. Man, I Want Sushi."
OH, SHE'S AWAKE TOO.
Pretending to sleep
SHE...
PAT PAT PAT
...MUST BE WONDERING HOW HER HAIR CAME LOOSE.
NOW SHE WONDERS WHY SHE HAS TWO BLANKETS.
Two?
THAT'S BECAUSE YOU STOLE MINE.

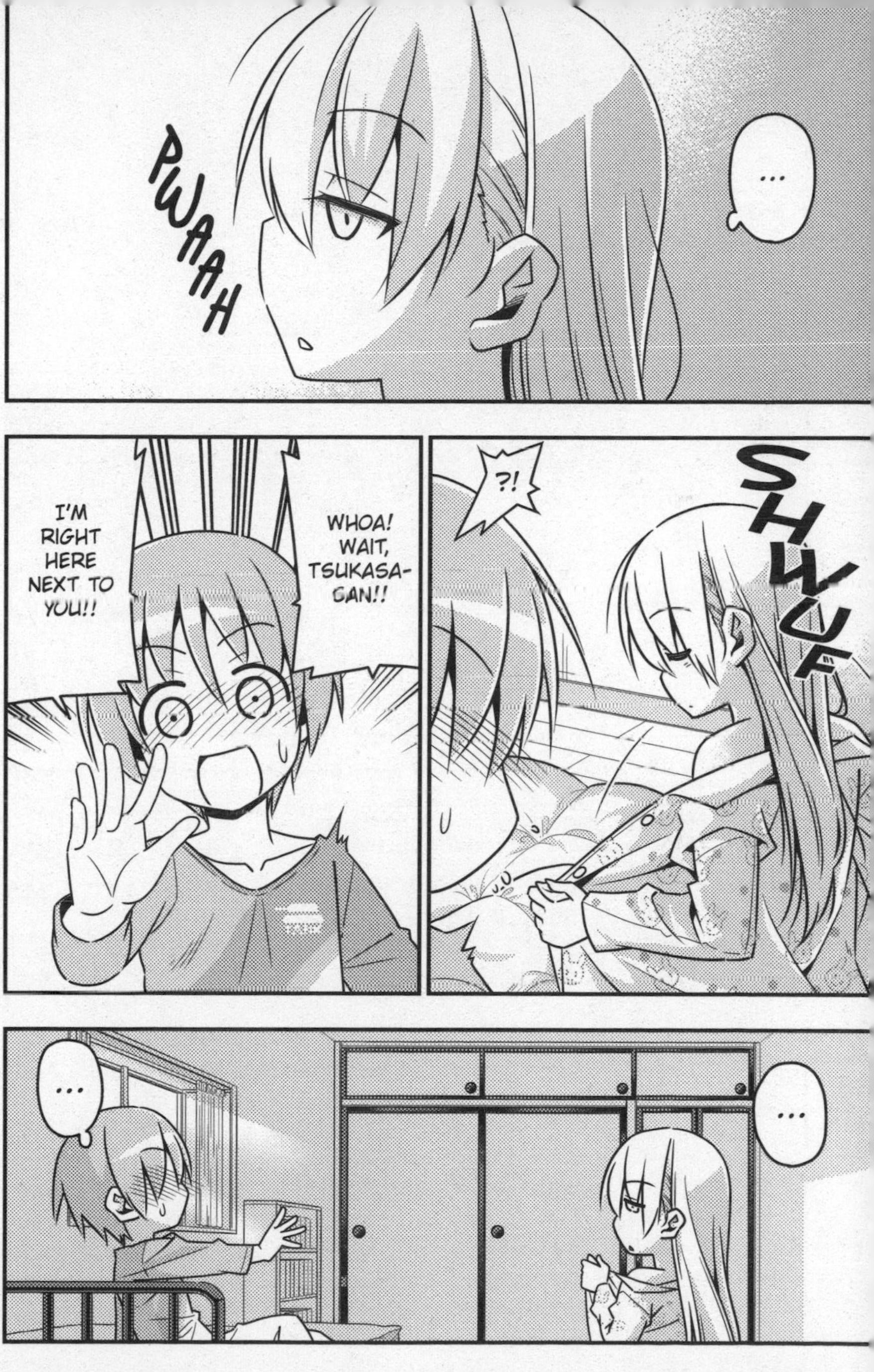
...
PWAAH
SHWUF
?!
WHOA! WAIT, TSUKASA-SAN!!
I'M RIGHT HERE NEXT TO YOU!!
...
...

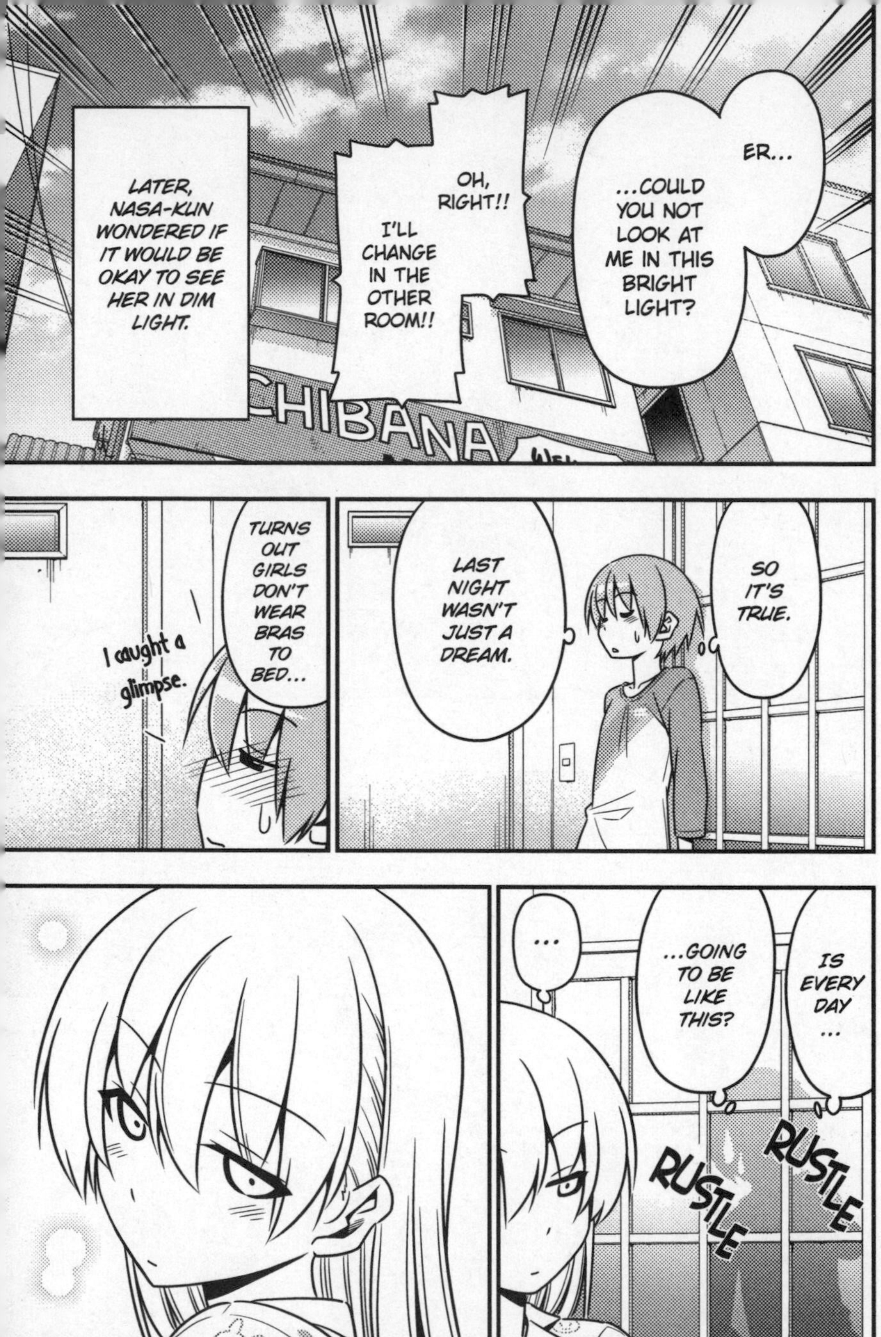
ER... ...COULD YOU NOT LOOK AT ME IN THIS BRIGHT LIGHT?
OH, RIGHT!! I'LL CHANGE IN THE OTHER ROOM!!
LATER, NASA-KUN WONDERED IF IT WOULD BE OKAY TO SEE HER IN DIM LIGHT.
CHIBANA
SO IT'S TRUE.
LAST NIGHT WASN'T JUST A DREAM.
TURNS OUT GIRLS DON'T WEAR BRAS TO BED...
I caught a glimpse.
IS EVERY DAY...
...GOING TO BE LIKE THIS?
...
RUSTLE
RUSTLE

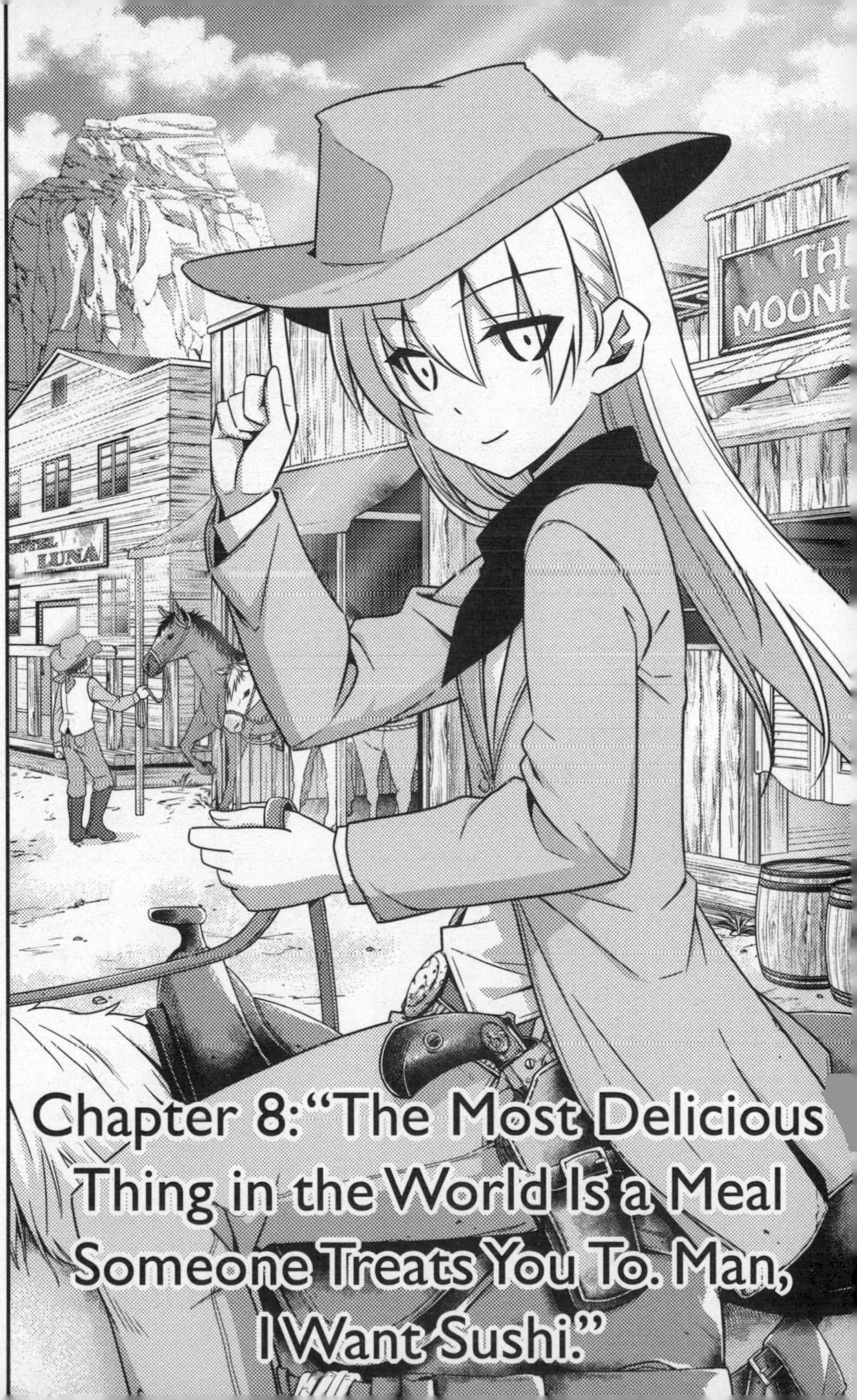
LUNA

Chapter 8: "The Most Delicious Thing in the World Is a Meal Someone Treats You To. Man, I Want Sushi."

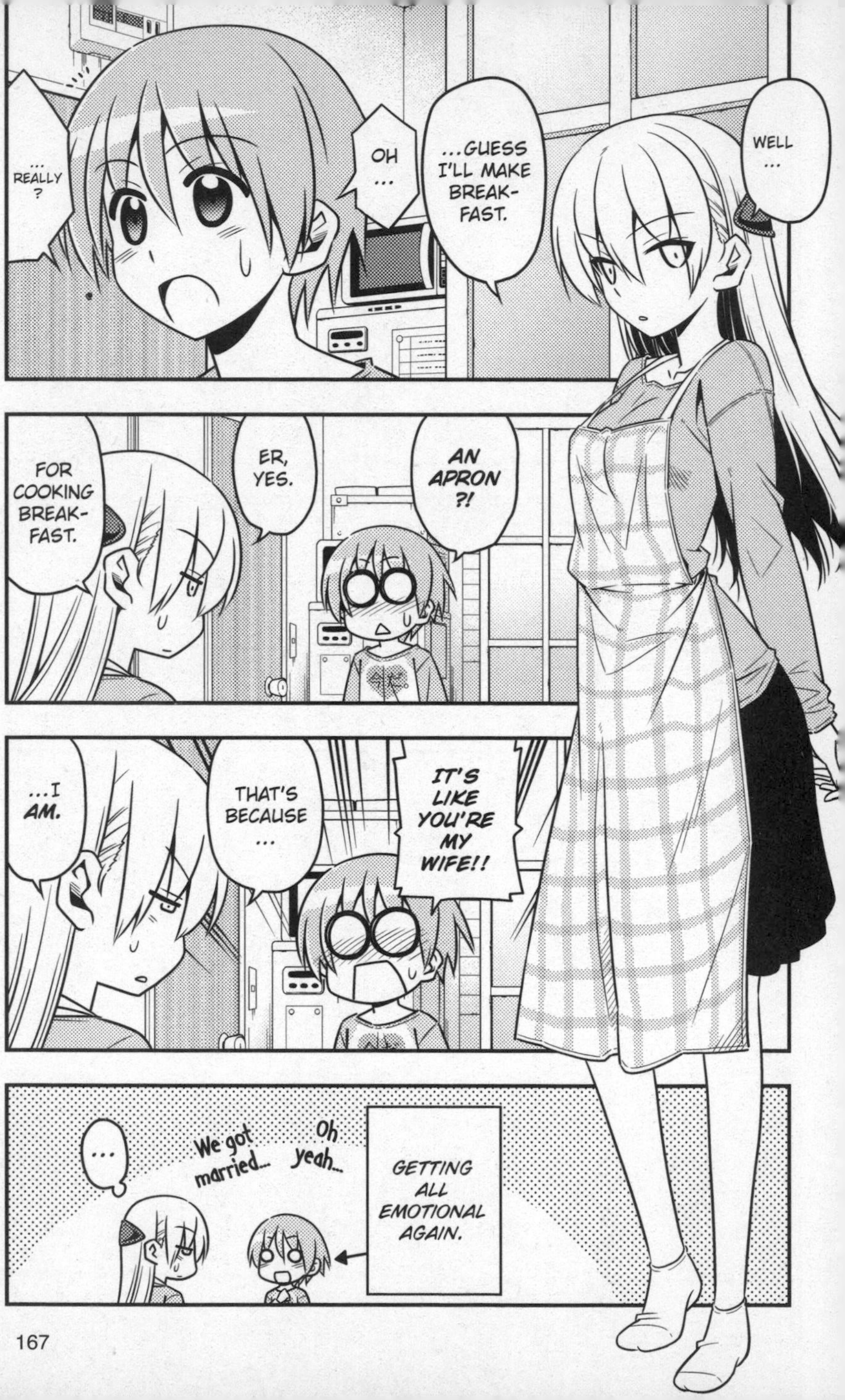
WELL ...
...GUESS I'LL MAKE BREAK-FAST.
OH ...
... REALLY ?
AN APRON ?!
ER, YES.
FOR COOKING BREAK-FAST.
IT'S LIKE YOU'RE MY WIFE!!
THAT'S BECAUSE ...
...I AM.
GETTING ALL EMOTIONAL AGAIN.
Oh yeah...
We got married...
...

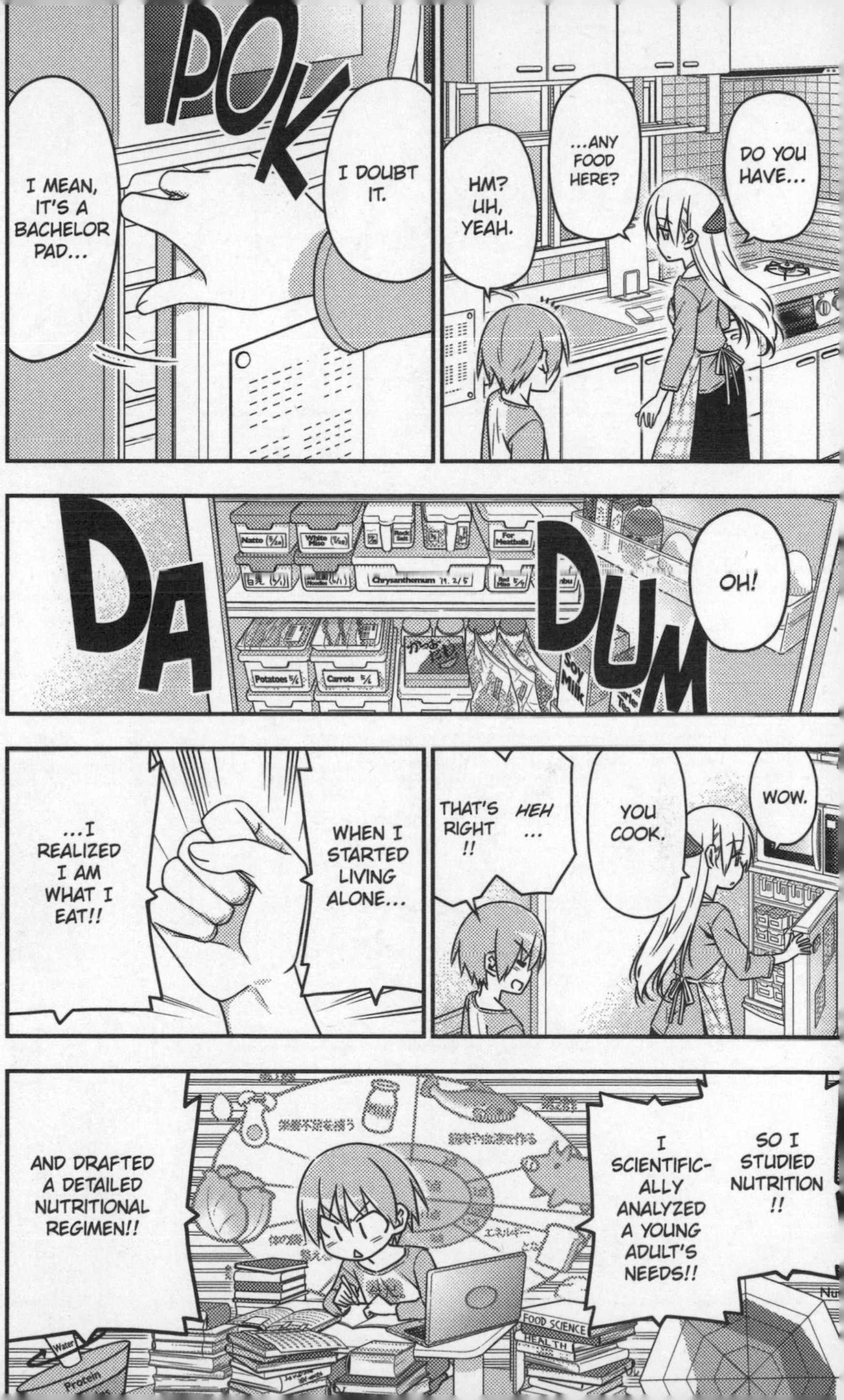
DO YOU HAVE...
...ANY FOOD HERE?
HM? UH, YEAH.
POK
I DOUBT IT.
I MEAN, IT'S A BACHELOR PAD...
OH!
DA
DUM
Natto
White Miso
Rock Salt
For Meatballs
Chrysanthemum '19. 2/5
Red Miso
Potatoes
Carrots
Soy Milk
WOW.
YOU COOK.
HEH...
THAT'S RIGHT!!
WHEN I STARTED LIVING ALONE...
...I REALIZED I AM WHAT I EAT!!
SO I STUDIED NUTRITION!!
I SCIENTIFIC-ALLY ANALYZED A YOUNG ADULT'S NEEDS!!
AND DRAFTED A DETAILED NUTRITIONAL REGIMEN!!
FOOD SCIENCE
HEALTH
Water
Protein

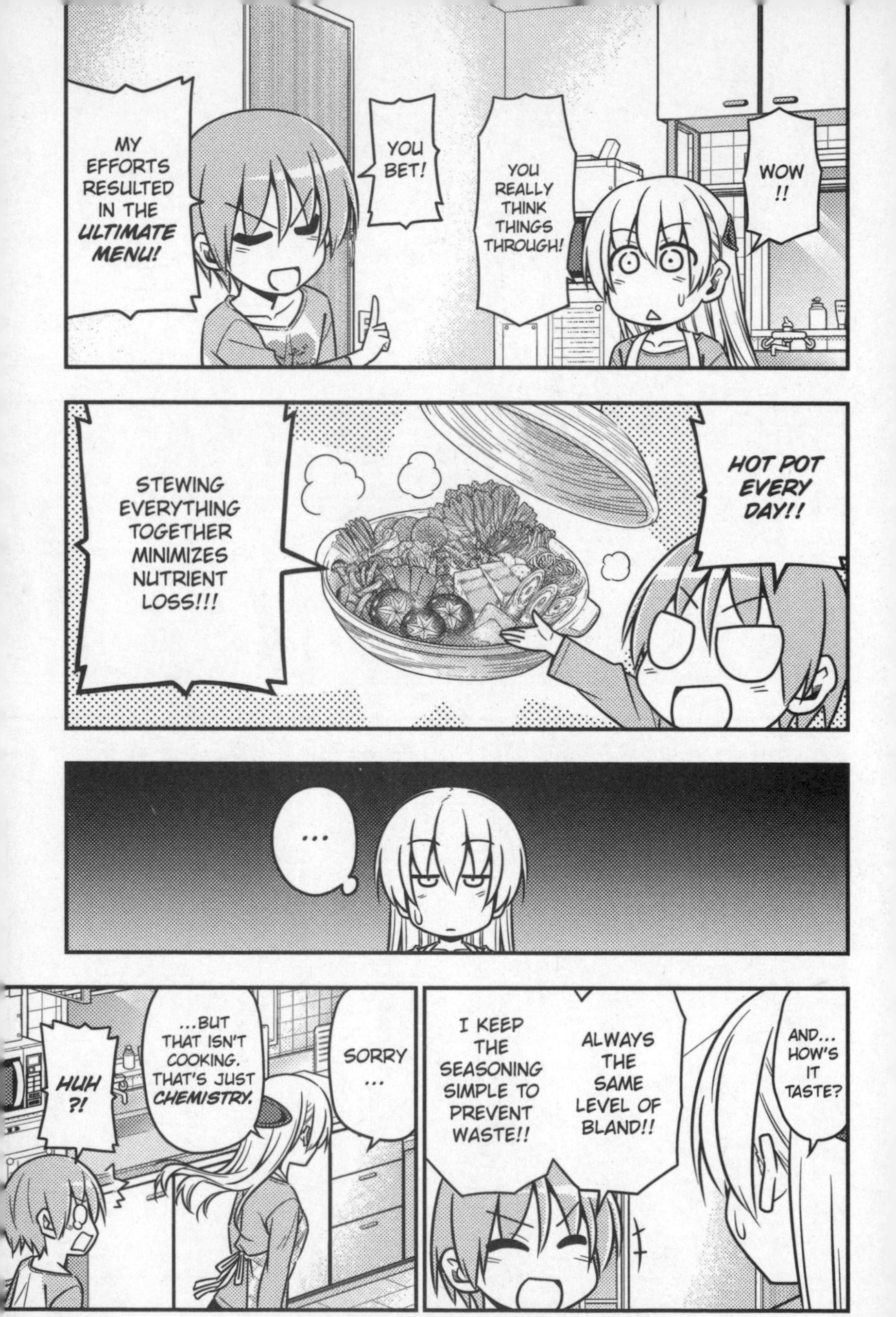
WOW!!
YOU REALLY THINK THINGS THROUGH!
YOU BET!
MY EFFORTS RESULTED IN THE *ULTIMATE MENU!*
HOT POT EVERY DAY!!
STEWING EVERYTHING TOGETHER MINIMIZES NUTRIENT LOSS!!!
...
AND... HOW'S IT TASTE?
ALWAYS THE SAME LEVEL OF BLAND!!
I KEEP THE SEASONING SIMPLE TO PREVENT WASTE!!
SORRY...
...BUT THAT ISN'T COOKING. THAT'S JUST *CHEMISTRY.*
HUH?!

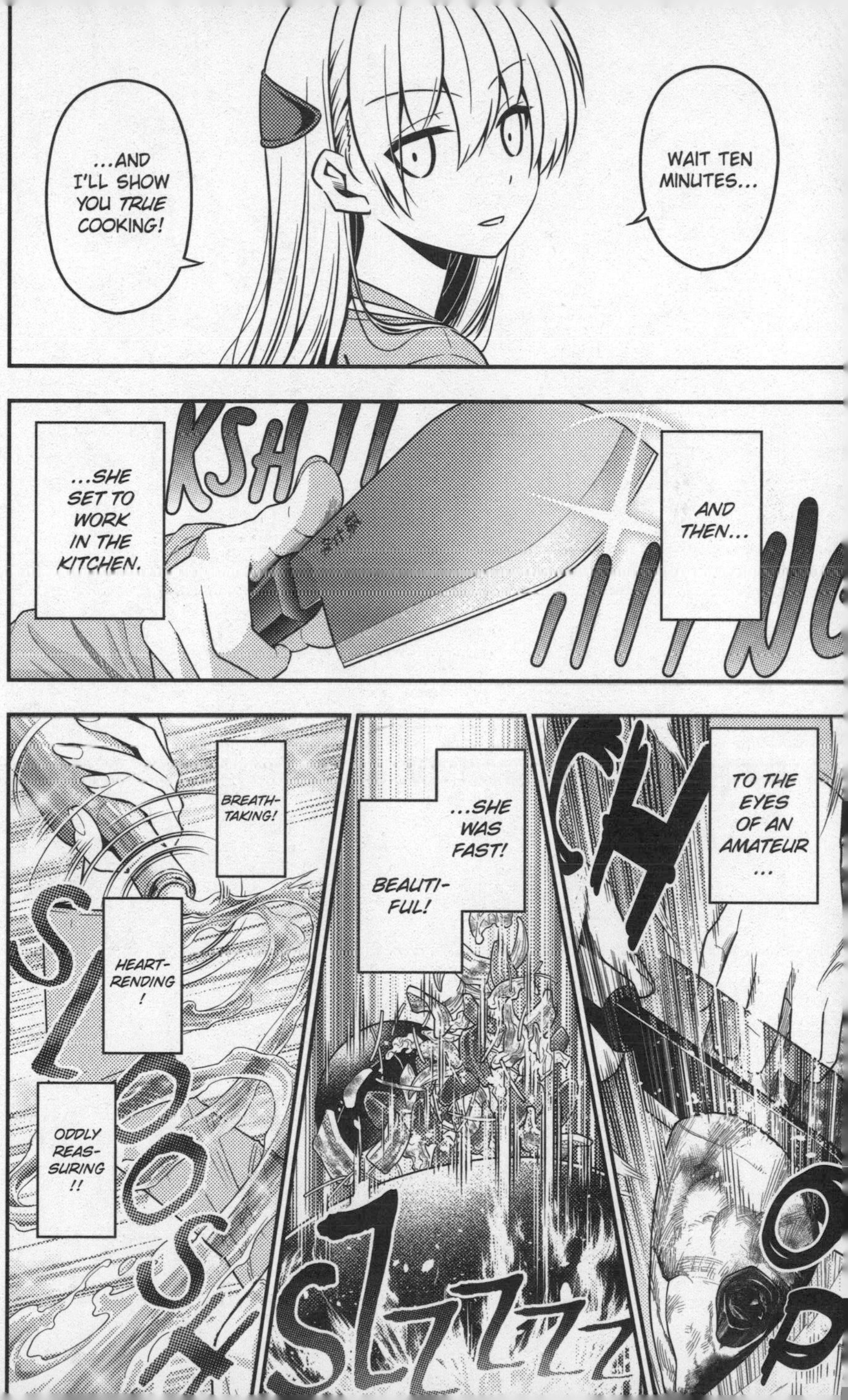
WAIT TEN MINUTES...
...AND I'LL SHOW YOU *TRUE* COOKING!
AND THEN...
...SHE SET TO WORK IN THE KITCHEN.
TO THE EYES OF AN AMATEUR ...
CHOP
...SHE WAS FAST!
BEAUTI-FUL!
SIZZZZ
BREATH-TAKING!
HEART-RENDING!
ODDLY REAS-SURING!!
SLOOOSH

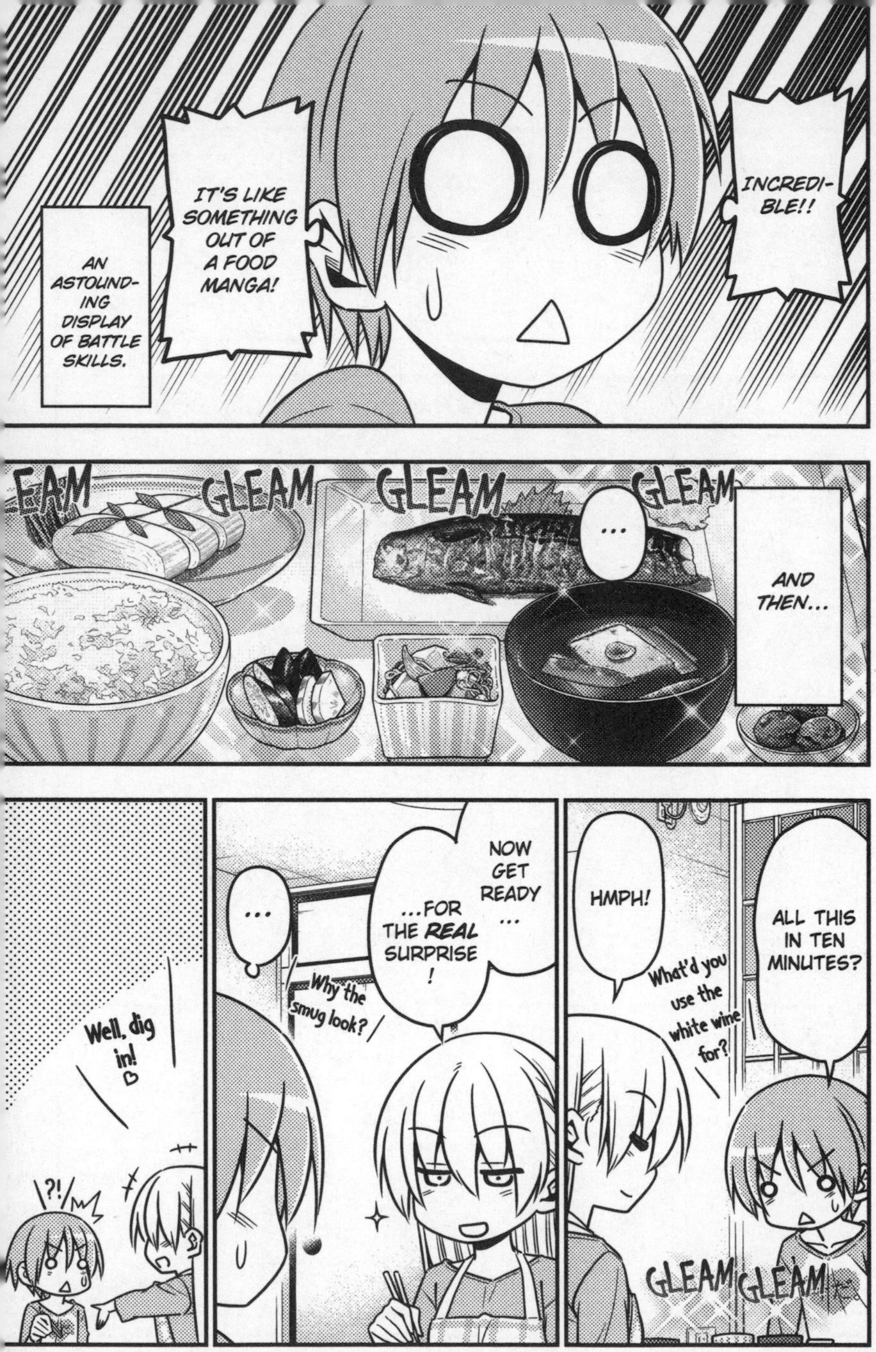

INCREDI-BLE!!
IT'S LIKE SOMETHING OUT OF A FOOD MANGA!
AN ASTOUNDING DISPLAY OF BATTLE SKILLS.
AND THEN...
GLEAM
...
GLEAM
GLEAM
EAM
ALL THIS IN TEN MINUTES?
HMPH!
What'd you use the white wine for?
GLEAM GLEAM
NOW GET READY ...
...FOR THE REAL SURPRISE!
Why the smug look?
...
Well, dig in! ♡
\?!/

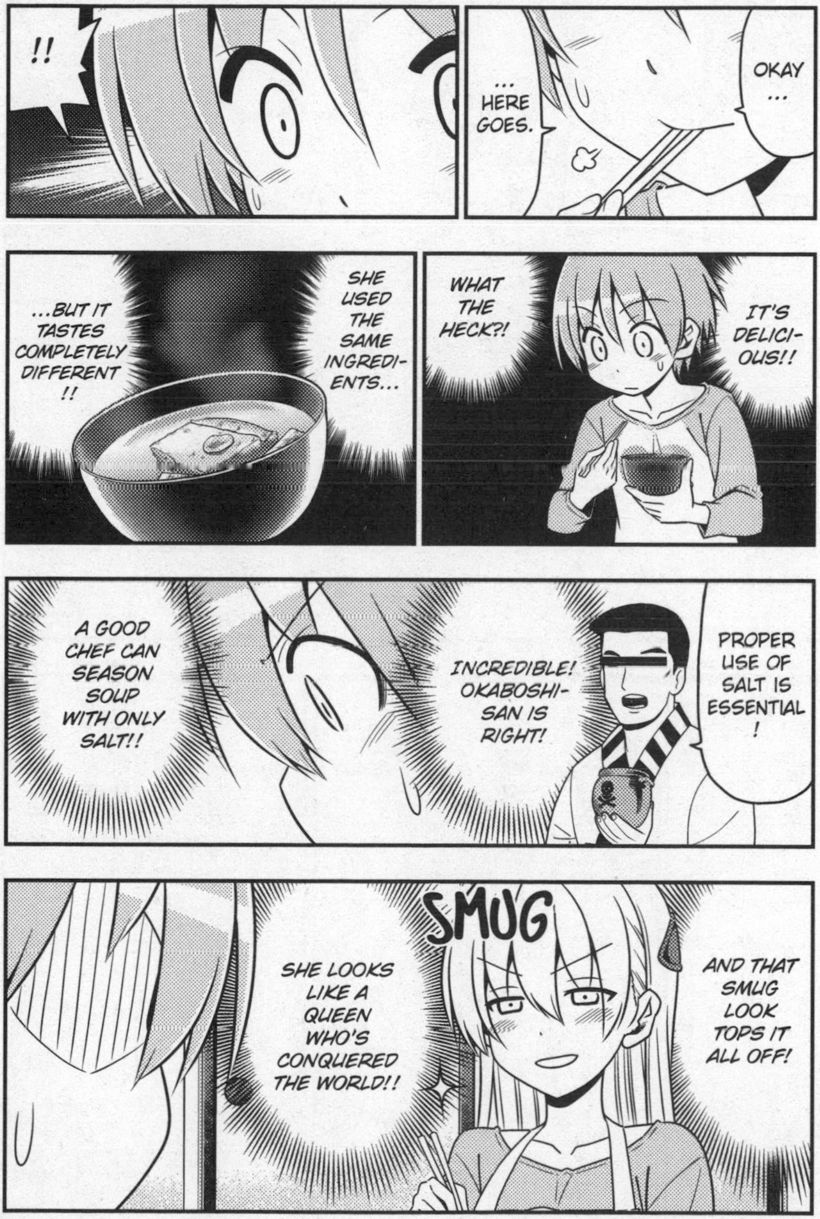
OKAY ...
... HERE GOES.
!!
IT'S DELICIOUS!!
WHAT THE HECK?!
SHE USED THE SAME INGREDIENTS...
...BUT IT TASTES COMPLETELY DIFFERENT!!
PROPER USE OF SALT IS ESSENTIAL!
INCREDIBLE! OKABOSHI-SAN IS RIGHT!
A GOOD CHEF CAN SEASON SOUP WITH ONLY SALT!!
AND THAT SMUG LOOK TOPS IT ALL OFF!
SMUG
SHE LOOKS LIKE A QUEEN WHO'S CONQUERED THE WORLD!!

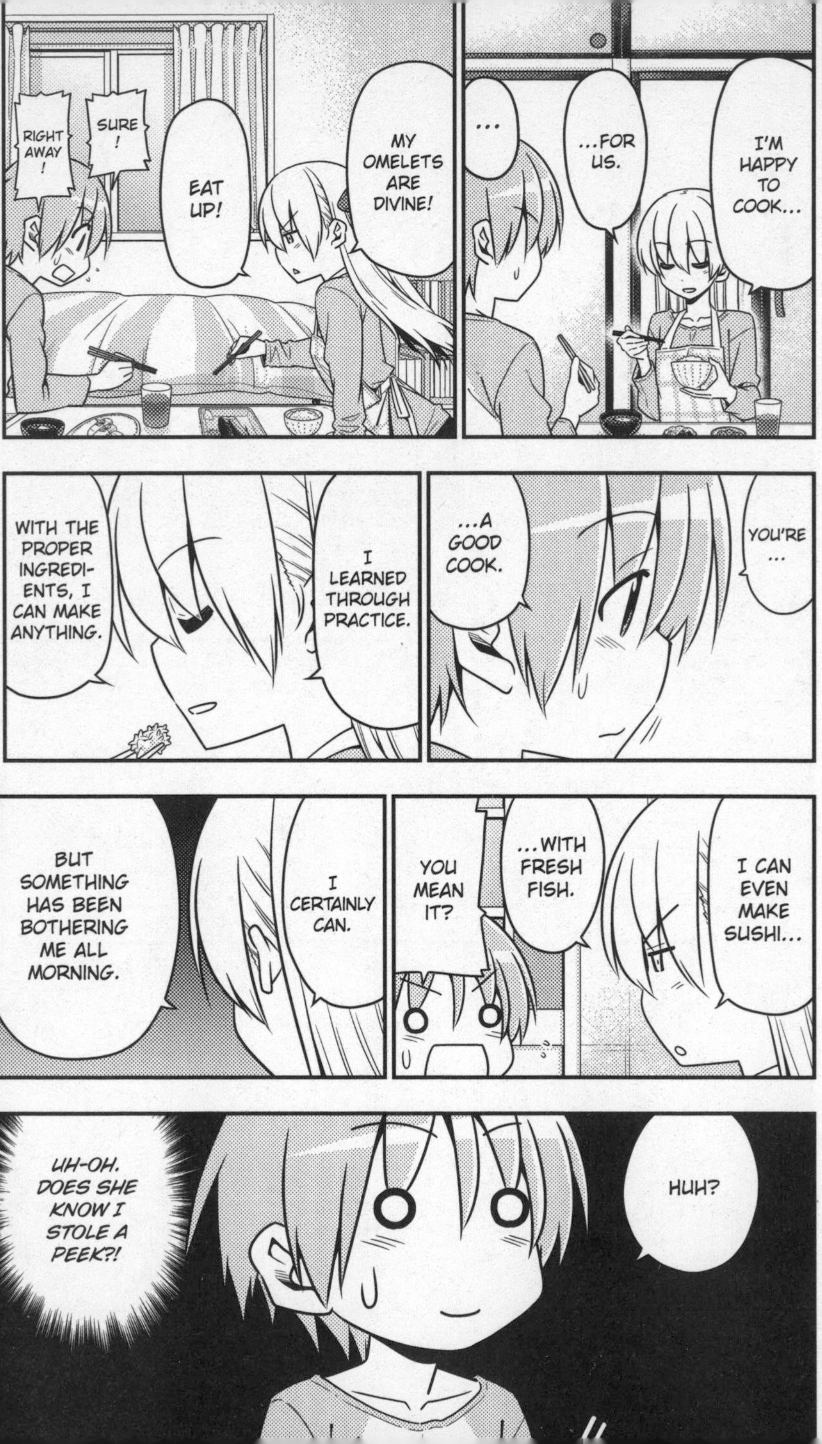
I'M HAPPY TO COOK...
...FOR US.
...
MY OMELETS ARE DIVINE!
EAT UP!
SURE!
RIGHT AWAY!
YOU'RE ...
...A GOOD COOK.
I LEARNED THROUGH PRACTICE.
WITH THE PROPER INGREDI-ENTS, I CAN MAKE ANYTHING.
I CAN EVEN MAKE SUSHI...
...WITH FRESH FISH.
YOU MEAN IT?
I CERTAINLY CAN.
BUT SOMETHING HAS BEEN BOTHERING ME ALL MORNING.
HUH?
UH-OH. DOES SHE KNOW I STOLE A PEEK?!

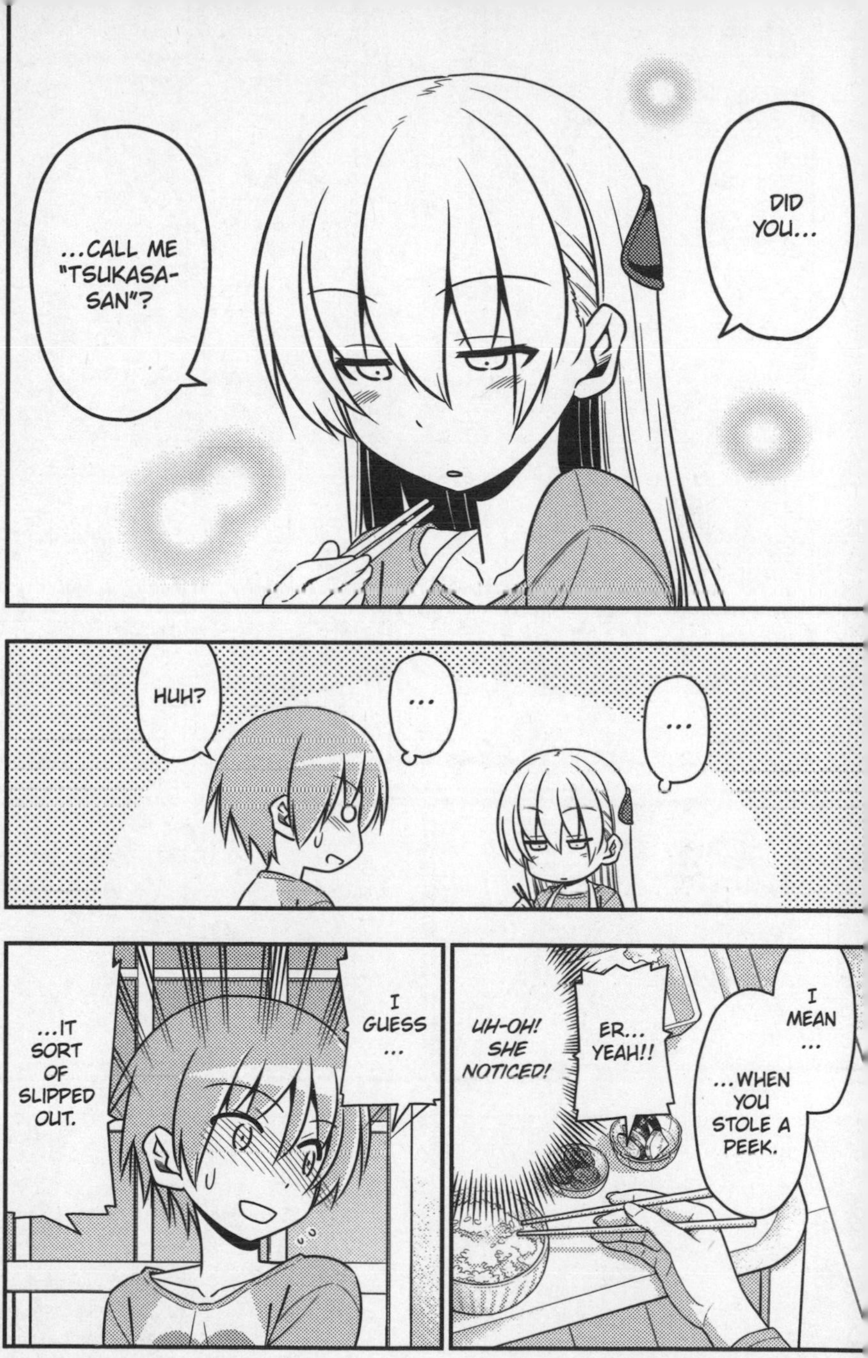
DID YOU...
...CALL ME "TSUKASA-SAN"?
...
...
HUH?
I MEAN ...
...WHEN YOU STOLE A PEEK.
ER... YEAH!!
UH-OH! SHE NOTICED!
I GUESS ...
...IT SORT OF SLIPPED OUT.

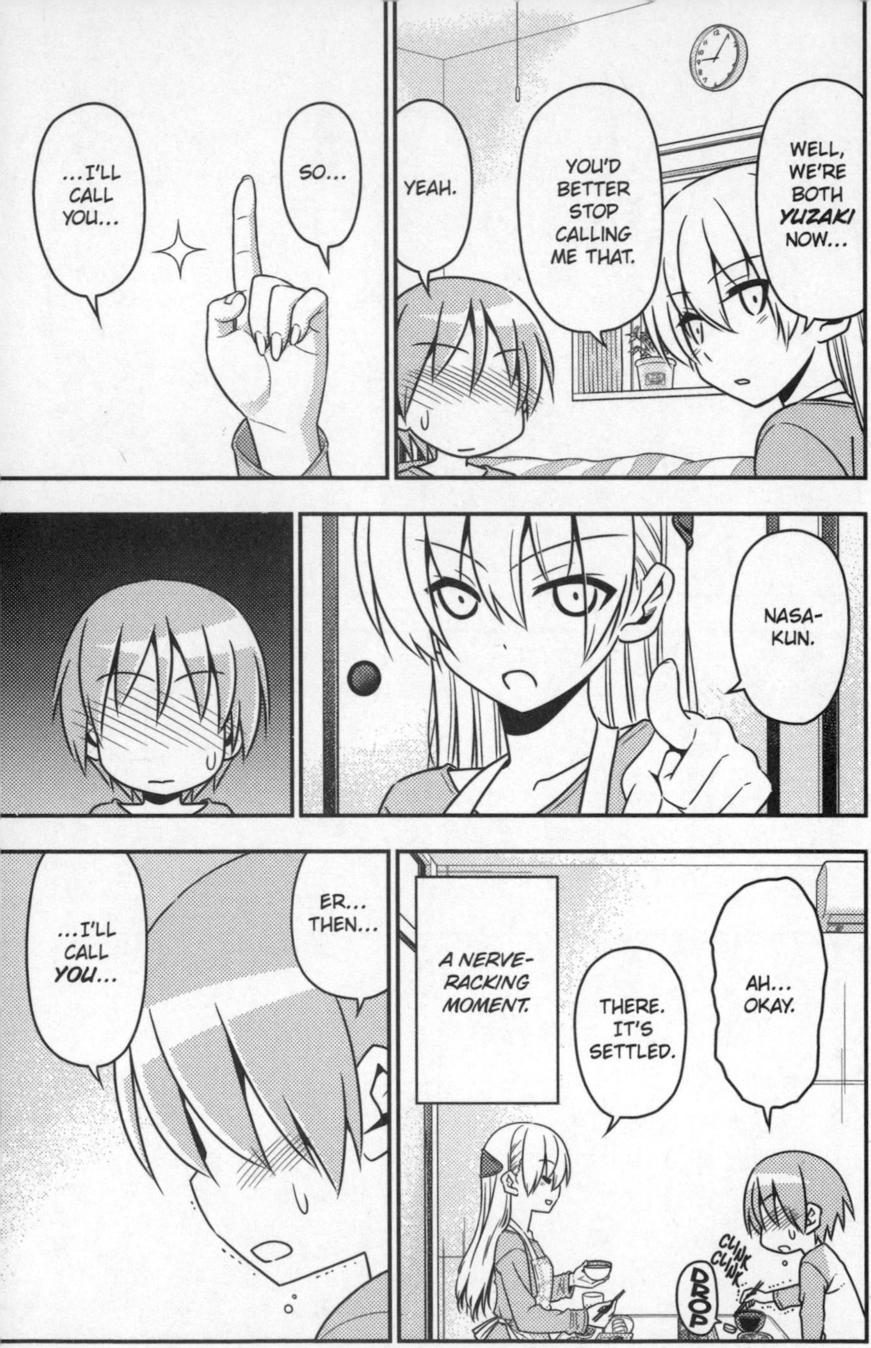
WELL, WE'RE BOTH YUZAKI NOW...
YOU'D BETTER STOP CALLING ME THAT.
YEAH.
SO...
...I'LL CALL YOU...
NASA-KUN.
AH... OKAY.
THERE. IT'S SETTLED.
A NERVE-RACKING MOMENT.
CLINK CLINK...
DROP
ER... THEN...
...I'LL CALL YOU...

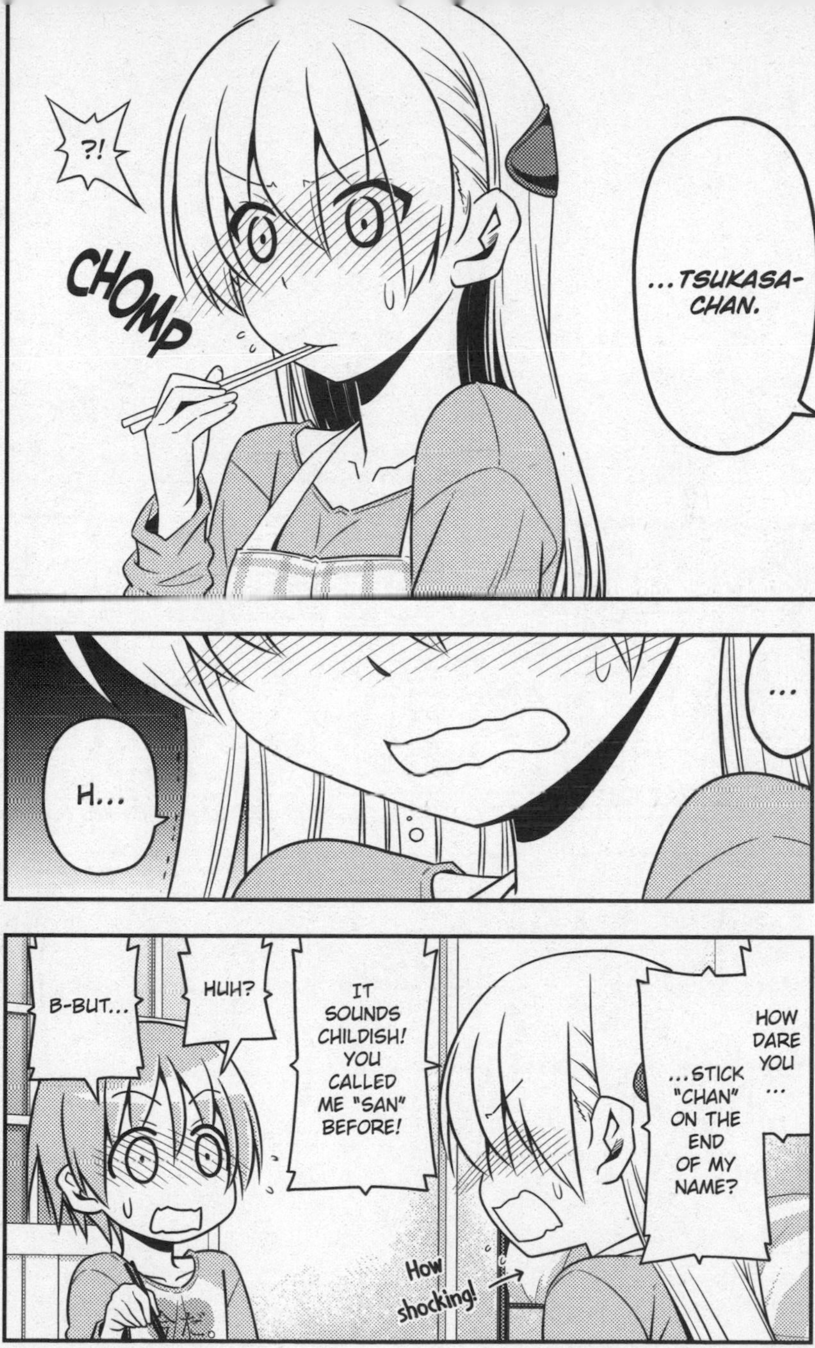
...TSUKASA-CHAN.
?!
CHOMP
...
H...
HOW DARE YOU ...
...STICK "CHAN" ON THE END OF MY NAME?
How shocking!
IT SOUNDS CHILDISH! YOU CALLED ME "SAN" BEFORE!
HUH?
B-BUT...

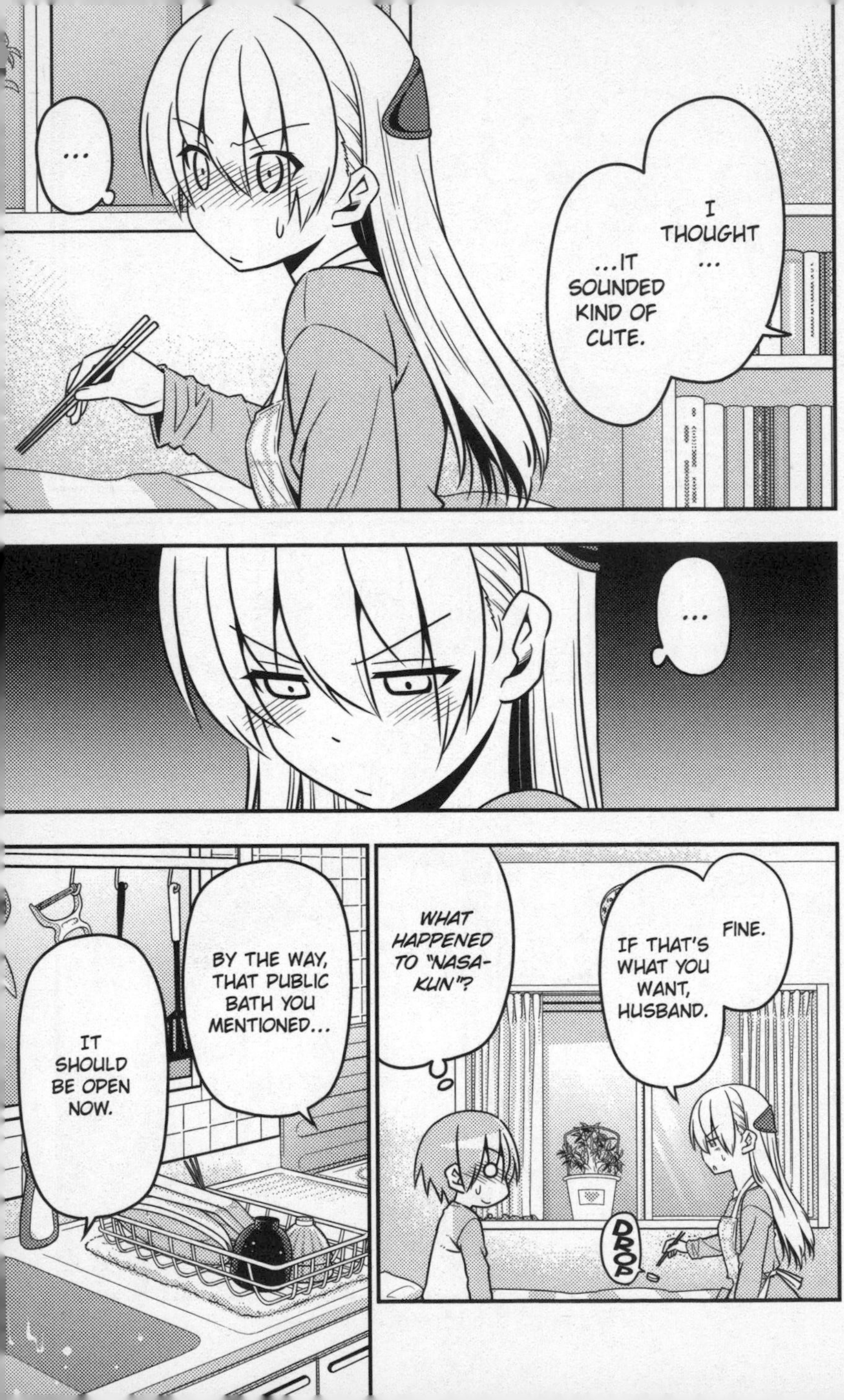
I THOUGHT... ...IT SOUNDED KIND OF CUTE.
...
...
FINE. IF THAT'S WHAT YOU WANT, HUSBAND.
WHAT HAPPENED TO "NASA-KUN"?
DROP
BY THE WAY, THAT PUBLIC BATH YOU MENTIONED...
IT SHOULD BE OPEN NOW.

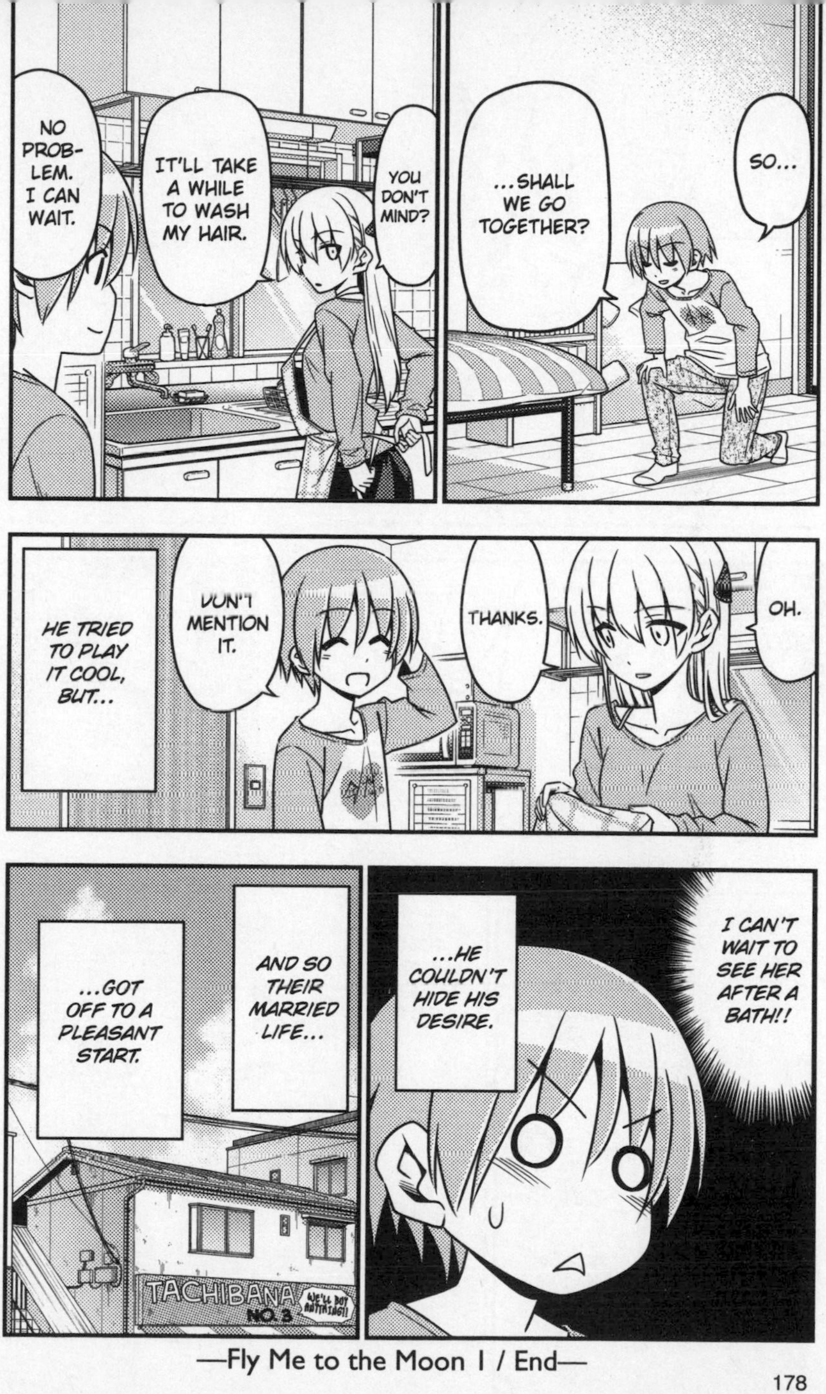
SO...
...SHALL WE GO TOGETHER?
YOU DON'T MIND?
IT'LL TAKE A WHILE TO WASH MY HAIR.
NO PROBLEM. I CAN WAIT.
OH.
THANKS.
DON'T MENTION IT.
HE TRIED TO PLAY IT COOL, BUT...
I CAN'T WAIT TO SEE HER AFTER A BATH!!
...HE COULDN'T HIDE HIS DESIRE.
AND SO THEIR MARRIED LIFE...
...GOT OFF TO A PLEASANT START.
TACHIBANA
NO. 3
WE'LL BUY ANYTHING!!

—Fly Me to the Moon 1 / End—

Bonus Manga
Daily Life at Yuzaki-san's House, Part 1

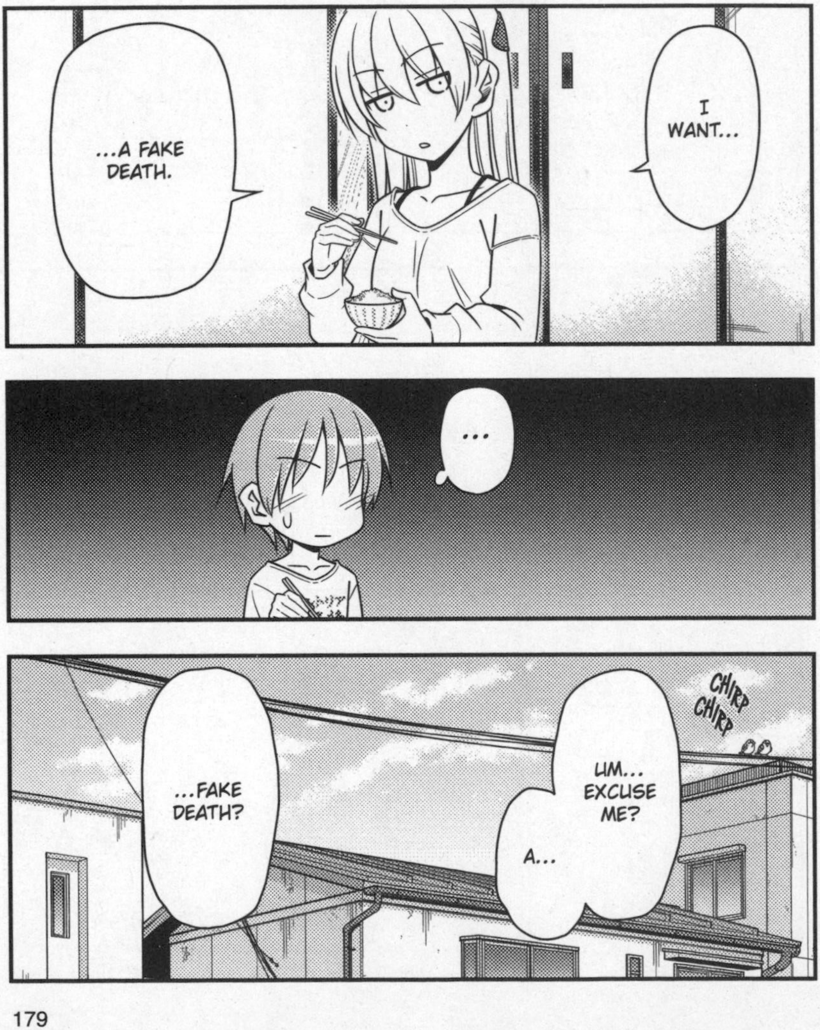
I WANT...
...A FAKE DEATH.
...
CHIRP CHIRP
UM... EXCUSE ME?
A...
...FAKE DEATH?

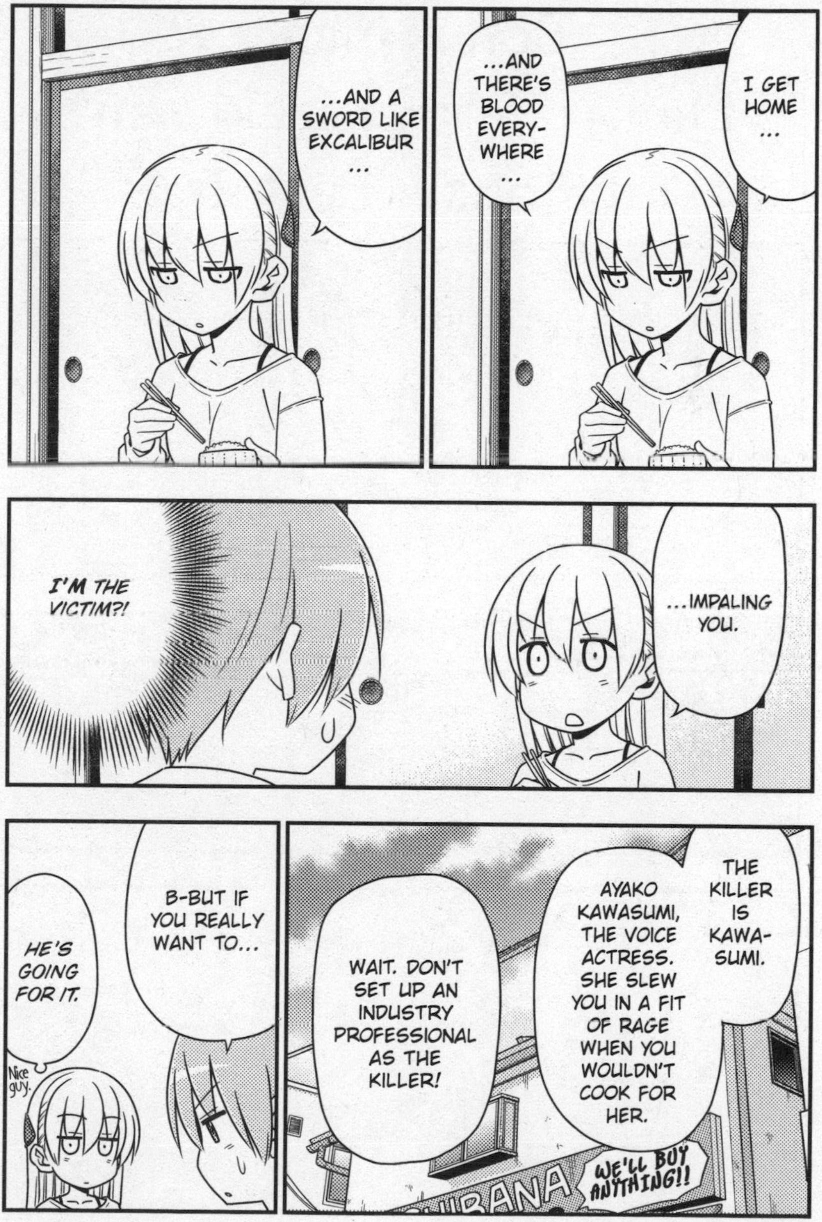
I GET HOME ...
...AND THERE'S BLOOD EVERY-WHERE ...
...AND A SWORD LIKE EXCALIBUR ...
...IMPALING YOU.
I'M THE VICTIM?!
THE KILLER IS KAWA-SUMI.
AYAKO KAWASUMI, THE VOICE ACTRESS. SHE SLEW YOU IN A FIT OF RAGE WHEN YOU WOULDN'T COOK FOR HER.
WAIT. DON'T SET UP AN INDUSTRY PROFESSIONAL AS THE KILLER!
WE'LL BUY ANYTHING!!
B-BUT IF YOU REALLY WANT TO...
HE'S GOING FOR IT.
Nice guy.

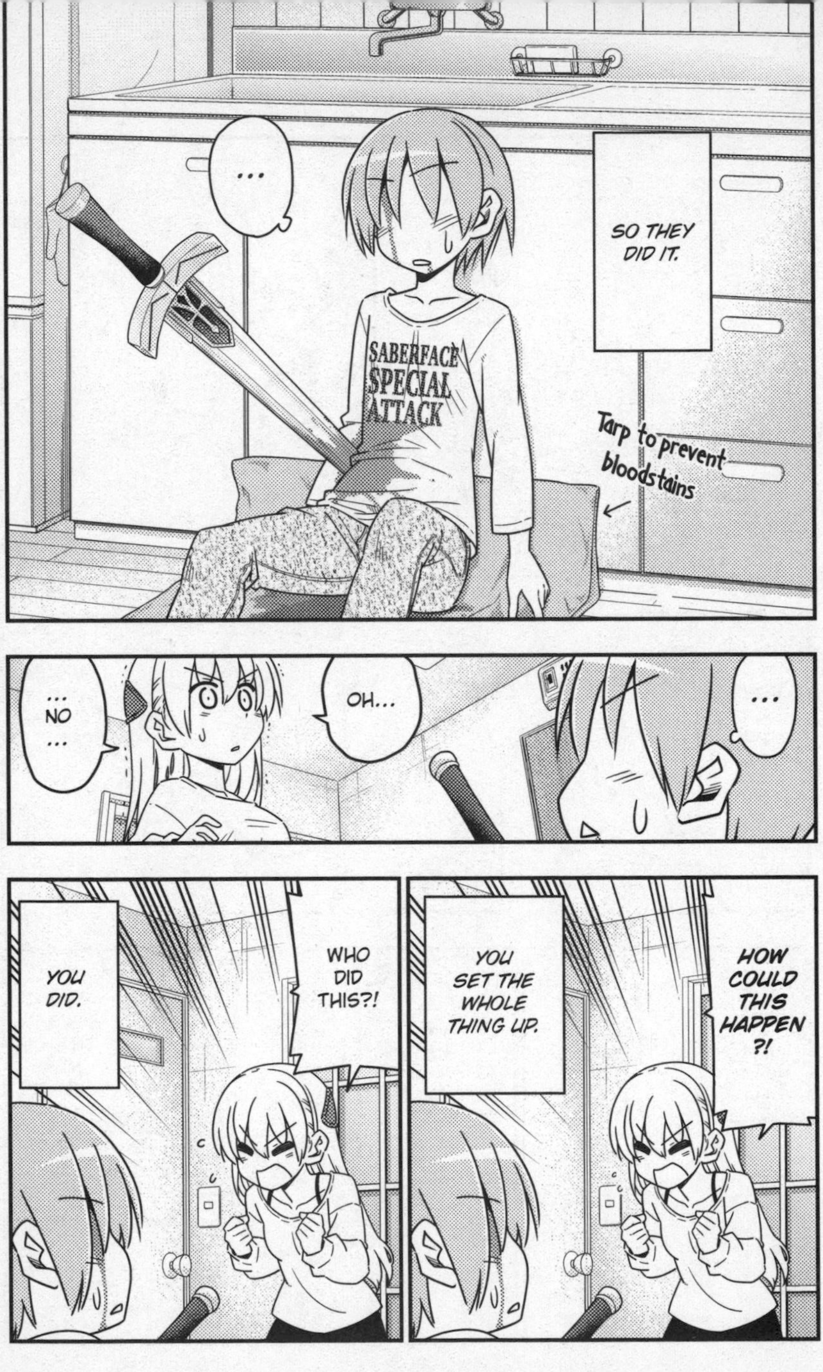
SO THEY DID IT.
...
SABERFACE SPECIAL ATTACK
Tarp to prevent bloodstains
...
OH...
... NO ...
HOW COULD THIS HAPPEN?!
YOU SET THE WHOLE THING UP.
WHO DID THIS?!
YOU DID.

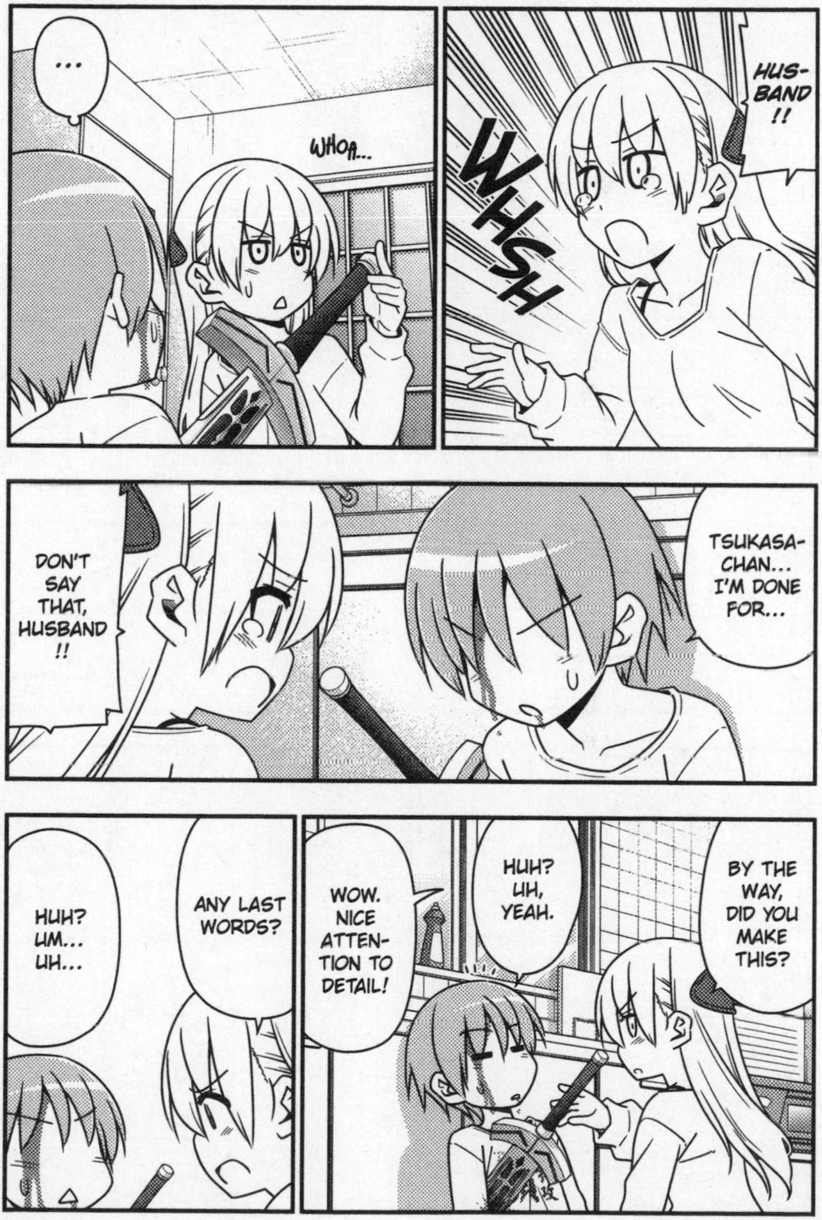
WHSH
HUS-BAND!!
...
WHOA...
TSUKASA-CHAN... I'M DONE FOR...
DON'T SAY THAT, HUSBAND!!
BY THE WAY, DID YOU MAKE THIS?
HUH? UH, YEAH.
WOW. NICE ATTENTION TO DETAIL!
ANY LAST WORDS?
HUH? UM... UH...

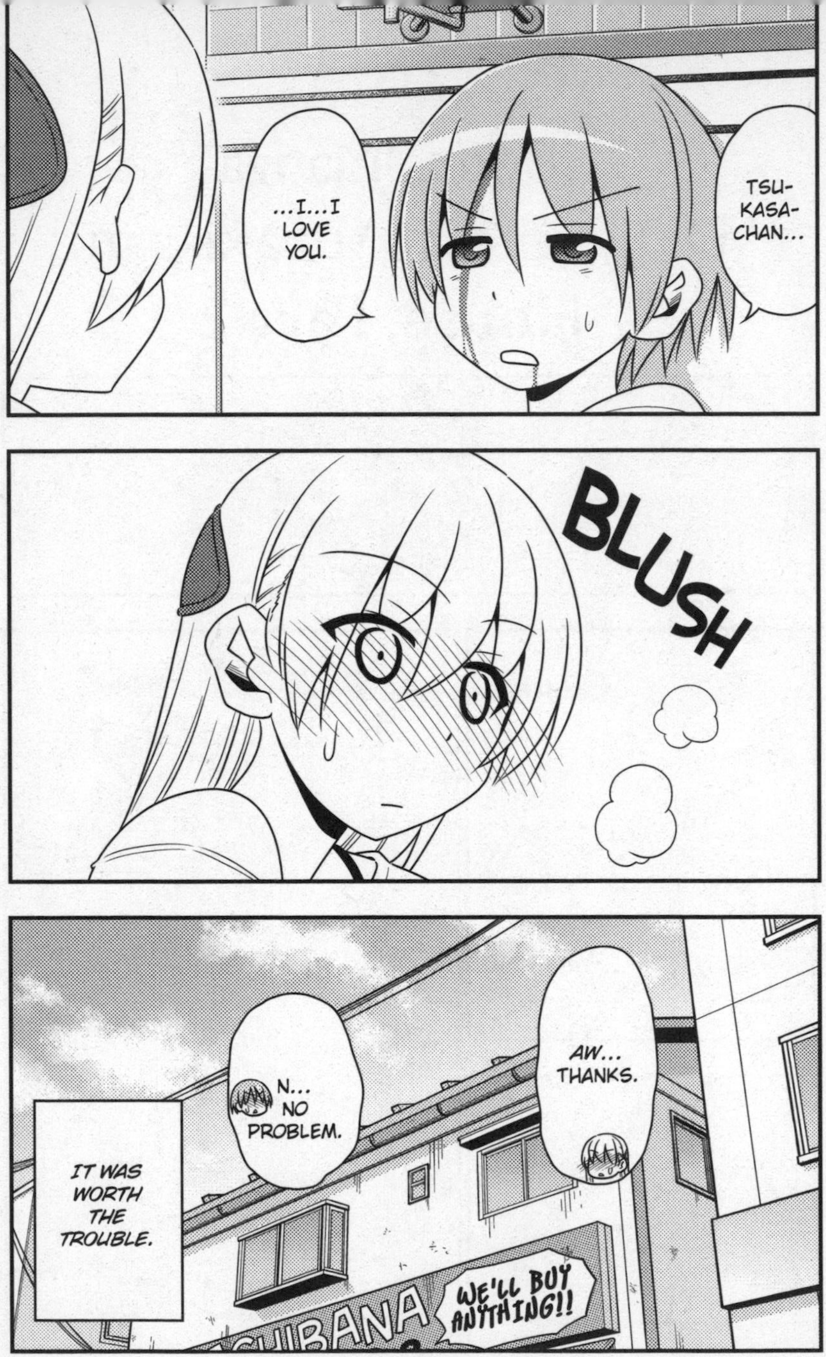
TSU-KASA-CHAN...
...I...I LOVE YOU.
BLUSH
AW... THANKS.
N... NO PROBLEM.
WE'LL BUY ANYTHING!!
IT WAS WORTH THE TROUBLE.

Bonus Manga
Daily Life at Yuzaki-san's House, Part 2

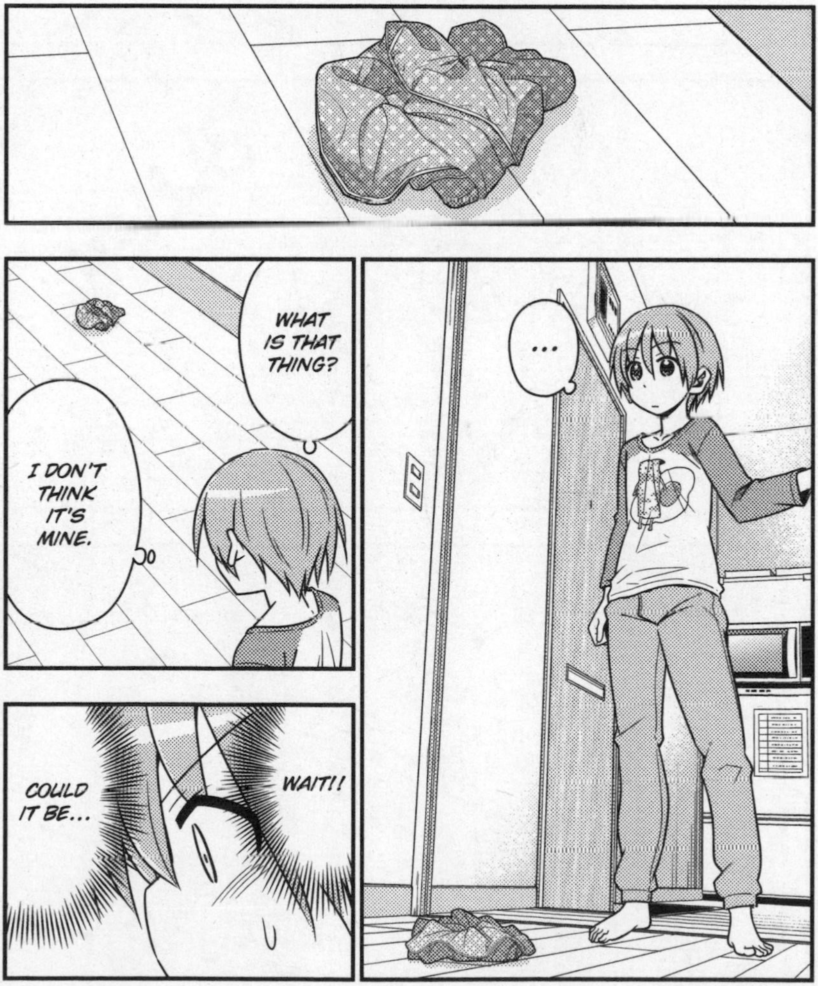
...
WHAT IS THAT THING?
I DON'T THINK IT'S MINE.
WAIT!!
COULD IT BE...

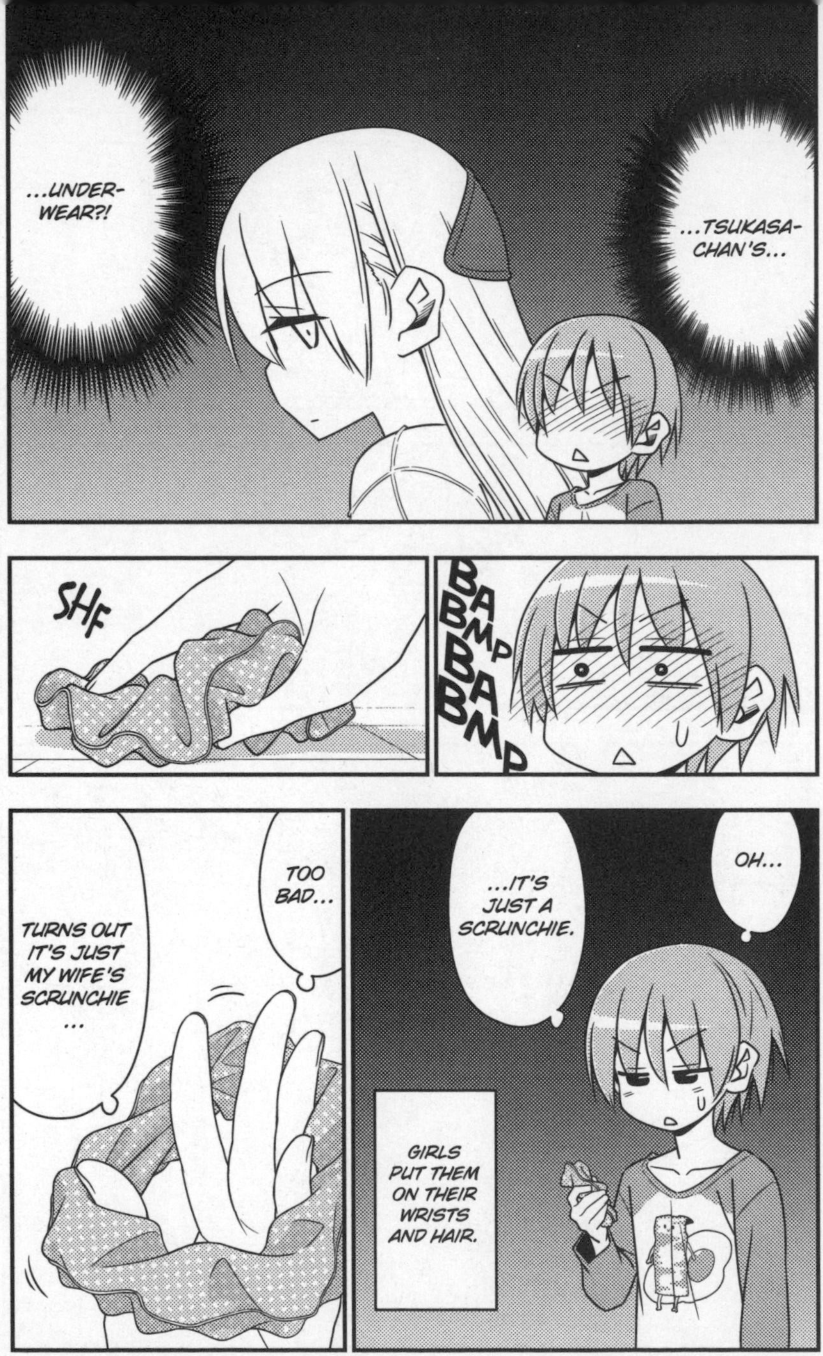
...TSUKASA-CHAN'S...
...UNDER-WEAR?!
BA BMP BA BMP
SHF
OH...
...IT'S JUST A SCRUNCHIE.
GIRLS PUT THEM ON THEIR WRISTS AND HAIR.
TOO BAD...
TURNS OUT IT'S JUST MY WIFE'S SCRUNCHIE ...

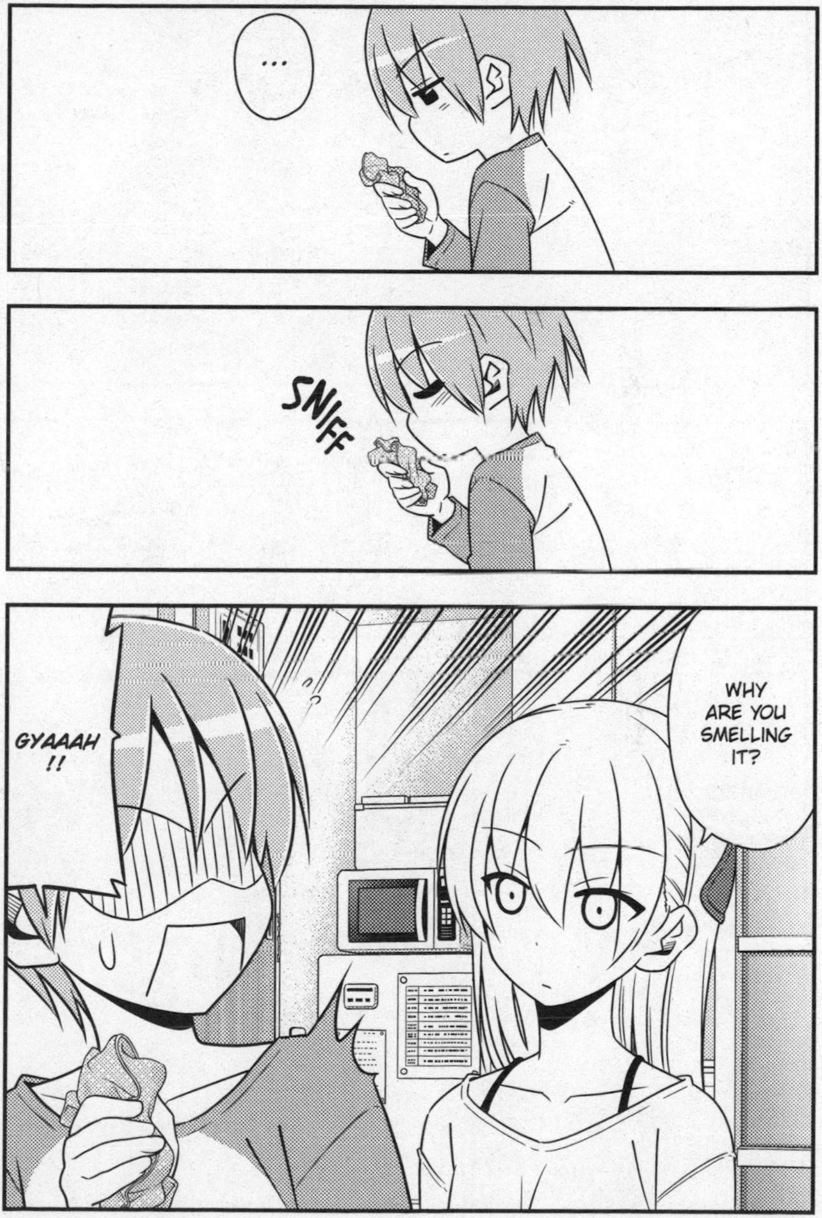
...
SNIFF
WHY ARE YOU SMELLING IT?
GYAAAH!!

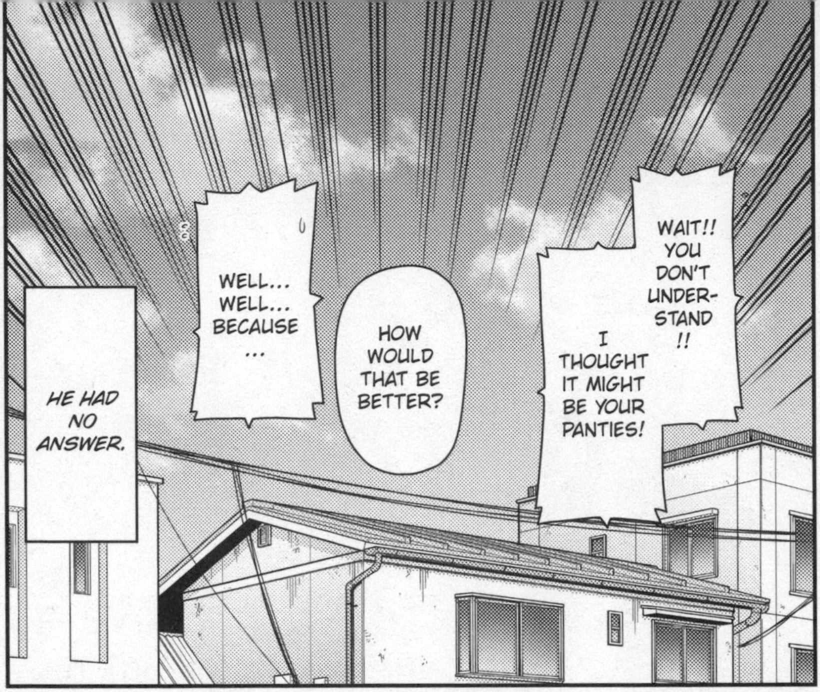
WAIT!! YOU DON'T UNDER-STAND!!
I THOUGHT IT MIGHT BE YOUR PANTIES!
HOW WOULD THAT BE BETTER?
WELL... WELL... BECAUSE...
HE HAD NO ANSWER.

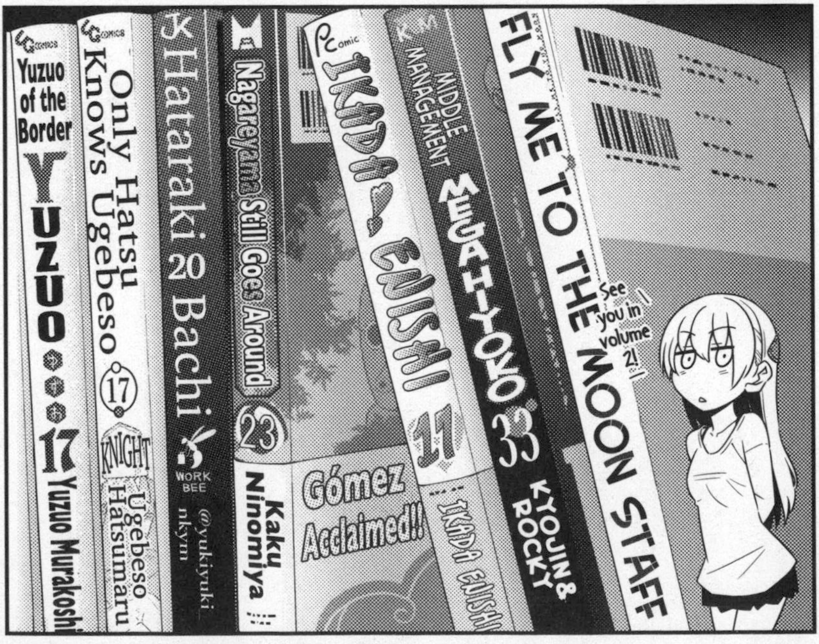
See you in volume 2!
FLY ME TO THE MOON 33 KYOJIN & ROCKY STAFF
MIDDLE MANAGEMENT MEGAHIYOKO
IKADA EVUSHI 11 IKADA EVUSHI
Gómez Acclaimed!!
Nagareyama Still Goes Around 23 Kaku Ninomiya
Hataraki 20 Bachi WORK BEE @yukiyuki_nkym
Only Hatsu Knows Ugebeso 17 KNIGHT Ugebeso Hatsumaru
Yuzuo of the Border YUZUO 17 Yuzuo Murakoshi

←Bonus content continues ♡

Notes from Hata!

FLY ME TO THE MOON

Original Designs

!!

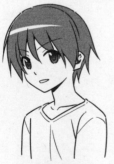

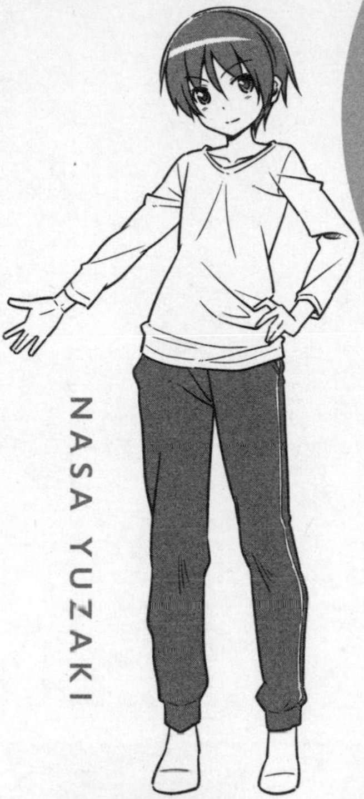

NASA YUZAKI

profile

Age: 18
Birthday: May 5
Height: 5'5" Weight: 115 lb.
Blood type: A
Likes: math, physics, finance

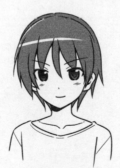

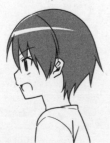

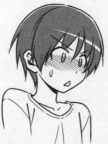

HATA'S COMMENTS

He's serious, logical and clearheaded to a fault. He's smart enough to be financially stable, but he's dumb in other ways, which causes different problems. He's crazy about his wife.

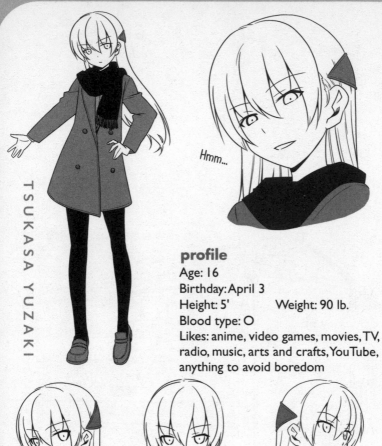

TSUKASA YUZAKI

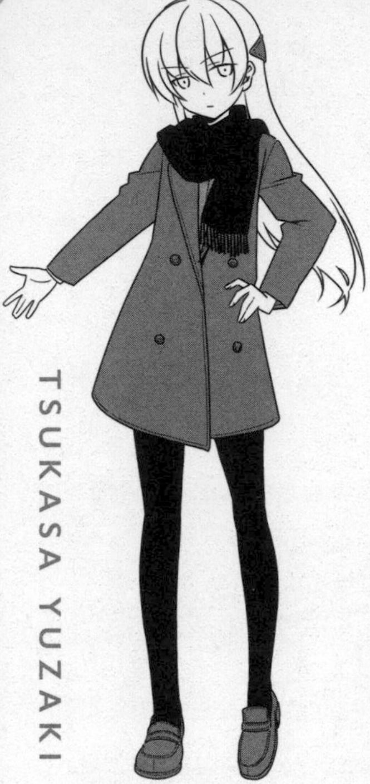

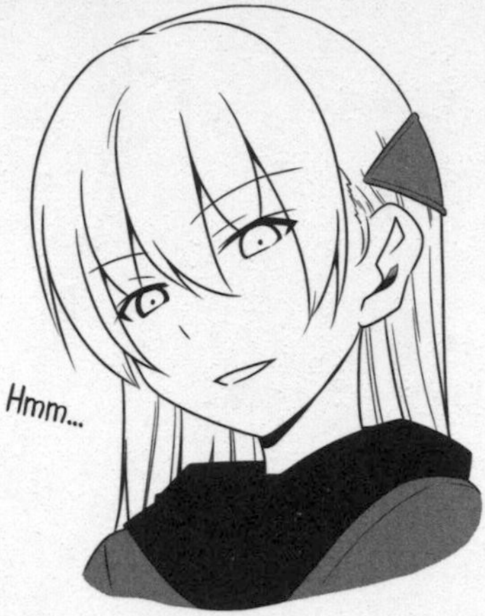
Hmm...

profile

Age: 16
Birthday: April 3
Height: 5' Weight: 90 lb.
Blood type: O
Likes: anime, video games, movies, TV, radio, music, arts and crafts, YouTube, anything to avoid boredom

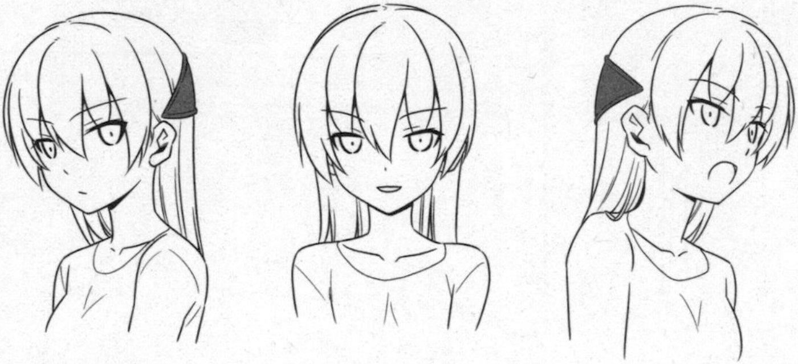

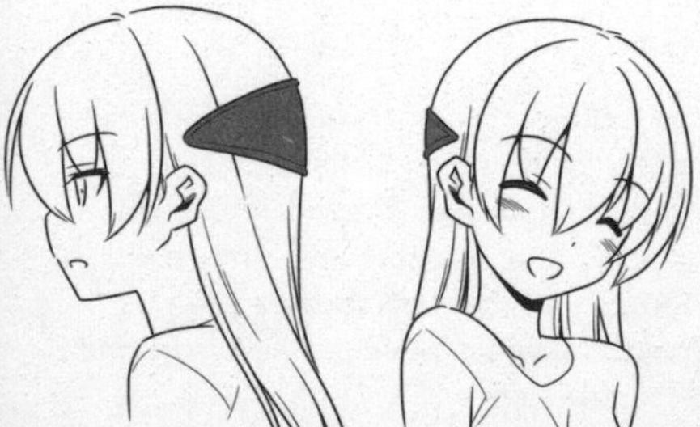

HATA'S COMMENTS

At present, she remains a mystery. I considered revealing her full identity before they started living together, but after some thought I decided to keep readers in the dark for a while. Later, when you go back and reread this volume, you may have a completely different impression.

This is what's over Tachibana No. 3!!

THE LOVE NEST

Check it out! ♪

EXTERIOR

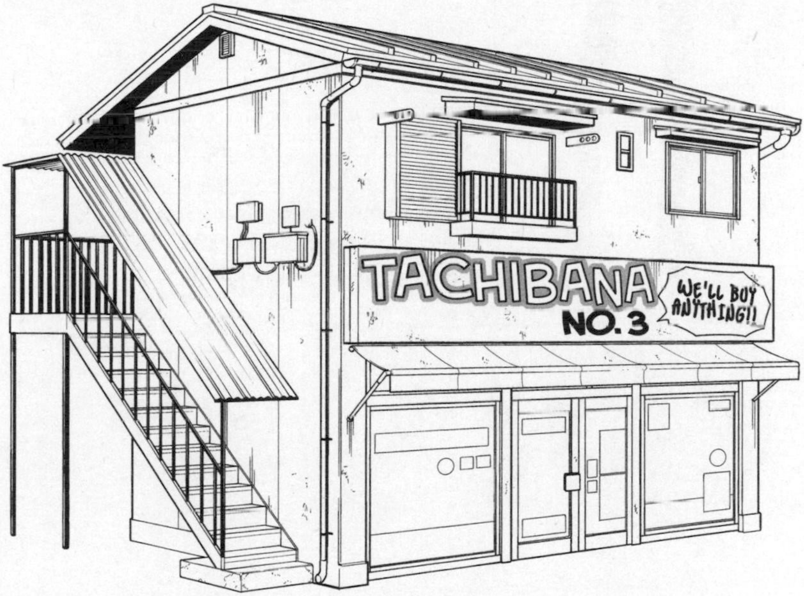
TACHIBANA
NO. 3
WE'LL BUY ANYTHING!!

HATA'S COMMENTS

Nasa-kun's apartment is located over a store called Tachibana No. 3, which doesn't appear to do much business. It's in Shibuya ward, but the rent is shockingly cheap because it's a converted attic and doesn't have a bath. Furthermore, it has a disturbing past. Several people claim to have seen a ghost dressed like a priest. The ghost seems to have stopped appearing since the latest exorcism.

INTERIOR

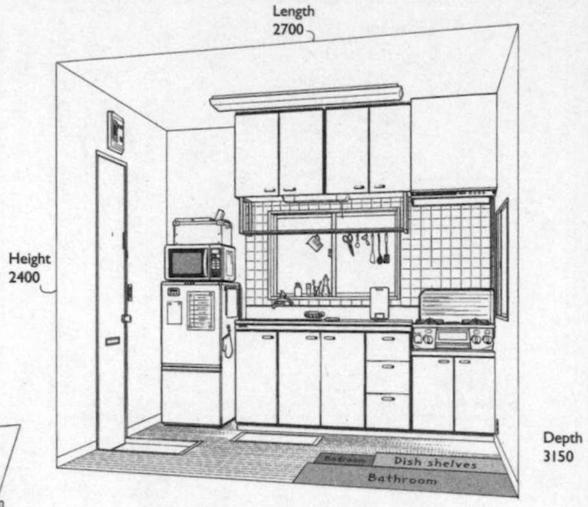
Length
2700
Height
2400
Depth
3150
Bedroom
Dish shelves
Bathroom

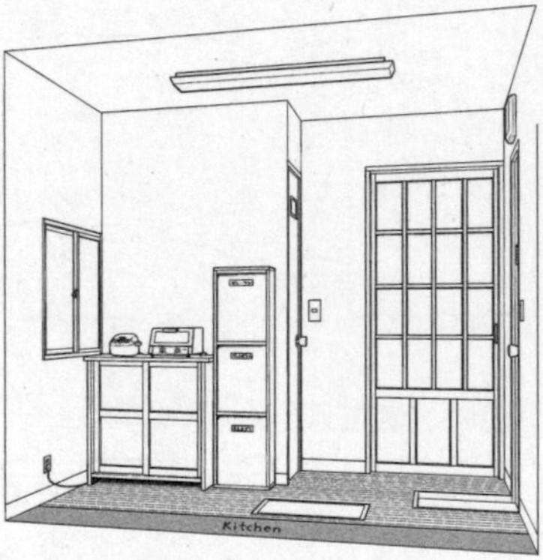
Kitchen

HATA'S COMMENTS

As you might expect, Nasa keeps his apartment clean and impeccably organized. However, he lacks a lot of the usual household items, much to Tsukasa's displeasure…

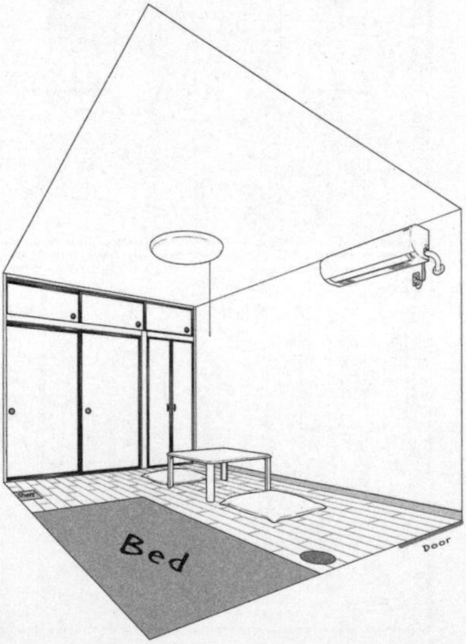
Bed
Door

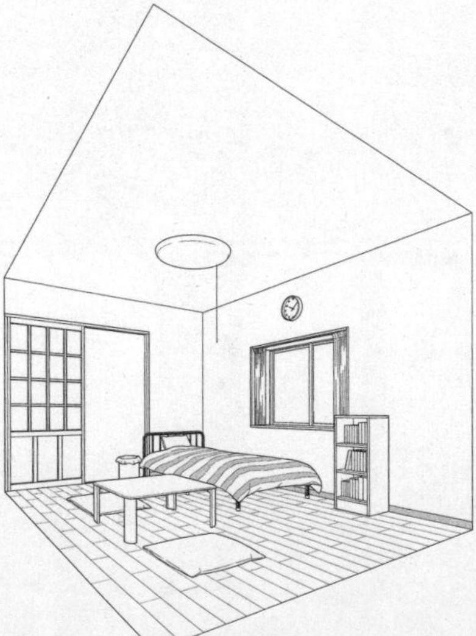

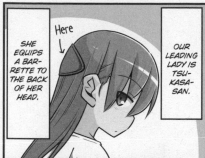

SHE EQUIPS A BARRETTE TO THE BACK OF HER HEAD.

Here ↓

OUR LEADING LADY IS TSUKASA-SAN.

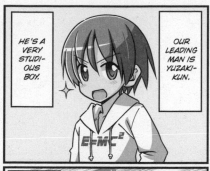

HE'S A VERY STUDIOUS BOY.

OUR LEADING MAN IS YUZAKI-KUN.

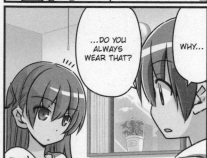

...DO YOU ALWAYS WEAR THAT?

WHY...

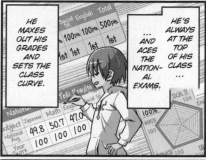

HE MAXES OUT HIS GRADES AND SETS THE CLASS CURVE.

...AND ACES THE NATIONAL EXAMS,

HE'S ALWAYS AT THE TOP OF HIS CLASS...

Subject	Japanese	Math	English	Social St.
National Avg.	49.8	50.7	47.0	
Your Score	100	100	100	

100%

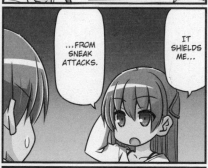

...FROM SNEAK ATTACKS.

IT SHIELDS ME...

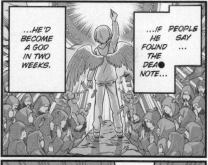

...HE'D BECOME A GOD IN TWO WEEKS.

...IF PEOPLE SAY...

...HE FOUND THE DEA● NOTE...

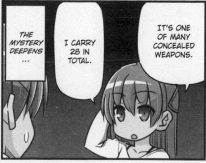

THE MYSTERY DEEPENS...

I CARRY 28 IN TOTAL.

IT'S ONE OF MANY CONCEALED WEAPONS.

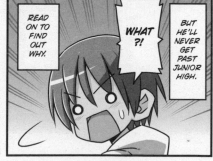

READ ON TO FIND OUT WHY.

WHAT?!

BUT HE'LL NEVER GET PAST JUNIOR HIGH.

Fly Me to the Moon

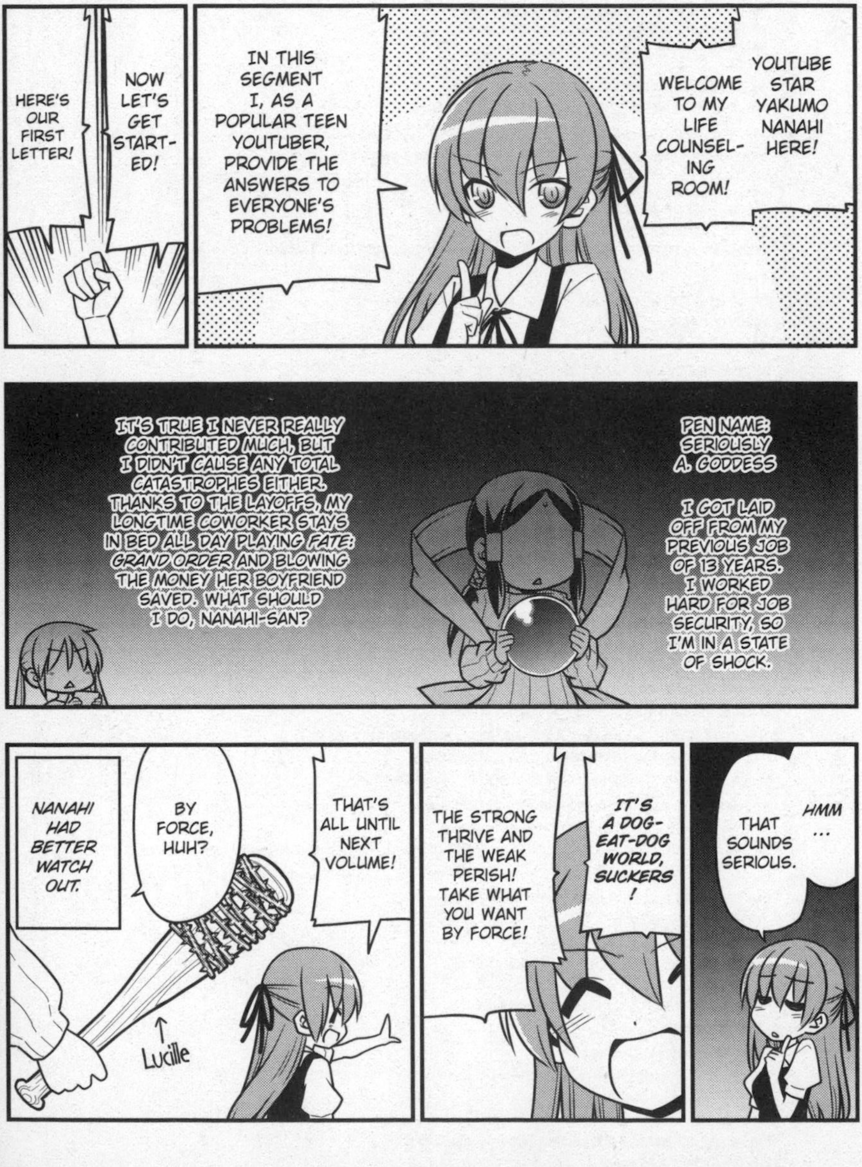
YOUTUBE STAR YAKUMO NANAHI HERE!
WELCOME TO MY LIFE COUNSELING ROOM!
IN THIS SEGMENT I, AS A POPULAR TEEN YOUTUBER, PROVIDE THE ANSWERS TO EVERYONE'S PROBLEMS!
NOW LET'S GET STARTED!
HERE'S OUR FIRST LETTER!
PEN NAME: SERIOUSLY A. GODDESS
I GOT LAID OFF FROM MY PREVIOUS JOB OF 13 YEARS. I WORKED HARD FOR JOB SECURITY, SO I'M IN A STATE OF SHOCK.
IT'S TRUE I NEVER REALLY CONTRIBUTED MUCH, BUT I DIDN'T CAUSE ANY TOTAL CATASTROPHES EITHER. THANKS TO THE LAYOFFS, MY LONGTIME COWORKER STAYS IN BED ALL DAY PLAYING *FATE: GRAND ORDER* AND BLOWING THE MONEY HER BOYFRIEND SAVED. WHAT SHOULD I DO, NANAHI-SAN?
HMM...
THAT SOUNDS SERIOUS.
IT'S A DOG-EAT-DOG WORLD, SUCKERS!
THE STRONG THRIVE AND THE WEAK PERISH! TAKE WHAT YOU WANT BY FORCE!
THAT'S ALL UNTIL NEXT VOLUME!
BY FORCE, HUH?
NANAHI HAD BETTER WATCH OUT.
Lucille

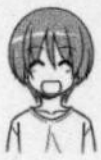

NASA AND TSUKASA

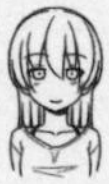

RESPOND TO READER QUESTIONS

(EVEN THOUGH THEY WERE DIRECTED TO THE AUTHOR)

WHAT DO YOU WISH YOU'D LEARNED WHEN YOU WERE YOUNG?

SHAOLIN BOXING. HUH?

NOVEMBER 23 IS LABOR DAY IN JAPAN. WHAT DO YOU WANT TO BUY YOURSELF AS A LITTLE REWARD?

A SINGLE-LENS REFLEX CAMERA SO I CAN TAKE CANDID SHOTS OF MY WIFE.

THE WALKING DEAD ON BLU-RAY.

WHAT'S THE WEIRDEST NICKNAME YOU'VE BEEN GIVEN?

ARMSTRONG GUN. I GET THAT ARMSTRONG WAS THE APOLLO MISSION CAPTAIN, BUT WHY "GUN"? I MEAN..."GUN"?

PIETÀ.

TELL ME YOUR FAVORITE NUMBER AND WHY.

ELEVEN. IT'S THE MOST ATTRACTIVE PRIME NUMBER.

646, THE YEAR JAPAN BECAME A NATION FOLLOWING THE TAIKA REFORM.

WHAT OLD STORIES OR FAIRY TALES DID YOU LOVE WHEN YOU WERE A CHILD?

THE DEATH OF ARCHIMEDES. IT'S ABOUT HOW FOOLS GET IN THE WAY OF SMART PEOPLE. IT TAUGHT ME THE IMPORTANCE OF WISDOM.

↑WHAT KIND OF CHILD *WERE* YOU?!

WHAT'S THE MOST EXCITING PART OF YOUR WEEK?

SEEING MY WIFE WHEN SHE WAKES UP BLEARY-EYED WITH HER HAIR A MESS.

↑HEY!

IS THERE A PHONE APP YOUR FINGERS AUTOMATICALLY OPEN?

YAHOO FINANCE.

YOUTUBE.

WHAT NON-JAPANESE NAME SOUNDS COOL TO YOU?

ZHUGE LIANG.

ALEXANDER MAHONE.

WHAT DID YOUR TEACHERS WRITE ON YOUR REPORT CARD?

"STOP PESTERING ME WITH SO MANY QUESTIONS AND MAKING ME CRY."

↑WHAT KIND OF CHILD *WERE* YOU?!

WHAT TV SHOW DO YOU WISH MORE PEOPLE WATCHED?

RUI YOSHIDA'S BAR CRAWL.

TELL ME SOMETHING USEFUL YOU LIKE.

GIT. IT'S USEFUL WHEN MULTIPLE PEOPLE HANDLE A PROGRAM'S SOURCE CODE.

↑THAT'S USEFUL? FOR ME, IT'S A VACUUM PUMP AND STORAGE BAGS FOR LEFTOVERS.

NEW'S YEAR'S, CHRISTMAS, SPRING FLOWER VIEWING...WHAT'S YOUR FAVORITE ANNUAL EVENT?

MY WEDDING ANNIVERSARY!

↑I LOOK FORWARD TO NEXT YEAR.

WHAT'S YOUR FAVORITE INSTANT FOOD?

INSTANT YAKISOBA, ESPECIALLY THE U.F.O. BRAND.

THE FIRST TIME I HAD INSTANT NOODLES, I WAS STUNNED.

TELL ME YOUR FAVORITE FOUR-KANJI PHRASE AND WHY.

NISSHIN GEPPO. IT MEANS "SLOW BUT STEADY PROGRESS."

YAKINIKU TEISHOKU. IT MEANS "BARBECUE THAT MAKES TSUKASA DROOL."

WHAT'S THE GREATEST LOSS YOU'VE EVER SUFFERED?

THE NEM CRYPTOCURRENCY HACK. BUT I BOUGHT IT CHEAP, SO I CAME OUT AHEAD.

GLENN FROM *THE WALKING DEAD.*

WHAT REMINDS YOU OF YOUR MOTHER'S COOKING?

YAKISOBA WITH KETCHUP.

↑IS THAT LIKE SPAGHETTI NAPOLITAN?

WHERE CAN YOU RELAX MOST AT HOME?

BY MY WIFE'S SIDE. ←*AWWW...*

WHAT ANIME MUSIC REALLY STIRS YOUR SOUL?

"ZENZENZENSE."

THE *GREAT MAZINGER* THEME.

WHAT'S THE MOST AMAZING INVENTION?

EULER'S FORMULA.

KENTUCKY FRIED CHICKEN.

WHERE WOULD YOU BUILD A SECOND HOME IF YOU COULD?

THE LUNAR SURFACE.

ABOUT THE AUTHOR

Without ever receiving any kind of manga award, Kenjiro Hata's first series, *Umi no Yuusha Lifesavers,* was published in *Shonen Sunday Super*. He followed that up with his smash hit *Hayate the Combat Butler*. His follow-up series, *Fly Me to the Moon,* began serialization in 2018 in *Weekly Shonen Sunday*.

FLY ME TO THE MOON
VOL. 1

Story and Art by **KENJIRO HATA**

SHONEN SUNDAY EDITION

TONIKAKUKAWAII Vol. 1
by Kenjiro HATA
© 2018 Kenjiro HATA
All rights reserved.
Original Japanese edition published by SHOGAKUKAN.
English translation rights in the United States of America,
Canada, the United Kingdom, Ireland, Australia and New
Zealand arranged with SHOGAKUKAN.

Original Cover Design: Emi Nakano (BANANA GROVE STUDIO)

Translation
John Werry

Touch-Up Art & Lettering
Evan Waldinger

Design
Jimmy Presler

Editor
Shaenon K. Garrity

Printed in the U.S.A.

Published by VIZ Media, LLC
P.O. Box 77010
San Francisco, CA 94107

10 9 8 7 6 5 4 3 2
First printing, September 2020
Second printing, January 2021

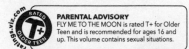

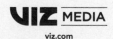

viz.com

shonensunday.com

A hilarious tale of butlers, love and battles!

Hayate the Combat Butler

Story and art by Kenjiro Hata

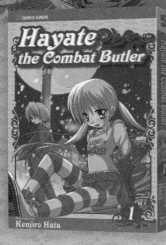

Since the tender age of nine, Hayate Ayasaki has busted his behind at various part-time jobs to support his degenerate gambler parents. And how do they repay their son's selfless generosity? By selling his organs to the yakuza to cover their debts! But fate throws Hayate a bone... sort of. Now the butler of a wealthy young lady, Hayate can finally pay back his debts, and it'll only take him 40 years to do it.

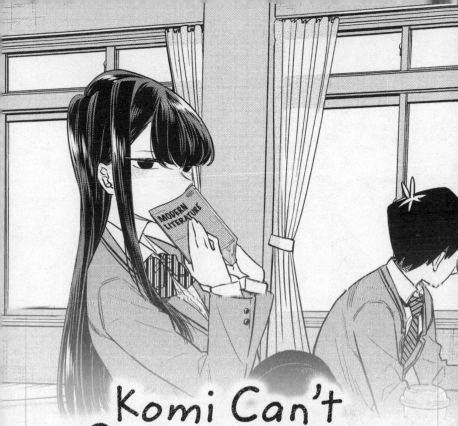

Komi Can't Communicate

Story & Art by Tomohito Oda

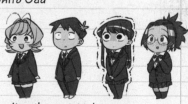

The journey to a hundred friends begins with a single conversation.

Socially anxious high school student Shoko Komi's greatest dream is to make some friends, but everyone at school mistakes her crippling social anxiety for cool reserve. With the whole student body keeping its distance and Komi unable to utter a single word, friendship might be forever beyond her reach.

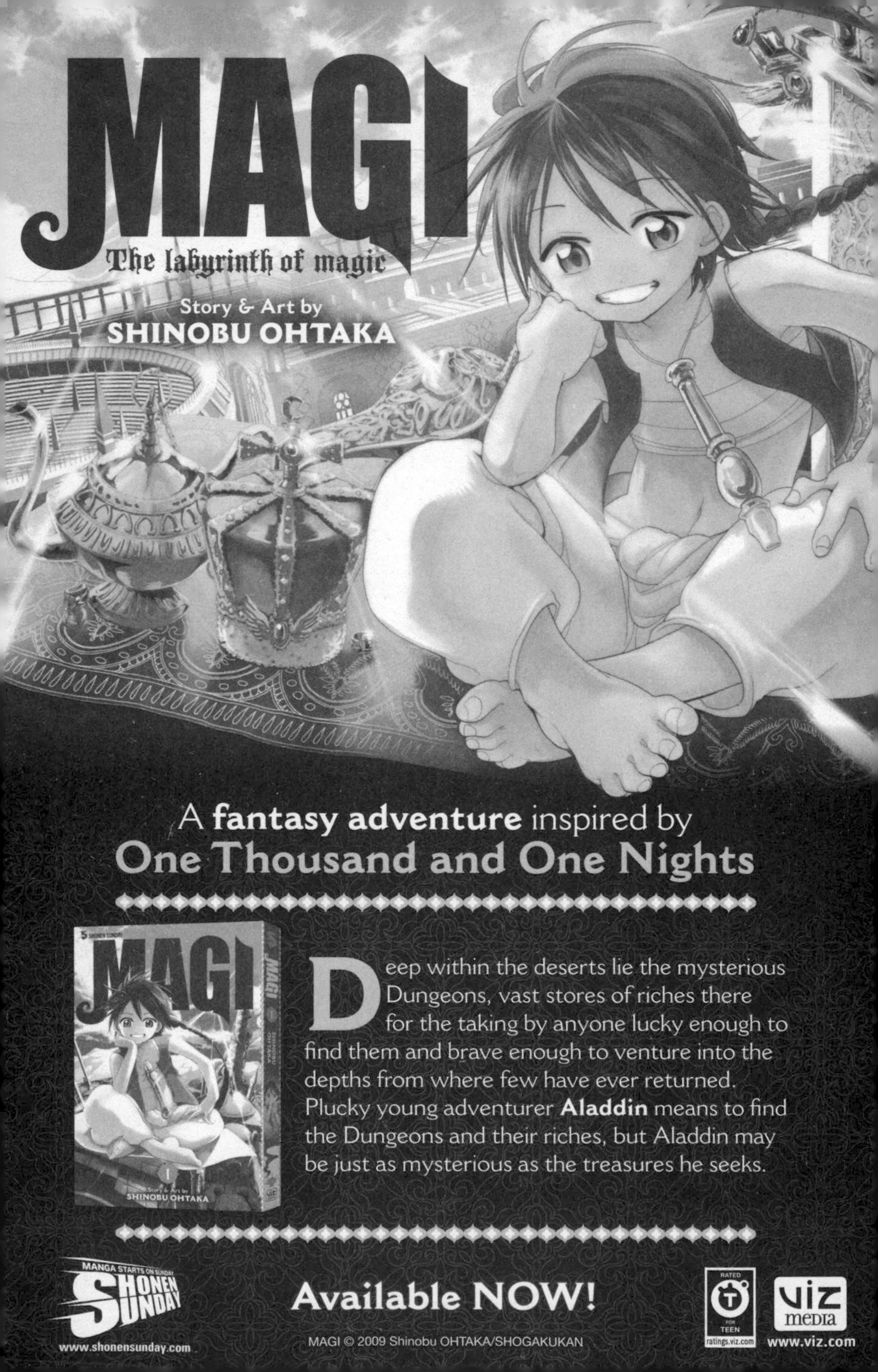
MAGI
The labyrinth of magic
Story & Art by
SHINOBU OHTAKA
A fantasy adventure inspired by
One Thousand and One Nights
MAGI
Story & Art by SHINOBU OHTAKA
Deep within the deserts lie the mysterious Dungeons, vast stores of riches there for the taking by anyone lucky enough to find them and brave enough to venture into the depths from where few have ever returned. Plucky young adventurer Aladdin means to find the Dungeons and their riches, but Aladdin may be just as mysterious as the treasures he seeks.
MANGA STARTS ON SUNDAY
SHONEN SUNDAY
www.shonensunday.com
Available NOW!
MAGI © 2009 Shinobu OHTAKA/SHOGAKUKAN
RATED T FOR TEEN
ratings.viz.com
VIZ media
www.viz.com

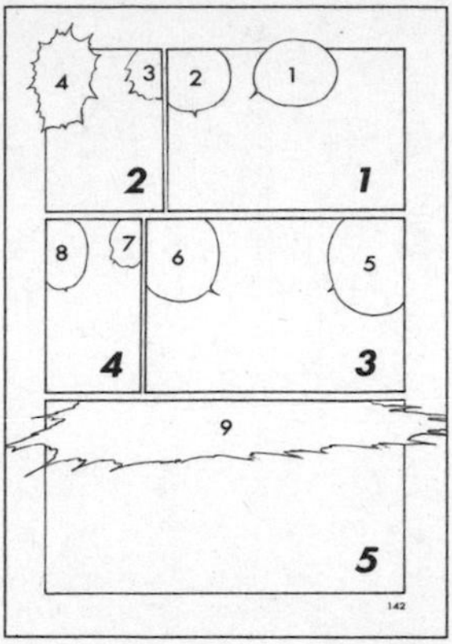

FOLLOW THE ACTION THIS WAY.

Fly Me to the Moon has been printed in the original Japanese format in order to preserve the orientation of the original artwork. Please turn it around and begin reading from right to left.

Unlike English, Japanese is read right to left, so Japanese comics are read in reverse order from the way English comics are typically read. Have fun with it!

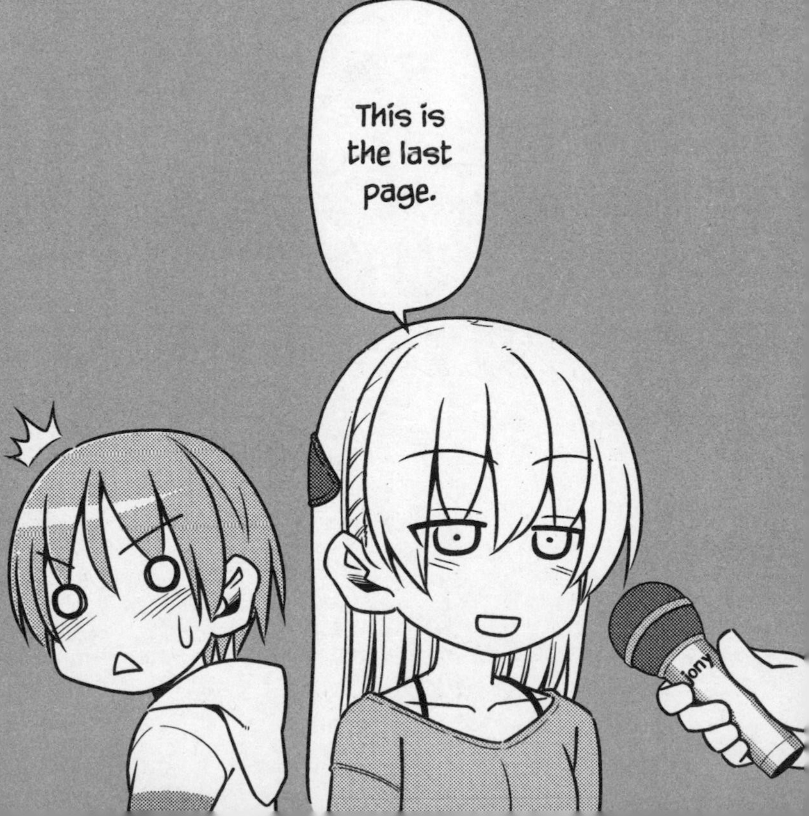
This is the last page.